an Introduction to

MIDDLE EAST POLITICS

SAGE has been part of the global academic community since 1965, supporting high quality research and learning that transforms society and our understanding of individuals, groups and cultures. SAGE is the independent, innovative, natural home for authors, editors and societies who share our commitment and passion for the social sciences.

Find out more at: **www.sagepublications.com**

an Introduction to

MIDDLE EAST POLITICS

Benjamin MacQueen

Los Angeles | London | New Delhi
Singapore | Washington DC

SAGE

Los Angeles | London | New Delhi
Singapore | Washington DC

SAGE Publications Ltd
1 Oliver's Yard
55 City Road
London EC1Y 1SP

SAGE Publications Inc.
2455 Teller Road
Thousand Oaks, California 91320

SAGE Publications India Pvt Ltd
B 1/I 1 Mohan Cooperative Industrial Area
Mathura Road
New Delhi 110 044

SAGE Publications Asia-Pacific Pte Ltd
3 Church Street
#10-04 Samsung Hub
Singapore 049483

Editor: Natalie Aguilera
Editorial assistant: James Piper
Production editor: Katie Forsythe
Copyeditor: Jane Fricker
Proofreader: Neil Sentance
Indexer: Avril Ehrlich
Marketing manager: Sally Ransom
Cover design: Francis Kenney
Typeset by: C&M Digitals (P) Ltd, Chennai, India
Printed by CPI Group (UK) Ltd, Croydon, CR0 4YY

© Benjamin MacQueen 2013

First published 2013

Library of Congress Control Number: 2012947812

British Library Cataloguing in Publication data

A catalogue record for this book is available from
the British Library

MIX
Paper from
responsible sources
FSC
www.fsc.org FSC® C013604

ISBN 978-1-4462-4948-2
ISBN 978-1-4462-4949-9 (pbk)

Table of Contents

Detailed Table of Contents

List of Figures

List of Tables

About the Author

Dr Benjamin MacQueen is a Senior Lecturer in the School of Political and Social Inquiry at Monash University. His research and teaching focuses on the politics of conflict, its resolution, and issues surrounding post-conflict reconstruction with a specific emphasis on the Middle East and North Africa, with publications including *American Democracy Promotion in the Changing Middle East: From Bush to Obama* (London: Routledge, 2013), with Shahram Akbarzadeh, James Piscatori, & Amin Saikal and *Political Culture and Conflict Resolution in the Arab World: Lebanon and Algeria* (Melbourne: Melbourne University Press, 2009).

Preface

The Middle East is a region of contradictory trends. Where repeated political crises appear to threaten regional or global stability, the defining political features of the region have proven remarkably resilient. Recent events, from the uprisings across the Arab world since 2010, the US-led invasion and occupation of Iraq, technological innovations, the global financial crisis, economic and cultural globalisation, and many other forces have come to re-shape the Middle East.

This volume is an effort to capture the dynamics of a changing Middle East for a new generation of students and readers. In particular, this volume presents a new format of Middle East studies textbook which captures the importance of issues such as democratisation, political change, human rights, political economy and environment, and the increased centrality of events in states such as Iraq, Egypt and those of the Gulf as well as recognising the importance of politics in 'non-core' areas such as Yemen, Sudan and the Maghreb, or North Africa. In saying this, it certainly does not seek to present a comprehensive re-writing of the modern political history of the region. The goals are much more modest: to reframe discussions, debates and themes in a way that make it more suitable and adaptable to a changed region and a changed world.

The lessons of the uprisings that have gripped the Arab world since late 2010, the so-called 'Arab Spring', are useful here. Where these events took both governments and analysts by surprise, they did not emerge from a vacuum. Indeed, one need only look at the events during and after October 1988 in Algeria to see how rioting over food prices, housing shortages, unemployment and general government misman-agement could push an established authoritarian regime to the brink of collapse and also result in a long-running civil war. A critical message here is that debates on democratisation, human rights and economic dependency were present but needed to be reinvigorated and given new dimensions with the emergence of the impacts of technological change, environmental concerns and the ever-changing pressures of globalisation.

In an effort to capture this *An Introduction to Middle East Politics* is divided into three parts. Part I is an examination of the formation of the modern state system in the Middle East with a particular focus on the interplay between the key periods of Ottoman imperial rule, colonial governance and the early years of independence. Where this historic background is critical, it is presented in such as way as to emphasise the political, social and economic legacies of these periods, particularly in terms of the emergence of the key political ideologies that have profoundly impacted the course of politics in the modern Middle East.

This is reflected in Part II, where the key themes in the political dynamics of the modern Middle East are explored in detail. This is centred on discussions relating to authoritarianism and political repression, economic dependency with a particular focus on the role of oil, and finally key security issues. In exploration of these themes, this volume combines a significant detail of specific events and cases grounded in the key debates that have sought to provide greater understanding to these phenomena. These debates revolve around the supposed authoritarian exceptionalism of the Middle East and North Africa, the impacts of economic dependency and rentier-style economies, and conventional and new security issues such as terrorism and political violence.

Part III then focuses on three of the continuing crises that have continued to define regional political affairs: US interventionism in the region, the Israeli–Palestinian conflict and the Arab uprisings. Where discussion over US interventionism in the region is dominated by the issues relating to both Afghanistan and Iraq, and is explored in depth in Chapter 8, this discussion also examines the controversies around patterns of intervention in Somalia and Yemen including the controversies related to new security tactics such as drone strikes. This thematic approach to these crises continues to the examination of the Israeli–Palestinian conflict, with a focus on the stalled Peace Process. Whilst this covers the key elements of the process, it also explores factors such as competing norms of self-defence and self-determination. Finally, the Arab uprisings are explored with emphasis on whether they represent a move toward a new democratic future for the Middle East and North Africa.

With the learning tools contained within this volume and on the companion website, including key learning objectives, extensive timelines, study questions and suggested further readings, it is hoped that this volume provides an engaging and thought-provoking overview of Middle East politics.

Acknowledgements

Whilst my name appears on the cover, this volume would not have been possible without the assistance of family, friends and colleagues. I would particularly like to thank my colleagues Associate Professor Brent Sasley of the University of Texas at Arlington, Associate Professor Özlem Tür at the Middle East Technical University in Ankara, Professor Shahram Akbarzadeh at the University of Melbourne, as well as my colleagues at the School of Political and Social Inquiry at Monash University as well as the invaluable assistance of Ms Siobhán Lyttle. I would also like to thank the anonymous reviewers who provided invaluable advice on the development of this manuscript. Many thanks must go to the commissioning, editorial, marketing and production team at Sage, including Natalie Aguilera, James Piper, Sally Ransom and Katie Forsythe. However, none of this was or is possible without my family. Kylie, Adele and Jeremiah, thank you.

Note on Transliteration

There are a number of transliterated terms used in this volume, particularly from Arabic to English but also from Farsi (Persian), Turkish and Hebrew. As with all transliteration, emphasis is placed on consistency. Where possible, explanatory notes will be given with the transliterated text (with the transliterated text in *italics*). For the Arabic transliterations, the letter ع ('ayn') is represented by the figure `, as in Shi`a or *Qur`an*. There is no equivalent letter in English, but it is conventionally understood as a 'glottal stop'.

Timeline

1517–1923: The Ottoman Caliphate (Constantinople)

1536: First of the Capitulations Treaties signed between France and the Ottoman Empire

1 July 1798: Napoleon's landing in Egypt

1805–49: Muhammad 'Ali's rule in Egypt

5 January 1820: The General Treaty of Peace establishing British dominance in the Persian Gulf

5 July 1830: Establishment of French rule in Algeria

1834: Introduction of the *tanzimat* reforms

16 November 1869: The opening of the Suez Canal

1876: Introduction of the first Ottoman constitution

13 June–13 July 1878: Congress of Berlin

1878: Suspension of the Ottoman constitution

12 May 1881: Establishment of the French Protectorate of Tunisia

1881: Creation of the Ottoman Public Debt Administration (OPDA)

13 July 1882: Establishment of British rule in Egypt after the Battle of Tel el-Kebir

1909: Reintroduction of the Ottoman constitution

1909–13: CUP control of the Ottoman government

30 March 1912: Establishment of the French Protectorate of Morocco

18 October 1912: Establishment of Italian colony in Libya

14 July 1915–30 January 1916: The Hussein–McMahon Correspondence

9 May 1916: The Sykes–Picot Agreement

2 November 1917: The Balfour Declaration

7 November 1918: The Anglo–French Declaration

8 March 1919–22 February 1922: The Egyptian Revolution

10 June–21 July 1919: The King–Crane Commission

28 June 1919: Treaty of Versailles

10 August 1920: Treaty of Sèvres

11 July 1921: Establishment of the Emirate of Transjordan

23 August 1921: Establishment of the British Mandate of Mesopotamia (Iraq)

3 June 1922: The 1922 (Churchill) White Paper

24 July 1923: Treaty of Lausanne

26 September 1923: Establishment of the British Mandate of Palestine

29 September 1923: Establishment of the French Mandate of Syria and the Lebanon

29 October 1923: Establishment of the Republic of Turkey

1928: Muslim Brotherhood founded in Egypt

15 April 1936–30 September 1939: The Arab Revolt in Palestine

11 November 1936–18 January 1937: The Peel Commission (Palestine Royal Commission)

17 May 1939: The 1939 (MacDonald) White Paper

2–31 May 1941: Anglo–Iraqi War

25 August 1941: Anglo–Soviet invasion of Iran

22 November 1943: Lebanese independence

22 March 1945: Arab League founded

17 April 1946: Syrian independence

25 May 1946: Jordanian independence

22 July 1946: King David Hotel bombing

7 April 1947: Baʿath Party founded in Syria

29 November 1947: UNGA Resolution 181

14 May 1948: Israeli independence

24 December 1951: Libyan independence

1951: Iraqi branch of the Baʿath Party founded

23 July 1952: Free Officers' Coup in Egypt

19 August 1953: US-backed overthrow of Mossadeq government in Iran

1 November 1954–19 March 1962: Algerian War of Independence

17 November 1954: Nasser becomes President of Egypt

1 January 1956: Sudanese independence

20 March 1956: Tunisian independence

7 April 1956: Moroccan independence

26 July 1956: Nasser nationalises the Suez Canal

29 October–6 November 1956: Suez Crisis

22 February 1958: Founding of the United Arab Republic

14 July 1958: Overthrow of Iraqi monarchy

15 July–25 October 1958: Civil war in Lebanon

27 May 1960: Military coup in Turkey

19 June 1961: Kuwaiti independence

28 September 1961: Dissolution of the United Arab Republic

3 July 1962: Algerian independence

1962–1970: Yemen Civil War

8 February 1963: Ba'ath Party coup in Iraq

1966: Split between the Syrian and Iraqi branches of the Ba'ath Party

5–10 June 1967: The Six-Day War

November 1967: Opening of the Tehran Nuclear Research Centre

30 November 1967: South Yemeni independence

1968: Israel achieves nuclear weapons capacity

17 July 1968: Ba'ath Party comes to power in Iraq

1 September 1969: Muammar Gaddhafi comes to power in Libya

15 September 1970–5 April 1971: Black September clashes in Jordan

13 November 1970: Hafiz al-Assad comes to power in Syria

12 March 1971: Military coup in Turkey

15 August 1971: Bahraini independence

3 September 1971: Qatari independence

30 November 1971: Iran takes possession of the islands of Abu Musa and Greater and Lesser Tunb

2 December 1971: UAE independence

5 April 1971: PLO moves to Lebanon

10 May 1973: POLISARIO Front founded

6–25 October 1973: October War

1975–90: Lebanese Civil War

31 October 1975: Morocco occupies positions in Western Sahara

10 June 1976: Syrian invasion of Lebanon

14 March 1978: First Israeli invasion of Lebanon

17 September 1978: Egyptian–Israeli Peace Treaty signed

1 April 1979: Islamic Republic of Iran proclaimed

16 July 1979: Saddam Hussein becomes President of Iraq

24 December 1979: Soviet invasion of Afghanistan

12 September 1980: Military coup in Turkey

22 September 1980–20 August 1988: Iran–Iraq War

7 June 1981: Israeli attacks on Osiraq facility

6 October 1981: Sadat assassinated, succeeded by Hosni Mubarak

1982: Hezbollah founded

xxxii AN INTRODUCTION TO MIDDLE EAST POLITICS

6 June 1982: Second Israeli invasion of Lebanon

18 April 1983: US Embassy bombing in Beirut

June 1983: Outbreak of Second Sudanese Civil War

23 October 1983: Beirut Marine Barracks bombings

1984: 'Office of Services' established by Abdullah Azzam and Osama bin Laden to coordinate foreign Islamist fighters in Afghanistan

September 1986: Mordechai Vananu's disclosure of Israel's nuclear programme revealed in *The Sunday Times*

March 1987: Founding of Hamas

December 1987–December 1993: First *intifada*

15 November 1988: Palestinian Declaration of Independence

1989: Al-Qaeda formally established in Afghanistan

22 May 1990: Yemeni unification

2 August 1990: Iraq invades Kuwait

8 August 1990: US-led 'Operation Desert Shield'

17 January 1991: 'Operation Desert Storm' is launched to remove Iraqi forces from Kuwait

3 April 1991: UN Security Council Resolution 687

30 October 1991: Madrid Peace Conference

1992: Osama bin Laden and al-Qaeda arrive in Khartoum, Sudan

20 August 1993: Signing of the Declaration of Principles from the Oslo Negotiations

29 December 1992: First 'official' al-Qaeda attack targeting US servicemen in Yemen

26 February 1993: Al-Qaeda associates bomb the basement of the World Trade Center, New York City

1994: Beginning of Taleban military operations

4 May 1994: Palestinian Authority formed

4 November 1995: Assassination of Israeli Prime Minister Shimon Peres by Israeli citizen Yigal Amir

May 1996: Al-Qaeda expelled from Sudan, move to Taleban-ruled Afghanistan

25 June 1996: Al-Qaeda bombing of the Khobar Towers, Dhahran, Saudi Arabia

27 September 1996: The Taleban take Kabul

17 January 1997: Signing of the Hebron Protocol

7 August 1998: Al-Qaeda bombs US embassies in Nairobi, Kenya and Dar-es-Salaam, Tanzania

20 August 1998: US aerial bombing of al-Shifa pharmaceutical factory in Sudan in response to the US Embassy bombings in Kenya and Tanzania

23 October 1998: Signing of the Wye River Memorandum

16–19 December 1998: UNSCOM inspectors withdraw from Iraq

16–19 December 1998: 'Operation Desert Fox'

7 July 2000: Israel withdraws from southern Lebanon

11–25 July 2000: Camp David negotiations

September 2000–May 2005: Second (al-Aqsa) *intifada*

12 October 2000: Al-Qaeda attack on the *USS Cole* off the coast of Yemen

21–27 January 2001: Taba Peace Summit

11 September 2001: Al-Qaeda attacks on the United States

7 October 2001: 'Operation Enduring Freedom' launched

5 December 2001: Bonn Agreement signed

19 January 2002: President Bush's 'Axis of Evil' State of the Union Address

20 January 2002: Machakos Protocol ends the Second Sudanese Civil War

24 June 2002: Road Map Peace Plan announced

August 2002: Information revealing Iran's nuclear facilities at Natanz and Arak

16 October 2002: Passing of 'Authorisation for Use of Military Force against Iraq Resolution' through the US Congress

8 November 2002: UN Security Council Resolution 1441

2003: Al-Qaeda in Iraq founded

2003: Al-Qaeda in the Islamic Maghreb founded

February 2003: Outbreak of conflict in Darfur

19 March 2003: 'Operation Iraqi Freedom' launched

9 April 2003: Baghdad falls to Coalition forces

21 April 2003: Establishment of the Coalition Provisional Authority

1 May 2003: Formal removal of Ba'ath Party from power

16 May 2003: CPA issues General Order Number 1 ('De-Ba'athification')

15–20 November 2003: Al-Qaeda bombings in central Istanbul, Turkey

4 April–1 May 2004: First Battle of Fallujah

8 May 2004: Transitional Administrative Law in Iraq

7 November–23 December 2004: Second Battle of Fallujah

11 November 2004: Yasser Arafat dies

9 January 2005: Mahmoud Abbas elected head of the PA

30 January 2005: First post-invasion elections in Iraq

14 February 2005: Former Lebanese Prime Minister Rafiq al-Hariri killed in bomb-blast in central Beirut

15 August 2005: Gaza withdrawal

15 October 2005: Iraq's post-Ba'ath constitution adopted

5 December 2005: Iraqi parliamentary elections

25 January 2006: Hamas wins Palestinian legislative elections

12 July–14 August 2006: July war between Israel and Hezbollah

25–31 March 2008: Battle of Basra

14 July 2008: ICC arrest warrant issued to Sudanese President Bashir for charges of war crimes and crimes against humanity

21 May 2008: Doha Agreement giving Hezbollah a veto over all government decision-making in Lebanon

27 December 2008–18 January 2009: Israeli invasion of Gaza ('Operation Cast Lead')

January 2009: Al-Qaeda in the Arabian Peninsula founded

12 July 2010: ICC arrest warrant issued to Sudanese President Bashir for charges of genocide

31 August 2010: Last US troops leave Iraq

7 December 2010: Self-immolation of Mohamed Bouazizi

27 December 2010: First mass protests in Tunis

4 January 2011: Death of Mohamed Bouazizi

14 January 2011: Tunisian President Ben Ali flees to Saudi Arabia

9 July 2011: South Sudan formally secedes from Sudan after January 2011 referendum

25 January 2011: First mass protests in Cairo's Tahrir Square

11 February 2011: Egyptian President Mubarak resigns

11 February 2011–30 June 2012: Egypt under the authority of the Supreme Council of the Armed Forces (SCAF)

14 February 2011: First mass protests in Bahrain

15 February 2011: First mass protests in Benghazi, Libya

27 February 2011: Resignation of Mohamed Ghannouchi as Tunisian Prime Minister

27 February 2011: Formation of the Libyan National Transitional Council

7 March 2011: Dissolution of the Tunisian Secret Police

9 March 2011: Dissolution of the Constitutional Democratic Rally in Tunisia

15 March 2011: Dissolution of the Egyptian State Security Investigations Service

17 March 2011: UN Security Council Resolution 1973

19 March 2011: Egyptian constitutional reforms approved at referendum

23 March–31 October 2011: 'Operation Unified Protector' in Libya

25 March 2011: First mass protests in Daraa', Syria

16 April 2011: Dissolution of the National Democratic Party in Egypt

29 July 2011: Free Syrian Army formed

23 August 2011: Syrian National Council formed in Istanbul

24 September 2011: PA submits request for full membership of the United Nations

20 October 2011: Death of Muammar Gaddhafi

23 October 2011: Tunisian Constituent Assembly elected

28 November 2011–11 January, 2012: Parliamentary elections in Egypt

26 February 2012: Ali Abdullah Saleh replaced by Abd al-Rab Mansur al-Hadi   as President of Yemen

23 May–17 June 2012: Presidential elections in Egypt

14 June 2012: Egyptian Supreme Court annuls vote of parliamentary elections

7 July 2012: Elections in Libya

About the Companion Website

An *Introduction to Middle East Politics* is also accompanied by a companion website, which is accessible at www.sagepub.co.uk/macqueen The website, which contains resources for both lecturers and students, intends to complement and build on the material here presented and includes the following material:

- PowerPoint Slides giving an overview of each chapter.
- Chapter summaries followed by study questions and suggested further readings.
- A consolidated timeline, with links.
- Links to relevant historical documents.
- Links to free journal articles.

PART I

The Formation of the Modern State System

Discussing the foundations of modern Middle Eastern politics is a fraught process. Deciding what factors have been more influential than others can lead to erroneous conclusions or, worse, determinism. Part I of this volume does not argue that the historic context presented here constitutes the sole factors shaping modern Middle Eastern politics. What it does argue is that there have been important legacies of the periods outlined below, particularly in terms of the formation of states in the region, the influence of religion in politics and the contests over identity and legitimacy.

In this regard, Part I differs from many texts in that it emphasises particular historic periods over others. In particular, it places greater emphasis on the legacies of the Ottoman period than is often done in modern political histories of the Middle East. This is particularly so where Chapter 1 outlines the reform period in the late Ottoman Empire and the interaction between the Empire, its subjects and Europe. In this regard, this volume argues that this period is of equal importance to that of the colonial period, discussed in Chapter 2.

From here, Part I moves to examine the influence of external and internal factors on how Middle Eastern politics was shaped through the 20th century. In Chapter 3, a focus on the dynamics of the Cold War highlights how, contrary to the assumed dynamic of the time, Middle Eastern states and communities were not passive players in this global 'Great Game' between the United States and the Soviet Union. Instead, local actors and regimes were able to exploit and even manipulate great power patrons to their own advantage, helping secure their rule and advance their strategic interests. In a similar vein, the examination of the main ideological currents in the Middle East through the 20th and into the

21st centuries, nationalism and Islamism, highlights the interplay between local, regional and global forces that have helped shape the region we see today.

In this regard, this volume seeks where possible to avoid a simple chronological outline of key events. As a result, there is a degree of overlap between the themes covered in each of the chapters. This is intentional, as key events have had multiple meanings in relation to different issues. For instance, the Arab–Israeli conflict or the Islamic Revolution in Iran mean different things for different groups both in the Middle East, and those outside the region. As such, this volume presents an innovative way of viewing the course of events in the Middle East, one that casts new light on regional politics.

No volume can give an exhaustive account of all the factors that have shaped regional politics. However, it is hoped that this context will give readers a fresh set of tools for understanding the immensely complex political dynamics of the modern Middle East, themes explored in Part II.

1

The Ottoman Empire and its Legacy in the Middle East

Learning Objectives

This chapter will enable a greater understanding of:

- The importance of religion and empire in the pre-Ottoman Middle East.
- The diversity of ethnic and religious communities in the Middle East.
- The ruling structures of the Ottoman Empire and their legacies for politics in the modern Middle East.
- The impacts of political and economic reforms during the late Ottoman period for states in the Middle East.
- The role of the military in politics in the Ottoman Empire and the influence of this today.
- The development of colonialism and economic dependency during the late Ottoman period and how this shaped Middle Eastern interactions with the outside world.

TIMELINE

70 CE: Roman conquest of the Jewish kingdom in Palestine

325 CE: Adoption of the Nicene Creed as the official Christian profession of faith

622 CE: The Muslim community flees Mecca for Medina (*hijra*)

630 CE: The Muslim community return to Mecca

632–61: The *Rashidun* Caliphate (Mecca)

661–750: The *Umayyad* Caliphate (Damascus)

756–1031: The *Umayyad* Caliphate in Cordoba (Cordoba)

750–1258: The *`Abbasid* Caliphate (Baghdad)

910–1171: The *Fatimid* Caliphate (Mahdia to 969, Cairo)

1250–1517: The *Mamluk* Caliphate (Baghdad)

(Continued)

(Continued)

1517–1923: The *Ottoman* Caliphate (Constantinople)	1876: Introduction of the first Ottoman constitution
1536: First of the Capitulations Treaties signed between France and the Ottoman Empire	1878: Suspension of the Ottoman constitution
1798: Napoleon's landing in Egypt	1881: Creation of the Ottoman Public Debt Administration (OPDA)
1805–49: Muhammad 'Ali's rule in Egypt	1909: Reintroduction of the Ottoman constitution
1834: Introduction of the *tanzimat* reforms	1909–13: CUP control of Ottoman government

INTRODUCTION

The pre-colonial, imperial history of the Middle East is often discounted as simply a long trajectory of decline that left the Middle East open for colonial exploitation. Whilst there is some truth in this, the pre-colonial period left profound legacies for the political, social and economic landscape of the region, legacies that intertwined with and often outlasted patterns of colonial rule in the modern Middle East. In particular, the slow decline of the Ottoman Empire and its efforts to resist territorial losses, economic decline, cultural malaise and the emergence of new identities and allegiances had immense impacts on the region. Through a brief overview of the people, identities and religions of the region this chapter will explore the patterns of Ottoman rule and its legacies. Understanding the legacies of the imperial era in the Middle East allows a greater comprehension of the impacts of colonialism and the formation of the state system in the region.

THE MIDDLE EAST IN THE IMPERIAL ERA

The Ottoman Empire was a multi-ethnic and multi-confessional realm. It reached its peak between the 17th and 18th centuries, during which time it developed an elaborate set of policies to manage relations between the many groups it ruled to ensure their political and economic representation, as well as to prevent challenges to its character as a Muslim Empire. This was challenging as the Empire ruled over a domain stretching throughout the Middle East, North Africa and into Southeastern Europe. This section will outline and discuss the religious and ethnic composition of the Ottoman Empire, with a focus on the Middle East and North African territories under Ottoman rule. This will include a brief discussion of the Middle East's religious heritage as the birthplace of the three dominant monotheistic faiths of Judaism, Christianity and Islam, the role of religious identity in the late Ottoman period, and the intersection of this with the emerging ideologies of ethnically based national identity.

THE MIDDLE EAST'S RELIGIOUS AND IMPERIAL HERITAGE

The Middle East is the cradle of the three monotheistic faiths of Judaism, Christianity and Islam. The common theme of monotheism, or belief in one God, along with their shared history in the Middle East, has tied these religious traditions together. They share a number of features outside this central tenet of monotheism, particularly in a focus on law, social justice and eschatology (life after death). In addition, religion and religious identity have been a key theme of Middle Eastern political life to today.

Judaism

The Jewish community traces its heritage to the 2nd millennium BCE. According to Jewish tradition, Abraham, as patriarch of both the Jews and Arabs, was directed by God (*yahweh*) to move from Harran in northern Mesopotamia (modern-day Iraq) to the land of Canaan (present-day Israel/Palestine). Here, the children of Abraham's grandson Jacob would establish the 12 tribes of Israel that would form the basis of the Jewish community before, during and after its exile and return from Egypt around the mid-13th century BCE. Between the 13th and 5th centuries BCE, the Jewish community would develop the core features of the faith, characterised by a focus on law and the inviolability of the oneness of God (Bayme, 1997: 282).

In addition, the Jewish community would pass through periods of self-rule, occupation and finally conquest at the hands of the Roman Empire in the year 70 CE and the imposition of Roman control over the former Jewish kingdom on the eastern shore of the Mediterranean Sea. From this point, the Jews became a diaspora community throughout the Middle East, North Africa, Europe, and later North America, Australia and elsewhere. This dispersal of the community would lead to the development of a range of different traditions, each of which referential to the core tenets of the Jewish faith.

The **People of the Book** (*ahl al-kitab*) is an Arabic term, referred to in the *Qur'an*, used to refer to the believers of the non-Muslim monotheistic faiths (Jews and Christians). The 'book' (*kitab*) is reference to the shared tradition of reverence for revealed scripture contained within a holy text (*Torah*, Bible, *Qur'an*). It was a concept developed by successive Islamic empires to show preference for these communities over followers of polytheistic faiths.

Christianity

In these latter years of independent Jewish rule, Christianity emerged as the second great monotheistic faith in the Middle East. Christianity was a faith founded by Jesus of Nazareth who was acclaimed as anointed by God by his followers as part of God's earlier covenants with the prophets Abraham, Isaac and Jacob. The designation 'Christ' is a translation from the Greek *khristos* or 'annointed' and translated from the Hebrew *mashiah*. As such, Christianity, or the followers of Jesus Christ, emerged directly out of Jewish tradition and clashed with both the Jewish religious hierarchy as well as the Roman state religious doctrine of polytheism.

Here, a key difference between Judaism and Christianity is worth noting in that the former developed alongside the establishment of a political entity in the first Jewish kingdom and its successors whilst the latter developed as a small sectarian movement with no political authority. Whilst this would change in the 4th century CE with the adoption of Christianity as the state religion of the Roman Empire under Emperor Constantine, references to specific prescriptions for political rule in Christianity are negligible compared to the elaborate legal system contained within Jewish doctrine. This would be a process formalised later with the various church councils convened by the Romans from the 4th century CE.

Islam

Indeed, the relationship between religion and politics highlights a closer connection between Judaism and the other great monotheistic faith to emerge from the Middle East, Islam. Judaism and Islam both seek to grapple directly and explicitly with the issue of temporal political authority and understand the relationship of this to spiritual authority and faith. Islam was founded by the Prophet Muhammad in the 7th century CE in the Hijaz, or the western Arabian Peninsula. After having developed a well-established trading network in the city of Mecca, Muhammad is said to have received direct revelation from God (*allah*) that was documented in the *Qur'an* (recitation or reading) as the direct word of God. The *Qur'an* developed over a number of years as Muhammad received more revelations. It is here that the relationship between Islam and politics began to develop through two distinct phases (Lapidus, 2002: 18–30).

The Caliphates

- The *Rashidun* Caliphate (632–61)
- The *Umayyad* Caliphate (661–750)
- The *Umayyad* Caliphate in Cordoba (756–1031)
- The *'Abbasid* Caliphate (750–1258)
- The *Fatimid* Caliphate (910–1171)
- The *Mamluk* Caliphate (1250–1517)
- The *Ottoman* Caliphate (1517–1923)

In this first phase, Muhammad drew a small group of followers to this new faith, but also drew the hostility of the authorities in Mecca, who saw the monotheistic message as a challenge to the dominant polytheistic practice in the region, as well as the themes of social justice as a challenge to their economic dominance of the region. This led to increasingly direct persecution of the community before it fled to the city of Medina in the year 622 CE. From here, Muhammad and his community grew, quickly becoming the dominant force in the city. It was during this second period that revelation and its documentation in the *Qur'an* began to deal explicitly with political matters as it was now the governing authority of a nascent political community.

Selections from the Constitution of Medina

- They are one community (*ummah*) to the exclusion of all men.
- God's protection is one, the least of them may give protection to a stranger on their behalf. Believers are friends one to the other to the exclusion of outsiders.
- Yathrib [Medina] shall be a sanctuary for the people of this document.
- If any dispute or controversy likely to cause trouble should arise it must be referred to God and to Muhammad the apostle of God.
- The Jews of al-Aus, their freed men and themselves have the same standing with the people of this document in purely loyalty from the people of this document.

Guillarme, Alfred (1967) *The Life of Muhammad: A Translation of Ibn Ishaq's Sirat Rasul Allah.* Oxford: Oxford University Press, p. 231

In addition to the increasingly specific revelations regulating the politics of the Muslim community, Muhammad also developed the Constitution of Medina (*al-dustur al-madina*), an agreement between the leader of the Muslim community and all the major tribes of the city including all Muslims as well as the significant Jewish population, the smaller Christian population, as well as the polytheist community. This model sought to replace tribal ties with membership in the Islamic community (*ummah*) with concurrent equal citizenship rights, to ensure religious freedoms within the community whilst positioning the head of the Muslim community as the head of the political community, to install a new taxation system that would alleviate social inequalities, and to allow for the accession of new groups. As such, this act and the context that it was articulated in, established a sense of unitary Islamic identity as well as a mode of Islamic governance that would incorporate a variety of other religions (Lapidus, 2002: 18–30).

> Today, it is estimated there are 1.57 billion Muslims globally, the world's second largest religion, with the vast majority of the Muslim global community (*ummah*) living outside the Middle East and North Africa (estimated 25%, or 407 million Muslims in the Middle East). Of this community, the majority are of the Sunni branch of the faith (85%–90%). Iran, Iraq and Bahrain have Shi`a majority communities with significant Shi`a communities in Lebanon, Yemen, Kuwait and Turkey.

This was not without challenge. Indeed, a number of Jewish tribes in Medina resisted the new government, leading to an unsuccessful rebellion and their exile from the city. In addition, the dominant tribes of Mecca, concerned about the emergence of a new regional centre of authority, engaged in a series of battles with the new community between 624 and 629 CE. Ultimately, the Muslim community defeated the Meccan forces and united the tribes of the western Arabian Peninsula under the banner of Islam by the time of the Prophet's death in 632 CE.

Islamic Empires

Challenges to the rapid growth of Islam as a religion and empire across the Middle East were not exclusively external. Contest over succession to Muhammad led to the outbreak of civil war over the method of selecting the leader of the community. The first three successors to Muhammad, Abu Bakr, Umar and Uthman, served to balance claims to succession based on political and economic ascendancy as opposed to lineage and proximity to Muhammad. These tensions broke open with the appointment of Ali as successor (*caliph*) in 656 CE, leading to challenges from members of the formally dominant *quraysh* tribe, members of whom had been appointed to prominent political positions across the growing Islamic empire. Ali was assassinated in 661 CE, seeing leadership pass to Mu`awiyyah, a member of the *quraysh* and governor of the Syrian territories conquered from the Byzantines. The supporters of Ali (*shi`atu `ali* or Shi`a) continued to rebel against this new government and were largely marginalised over the ensuing five centuries whilst the majority of the community (calling themselves the `*ahl us-sunnah wa`l-gama`ah* or Sunni) gave their allegiance to Mu`awiyyah and the newly established Umayyad *caliphate*.

The Umayyad *caliphate*, built on the conquests of the first Islamic empire and its immediate successors, spread its rule from the Arabian Peninsula and the Levant through North Africa, Andalusia (modern-day Spain) and east to the borders of India by the mid-8th century CE. Here, the Middle East, with the exception of Byzantine-held Anatolia (modern-day Turkey) became ruled by a succession of Islamic empires until the collapse of the Ottoman Empire at the end of World War I. This saw the region's political practices, symbology, literature, art and all other fields heavily imbued with reference to Islam, even when this was not specifically referential to religion. The glories of this period,

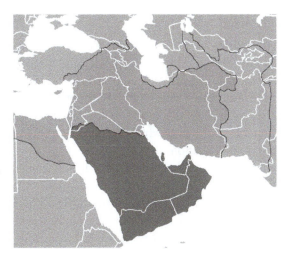

Figure 1.1 The expansion of Islamic rule in the Middle East and North Africa from the time of the Prophet Muhammad to the end of the Umayyad Caliphate in 750 CE

Source: Boston Public Library

particularly the `Abbasid 'Golden Age' between the 8th and 13th centuries CE put the Middle East at the centre of technological, artistic and political advancement. Nostalgia for this period, and discussions of how the Middle East and the Islamic world was challenged and increasingly dominated by the European colonial powers by the 18th and 19th centuries, is a common reference point for the emergence of modern political dialogue in the region and still shapes many discussions today (Donner in Esposito, 1999; Lapidus, 2002: 67–80).

THE PEOPLE OF THE OTTOMAN EMPIRE

Of the imperial rulers in the Middle East, it was the Ottomans who arguably left the most lasting political, economic and social legacy in the region. The Empire, founded in the 14th century CE in Anatolia before the conquest of the Byzantine capital at Constantinople (renamed Istanbul) in 1453 CE, was based on the military might of the Turkish population who had migrated from Central Asia and converted to Islam from the 9th century CE. Between the 14th and 16th centuries, the Ottoman Empire expanded to control the Fertile Crescent, the Red Sea coast, the North African coast to modern-day Morocco, all of Anatolia and all of the Balkan Peninsula, famously pushing to the gates of Vienna twice, in 1529 and 1683 CE.

The *Millet* System

Across this vast territory, the Empire ruled over a variety of ethnic groups such as the Turks, Arabs, Tartars, Kurds, Turkomans, Berbers, Mamluks, Bosnians, Albanians, Greeks, Bulgarians, Armenians and Georgians, amongst many others. However, religion was used as the primary tool of personal identification in the Empire. This was institutionalised in the *millet* system, a method of administration where the non-Muslim population of the Empire was organised according to religious affiliation.

Here, the *millet* system established categories for the Greek Orthodox, the Armenian (including Armenian Catholic, Evangelical and Apostolic), the Syriac Orthodox and the Jewish communities. This system was designed to ensure their protection as each community would exercise its own personal status law as administered by the relevant religious authorities. Whilst this was an exercise in promoting a sense of equality, the *millet* system contained within it an institutionalisation of preferential treatment for the Muslim citizens of the Empire until the *tanzimat* reforms of the 19th century discussed below. Up to this point, all disputes between non-Muslims (*dhimmi*) and Muslims were to be administered under Muslim law,

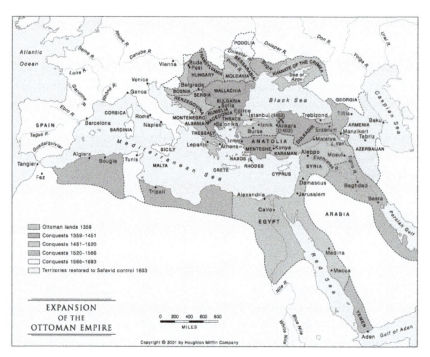

Figure 1.2 Expansion of the Ottoman Empire, 14th to 17th centuries CE

Source: Naqshbandi.org

non-Muslims could not officially hold positions within the imperial government (although many non-Muslims held critical advisory roles throughout the history of the Empire), and non-Muslims had to pay a tax, the *cizya*.

Somewhat ironically, for the bulk of its history the Ottoman Empire had a minority Muslim population. Until the loss of the majority of its European territories through the 19th century, the population of the Empire peaked at over 70 million inhabitants, with an estimated 40 million members the various non-Muslim *millets*. On the eve of the collapse of the Ottoman Empire, and after the bulk of its European and North African territories had been excised by the European powers, the population stood at an estimated 20 million. Of this, an estimated 15 million, or 75% were Muslim; 1.8 million, or 9% were Greek Orthodox; 1.3 million, or 7% were Armenian; 190,000, or 1% were Jewish; with the remainder being a range of smaller groups, largely members of Eastern Christian churches (Lapidus, 2002: 265).

> The term **millet** comes from the Arabic *millah* (nation). The enshrinement of religious identification as the source of personal law has its roots in pre-Ottoman imperial rule, but was formalised during the *tanzimat* reform period (1839–76). Until the rise of 'Ottomanism' during the 19th century and efforts to formalise equality for all members of the Empire, the *millet* system worked to both protect religious identity and enshrine Muslim predominance.

THE EMERGENCE OF NATIONAL IDENTITIES

Ethnic identity was present, in one form or another, throughout the Ottoman Empire. In particular, language as a vehicle of identity helped define and categorise the many communities within the Empire. However, ethnicity as the primary form of identity, or what we know commonly today as national identity, only began to crystallise amongst communities in the Empire during the mid- to late-19th century CE. As with most nationalist doctrines, the emergence of national identities in the region materialised largely in response to challenges from other groups, particularly from Europe. In this dynamic, contemporary Turkish and Arab identity developed together.

Origins of Turkish National Identity

The origins of contemporary Turkish identity grew not from a specific government policy but from education and economic interactions between the Ottoman Empire and Europe. Here, the ideas of nationalism as an identity that superseded both

Figure 1.3 Intellectual, artist and Turkish nationalist, Osman Hamdi Bey (1842–1910)

Source: Public domain

religious and, later, imperial allegiance would take root in the Anatolian Peninsula and, consequently, across the Middle East. Whilst we will discuss this in more detail in Chapter 4, nationalism can be briefly defined as an ideology that focuses on the unity and equality of all members of an ethnic or cultural community, with the aim that these communities, or nations, would be represented by their own nation-state.

This quintessentially modern form of political organisation was born out of the French Revolution in the late 18th century and quickly spread through Europe and North America before finding its way to the Middle East, largely through Turkish and Arabic scholars and military officers in training who were studying at European institutions through the 19th century. Initially, early ideas of national identity in the Ottoman Empire sought to preserve the multi-ethnic character of the Empire. This was articulated through the various strands of the 'Young Ottoman' movement where the central idea was one of allegiance to the Ottoman 'homeland' regardless of religious affiliation (Kayali, 1997: 18).

Whilst this became formalised through the various reform processes during the 19th century, it also led to a sharpening of ethnic divides within the Empire, largely between the dominant Turkish communities and their representatives in the higher ranks of the Ottoman military and the Arab community in the south of the Empire. This saw the idea of Ottoman nationalism, or 'Ottomanism', decline through the 19th century to be replaced by an increasingly potent sense of Turkish and Arab identity. Turkish ethnic identity crystallised with the Young Turk movement, an amalgam of various protest movements seeking the implementation of a constitutional regime to temper the power of then-Sultan Abdul Hamid II (1876–1909) that had grown as a result of the centralisation policies of the *tanzimat*.

Indeed, Abdul Hamid had dissolved the former Ottoman constitution and parliament in 1878. Whilst it was made up of a number of groups both inside and outside the Empire, its driving force were European-educated army officers largely from the Third Army in Salonika. Their pressure on the Sultan led to the reinstigation of the constitution in 1908. In 1909, counter-protests erupted amongst conscript soldiers and members of the religious establishment calling for the

Figure 1.4 Members of the Young Turks in the early 20th century with future President of the Republic of Turkey, Mustafa Kemal ('Atatürk'), centre

Source: Runnymede Institute

constitution to be dissolved and religious law to be introduced. These protests were also an effort to counter what was seen as an increasing Europeanisation of the political life of the Empire through this officer corps. In response, the officers confronted the Sultan, who they claimed had stirred this unrest, and forced him from office, replacing him with Mehmet V as a figurehead for a new military-backed regime (Allen Butler, 2011: 37).

Whilst the protest movement initially also included a range of other voices, the military leadership through the Committee for Union and Progress (CUP), founded in 1889, soon took full control of the new government. In their efforts at reforming the government between 1909 and 1913, the CUP slashed the bureaucracy, targeting high-ranking Arab officials in the name of enhancing efficiency. This saw the increasing alienation of both the civil service and the Arabs more generally from the imperial authority in the lead-up to World War I.

This fracturing of Ottoman authority was accelerated by a loosening of controls over press censorship that allowed for both greater criticism of the government and for the articulation of counter-narratives, particularly through the emergence of a greater sense of Turkish and Arab nationalism based on linguistic unity around the key urban areas in Anatolia and the Arab east. This was also compounded by the increasing interference of the British and French in the Ottoman-held Arab territories in the Levant and Arabian Peninsula.

In this regard, the CUP and the Young Turk movement more generally were not a nationalist movement as such, at least initially. They saw their heritage in line with their predecessor movement in the Young Ottomans, and sought the promotion of a multi-confessional sense of Ottomanism. However, as they oversaw the steady erosion of Ottoman holdings in the Balkans, the idea of a multi-confessional identity become increasingly moot as the Empire was reduced to an Anatolian, largely ethnically Turkish core (with large Armenian, Kurdish and Greek minorities) with a significant Arab southern flank. Indeed, as ethnic identity became increasingly salient in Southeastern Europe, it also began to resonate with the people of the late Ottoman Empire. Coupled with the articulation of a sense of Turkish identity within key elements of the CUP leadership, the movement towards rearticulating the Ottoman Empire as a Turkish domain began to take root (Kayali, 1997: 38).

Origins of Arab National Identity

This struggle between ethnic identity, religious affiliation and regional links is an issue that reflects many of the issues that underlie the fragility of regional identities and political affiliations today. This is particularly so amongst the Arab community where the growth of a unitary identity, particularly in the Arab east, based primarily on linguistic unity has sat in tension with the political division of the region. Whilst a sharper sense of Arab national identity emerged in reaction to the growth of the Young Turk movement and its turn to Turkish nationalism, Arab identity had began to establish itself particularly in the literary and intellectual circles of the main cities of Damascus, Cairo, Baghdad, Beirut and elsewhere through the 19th century (Dawisha, 2003: 14–48).

This notion of Arab identity did not articulate a clear and unified sense of political identity, whether the Arabs should remain part of the Ottoman Empire, whether they should form their own renewed *caliphate* or republic, or what the territorial limits of their community were. However, the revival and dissemination of literary Arabic in the late 19th century laid the foundations for a cross-confessional sense of Arab identity that would emerge in clearer form in response to the early stages of creeping European colonialism, the final stages of Ottoman decline and the imposition of direct forms of colonial rule during the 20th century.

Arab identity has always been a contested term, and one that seeks to identify elements of unity within a highly culturally and geographically diverse community. The Arab people populate a vast and varied geographic area, stretching from the deserts and mountains of the Arabian Peninsula, through the Fertile Crescent, along the Mediterranean coast from Lebanon through Africa, to the Atlas Mountains of Algeria and Morocco to the coast of the Atlantic Ocean. They are not the sole community in these areas, sharing North Africa with the various Berber (Amazigh) communities and the Levant with other groups such as the

Figure 1.5 Pictured in Damascus, members of *al-Fatat* (Young Arab Society), an association of intellectuals, artists and politicians formed in Paris in 1911. Members of this group would go on to become leading Arab politicians, including Riad as-Solh, the first Prime Minister of Lebanon in 1943 and Shukri al-Quwatlu, the first President of Syria in 1943

Source: Public domain

Kurds, a large Armenian diaspora, Greeks, Turkmen, Assyrians, Jews and others. However, they are the dominant community in the region and, up to the early 20th century, in the southern tier of the Ottoman Empire.

Whilst there is religious diversity amongst the Arab people, around 90% of Arabs are Muslim, with the majority of these being Sunni Muslim. Indeed, Arab and Muslim histories are inextricably tied together. The Arab people, prior to the founding of the religion in the 7th century CE, populated the Arabian Peninsula with scattered communities further north across the Levant. It was only with the expansion of the Islamic religion up to the 10th and 11th centuries that the Arab people became the dominant social group in the Middle East and North Africa. However, Arab Christians and Arab Jews have been central players in the political life of the region, including in the development of early nationalist movements.

Emerging Ethnic and Nationalist Tensions

This sense of modern Arab national identity grew at the same time and, indeed, in competition with the development of the sense of modern Turkish national

Figure 1.6 Enver Pasha (1881–
1921), Ottoman officer
and leader of the
Young Turk movement

Source: Public domain

identity. It primarily drew on a shared language and history, even where both of these factors vary for Arabs in Morocco to those in Iraq, Lebanon, or Oman. This balance or, as some historians argue, tension between the broader sense of Arab identity and local identities based around emerging states or tribal/familial associations is a key characteristic of the Arab community (Barakat, 1993: 32–47).

Early manifestations of Arab national identity largely downplayed this due to the immediate sense of confrontation with the increasingly unpopular Ottoman rule. This led to two initial streams of resistance to the Ottomans based on Arab identity, one expressive of 'traditional' allegiances as manifested in the Arab Revolt during World War I and another growing out of more secular intellectual groups and movements in the cities of Damascus, Baghdad and Cairo.

Both Turkish and Arab nationalism would become highly influential in the latter years of the Ottoman Empire and immediately after its collapse in the wake of World War I. However, the political trajectory of the region and the allegiances people adhered to have been deeply influenced by the political systems and practices of the Ottoman period. Indeed, the legacies of Ottoman rule in the Middle East continue to be debated by historians, with emergent and recurring patterns in contemporary Middle Eastern politics reflective of the policies of the Empire and their political, economic and social consequences.

THE LEGACY OF OTTOMAN RULE IN THE MIDDLE EAST

Whilst the Ottoman legacy in the Middle East was profound, this section will focus on four areas where patterns of Ottoman rule as well as Ottoman engagement with Europe left imprints on the future political, social and economic trajectory of the Middle East. First, the core political institutions of the Empire highlight a tradition of centralised, bureaucratic rule in the region. Second, the Ottoman response to European dominance and development led to a series of policy reforms known as the *tanzimat*. These reforms led to changes in patterns of rule that have been highly influential for the forms of rule and statehood that emerged in the Middle East during the 20th century. Third, the role of the Ottoman military left an important legacy not just for the way the institution was organised, but for how it saw its role in politics and as a vehicle for change, by force if necessary. Fourth, the Ottoman economic dependency on Europe that emerged through the 19th century has helped shape the pattern of contemporary economic relations between the Middle East and the outside world, as well as fostering particularly sharp resentment of consistent external interference in the region.

OTTOMAN RULE IN THE MIDDLE EAST

Ottoman rule went through various phases, but maintained core institutional elements over the seven centuries it dominated the Middle East. Here, three institutions were central: the Sultan, the Grand Vizier and the Grand Mufti. The Sultan sat atop the ruling hierarchy in the Ottoman Empire. This was a title inherited from the Seljuqs to denote the ruler of a Muslim Empire who did not claim the *caliphate*, or succession to the Prophet Muhammad. However, Sultan Selim I (1512–20) induced the former claimants, the remnants of the `Abbasid dynasty, to cede their claims to the Ottoman ruler with the Ottoman defeat of the Egyptian-based Mamluk Empire in 1517 CE, where the former imperial dynasty had sought refuge.

The degree of authority wielded by the Sultan varied during the course of the Empire; however, the Sultan's court (*saray*) and his high officers held considerable sway over decision-making during the lifespan of the Ottoman Empire. The *saray* was the centre of government and also served as a training ground for administrators and military officers who governed the Empire. The Ottomans sought to implement an increasingly centralised bureaucracy, particularly during and after the 19th century CE, administered through the *saray* with the Grand Vizier at its head. The day-to-day political affairs of the government were administered by the Grand Vizier, a position roughly equivalent to a modern-day prime minister (Ágoston and Masters, 2009: 617). Whilst the Vizier wielded

Figure 1.7 Ahmed Tewfik Pasha (1845–1936), the last Grand Vizier of the Ottoman Empire

Source: Public domain

considerable power, he was also vulnerable as scapegoat should there be outbreaks of public discontent or major government failures. This was an all-too common theme towards the latter decades of the Empire, leading to greater political instability and further vulnerability of the Empire to external and internal challenges.

The Ottoman government sought to regulate religion, specifically Islam, across the Empire through the religious establishment headed by the Grand Mufti, or *sheikh al-'ulama*. The Empire's private law code was run according to religious identity in line with the categories of the *millet* system. Outside of this, Islamic law (*shari'ah*) was dominant, administered by religiously educated judges, or *qadi*. The Grand Mufti had the power to appoint the *qadi* as well as the extraordinary power to veto any other ruling of the government, even one issued by the Sultan, should he deem it contradictory to the *shari'ah*. However, as the Mufti was appointed by the Sultan and served at his pleasure, there are no notable instances where the Sultan's authority was challenged in this way (Ágoston and Masters, 2009: 617).

THE *TANZIMAT* REFORMS AND 'MODERNISATION'

It was the last decades of Ottoman rule, and the reforms undertaken during this time to stem the territorial losses and increasing economic dependency on Europe, that left the most pronounced legacy on the contemporary Middle East. As the borders of the Empire contracted, the imperial administration in Istanbul sought to impose a greater degree of centralised control over the remaining territory. This was an effort to mirror the centralised bureaucracies of the European powers, an effort at political modernisation. In particular, the imperial government sought to extend its control over education, charity and social services, areas that were previously the almost exclusive domain of local administrations.

The *Tanzimat*

The centrepiece of this centralisation programme was the *tanzimat* (reorganisation). The *tanzimat* were a series of often disorganised policy programmes designed to ensure the territorial integrity of the Empire against both external threats and internal rebellions as well as to reinvigorate the Ottoman economy and free it from its increasing dependency on Europe. The mechanisms for achieving this focussed on tax standardisation, the enshrinement of private property rights, a centralisation of the bureaucracy and the introduction of conscription. In essence, it broadened the role of the Ottoman state considerably, granting it a presence in many areas that had previously been delegated to local notables, religious institutions and the private sphere (Finkel, 2007: 3).

The *tanzimat* (reorganisation) reforms were an effort to resist increasing European dominance whilst emulating more effective European models of rule. It symbolised efforts to reform the administration of the Empire towards notions of citizenship, modernisation of the finance system and strengthening the institution of the military. It had some success in developing a more effective centralised rule; however this also bred greater resentment of the increasingly powerful position of the Sultan. Ultimately, these reforms could not prevent the external and internal pressures that led to the collapse of the Empire after World War I.

The reforms sought to standardise and centralise the structure of the Empire through the imposition of new administrative units, the *vilayets* (provinces). This effort at standardisation was introduced with the first set of reforms in 1834. In the areas closest to the Ottoman capital (Anatolia and the Balkans), relatively centralised administration could be implemented. However, in the more peripheral *vilayets* (notably around Cairo, Baghdad, Algiers, Tunis and even Aleppo and Damascus), the Ottomans sought to rule through local leaders and administration functioned around and through these local urban centres. This led to the creation of some sense of political community based on these areas. In particular, Egypt remained a distinct cultural and, at times, political entity drawing particularly on its Mamluk heritage (Lapidus, 2002: 354–8).

This had a myriad of effects across the Empire. In terms of education, many Ottoman public servants were dispatched to European learning institutions to acquire necessary skills for these new tasks. In this environment, these new public servants, as well as the officer class, encountered a variety of new political ideologies that would shape regional political discourse through the late 19th and early 20th centuries. Here, nationalism, socialism and the principles of industrialisation would begin to take root amongst the political elites across the Middle East. The general increase in the size of the public service in the late Ottoman Empire saw this sector become the primary avenue for social mobility (Evered, 2012). This was a critical change for the social patterns of the Middle East where social mobility previously had been hindered by the hierarchical nature of the imperial system. Now, the institutions of state allowed those who had previously been excluded from access to political and economic advancement the chance for greater social mobility.

The Reform Process and the Decline of Ottoman Authority

This played into the fraying of Ottoman authority outside the core territories in Anatolia and the Levant. For instance, in seeking to mitigate the growth of opposition across its vast territory, the reforms also developed a new system of provincial administration. This new system was, in varying degrees, later used by the European powers as a framework for the colonial division of the Arab Middle East. Prior to the 19th century, the provincial policy focussed on building Ottoman authority around pre-existing administrative areas. Here, the Sultan's sons were allocated provinces (*sančaks*) and acted as governors (*beylerbeys*) which they ruled in conjunction with high-ranking military officers (*sančakbeys*) (Ágoston and Masters, 2009: 616).

Regionalism and Centralisation

Despite efforts to maintain links back to the central government, this system tended to emphasise the role of particular urban areas and the links between these areas and their immediate hinterlands (i.e. Cairo to Egypt, Damascus to the Levant and Baghdad to the Tigris–Euphrates river valley). Control was often divided between local leaders and Ottoman officials, with Ottoman control greatest in the urban areas and local autonomy asserting itself most in the rural areas. In the 18th and 19th centuries, despite these efforts at centralisation, Ottoman control over these areas waned, and the local authorities and elites began to assert themselves over the local population (Quataert, 2007: 90–110).

This was fostered by the ideological growth of the notion of nationalism imported from Europe which accompanied the increasing European interventions in the Empire. However, this notion of national identity was tempered by the strong presence of family and region-based allegiances which were deeply influential over social and political organisation across the region. The reform process was further complicated due to the lack of strong political institutions outside the personalised rule of the Sultan and the Grand Vizier. Here, efforts were made to construct new political institutions that would, on one hand, address the growing calls for political representation and, on the other, reinforce the need for greater centralised rule in the face of both internal and external challenges. In this regard, efforts were made to introduce a parliament in the latter stages of the Empire.

The 1876 constitution introduced a two-chamber parliament, guarantees on freedom of religion and a gesture towards a formal division of powers. However, the Sultan retained control over all core political and economic decisions, without the need to consult with the newly formed

Figure 1.8 Decline of the Ottoman Empire, 18th to the 20th centuries

Source: Public domain

parliament. This qualification undermined the ability of this new institution to serve as a formal mechanism for popular will, compounded by the deteriorating relations between the central government and the regions on the periphery of the Empire who saw little incentive in participating in a process that might hinder their own chances at greater autonomy or independence.

Therefore, the overarching theme of the late Ottoman period was an effort to centralise the rule of the imperial government. It was hoped that implementing this programme as a form of political modernisation would stem the territorial losses of the Empire, insulate it against further economic and cultural penetration and preserve it into the future. Whilst this failed, with Ottoman involvement in World War I leading to the collapse of the Empire, it did leave a legacy for the successor states across the region.

This is particularly so in terms of total, direct rule backed by a large military and state bureaucracy and the emerging political model. As the late imperial administration pursued a policy of centralisation, tensions arose as established patterns of social and economic authority were increasingly challenged across the Middle East. This was particularly so in the outlying provinces where the imperial administration struggled to impose centralised rule whilst not alienating local elites, for fear of their involvement in challenges to an already fragile government in Istanbul (Palmer, 2011).

THE MILITARY AND POLITICAL AUTHORITY

The role of the military as an institution was a central part of the functioning of the Empire. Indeed, succession to the throne in the Ottoman Empire was a process deeply embedded in the military institution as well as through the direct use of violence. Unlike many other empires, the Ottoman throne did not automatically pass to the eldest son of the monarch. Instead the Sultan's sons were sent to various parts of the Empire to act as governors and receive a military and political education. Upon the death of the Sultan, each of the sons would engage in a contest for the throne, with the position passing to the victor (Quataert, 2007).

During the reign of Sultan Mehmet II (1451–81), this process took a more violent turn. After acceding to the throne, Mehmet ordered the execution of all his brothers as a means to ensure that there would be no direct challenge to his rule. This act of fratricide became institutionalised through to the 17th century CE before giving way to succession of the throne to the eldest male in the royal family. However, whilst the act of fratricide did not continue, all males in the royal family were cloistered in the royal palace, away from potential political activity. This process mirrored the changing nature of the Empire, where militaristic expansion ceased during the 17th and 18th centuries, and the Sultan assumed a less martial role in favour of maintaining the political status quo through symbolic power.

The Military and Politics in the Ottoman Empire

With the change away from the use of fratricide came many more challenges, often successful, to the rule of the Sultan. However, this did not see a collapse of the system, as challenges all emerged from within the key institution of the royal household. This highlights continuity to today in terms of the rotation of leadership in many regional states, particularly during the Cold War, without real changes to the patterns of rule or systems of governance. Here, the institution of the military provided those who would emerge to challenge existing authority.

The increased power of the military in the latter period of the Ottoman Empire, particularly the role of the military in sponsoring political and economic reforms, established a pattern whereby regional militaries have continued to intervene in politics since independence (Quataert, 2007: 90–110). This has been somewhat of a contradictory pattern whereby the military has seen itself as the champion of modernisation and Western-style reforms (such as bureaucratisation and industrialisation), whilst at the same time being an institution that, when taking control of the state, has articulated a foreign policy hostile to Western powers. In many ways it was this dependency on the European powers during the latter years of the Ottoman Empire, and the humiliation that this brought, that fostered a sense of resentment combined with a desire for emulation.

Muhammad `Ali in Egypt

This dynamic can be seen in the reforms in Egypt under Muhammad `Ali in the early 19th century. War between Britain and Napoleonic France raged across Europe in the late 18th and early 19th century. In 1798, this conflict came to Egypt in the form of a French expeditionary force which sought to disrupt British maritime dominance of the Mediterranean and disrupt their links to the growing colonial holdings in India. The French presence in Egypt ended at the hands of a joint British–Ottoman action in 1801. Muhammad `Ali, an Albanian officer in the Ottoman forces, quickly emerged as the dominant force and imposed his rule in the vacuum left by the French withdrawal and the inability of the Ottomans to subsequently assert their direct authority over the increasingly independent territory.

Over the next 40 years, `Ali, who remained under nominal Ottoman authority, thoroughly reformed both the military and political institutions in Egypt, introduced programmes of economic development and industrialisation, and even waged a series of campaigns against the government in Istanbul that saw him gain control over the Sudan, the Hijaz and the eastern shore of the Mediterranean.

The Impacts of Muhammad `Ali's Reforms

Whilst `Ali's rule did not see the introduction of a plural-ist political system, preferring to seek the establishment of a dynasty in Egypt, his reforms of the military and his use of the military as the engine of politi-cal, economic and social reor-ganisation in Egypt set a trend for others ruling in the peripher-ies of the Empire as well as for post-independence rulers in the Middle East. The Ottoman and Mamluk military establishment that dominated Egypt prior to the 19th century was completely dismantled in favour of a new organisation built directly on the European model.

To facilitate this, officers were sent to Europe for training whilst the government contributed mas-sive resources to the development of an educational infrastructure that could support, at first, mili-tary training and then broader education in the future. Here, the military-led model of develop-

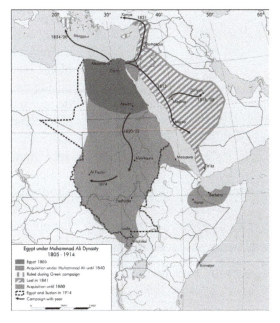

Figure 1.9 Muhammad `Ali (1769–1849), ruler of Egypt from 1805 to 1849, led a series of modernising reforms in Egypt. These reforms continue to define the place of this institution in Egyptian society and its relationship to politics. `Ali broke from Ottoman rule in the early 19th century, conquering the territories of today's Sudan, Israel/Palestine, Jordan, Lebanon, western Syria, the western and central Arabian Peninsula and parts of Anatolia, Cyprus and Greece before being forced, with British and French backing, to resubmit to Ottoman authority

Source: Public domain

ment established by `Ali would be replicated in the last years of the Ottoman Empire and during the early years of independence through the 20th century.

The success of Muhammad `Ali's reforms and the strength of the military as the vehicle for modernisation prompted international intervention in 1841 when the British, concerned about the growing power of this new regime, cooperated with the Ottomans in defeating `Ali's forces in Syria and forced him to withdraw back to

Figure 1.10 Muhammad 'Ali (1769–1849), ruler of Egypt from 1805 to 1849

Source: Public domain

Egypt. The British intervention was based on their concern over the instability it had caused in the region, potentially undermining the viability of the increasingly weak Ottoman Empire and raising the fear of regional instability that would disrupt trade and disrupt British links to India (Cleveland and Bunton, 2009: 64–74). As a result, the British imposed a settlement that not only limited the size of the Egyptian military and placed it back under Ottoman control, but also forced the Ottoman government to accept a series of economic reforms that allowed for European control over the Ottoman economy. The once-great Empire was increasingly living up to its moniker as the 'sick man of Europe'.

EUROPE AND THE OTTOMAN 'SICK MAN'

It was as early as 1536 that the Ottomans, under Sultan Suleiman I, signed the first of what would become known as the 'Capitulations Treaties' with the European powers. This treaty, signed with France, created a fifth category in the *millet* system for French citizens, largely Catholic, who had taken up residence in the Empire. This group would be tax exempt and answerable to the French king via the French ambassador. Whilst this was a reciprocal process, there was little in the way of movement of Ottomans to Europe, representative of the dominance of the Empire at the time (Palmer, 2011).

> The **capitulations** (*ahdnâmes*) were a series of bilateral treaties that granted exemptions from taxes and other liabilities for the subjects of European empires or their representatives in the Ottoman Empire. Signed between the 16th and 19th centuries, the treaties bestowed autonomy on these groups allowing the European powers to gain control over trade with the Ottoman Empire.

Over the intervening centuries the British, Dutch and others also signed these treaties with the Empire, seeing the growing expatriate communities take increasing control over the Ottoman export market. This process accelerated through the 18th and 19th centuries whereby the European states began to grant citizenship to particular non-Muslim groups within the Empire under the auspices of these treaties. This broadened out further as the European powers, as well as Russia, claimed the right of protection over particular non-Muslim communities throughout the Empire. As such, the sovereignty of the Sultan over his subjects was steadily eroding whilst the economy of the Empire became increasingly dependent on governments in Europe and their protected representatives within the Empire.

In response, the Empire sought to implement economic reforms that would counter this trend. The logic behind the first foreign loans was twofold: to finance immediate war efforts, particularly in the Crimea, and to foster development that would lead to greater revenues in the future. However, the continuation of hostilities, lack of spending and the intent of foreign powers to gain greater control over the Ottoman economy led to the failure of these efforts to reform the Ottoman financial system. This was further hindered by the territorial scope of the Empire making it difficult to implement consistent taxation collection, combined with the increasing economic dependency on European industry and manufactured goods (Kasaba, 1988).

Figure 1.11 A Capitulation Treaty between France and the Ottoman Empire from 1615. These treaties would severely curtail the economic viability of the Ottoman Empire, and lay the groundwork for continued patterns of economic dependency of, first, the Ottoman Empire then, later, Middle Eastern states, on the West

Source: Public domain

Economic stagnation saw the Ottomans default on their mounting debts to Europe leading to the creation of the Ottoman Public Debt Administration (OPDA) in 1881. The OPDA was a large organisation, employing over 5000 staff, which was created and controlled by European financial institutions that would manage Ottoman state revenues in exchange for the forgiveness of half of the Ottoman debt and a renegotiation of the remaining liability. The OPDA had enormous powers, including the right to collect tax revenue and distribute this to financers of Ottoman debt as well

Figure 1.12   Sultan Abdul Hamid II (1876–1909) oversaw the final period of Ottoman decline

Source: Public domain

as financing development projects. It was run by representatives from Britain, France, the Netherlands, Italy, Austria–Hungary, Germany and a member from the Ottoman private sector.

The Ottoman government was represented on the council, but did not have voting rights. Whilst there was some streamlining of the collection of taxes and spending on development projects, the creation of the OPDA essentially deprived the Empire of an independent source of revenue, leaving it at the mercy of the powers that controlled the OPDA leadership committee. This created a cycle of dependency whereby European states and financial institutions continued to lend to the Empire, backed by OPDA guarantees, and leaving the Empire in greater debt and with greater reliance on the OPDA and its backers.

This was compounded by the terms of trade between the Empire and Europe that were heavily weighted in favour of the Europeans as the Ottomans almost exclusively exported agricultural products and relied on imports of manufactured items. The Ottoman government and, later, the OPDA did implement some development projects. However, such was the dominance of Europe economically that Ottoman industrial development would never have advanced sufficiently to alter this situation. Indeed, the fact that the Ottoman economy was controlled by Europe through the OPDA in its latter years effectively prevented this from happening. As such, the situation of economic dependency of the region on Europe was established at this time, and was deeply embedded in the political structures of the region. It also fostered a deep sense of resentment towards the European powers coupled with a desire for independent economic advancement across the Middle East (Kasaba, 1988).

The European powers, informally at first, dealt with the Christian subjects of the Ottoman Empire in the establishment of trade relationships. In particular, the use of Ottoman Christian intermediaries greatly enhanced the economic power of these groups within the Empire. This position was enhanced as they were able to gain tax exemptions because of their connections to the increasingly powerful European markets, enabling them to sell their goods at a cheaper rate than Muslim merchants.

By the late 19th century, a seemingly contradictory political situation prevailed where the Ottoman Empire itself was highly fragile and dependent on European support. However, the size of state institutions had expanded significantly as well as the roles they sought to fulfil. This was particularly so in terms of the army and intelligence services. This fragile, highly militarised and paranoid form of state rule would be replicated across the region on independence. These patterns also set and amplified tension across the region, particularly in terms of religious identification and tension between land-owning elites and the peasantry. In terms of religious identity, the late Ottoman Empire sought to rein in control over the religious authorities across the remainder of the Empire during the late 19th and early 20th centuries. This was a move against the traditional structure of the *millet* system where authority was delegated through local religious leaders.

CONCLUSION

The Ottoman Empire's legacy is still a point of intense debate. However, the basic importance of this period is undeniable. Whilst centralised and bureaucratic rule, the role of military in politics, economic dependence on Europe and the antagonism this created, cultural influence and resentment and external infiltration are not exclusive to the Middle East, the specifics of Ottoman rule and the intensity of European engagement with the people of the Middle East gave this a particular form. Indeed, many of the core issues that continue to shape Middle Eastern politics grew from this period, and became increasingly salient with the collapse of the Ottoman Empire, the imposition of colonial rule across the region and the subsequent emergence of the regional state system.

Study Questions

- In what ways has the Middle East's religious heritage impacted on its political development?
- What factors have impacted on the formation of identities in the pre-colonial Middle East?

(Continued)

(Continued)

- Did the structures of Ottoman rule, particularly that of the Sultan and the Grand Vizier, create a legacy of personalised rule in the Middle East?
- In what ways did the *tanzimat* reforms, particularly administrative centralisation, ultimately undermine Ottoman authority?
- How did the role of the military change during the latter years of the Ottoman Empire and in what ways did it impact on the political trajectory of the Middle East?
- How did economic dependency feed into dynamics of resentment and emulation that shaped emerging political ideologies and rhetoric in the Middle East?

FURTHER READING

Dale, Stephen (2010) *The Muslim Empires of the Ottomans, Safavids, and Mughals.* Cambridge: Cambridge University Press.
An inclusive and detailed overview of three major Muslim empires who were seminal in shaping the relationship between Islam and politics.

Gerber, Haim (2010) *State and Society in the Ottoman Empire.* Farnham: Ashgate.
An examination of the interplay between the socioeconomic history of Turkish society, the *tanzimat* and the development of Turkish and Arab nationalist identities in the late Ottoman Empire.

Hanioğlu, M. Şükrü (2008) *A Brief History of the Late Ottoman Empire.* Princeton, NJ: Princeton University Press.
Focussed on broad themes relating to local trends and the interplay with global forces, this volume unpacks the emerging trends in the late Ottoman Empire and its legacies for the modern Middle East.

Kayali, Hasan (1997) *Arab and Young Turks: Ottomanism, Arabism, and Islamism in the Ottoman Empire.* Berkeley: University of California Press.
Through exploring the relationship between various communities and central authority in the Ottoman Empire, this volume provides critical insights into emerging political forces in the Middle East.

Shaw, Stanford J. (1977) *History of the Ottoman Empire and Modern Turkey.* Cambridge: Cambridge University Press.
A seminal work on the transition from Ottoman to Republican rule in Turkey forming the basis of the modern state of Turkey.

Go to the companion website at www.sagepub.co.uk/macqueen for further material including free journal articles and links to other relevant documents.

REFERENCES

Ágoston, Gábor and Masters, Bruce (2009) *Encyclopedia of the Ottoman Empire.* New York: Facts on File.

Allen Butler, Daniel (2011) *Shadow of the Sultan's Realm: The Destruction of the Ottoman Empire and the Creation of the Modern Middle East.* Dulles, VA: Potomac Books.

Barakat, Halim (1993) *The Arab World: Society, Culture, and State.* Berkeley: University of California Press.

Bayme, Steven (1997) *Understanding Jewish History: Text and Commentaries.* New York: Ktav Publishing.

Cleveland, William L. and Bunton, Martin (2009) *A History of the Modern Middle East*, 4th ed. Boulder, CO: Westview Press.

Dawisha, Adeed (2003) *Arab Nationalism in the Twentieth Century: From Triumph to Despair.* Princeton, NJ: Princeton University Press.

Esposito, John L. (ed.) (1999) *The Oxford History of Islam.* Oxford: Oxford University Press.

Evered, Emine (2012) *Empire and Education Under the Ottomans: Politics, Reform and Resistance from the Tanzimat to the Young Turks.* London: I.B. Tauris.

Finkel, Caroline (2007) *Osman's Dream: The History of the Ottoman Empire.* New York: Basic Books.

Guillarme, Alfred (1967) *The Life of Muhammad: A Translation of Ibn Ishaq's Sirat Rasul Allah.* Oxford: Oxford University Press.

Kasaba, Reşat (1988) *The Ottoman Empire and the World Economy: The Nineteenth Century.* Albany: State University of New York Press.

Kayali, Hasan (1997) *Arab and Young Turks: Ottomanism, Arabism, and Islamism in the Ottoman Empire.* Berkeley: University of California Press.

Lapidus, Ira M. (2002) *A History of Islamic Societies.* Cambridge: Cambridge University Press.

Palmer, Alan (2011) *The Decline and Fall of the Ottoman Empire.* London: Faber & Faber.

Quataert, Donald (2007) *The Ottoman Empire, 1700–1922.* Cambridge: Cambridge University Press.

2

The Colonial Period in the Middle East

Learning Objectives

This chapter will enable a greater understanding of:

- The interplay between the Ottoman and the colonial periods and how they impacted on the modern Middle East.
- The origins of the state system of the Middle East, particularly in terms of patterns of centralised rule, new political institutions and elites and the role of religion in politics.
- The formation of political discourse in the Middle East, with particular reference to its relationship with the outside world.
- The cultural challenge of colonialism and how this affected political and social life within the Middle East.
- The sources of current issues in Middle Eastern politics, with particular emphasis on the question of dependency and the sources of the Arab–Israeli conflict.

TIMELINE

1 July 1798: Napoleon's landing in Egypt

5 January 1820: The General Treaty of Peace establishing British dominance in the Persian Gulf

5 July 1830: Establishment of French rule in Algeria

16 November 1869: The opening of the Suez Canal

13 June–13 July 1878: Congress of Berlin

12 May 1881: Establishment of the French Protectorate of Tunisia

13 July 1882: Establishment of British rule in Egypt after the Battle of Tel el-Kebir

30 March 1912: Establishment of the French Protectorate of Morocco

18 October 1912: Establishment of Italian colony in Libya

14 July 1915–30 January 1916: The Hussein–McMahon Correspondence

9 May 1916: The Sykes–Picot Agreement

2 November 1917: The Balfour Declaration

7 November 1918: The Anglo–French Declaration

8 March 1919–22 February 1922: The Egyptian Revolution

10 June–21 July 1919: The King–Crane Commission

28 June 1919: Treaty of Versailles

10 August 1920: Treaty of Sèvres

11 July 1921: Establishment of the Emirate of Transjordan

23 August 1921: Establishment of the British Mandate of Mesopotamia (Iraq)

3 June 1922: The 1922 (Churchill) White Paper

24 July 1923: Treaty of Lausanne

26 September 1923: Establishment of the British Mandate of Palestine

29 September 1923: Establishment of the French Mandate of Syria and the Lebanon

29 October 1923: Establishment of the Republic of Turkey

15 April 1936–30 September 1939: The Arab Revolt in Palestine

11 November 1936–18 January 1937: The Peel Commission (Palestine Royal Commission)

17 May 1939: The 1939 (MacDonald) White Paper

INTRODUCTION

The colonial period was central to the formation of the modern Middle East. We have already seen how the Ottoman period left important legacies for the political landscape of the region. These legacies intertwined with patterns of colonial authority as well as local forms of political organisation in shaping the modern Middle East. A variety of approaches to colonial rule were employed, from attempts to formally annex parts of the region into European states themselves, to the use of proxy local leaders as the vehicle for European domination, through to a focus on economic control. In sum, patterns of colonial rule were not uniform, yet centred on enforcing external control on the Middle East and North Africa.

This chapter will explore these themes, outlining the interplay between Ottoman and colonial legacies to explore the formation of the modern state system in the Middle East. This will enable an exploration of specific issues such as the emerging forms of politics in the region that facilitated the growth of authoritarian governments, established patterns of economic dependency and political tension with Western states, as well as the emergence of specific issues such as the Arab–Israeli conflict.

THE DAWN OF EUROPEAN COLONIALISM IN THE MIDDLE EAST

Early European Colonialism

European presence was first felt before the collapse of the Ottoman Empire with the landing of Napoleon's army in Egypt in 1798. Whilst this was a short-lived venture, it showed the ease with which Europe could subvert Ottoman authority. This symbolised the shifting global balance of power towards the Europeans and away from the Ottomans from the 15th to the 19th centuries. European sponsorship assisted Serbian (1830) and Greek (1832) independence with the 1878 Congress of Berlin leading to Romanian, Montenegrin and Bulgarian independence, as well as British control over Cyprus and Austrian control over Bosnia. The Congress of Berlin also formalised the dependent status of the Ottoman Empire in the eyes of the Europeans, fostering a set of motives for Ottoman involvement in World War I.

Figure 2.1 Napoleon soon after the French landing in Egypt in 1798

Source: Public domain

However, prior to World War I, the colonial process was well under way. In these early cases, focused on the former Ottoman territories in North Africa, we can see the implementation of distinct forms of colonial rule, each of which would impact their societies in particular ways. In Algeria, French rule saw an effort to implement what was termed 'total colonisation', including the incorporation of Algerian territory into France, widespread displacement of the local population and the settlement of large numbers of Europeans in Algerian territory (Sessions, 2011). In Tunisia, a much more limited form of colonialism was implemented, with French authority focused on ruling through local proxies and extracting resources. Finally, British rule in Egypt did not seek the official annexation of territory as happened in Algeria, but presented a different form of deep colonial experience, particularly in terms of the cultural impacts on the local population.

'Total Colonisation' in Algeria

The first colony established by the French in the region came in the North African territory of Algeria in 1830. The French colony of Algeria would represent a particular type of colonial process, one that marks the country until today. Between 1830 and 1870, the French limited their authority in Algeria to the urban areas and operating largely through existing authorities. Whilst colonial authority was limited to the main urban areas of Oran in the west, Algiers in the centre and Constantine in the east, the French also implemented a policy of land acquisition in the main agricultural producing areas of the Tellian ('Inner') Atlas Mountains, displacing the indigenous Arab and Berber (Amazigh) communities to less fertile regions. This resulted in major food shortages and outbreaks of disease that saw the indigenous population decline by over one-third from 1830 to 1870 (Sessions, 2011).

French colonialism in Algeria also led to a major rupture in the Algerian social fabric, including the collapse of the local economy, the education system and a systematic dismemberment of local cultural traditions. In addition, the French sponsored the migration of large numbers of European migrants to Algeria. These migrants were settled in the lands of dispossessed Algerians. The majority of these migrants came from the poorer regions of southern France, as well as a smaller number from Spain and Italy. By the end of the 19th century, this community, known colloquially as the *pieds noirs* ('black feet'), grew to several hundred thousand, dominated all aspects of Algerian political and economic life and was granted full French citizenship (Evans, 2012).

Beyond Colonisation in Algeria

Whilst the French initially limited their colonial presence in Algeria, early resistance, such as `Abd al-Qadir's uprising in the west, combined with changing priorities in Paris, saw the implementation of what came to be known as a policy of 'total colonisation' by 1870. This new approach amplified many of the policies mentioned above, with the broad logic being an effort to incorporate Algeria as part of the French *metropole*. The French General Raoul Salan encapsulated this notion of *Algérie Français* when he declared on the eve of the outbreak of the Algerian War for Independence in 1954 that 'the Mediterranean runs through France as the Seine runs through Paris' (cited in Andrew, 1981: 35).

The connection between Algeria and France not only included colonial domination and the settlement of Europeans in North Africa but also the migration of large numbers of Algerians, both Arab and Berber, to France. It was this community, who came to work in large numbers in the French manufacturing industry, who began to first agitate for Algerian independence. In particular, the service of many Algerians in the French army during World War I and World War II, as well

Figure 2.2 Early Algerian nationalist Messali Hadj (1898–1957), leader of a trade union representing the large Algerian migrant community in France (*ÉtioleNord-Africaine*) before founding the nationalist party, the *Parti du Peuple Algérien* in 1937 and his subsequent imprisonment by the French

Source: Dzlinker

as the continuing lack of representation for Algerians in the French parliament, despite the formal inclusion of Algeria into France, saw the crystallisation of Algerian nationalist sentiment, one distinct from a broader Arab nationalist sentiment, through the early 20th century.

In this regard, the colonial process in Algeria was unique compared to the rest of the Arab world. This is not to say that the colonial period did not have profound impacts across the region. However, the specific model employed by the French, that of seeking to incorporate the very territory of Algeria into France proper, was distinct from other policies. The symbolism of this would feed directly into the emergence of the Algerian nationalist opposition in the early 20th century, particularly amongst the working-class Algerian émigrés in France who would act as the core of the early anti-colonial movement (Silverstein, 2004). In addition to the particular type of colonial practice in Algeria pursued by the French, the sheer length of the colonial experience here was unprecedented. Whilst the uprising that overthrew French rule will be discussed later, French domination of Algeria lasted 132 years, from 1830 to 1962, only to be ended through a bloody revolutionary uprising that had deep ramifications not only for Algeria but also within France itself.

Economic Domination in Tunisia

The French Protectorate in Tunisia presented a markedly different model of colonialism to that of Algeria. Specifically, it represented an effort to ensure commercial interests in the Mediterranean whilst maintaining the semblance of Tunisian autonomy. This autonomy was undermined, however, by effective French control via the French Resident-General who controlled the Tunisian economy and armed forces. The French presence in Tunisia began with the 1878 Congress of Berlin where the French negotiated for control over Tunisia in exchange for British control over

Figure 2.3   A group of French *Chasseurs d'Afrique* (Huntsmen of Africa) on patrol in
               Tunisia in 1881

Source: Public domain

Cyprus. This was initially opposed by various groups in the country, a resistance that
was broken after an incursion of tribal forces into Algeria in 1881.

The French, who considered this a violation of French territorial integrity, used
this as a pretext for the imposition of French control with Tunisia as a French 'protectorate'. This came on the back of pre-existing French presence in Tunisia as a
result of the declaration of bankruptcy in 1869 by the administration of Muhammad
III as-Sadiq. Muhammad III ruled with nominal Ottoman authority as the *bey*
(governor), but had exercised effective independence since the mid-19th century.
This led to the imposition of a French-controlled international commission taking
charge of the Tunisian economy.

Political Control for Economic Control in Tunisia

French control was formalised in 1883 with the La Marsa Convention that bound
the *bey* to implement policies dictated by Paris. This formalised the role of the
Resident-General, permitting the office holder to issue executive orders independent of consultation with the Tunisian authorities that were bound to execute them.
As such, whilst the French left the pre-existing institutions intact, they positioned
them as conduits for French policy priorities. In this process, they were effective at
co-opting local elites to act as proxies for French interests, ensuring they received

income and other benefits. These elites were receptive to this as the dire state of the Tunisian economy prior to the French arrival threatened to upset the established political, social and economic order.

The French, therefore, shored up this order to ensure their cooperation. Also in contrast to the colonial policy in Algeria, the French invested in the Tunisian education system, encouraging the participation of locals in the acquisition of French and other disciplines that would enable them to staff the French-controlled civil service. This policy only had limited success, leaving the majority of Tunisians without access to state employment. However, an educated local elite with an investment in the new administration of the Protectorate did help mitigate the emergence of popular movements seeking to overthrow French domination through to World War II. It was only with the end of World War II and the consolidation of opposition behind the 'pragmatic' leadership of Habib Bourguiba and the Neo-Destour Party that Tunisia moved towards independence by the mid-20th century (Perkins, 1986: 180).

Culture, Politics and British Rule in Egypt

In contrast, initial British colonial intervention in the Middle East was not initially premised on control of the region *per se*, but control of strategic points to facilitate contact with their vast colonial holdings in India. Central to this was Egypt, particularly after the completion of the Suez Canal in 1869. Construction of the canal began in 1858 by a French-owned company with permission of Muhammad `Ali's successor Sa`id Pasha. Using largely local labour, and working under initial opposition from the British who saw the French role as a threat to their maritime dominance, construction was completed in 1868 with the canal opening in November 1869. Whilst the opening of the canal was hailed as a success, its cost saw the Egyptian administration accumulate large debts to European banks, debts it sought to service through Sa`id Pasha's successor, Ismail Pasha, raising taxes for Egypt's nascent but growing middle classes (Wright, 2010).

> Islamist and liberalist blocs, represented by contemporary forms of the *Wafd* and the Muslim Brotherhood, would be the largest groups competing in the 2011 Egyptian legislative elections, the first after the fall of President Hosni Mubarak in the wake of the 25 January uprising. This will be discussed in Chapter 10.

As Ismail's government was not able to service the debt, and he was wary of the effects an increased taxation regime was having on the stability of his government, he sold the Egyptian government's share to the British in 1875 with the French government holding the remaining majority ownership. This allowed the British to exercise further control over the canal and, by extension, Egypt itself through the late 19th century.

Egypt's 'New' Opposition: Liberalists

These developments led to the formation of the first 'modern' opposition movements in Egypt under Ottoman General Ahmed Urabi. In 1879, Urabi formed the Egyptian Nationalist Party in opposition to the exclusion of peasants from the officer corps by Ismail Pasha's successor, Tewfik Pasha. This was tied to a broader narrative resisting foreign domination of the Egyptian economy, foreign control over the Suez Canal and broader patterns of European imperialism. Urabi eventually gained control over the Egyptian army and launched a rebellion against Tewfik and the increasingly tight British control over Egypt. This, along with the legacy of the army as a modernising force under the rule of Muhammad `Ali, enshrined this institution as the vehicle for change, and gave it an esteemed place within Egyptian political life through to the early 21st century (Cleveland and Bunton, 2009: 74).

Urabi and his supporters began planning for the installation of a new parliament that would limit the power of the *khedive*, or viceroy, and install the leader of the rebellion as Prime Minister. In response, Tewfik called at first for Ottoman support. When the Ottomans, who were still the nominal rulers of Egypt, hesitated, the British and the French took action against the nationalist forces. After an initial defeat, the British took the Suez Canal and, later, Cairo, imposing their authority over Egypt by the end of 1882. The British then reinstalled Tewfik as *khedive* under British control.

The *de facto* nature of British authority in Egypt does not discount the extent of British colonial policy in Egypt. This was more similar to the policy in India than, for instance, French colonial activity in Tunisia. After 1882, the British formalised

Figure 2.4 Ahmed Urabi (1841–1911), former army general and leader of an uprising against the British-backed government of Tewfik Pasha in 1879

Source: Public domain

their influence with the establishment of the position of Consul-General, a representative of the British crown who effectively ruled through the *khedive*. In effect, the Consul-General wielded ultimate power in Egypt backed up by British military might. Through the so-called 'Organic Law' (1883–1913), a two-chamber parliament was established. However, this operated in an advisory capacity only, with ultimate decision-making left with the British and the Consul-General (Powell Eve, 2003).

In this context, various political trends began to crystallise, trends that mirrored the development of local political trends across the region. These focused on three broad themes: secular liberalism, religious revivalism and nationalism. These were not discrete ideologies, each borrowing ideas, rhetoric and strategy from the other. Egypt's liberalist movement drew from the political and economic elites particularly segments of the land-owning class and urban intellectuals. Where the large landowners had been mixed in their attitudes to the reforms of Muhammad `Ali's rule, this continued under the British.

Figure 2.5 Saad Zaghlul (1859–1927), founder and leader of the *Wafd* Party and Egypt's first Prime Minister in 1924

Source: Public domain

Here, a core of elite large landowners supported British rule as a means of retaining their control over Egypt's critical agricultural sector, a stance opposed by smaller and some large landowners who favoured greater autonomy or independence. This group would form the core of the *Wafd* ('Delegation') Party, a movement that called for the end of the British occupation and was the most potent force in Egyptian politics from World War I through to the end of World War II (Deeb, 1979).

The *Wafd*'s high point, it may be argued, was during the 1919 Revolution. Hopes for independence across the region grew during World War I, particularly as many colonial communities participated in the war effort. Egypt served as a base for British activity against the Ottomans and hundreds of thousands of Egyptians serving as labourers for the British army. However, the lack of action on Egyptian independence at the end of the war led to a wave of popular unrest. The *Wafd* were central to this process, leading a delegation to the postwar negotiations as well as organising petitions and other measures in support of independence.

In response, the British arrested *Wafd* leader Saad Zaghlul, prompting the eruption of civil unrest across Egypt that included a cross-section of Egyptian society. In response, the British offered qualified independence, where they would retain effective control over Egypt's security and foreign policy. *Wafd* acceptance of this would see Zaghlul form the first independent Egyptian government in 1924, but also undermine the popularity of the party who were increasingly viewed as a front for continued British domination.

Egypt's 'New' Opposition: The Muslim Brotherhood

The other important source of opposition to the British in Egypt at this time was the Muslim Brotherhood. Whilst this movement will be dealt with in greater detail in Chapter 4, their genesis reflects an important part of the Egyptian colonial experience. The movement was founded in 1928 by schoolteacher Hasan al-Banna in the city of Ismailia in the Suez Canal region. This area witnessed the most concentrated presence of British forces in Egypt.

As such, the impacts of British political, economic and cultural domination were felt sharply. Al-Banna articulated his opposition to British rule differently from the *Wafd* Party in calling for the implementation of *shari'ah* law as a means to subvert British domination. This message reflected a particular interpretation of colonial dominance in Egypt, one that sought to counter the British vision of a superior Western culture bringing a 'backward' Islamic culture into the modern era.

This cultural challenge will be discussed in detail below; however, its resonance here is critical for understanding the impacts of this form of colonialism on political discourse in the Middle East. In particular, where the *Wafd* and others sought to achieve independence for Egypt based on a liberal ideology, the Muslim Brotherhood accused these groups of essentially reinforcing European domination. This was not merely recourse to religious law as a retreat to some idealised past, however.

The Muslim Brotherhood established branches across the Middle East and North Africa after 1928 as well as having offices in a number of states in the West. The Muslim Brotherhood branch in the Mandate of Palestine and, later, the Occupied Territories, reformed as the 'Islamic Resistance Movement', or Hamas, in 1987.

Instead, al-Banna and his contemporaries used Islamic discourse, one that appealed to the majority of Egyptians, as a means to criticise the actions of foreign companies and their government sponsors in the exploitation of Egyptian workers, with particular reference to their role in the construction and maintenance of the Suez Canal. The canal was vital to the maintenance of the British commercial empire, yet relied on what the Brotherhood saw as the sweat and blood of Egyptian workers. This ideology was fused with a range of other ideological messages rooted in Islamic doctrine, from the importance of charity to socially conservative views on gender rights (Mitchell, 1993).

Colonialism and Independence in the Gulf

Further east, this diversity of European intervention was also on display, from the British establishing a formalised colony in South Yemen in 1886, to forms of protectorate in the Gulf from the early 19th century, and resistance to this in the territories that would become Saudi Arabia, an area that avoided a formal colonial relationship. In this regard, the Arabian Peninsula had become largely peripheral to the politics of the region by the 19th century despite its religious centrality for Muslims. In this regard, the Ottomans served as custodians of the Holy Cities in the Hijaz (Mecca and Medina) through the authority of local notables, particularly the Hashemite descendants of the Prophet Muhammad.

However, outside these centres, the peninsula was ruled by tribally based confederations tied together through political allegiances and religious affiliation. As will be discussed in Chapter 4, the most notable of these groups were the al-Saud family who had linked themselves to the teachings of 18th-century religious figure Ibn `abd al-Wahhab. The Wahhabi/Saudi alliance would emerge from the northern portion of the peninsula to establish itself as the pre-eminent force on the peninsula by the early 20th century.

Here, the links between religion and state were strong in Yemen, Oman and the fledgling Saudi state whilst kinship ties dominated in the Sheikhdoms of the Gulf. These political units would form the basis of the British colonies and subsequent states that would succeed them in the 20th century. Perhaps only Yemen exhibited the tendencies towards a clear state structure with deep historic roots of independence and a clear territorial definition, particularly in the north under the Shi`a Zaydi dynasty that ruled from 893 to 1962. However, the growth of modern political ideologies did not permeate the peninsula until after independence with political organisation predominantly based on these more 'traditional' forms of organisation to this point (Davidson, 2012).

Figure 2.6 The expansion of Saudi rule during the early 20th century

Source: Universal Mapping Pty Ltd

WORLD WAR I AND TURKEY

The British presence in the Levant and in the Arabian Peninsula would be at the root of some of the most problematic issues facing the modern Middle East. This centred on the British Mandate in Palestine and their role in the Arab Revolt during World War I. During the war, the British were active in the Arabian Peninsula and the Levant in agitating anti-Ottoman sentiment amongst Arab elites. This agitation was based on appeals to Arab national identity led by British agent T.E. Lawrence who sought to promote Arab unity under the leadership of the Hashemites, the custodians of the Holy Cities during the latter period of the Ottoman Empire and descendants of the Prophet Muhammad.

However, the release of details of the 1916 Sykes–Picot Agreement and the 1917 Balfour Declaration alongside the Hussein–McMahon Correspondence highlighted the contradictory promises that Britain was following in the region.

Figure 2.7   From left: Sir Henry McMahon (1862–1949), High Commissioner in Egypt during World War I and Sherif Hussein bin Ali (1854–1931), leader of the Arab Revolt during World War I

Source: Public domain

The subsequent division of the region into a series of separate states based on their colonial identities would lie at the root of much opposition that would develop in the Middle East, particularly the Arab Middle East, during the colonial period.

The following section will outline British and French activity in the Levant during and after World War I, with a particular focus on how the British and French began to shift from an effort to maintain a semblance of Ottoman territorial integrity to planning for a post-Ottoman Middle East that would ensure their own interests. The British took the lead in developing a set of policies that sought to foster alliances within the Arab world, also with the growing Jewish migrant community in the territory known as Palestine, as well as acting in their own direct interests. The contradictory nature of these policies would foster resentments that persist to today.

THE ARAB REVOLT AND THE HUSSEIN–MCMAHON CORRESPONDENCE

As noted in Chapter 1, the growth of an Arab nationalist sentiment had accelerated through the 19th century in opposition to the hardening of Turkish national identity primarily through the Young Turk movement. Despite this, a nationalist movement as such is hard to identify outside a number of urban elites and traditional leaders, many of whom sought greater autonomy within the Ottoman

Empire rather than full independence. This is not to discount the importance of these figures, who ranged from traditional tribal leaders to urban intellectuals, artists and early trade union figures. However, low literacy rates and the fluctuating political atmosphere hindered this nationalist sentiment permeating beyond the elite levels of society.

Text of a letter from Sir Henry McMahon to Sherif Hussein on 24 October 1915:

The districts of Mersin and Alexandretta, and portions of Syria lying to the west of the districts of Damascus, Homs, Hama and Aleppo, cannot be said to be purely Arab, and must on that account be excepted from the proposed delimitation. Subject to that modification, and without prejudice to the treaties concluded between us and certain Arab Chiefs, we accept that delimitation. As for the regions lying within the proposed frontiers, in which Great Britain is free to act without detriment to interests of her ally France, I am authorised to give you the following pledges on behalf of the Government of Great Britain, and to reply as follows to your note: That subject to the modifications stated above, Great Britain is prepared to recognise and uphold the independence of the Arabs in all the regions lying within the frontiers proposed by the Sherif of Mecca.

The Ottoman entry into World War I saw the arrest of many Arab nationalist leaders who were accused of collaboration with the British and French. In response, the custodian of the Holy Cities of Mecca and Medina, the Hashemite Sherif Hussein bin Ali, began a correspondence with the then British High Commissioner in Egypt, Sir Henry McMahon. An exchange of letters between July 1915 and January 1916 between Hussein and McMahon led to an agreement in June 1916 (the Damascus Protocol) where the British would cooperate with Hussein's Arab forces to overthrow Ottoman rule in exchange for British sponsorship of Arab independence (Pappé, 2006: 61–70).

Attacks against the Ottoman forces in Mecca and Medina began soon after, launching the Arab Revolt. The revolt involved coordination with British and French armed forces, with the close involvement of a number of officers such as Colonel Cyril Wilson and the famed T.E. Lawrence from the British and Captain Muhammad Raho from the French. In addition, the British drew on the local knowledge of scholars such as Gertrude Bell in establishing contacts across the region. The revolt continued until the defeat of the Ottomans at the end of World War I, raising hopes for the fulfilment of the vision outlined by McMahon for British sponsorship of a large, independent Arab state in the Levant and the western Arabian Peninsula. However, other factors would emerge to complicate this vision.

BALFOUR DECLARATION

In November 1917, British Foreign Secretary Sir Arthur James Balfour issued a communiqué to Baron Lionel Walter Rothschild, a prominent British financier, supporting the creation 'in Palestine of a national home for the Jewish people'. Issued from the office of the Foreign Secretary, the Balfour Declaration, as it has come to be known, was viewed as reflective of official British government policy in support of the cause of Zionism. Whilst Zionism will be discussed in detail below, it can be broadly understood as the movement for the re-establishment of Jewish life on a national basis.

This caused great antagonism amongst those involved in the Arab Revolt, as it appeared to run directly contrary to the sentiments expressed in the Hussein–McMahon Correspondence and the subsequent Anglo–French Declaration in 1919. Indeed, the issue of Jewish migration to the Ottoman territory of Palestine had already become one of great controversy for the largely Arab population in this area. The policy of *aliyah*, or migration to the territory of Palestine, had been active since 1882, sponsored by European Zionist organisations. In 1914, an estimated 8% of the roughly 800,000 residents of the area were Jewish, a community that grew to an estimated 30% of the community by 1941 (Morris, 2009).

Figure 2.8　From left: Baron Lionel Walter Rothschild (1868–1937), Zionist leader and Sir Arthur Balfour (1848–1930), former British Foreign Secretary

Source: Public domain

Text of the Balfour Declaration (2 November 1917)

Dear Lord Rothschild,

I have much pleasure in conveying to you, on behalf of His Majesty's Government, the following declaration of sympathy with Jewish Zionist aspirations which has been submitted to, and approved by, the Cabinet.

'His Majesty's Government view with favour the establishment in Palestine of a national home for the Jewish people, and will use their best endeavours to facilitate the achievement of the object, it being clearly understood that nothing shall be done which may prejudice the civil and religious rights of existing non-Jewish communities in Palestine, or the rights and political status enjoyed by Jews in any other country'.

I should be grateful if you would bring this declaration to the knowledge of the Zionist Federation.

Yours sincerely,

Arthur James Balfour

Whilst this issue will be explored in detail below, it is important to note the timing of the declaration and the environment in which it was received, particularly amongst the Arab communities in the Levant. As European domination was formalised with the end of World War I, there was little clarity as to the intentions of these powers. This fostered widespread suspicion and overt hostility to this external influence, a factor that impacted deeply on the political rhetoric of the time, and became a tool that local political elites would use with great effect both prior to and after independence.

SYKES–PICOT AGREEMENT

Confirming these sentiments, secret negotiations between a British delegation led by diplomat Sir Mark Sykes and a French delegation led by diplomat François Georges-Picot, concluded on 16 May 1916, would largely define the political map of the modern Middle East. This negotiation, that came to be known as the Sykes–Picot Agreement, formally divided the eastern Arab world into spheres of British and French influence, contradicting the British position of sponsoring Arab independence in this area as outlined in the Hussein–McMahon Correspondence.

Figure 2.9   From left: François Georges-Picot (1870–1951), French diplomat and Col. Mark Sykes (1879–1919), British diplomat

Source: Public domain

It granted the French direct control over the eastern Mediterranean coast including all of current-day Lebanon, the coastal region of Syria and a portion of southern Turkey with the hinterland region, the rest of modern-day Syria, to be under a French sphere of influence. The British gained 'direct control' over the southern portions of today's Iraq with a broader sphere of influence that ran from the coastal areas between Lebanon and Egypt, over the Jordan River, through to Baghdad and Kirkuk.

Imperial Russia was a party to the original secret negotiations in an effort to pursue their claims over Ottoman territory around the Black Sea Straits. However, after the triumph of the Bolshevik Revolution in 1917, the new regime in Moscow renounced all these claims. In addition, they released the details of these hitherto secret negotiations in November 1917, causing a wave of anti-European sentiment across the region. The Anglo–French Declaration released 12 months later would be a formalisation of this, stating that the British and French sought to 'assist in the establishment of indigenous Governments and administrations in Syria and Mesopotamia which have already been liberated by the Allies'.

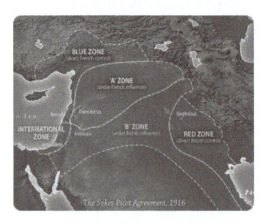

Figure 2.10   The Sykes–Picot Agreement

Source: Public domain

The Hussein–McMahon Correspondence, the Balfour Declaration and the Sykes–Picot Agreement all fed into a growing atmosphere of mistrust leading up to the end of World War I. Whilst these actions sat at odds with one another, they also confirmed the growing suspicion that the European powers had little intention of granting any meaningful form of independence in postwar negotiations, fears that would be confirmed in 1919.

VERSAILLES TREATY AND THE LEAGUE OF NATIONS MANDATES

The Versailles Treaty of June 1919 that ended World War I also saw the creation of the League of Nations, an effort to create an international organisation to help prevent another global conflict. The League was also given a range of other duties, including what it called 'just treatment of native inhabitants', particularly for territories previously under control of those states defeated in World War I, including the Ottoman Empire. Officially, the former Ottoman territories were deemed 'Class A Mandates' at the subsequent San Remo Conference in 1920

Figure 2.11 Faisal bin Hussein bin Ali al-Hashemi (1885–1933), future king of Iraq, at the Versailles Peace Conference (centre). T.E. Lawrence, British officer and liaison with the leaders of the Arab Revolt during World War I, is third from right

Source: Public domain

where independence would be supported 'subject to the rendering of administrative advice and assistance by a Mandatory until such time as they are able to stand alone'. In other words, the independence of the Arab territories formally under Ottoman rule would be managed by the European powers victorious in World War I. The arrangement for this had been worked out previously, in the secret negotiations between Sykes and Picot.

In addition, whilst independence was pushed back further, the division of the region was also formalised in five new entities. Britain administered the Mandate of Mesopotamia from 1920 to 1932 before the creation of the Kingdom of Iraq as well as the Mandates of Palestine, from 1923 to 1948, and Transjordan, from 1921 to 1946. The relationship between these two Mandates is one of the many debated issues around the British stance in relation to the independence of Israel, discussed below. The French, adding to their extensive holdings in North Africa, administered the Mandate of Syria from 1923 to 1944. This Mandate included the territory of modern-day Lebanon that became a separate republic upon the end of the Mandate in 1943.

During negotiations at the Versailles Peace Conference, Sherif Hussein remained largely deferent in seeking to pursue the interests of Arab unity. It has been contended that the British had assured Hussein that the promises of the Hussein–McMahon Correspondence would be upheld, leading him to the conclusion that intervention at these negotiations might have jeopardised promises for his installation as king of an Arab state centred on the Hijaz and Levant. This corresponds with statements by British Prime Minister Lloyd George in 1919 that the Hussein–McMahon Correspondence was a treaty, therefore the British were bound to honour it (Tessler, 1994: 146).

These statements, however, also worked to offset pressure on Prince Faisal, Hussein's son who served as representative of the Arabs at post-World War I negotiations and was elected leader by the newly formed 'Pan-Syrian Congress' that formed in Damascus in 1918 as a proxy government of the envisioned new Arab state. The congress sought results from Faisal at the postwar negotiations on independence as well as the apparent British support for the creation of a Jewish state in Palestine. However, divergence over how direct external authority should be imposed saw the French move to impose themselves more directly by deposing the short-lived Pan-Syrian Congress and the authority of Faisal.

THE REPUBLIC OF TURKEY

Between 1911 and 1922, the Ottoman Empire was in an almost constant state of warfare with only 22 months of peace in this period, facing internal insurrections and external threats. The final Ottoman defeat came in 1918, leading to the removal of the Sultan and the installation of the Grand National Assembly that ruled during the transition to the establishment of the Republic of Turkey in 1923 with Mustafa Kemal 'Atatürk' as Head of State. However, this transition was a tumultuous process, and one that would lay the foundations for the modern Turkish republic as well as witnessing a number of deeply controversial events.

The 1920 Treaty of Sèvres was the initial postwar settlement dealing with the Ottoman Empire, in conjunction with the aforementioned 1920 San Remo Conference. In sum, the treaty sought the full partition of the Ottoman Empire, including the creation of an Armenian state in the northeast, an autonomous Kurdish area under joint British and French supervision in the southeast, Italian influence in southern Anatolia, Greek annexation of a number of territories in eastern Anatolia and north of Istanbul with British control over a demilitarised area around the Black Sea Straits.

Figure 2.12 Mustafa Kemal 'Atatürk' (1883–1938), founder and first President of the Republic of Turkey

Source: Public domain

Whilst the monarchy in Istanbul remained after the war, and agreed to the terms of the treaty, Atatürk and his supporters under the Turkish National Movement split from Istanbul and established a separate authority in Ankara. Over the course of the next two years, Atatürk led a series of campaigns that rolled back the areas of foreign occupation in the south. In addition, Atatürk's forces continued a campaign against the establishment of an independent Armenian state in the northeast.

This campaign is a point of heated debate not just amongst historians, but between governments, with the Armenian community claiming that the Turkish forces engaged in a campaign of genocide, leading to the death or forcible displacement of up to 1.5 million Armenians from the future Turkish state. The Turkish government continues to vehemently oppose this, arguing that the deaths were not part of an official government policy (Dadrian, 1995). As a result of Atatürk's campaign across Anatolia, the new Turkish government signed the Treaty of Lausanne in July 1924. The new constitution of the Republic officially abolished the *caliphate* and the use of the *shari`ah* as the basis for the legal system. Whilst democracy was enshrined in the constitution, the new Republic

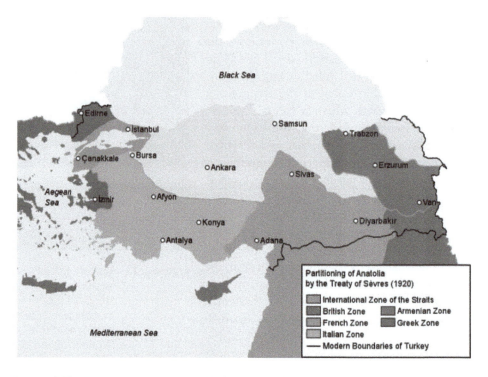

Figure 2.13   The allocations of the 1920 Treaty of Sèvres
Source: Public domain

was effectively a one-party state under the Revolutionary People's Party (RPP), Atatürk and Prime Minister Ismet Inönü. At the core of the new constitution were the 'six principles' of the new Republic.

The 'Six Principles' of the Turkish Republic

1. Republicanism; 2. Secularism; 3. Populism; 4. Nationalism; 5. Statism; 6. Reformism
   The Turkish military have traditionally seen themselves as defenders of these 'Principles of Kemalism'. This has led to military coups in 1960, 1971, 1980, and the so-called military memorandum in 1997 that bought down the sitting government of Necmettin Erbakan. Most often, the military has acted in protection of the principle of secularism. The election of the nominally Islamist *Adalet ve Kalkinma Partisi* (Justice and Development Party, or AKP) in 2002 led to renewed debate on this principle.

As such, Turkey emerged as a different political entity, and one that sought to avoid involvement in any major military engagement, including opting for neutrality in World War II. Turkey also avoided colonial rule. However, these campaigns, particularly the debate over the Armenian genocide, the status of ethnic minorities such as the Kurds and the relationship of both religion and the military to the democratic system, in many ways defined Turkish politics through the 20th century.

COLONIES, PROTECTORATES AND CLIENT STATES

As we have seen, the most intense period of colonial activity took place between World War I and World War II, with the division of the former Ottoman Arab territories. It was here that the political map of the Middle East, the creation of the modern-day states, took place and has remained largely unchanged to this day. In this regard, the period of European colonialism was relatively short compared to, for instance, sub-Saharan Africa or the British presence in India. Interestingly, French Algeria, Italian Libya and Britain in the southern Yemeni city of Aden were the only 'official' colonies.

The logic behind this was that the European powers, whilst easily intervening within the Empire, and occasionally taking portions of territory, were concerned about the implications for regional stability should the Ottoman Empire collapse. Therefore, they consciously maintained the territorial integrity of the core of the Empire whilst at the same time took control over the economy of the region. Despite this short period of formalised rule, a particularly virulent form of domination that permeated the political, social, economic and cultural discourses of the region marked the colonial period. There was little ambiguity in the reality of European domination of the region.

Regardless of the type of rule, it was the colonial power that dictated the political arrangements across the region, be they monarchical or republican, centralised or decentralised, secular or religious. This is not to say that there was no consultation with the local population, many of whom were active participants in the colonial administration. However, their participation worked to facilitate continued European political and economic control.

THE INTERPLAY OF OTTOMAN AND COLONIAL LEGACIES

The most direct manifestation of European control was the territorial definition of the new political entities, each of which would form the modern-day states of the Middle East and North Africa. This was not purely artificial, with Ottoman policies of centralised bureaucracy around major urban areas, as well as deeper historical communities helping provide the logic for these new polities. This was notable with respect to the relationship of Cairo, Damascus, Algiers and Tunis to their hinterland regions. Each entity exhibited particularities in its methods of rule, which fed into specific political dynamics for each state. Amongst the Arab states, this laid the groundwork for the tension between the broader Arab drive for unity and the parochialisms of each regime.

As such, the combination of Ottoman and colonial rule left a vast array of social, political, cultural and economic legacies for the Middle East. The contemporary state system in the region captures many of these legacies. Whilst these impacts may not be, in and of themselves, unique to the Middle East, their combination has given the contemporary Middle East a particular dynamic. For instance, the modern Middle East is a region that is commonly perceived as conflict-prone, unstable and unpredictable. In addition, it is one that suffered immense colonial impact. Whilst this may be true in some respects, the state system in the Middle East has proven remarkably resilient, with the 'Arab Spring' uprisings from late 2010 presenting the first real region-wide challenge to the established political order since the independence era. In addition, the period of European colonial rule

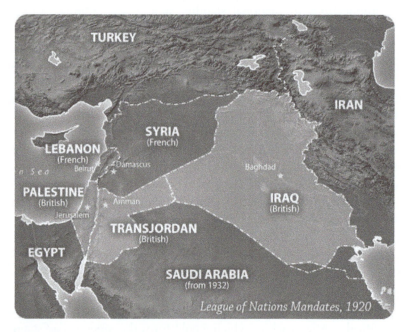

Figure 2.14 The League of Nations Mandates

Source: Public domain

was relatively short by global standards but had profound impacts on all aspects of life for those in the Middle East.

Understanding this dynamic is essential to fully comprehending the environment in which the modern Middle East emerged. In particular, as Roger Owen has argued, the creation of these colonial and pseudo-colonial entities created a new reality in the Middle East, one that led to the creation of new forms of organisation, identities and allegiances. Here, focus will be on a number of legacies that are primarily political, but had implications socially, culturally and economically (Owen, 1992). Specifically, efforts at creating centralised, highly bureaucratic states also saw the emergence of largely hollow political institutions where there was little, if any, separation between the state and the regime. Also, the emergence of new political elites, often sponsored by European powers, was complemented with efforts to control the religious institutions in each territory. Finally, economic dependency and a permeating sense of cultural tension all fed into the political environment that would emerge with the independence of the Middle Eastern states in the 20th century.

CENTRALISED RULE

Efforts at establishing centralised rule were a key feature of European activity in the Middle East. This built on the reforms of the late Ottoman period that gave key urban centres a greater degree of control over their immediate hinterlands. As with each of these processes, this was not uniform. As Roger Owen has outlined, this built on more established territorial entities such as authority from Algiers in what would become the state of Algeria in 1964, creating new entities as an amalgam of former Ottoman provinces, such as the extension of Damascus and Baghdad's authority over what would become Syria in 1946 and Iraq in 1932, or the creation of new entities such as Amman's administration of what would become the state of Jordan in 1946 (Owen, 1992: 9).

Into each of these entities, European powers sponsored the development of centralised bureaucracies that often built on the framework of Ottoman rule, with a particular focus on the establishment of effective security services and economies. The main features of centralised administration revolved around the security services (Owen, 1992: 10). Indeed, there was little focus on the development of public education systems, health services and other state functions that have traditionally been the drivers of integration. This, combined with the emerging narrative that criticised the very existence of these new entities as artificial European creations, led these entities to increasingly exhibit tendencies towards basing their rule increasingly on coercive means.

A Focus on Security

Ironically, the reliance on state coercion would see the development of powerful security services in many of the new states in the Middle East. It would be from these institutions that many of the successful challengers to European dominance, whether the overthrow of direct European rule or the overthrow of proxy regimes, would emerge in Egypt, Iraq, Syria and elsewhere. As Kamrava contends, the 'very genesis of most modern Middle Eastern states is traced back to the armed forces' (Kamrava, 2000: 68) where this military heritage permeates most, if not all, aspects of the current character of these states.

> The military has ruled a large number of Middle Eastern states since independence. In addition, it has been active in subverting the fragile political institutions through a number of military coups, including in Egypt in 1952 and 2011, Algeria in 1965 and 1992, and Iraq in 1933, 1937, 1949, 1952 and 1958. This will be discussed in more detail in Chapter 6.

In particular, most current regimes continue to rely, in one way or another, on the institution of the military to buttress its rule, continue to exist only through trade-offs with the military, or serve as proxy regimes for a 'shadow' military administration. Whilst this may be an extreme view of the power of the military in the Middle East, even in the wake of the uprisings since late 2010, it does capture the importance of the military in the formation of the modern Middle East.

In addition, existing power dynamics were also exploited to maintain order. In Egypt and Iraq, the British sought to favour large landowners through the implementation of favourable land laws and taxation. Whilst this had the effect of fostering resentment amongst the bulk of the population and shaping much of the populist discourse of nationalist movements that would emerge prior to and after World War II, it also set in train a dynamic whereby central authorities would be viewed as the holders and distributors of power and wealth, a pattern that would continue after independence.

These were not wholly uniform approaches. Indeed, there was a variety of local proxies employed by the Europeans as well as new systems of government developed under their League of Nations authorised tutelage. For instance, the British reliance on monarchical authority in Egypt, Transjordan, Iraq and the Gulf with the French favouring republican models in Syria and Tunisia. Despite this, centralised rule was pursued, but through different means: the sponsorship of monarchies saw some delegation of powers to the monarch where this institution would be subject to influence from the colonial authority. In republican systems, the colonial power would seek to exert more direct influence on compliant regimes.

NEW ELITES AND NEW INSTITUTIONS

Where debate continues to exist over the notion of the artificiality of these states, there is little disagreement in terms of the recent origin of the new political institutions in each state. The colonial powers, in essence, sought to create new institutions within new territorial entities in a relatively short period of time. As was outlined above, this was not a terribly effective process, one that led to an over-emphasis on state security services and an under-development of other areas such as education, health and social services.

Syria captures these themes in a variety of ways. Nazih Ayubi has defined Syria as a 'residual state' (Ayubi, 1999: 114) after the divisions of Sykes–Picot and the Mandate system. As such, even where there had been moves towards the centralisation of authority around the area of Damascus, the territorial scope of this was markedly different from what had been envisioned by local elites or what was reflected in the established patterns of local cultural, economic and even familial relations on the ground. As a result, existing patterns of authority and economy sought to adapt whilst new groups pushed to move from positions of marginalisation to take control of this new environment.

New Political Elites

In this regard, these arrangements saw the emergence of a range of new political elites. For instance, the reliance on coercive policies saw a continuation of the Ottoman efforts at exploiting ethnic and religious diversity as a means to maintain their authority. In Syria, the French sponsored the enlistment of large numbers of the Alawite minority, a group that had previously been on the margins of power in the region, to key posts within the new military. Combined with an exploitation of class cleavages, the colonial process both amplified existing antagonisms as well as created new players in the political system. As such, the view of historians such as Elie Podeh captures what was an interplay between a series of pre-existing identities and new allegiances during this period (Podeh, 1998). This dynamic would in many ways be frozen upon independence or overthrow of the many Western-backed governments across the region.

In terms of economic development, the European powers tied the economies of these territories closely to their own, including the direct management of economies out of European capitals rather than through the colonial capital. As a result, any move towards local control or regulation of the local economy was undermined. This saw the development of new economic elites, a small group who were able to take advantage of this form of colonial mercantilism. This created tension with existing economic elites, often large landowners, who tried to

Figure 2.15 From left: images of central Damascus and central Baghdad in the early
20th century

Sources: Maher Sayadi, Public domain

shore up their dominant position in the rapidly changing political and economic environment.

However, even with independence or revolutionary change, the emerging states in the Middle East would carry the legacy of the institutions of this time through to today. Centralised rule based largely on coercive means, a prominent military role in politics, tense class and ethnic divisions, under-developed education systems and strong yet volatile links to European powers played a key role in the various forms of populist, autocratic politics that would emerge in the Middle East after World War II.

CONTROL OF THE RELIGIOUS SPHERE

Another key part of this process was an effort to control the religious sphere through a variety of means, such as official secularisation policies and reforms of religious institutions. As Halliday has pointed out, this was not necessarily an ideological commitment to the idea of a separation of mosque and state but an effort to strengthen state or, more specifically, regime, authority (Halliday, 2005). With some exceptions, religious institutions were a source of authority and legitimacy that was largely outside the control of these new regimes. Therefore, installing secularism as a priority of the political process sanctioned efforts to undermine religious authorities or establish state-sanctioned religious institutions.

This was not a one-way process in terms of external parties or new regimes simply shaping society, nor was there a uniform trend towards secularisation across the region. Indeed, the very weakness of these new states required some accommodation with popular sentiment. The establishment of state-sanctioned religious institutions was one means by which new states sought to manipulate popular religiosity for their own ends. This was a continuation of the Ottoman policy of seeking to bring the religious establishment under state control, particularly during the reforms of the 18th and 19th centuries.

Here, colonial authorities continued the practice of putting an official clergy (`ulama`) on the government payroll and administering real estate holdings of the various religious establishments through the central government (Owen, 1992: 29). This was complemented with the creation of secular education systems and civil law codes in areas such as Syria, Jordan, Tunisia and Egypt to mitigate the influence of religious authorities. This policy also blended the religious and governmental, with the use of religious edicts, or *fatwas*, to legitimate government policy and, by proxy, the very existence of these new governments.

Figure 2.16 Cairo's Al-Azhar mosque in the early 20th century

Source: Public domain

THE CULTURAL CHALLENGE

Perhaps the most subtle, yet controversial impact of this period was not so much in the reshaping of the political landscape, or the creation of economic dependency on colonial powers, but the cultural challenge to the people of the region. Indeed, the rationale employed by the European powers for their dominance of the region in many ways shaped the political discourse of the modern Middle East and laid the foundations for the particularly volatile relationship between the region and Western states.

Lord Evelyn Baring Cromer, Consul-General in Egypt from 1883 to 1907:

The European is a close reasoner his statements of fact are devoid of ambiguity; he is a natural logician; ... his trained intelligence works like a piece of mechanism. The mind of the Oriental, on the other hand, like his picturesque streets, is eminently wanting in symmetry. His reasoning is of the most slipshod description. Although the ancient Arabs acquired in a somewhat higher degree the sciences of dialectics, their descendants are singularly deficient in the logical faculty.

Figure 2.17   Born in Jerusalem, Edward Said (1935–2003) was Professor of English and Comparative Literature at Columbia University, New York. Said's work has had profound impacts on the way in which culture and politics in the Middle East are understood

Source: Columbia News

This challenge can perhaps best be understood through the notion of the 'civilising mission'. Whilst this was a concept predominantly employed by the French, it does help understand the efforts to justify the imposition of European domination over the Middle East as well as in Africa, South and East Asia and Latin America. Central to this was an understanding of human societies each on a path of 'development', with the European states leading the way towards a more 'civilised' future.

Overlaid with ideas of Social Darwinism and the supposed innate superiority of particular ways of life, the European powers continually justified their presence in the region in terms of laying the groundwork for development and civilisation. Indeed, the very idea behind the Mandate system sponsored by the League of Nations is built on this principle, where the European states would sponsor a 'backward' culture in its search for 'modernity'.

Said and Orientalism

The prejudice of this perspective is clearly evident. However, as Edward Said has famously contended, this ran deeper than statements justifying immediate political and economic domination. Said's *Orientalism* argued that the very notion of an uncivilised Orient, or other, was a construction of stereotypes used not to understand other cultures and peoples, but to claim the idea of 'modernity' as an exclusively Western possession. Indeed, this construct of the 'Orient' was used to 'define Europe' (Said, 1979: 1) as modern, rational and possessing of a capacity for reasoned thought as opposed to the constructed 'Oriental'.

This discourse permeated almost all aspects of European activity in the Middle East, and fed into the emergence of new political trends in the region. For instance, the focus on the supposed superiority of Western culture and Western religious culture was used as justification for the attempts to dismantle the religious institutions in many Middle Eastern societies as incompatible with modernity. This debate over religion, particularly Islam, and modernity facilitated the various discourses around the emergence of Islamic reformist movements and secularist movements across the region through the 19th and 20th centuries, with many elements of this discourse still resonating today.

DEPENDENCY

As a result of these factors, a sense of dependence was the dominant feature of the relationship between the Middle East and Europe. Even before the independence of these states, they had been developed in such a way as to leave them at the mercy of developments outside their borders and beyond their control. Even issues directly relevant to the future of these communities were either removed from their decision-making or were decided on by local elites who acted in concert with European powers.

As such, we can see the emergence of patterns of rule at this time that resonated through the rest of the 20th century – really only substantially challenged by the early 21st century during the so-called 'Arab Spring' – whereby Middle Eastern states relied on a mixture of external support, patronage, wealth distribution, symbology, direct coercion and indirect or threatened coercion to maintain their rule. This is certainly not an exceptional dynamic, as these methods of rule are present amongst most regions across the globe. What is important and perhaps exceptional is the degree to which these regimes, all of which were characterised by some form of authoritarianism or autocracy, have been able to survive almost unchallenged since independence.

PALESTINE AND ISRAEL

Encapsulating these trends, particularly in terms of external interference, the emergence of new political trends and their interplay with pre-existing ideologies, the impacts of new political institutions, elites and communities, was the controversy surrounding the British Mandate of Palestine and the early steps towards the founding of the State of Israel in 1948. Whilst the immediate circumstances and controversies around the establishment of Israel will be discussed in Chapter 3, this section will outline the ideological basis for Jewish settlement in the Palestine Mandate and how this is connected to statehood. In addition, it will explore how the role of the British worked to amplify the tensions between the Arab and Jewish communities, leaving the status of the Palestine Mandate in a highly ambiguous state on the eve of World War II.

ZIONISM

The philosophical origins of the movement towards the establishment of the state of Israel in 1948 can be found in the Zionist movement. Broadly, Zionism emerged amongst Jewish intellectuals in Eastern and Central Europe as an ideology calling for the reconstitution of Jewish life on a national basis. That is, a focus on the creation of a nation-state to secure the survival and livelihood of the Jewish community. Whilst there was some debate as to where this new state would be created, the focus on the Biblical Holy Land, the territory that would become the Palestine Mandate, was present from early on.

Figure 2.18 From left: Theodor Herzl (1860–1904) and Leon Pinsker (1821–91)
Source: Public domain

As with other nationalist ideologies of the time, Zionism was a response to the emergence of European national identities. However, the emergence of these identities posed a particular threat to Jewish communities who had often existed in these communities in the face of intense hostility. This hostility, as anti-Semitism, increased markedly throughout Europe in the 19th century, providing the impetus for the growth in popularity of the Zionist movement. Whilst there was a uniform focus on the creation of a Jewish state, the Zionist movement displayed a great deal of diversity, including streams with a more class-based Marxist focus and others with a more explicitly religious focus. However, it was the liberal stream, most clearly articulated by Theodor Herzl and Leon Pinsker, that would articulate the dominant Zionist vision through the late 19th and early 20th century.

Anti-Semitism in Germany peaked through the early decades of the 20th century, before its climax in the devastation of the Holocaust. Anti-Semitism was not limited to Germany, but became part of the Nazi regime's policy platform when the Jewish community was stripped of citizenship rights and the state sponsored organised violence against the community. Upon the outbreak of World War II, the Nazi regime implemented a programme of genocide that led to the death of 6 million of Europe's estimated 9 million Jewish population.

Debates on how the Zionist vision would be achieved are one of the many intense controversies surrounding the establishment of Israel, with this debate continuing to shape political debates in contemporary Israel (see Chapter 9). Here, the central aim of the Zionist movement, to 'construct in Palestine a distinct Jewish community', linked to the Balfour Declaration's facilitation of the creation of a 'Jewish national home' in Palestine left a range of issues ambiguous. In particular, how would this new 'home' be constructed in terms of the existing population of the area? In this regard, Shima Flapan outlines a range of Zionist goals that centre on the importance of external sponsorship of Jewish statehood, the creation of a Jewish community distinct from the Arab community in Palestine, an effort to undermine the emergence or emphasis on a distinct Palestinian Arab national identity that may compete with Zionist territorial claims and the sponsorship of Jewish migration to strengthen the Zionist claims to the territory (Flapan, 1979).

An important element of this debate in Zionism includes the perspectives of so-called 'revisionist' Zionism. Drawing primarily on the writing of Ze'ev Jabotinsky, revisionist Zionism is a perspective that focussed on the establishment of a Jewish state in the entire original British Mandate, one that included the future Mandate and modern-day state of Jordan. As is discussed in Chapter 9, Jabotinsky's ideas were highly influential on the ideologies of Israel's right-wing parties, particularly Likud, and their reticence to negotiate over the partition of any part of the Israeli state in negotiations with the Palestinians.

THE KING–CRANE COMMISSION

In line with the creation of a Jewish state, the Zionist movement began to finance the migration (*aliyah*) of Jews to the Ottoman-held territories in the eastern Mediterranean, a process that would accelerate after the creation of the Palestine Mandate in 1923. Indeed, elements of the Balfour Declaration were included in the British Mandate of Palestine, retaining reference to a 'national home' as opposed to the creation of a Jewish 'state'. As mentioned previously, this policy saw the Jewish community in Palestine grow to 60,000, or 8% of the total population in 1914, a community who held an estimated 10% of the land in the territory.

As the Balfour Declaration fed into the broader controversy over European interests, the United States launched an investigation into the process by which former Ottoman territories were being managed after World War I. This commission, established by US President Woodrow Wilson and headed by Henry Churchill King and Charles Crane, was guided by Wilson's stated desire, outlined in the famous 'Fourteen Points' speech of 1918, to allow the non-Turkish communities of the Ottoman Empire the 'unmolested opportunity of autonomous development'.

The Ambiguity of the King–Crane Commission

Whilst the findings of the King–Crane Commission in relation to the broader region argued for the US to replace the British and French in occupying the region, it famously questioned the viability of the creation of a Jewish state in the area to become the Palestine Mandate. Indeed, in surveying the largely hostile attitudes of the Arab community to a growing Jewish presence and particularly to the rising popularity of the Zionist movement alongside the growing, yet nascent size of the Jewish community in the region, the commission concluded that the only means by which such a state could be established would be through 'a practically complete dispossession of the present non-Jewish inhabitants of Palestine'. Instead, the commission argued for the creation of a 'Greater Syria', inclusive of the Syrian, Jordanian and Palestinian Mandates that would have protection for minorities enshrined in any future constitution. Despite this, as we have seen, the commission did not affect the outcome of the post-World War I negotiations that saw a division of the region and an incorporation of the goals of the Balfour Declaration in the Palestine Mandate. However, it did feed into the growing antagonism between the communities as each fought to establish the validity of their claims over the Biblical Holy Land.

THE BRITISH WHITE PAPERS AND THE ARAB REVOLT

On the eve of the formal establishment of the Palestine Mandate in 1923, and in the wake of unrest amongst the Arab community in Palestine during 1920 and 1921, British colonial policy became increasingly mired in confusion. In an attempt to clarify its stance in relation to the question of Palestine, then Colonial Secretary Winston Churchill and British High Commissioner in Palestine Herbert Samuel released a White Paper to clarify the official British government's stance.

The 1922 (Churchill) White Paper

In brief, whilst the White Paper reiterated the British government's support for the sentiments contained in the Balfour Declaration, it also sought to distance the British position from the establishment of a separate Jewish state. Here, the White Paper focussed on the use of the phrase 'national home' in the document, one that would have international guarantees for the protection of Jewish rights. However,

the White Paper also sought to counter the claims of those who pointed to the provisions of the Hussein–McMahon Correspondence, arguing that the area to the west of the River Jordan was never part of the original discussions. Acting on this, the British subsequently moved to formally separate these territories from the Mandate of Jordan, leading to the creation of the two separate Mandates of Palestine and Transjordan in 1923.

In an attempt to court relations with both sides, the White Paper also outlined limits for Jewish migration to the territory whilst also enshrining the right of the *aliyah* process. This had little effect

Figure 2.19 The British Mandates of Palestine and Transjordan in 1922

Source: Seblini

on the growth of the Jewish migrant population in Palestine or the increasing rate of land transfer from the Arab to the Jewish community. It also did little to undercut the growing suspicion amongst the Jewish community that the British were backing away from what they saw as a promise for the support for an independent Jewish state as expressed in the Balfour Declaration. It is here that we can see how a lack of trust with which external powers are viewed in relation to this issue was founded. Indeed, it is the very mishandling by the colonial power and the confused policies that it pursued that helped created the volatile environment leading up to the creation of the State of Israel in 1948.

Figure 2.20   Winston Churchill (1874–1965) as Colonial Secretary

Source: Public domain

The Arab Revolt and the 1937 Peel Commission

The tensions between the two communities and from both communities towards the British grew through the 1930s. For the Arab Palestinian community, a severe deterioration of the economic environment, particularly for the poorer rural communities, combined with the increasing rate of Jewish migration and land acquisition and a seeming British deference to these issues, led to the outbreak of conflict in 1936. Initially manifesting as a series of strikes across the Mandate, the Arab Revolt escalated into a full-scale yet highly disorganised insurrection by 1937 that left an estimated 4000–5000 dead (Hughes, 2009: 235).

In the wake of the outbreak of the Arab Revolt, the British government dispatched Earl William Peel to Palestine in November 1936 to investigate the causes of the uprising. The report of the Peel Commission (officially known as the Palestine Royal Commission) established one of the seminal themes of this conflict, partition. Specifically, the commission recommended that the Palestine Mandate be abolished, to be replaced by two new entities, a Jewish state along the central and northern coast of the Mandate, including the Galilee region, and an Arab state in the remaining portions of the territory with an internationally administered area around Jerusalem through to the coast south of Tel Aviv. Controversially, the report also recommended a population exchange along the lines that took place in western Turkey between the Greek and Turkish communities and that would later take place with the partition of India (cited in Rabinovich and Reinharz, 2008: 44).

Whilst Arab opinion was almost unanimous in its rejection of the proposal, Zionist opinion was divided, with some arguing that it did not achieve the aims of Zionism in all of *Eretz Israel* (Hebrew for the Land of Israel) and others arguing that it was a critical first step in the realisation of a Jewish state in the territory. This would be a trend mirrored later when the newly established United Nations proposed partition of Palestine in 1947. Also, this notion of partition still resonates in current discussions of a 'two state solution' for the Arab–Israeli conflict. Ultimately, however, the subsequent British-led 1938 Partition Commission, whilst outlining a series of other partition recommendations, concluded that population transfers and the financial fragility of these new entities would make this process too difficult.

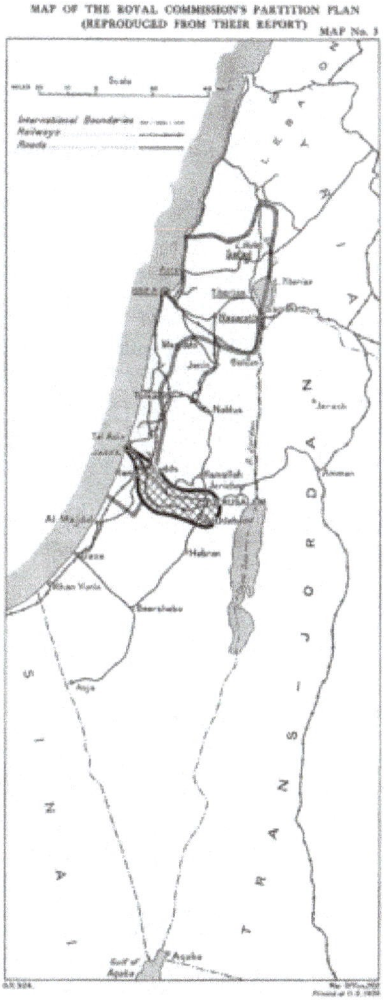

The 1939 (MacDonald) White Paper

With the collapse of discussions on partition, and war looming in Europe, the British sought to quell the violence through the convening of a conference in 1939 with both Arab and Jewish leaders. The failure of this conference to reach any meaningful agreement led British Colonial Secretary Malcolm MacDonald to issue a new White Paper in 1939, one that was framed in the context of courting Arab opinion in the

Figure 2.21 The map of the Partition Proposal from the 1937 Peel Commission

Source: Public domain

lead-up to World War II. Essentially, the new British government stance was to detach itself from any move towards the establishment of a Jewish state, whilst still supporting the idea of Jewish rights enshrined in any post-independence arrangement.

Figure 2.22 A 1936 labour strike in Jerusalem during the Arab Revolt
Source: Public domain

Figure 2.23 Jewish settlers in Palestine in the early 20th century
Source: Public domain

Significantly, the 1939 White Paper sought strict limits on Jewish migration and land acquisition. The Jewish community had increased to around 30% of the population by the late 1930s, whilst owning between 5% and 7% of the land in the Mandate. The majority of the Arab land was owned by large landowners, often absentee, who appeared increasingly willing to sell large sections of arable land to the new settlers. This act, particularly the provisions relating to land ownership, did have the effect of mitigating some of the antagonism behind the Arab Revolt. However, it led to the British becoming the focus for Zionist agitation.

As such, on the eve of World War II the British had overseen a situation in Palestine that led to simmering tensions between the two major communities there as well as highly strained relations between the colonial authority and these communities. This in many ways captured the broader themes of this period in terms of the creation of largely arbitrary borders, the creation of an environment of dependency and cultural antagonism, an ineffective management of local community interests and a confused, self-interested colonial policy.

BRITISH COLONIALISM IN IRAQ

Where the controversies surrounding the Mandate system and external intervention gained considerable attention in Palestine, the British presence in Iraq, or the 'British Mandate of Mesopotamia', was in many ways equally important. Indeed, the British presence in Iraq between 1916 and 1932 and then again during the early years of World War II laid the groundwork for the suspicion and hostility with which successive Iraqi regimes viewed the UK and later the US.

> Lt. Gen. Stanley Maude – proclamation of Baghdad in 1917 – 'I am charged with absolute and supreme control of all regions in which British troops operate; but our armies do not come to your cities and lands as conquerors or enemies, but as liberators.'

As was discussed above, Faisal bin Hussein was active in cooperating with the British in the Arab revolt against the Ottomans during World War I. Faisal ruled the short-lived Arab Kingdom of Syria centred on Damascus, a kingdom that lasted from March to July 1920. However, despite support for the creation of an independent and unitary Arab state in the King–Crane Commission, the British and particularly the French pursued the division of the Levant according to the tenets of the Sykes–Picot Agreement, seeing the end of the short-lived kingdom.

British authority was established in Iraq in 1920, seeing the emergence of a new territorial entity out of the three former Ottoman *vilayets* of Mosul in the north, Baghdad in the centre and Basra in the south. This included highly diverse communities, including Kurdish, Turkmen and Assyrian populations in the north, a large

Arab Sunni community through the centre of the country, an Arab Shi`a in the south that was the largest single group, as well as a highly diverse population in the new capital of Baghdad. The borders of the new state were also controversial in that they limited Iraq to 58 kilometres of coastline along the Gulf, allocating this to the British-controlled territory of Kuwait (Cleveland and Bunton, 2009: 204–5). This would be a source of tension that culminated in the ill-fated 1990 Iraqi invasion of Kuwait and subsequent US-led military intervention (see Chapters 7 and 8).

The British initially ruled through the Foreign Office, however this became untenable with the outbreak of the 1920 Iraqi Revolution, an anti-British revolt that spanned the country's Sunni and Shi`a communities seeking British withdrawal. It was a critical event in modern Iraqi history, one that some consider as forming a key narrative in the formation of a separate Iraqi identity (Tripp, 2002: 44). This was built on the severity of the British response to the armed uprising. In excess of 6000 Iraqis died during the height of the conflict between July and October 1920 along with over 500 British soldiers (Tauber, 1995: 15).

With their authority established in Iraq after crushing the 1920 uprising, the British installed Faisal as king in Baghdad in August 1921. Whilst the new king had nominal authority, the 1922 Anglo–Iraqi Treaty limited his powers, with the British maintaining a military presence in the country and increasing dominance of the new Iraqi oil industry (Cleveland and Bunton, 2009: 208). This close relationship with Britain continued after Iraqi independence in 1932, a relationship that

Figure 2.24   From left: King Faisal I (23 August 1921–8 September 1933), King Ghazi I (8 September 1933–4 April 1939) and King Faisal II (4 April 1939–14 July 1958)

Source: Public domain

also bred a degree of popular resentment, particularly over the meagre returns from what was increasingly seen as vast potential oil wealth. As such, without the astute leadership of Faisal I after his death in 1933, the institution of the monarchy under his successors, Ghazi I (1933–9) and Faisal II (1939–58) were increasingly portrayed as leaving Iraq open to continued exploitation and foreign control, a theme that would be prominent in the 1958 Revolution that fundamentally changed Iraqi politics and society (see Chapter 3).

CONCLUSION

This chapter has sought to outline the interplay between the legacies of the Ottoman period and the impacts of increasing European dominance. Here, the foundations for the modern state system were forged based on a questionable territorial division of the region as well as trends towards the establishment of authoritarian regimes. This period also saw the crystallisation of many of the issues that continue to define the region's political landscape including the origins of the Israeli–Palestinian conflict as well as controversies over the role of foreign powers in the region. It was from here that, as we shall see in Chapter 3, the region moved towards independence within the changed international environment of the Cold War, an era that would see the Middle East increasingly viewed as a region in crisis.

Study Questions

- In what ways did Ottoman rule combine with colonial and imperial activity to shape the modern state system in the Middle East?
- In what ways were contemporary political ideologies and political rhetoric in the Middle East shaped by this 'colonial encounter'?
- How did colonial patterns differ across the Middle East and what impacts did this have?
- What are the controversies surrounding the establishment of the Republic of Turkey and how do they shape current issues?
- Was there a significant difference in the relationship between Middle Eastern states and Western states through the 20th and into the 21st centuries as there was during the colonial period?
- What were the impacts of the cultural discourses of colonialism on the relations between the Middle East and Western states and societies?
- In what ways did the issues of the Mandate period shape the controversies surrounding the establishment of the State of Israel?

FURTHER READING

Choueiri, Youssef (ed.) (2005) *A Companion to the History of the Middle East.* New York: Wiley-Blackwell.
A comprehensive volume that covers the key themes that dominated the religious, social, cultural, economic, political and military origins of the modern Middle East.

Cleveland, William L. and Bunton, Martin (2009) *A History of the Modern Middle East*, 4th ed. Boulder, CO: Westview Press.
Now in its fourth edition, this seminal volume provides a highly detailed account of the modern political history of the region.

Fromkin, David (2001) *A Peace to End All Peace: The Fall of the Ottoman Empire and the Creation of the Modern Middle East.* New York: Owl Books.
A compelling account of the specific events around the collapse of the Ottoman Empire, providing critical insight into the dynamics that shaped the emergence of the modern state system in the Middle East.

Khalidi, Rashid (2005) *Resurrecting Empire: Western Footprints and America's Perilous Path in the Middle East.* New York: Beacon Press.
A critical examination of the patterns of Western interventionism in the Middle East, a trend that has impacted greatly on the rhetoric and ideologies of the region today.

Rubin, Barry (1981) *The Great Powers in the Middle East 1941–1947: The Road to the Cold War.* London: Routledge.
Based on extensive archival research, this volume details the machinations between 'Great Powers' during the World War II period and its impacts on the Middle East.

 Go to the companion website at www.sagepub.co.uk/macqueen for further material including free journal articles and links to other relevant documents.

REFERENCES

Andrew, Christopher M. (1981) *The Climax of French Imperial Expansion: 1914–1924.* Stanford, CA: Stanford University Press.
Ayubi, Nazih (1999) *Overstating the Arab State: Politics and Society in the Middle East.* London: I.B. Tauris.
Cleveland, William L. and Bunton, Martin (2009) *A History of the Modern Middle East*, 4th ed. Boulder, CO: Westview Press.
Dadrian, Vahakn N. (1995) *The History of the Armenian Genocide: Ethnic Conflict from the Balkans to Anatolia to the Caucasus.* Oxford: Berghahn Books.

Davidson, Christopher (2012) *Power and Politics in the Persian Gulf Monarchies.* New York: Columbia University Press

Deeb, Marius (1979) *Party Politics in Egypt: The Wafd and its Rivals, 1919–38.* Ithaca, NY: Ithaca Press.

Evans, Martin (2012) *Algeria: France's Undeclared War.* Oxford: Oxford University Press.

Flapan, Shima (1979) *Zionism and the Palestinians.* London: Croom Helm.

Halliday, Fred (2005) *The Middle East in International Relations.* Cambridge: Cambridge University Press.

Hughes, Matthew (2009) 'A Very British Affair? The Repression of the Arab Revolt in Palestine, 1936–39 (Part One)', *Journal of the Society for Army Historical Research*, 87 (351): 234–55.

Kamrava, Mehran (2000) 'Military Professionalization and Civil–Military Relations in the Middle East', *Political Science Quarterly*, 115 (1): 67–92.

Mitchell, Richard P. (1993) *The Society of the Muslim Brothers.* Oxford: Oxford University Press.

Morris, Benny (2009) *1948: A History of the First Arab–Israeli War.* New Haven, CT: Yale University Press.

Owen, Roger (1992) *State, Power and Politics and the Making of the Modern Middle East.* London: Routledge.

Pappé, Ilan (2006) *A History of Modern Palestine: One Land, Two Peoples.* Cambridge: Cambridge University Press.

Perkins, Kenneth A. (1986) *Tunisia: Crossroads of the Islamic and European Worlds.* Boulder, CO: Westview Press.

Podeh, Elie (1998) 'The Emergence of the Arab State System Reconsidered', *Diplomacy and Statecraft*, 9 (3): 50–82.

Powell Eve, M. Troutt (2003) *A Different Shade of Colonialism: Egypt, Great Britain, and the Mastery of the Sudan.* Berkeley: University of California Press.

Rabinovich, Itamar and Reinharz, Jehuda (2008) *Israel in the Middle East: Documents and Readings on Society, Politics, and Foreign Relations, Pre–1948 to the Present.* Lebanon, NH: Brandeis University Press.

Said, Edward (1979) *Orientalism.* New York: Penguin.

Sessions, Jennifer E. (2011) *By Sword and Plow: France and the Conquest of Algeria.* Ithaca, NY: Cornell University Press.

Silverstein, Paul A. (2004) *Algeria in France: Transpolitics, Race, and Nation.* Bloomington: Indiana University Press.

Tauber, Eliezer (1995) *The Formation of Modern Syria and Iraq.* London: Frank Cass.

Tessler, Mark (1994) *A History of the Israeli–Palestinian Conflict.* Bloomington: Indiana University Press.

Tripp, Charles (2002) *A History of Iraq.* Cambridge: Cambridge University Press.

Wright, William (2010) *A Tidy Little War: The British Invasion of Egypt 1882.* Stroud: The History Press.

3

Superpower Rivalry and the Cold War in the Middle East

Learning Objectives

This chapter will enable a greater understanding of:

- The impacts of World War II on the Middle East and the emergence of independent states in the region.
- The emergence of the State of Israel and the core controversies of the Arab–Israeli conflict.
- The decline of colonial influence in the region and the transfer to the Cold War environment.
- The impacts of the Cold War, particularly the impacts of superpower foreign policy on regional political dynamics.
- How regional events, such as the Yemen Civil War, the Lebanese Civil War and the Iran–Iraq War, capture the impacts of the Cold War on the Middle East.

TIMELINE

2–31 May 1941: Anglo–Iraqi War

25 August 1941: Anglo–Soviet invasion of Iran

22 November 1943: Lebanese independence

17 April 1946: Syrian independence

25 May 1946: Jordanian independence

22 July 1946: King David Hotel bombing

29 November 1947: UNGA Resolution 181

14 May 1948: Israeli independence

24 December 1951: Libyan independence

23 July 1952: Free Officers' Coup in Egypt

19 August 1953: US-backed overthrow of Mossadeq government in Iran

1 November 1954–19 March 1962: Algerian War of Independence

17 November 1954: Nasser becomes President of Egypt

1 January 1956: Sudanese independence

20 March 1956: Tunisian independence

7 April 1956: Moroccan independence

26 July 1956: Nasser nationalises the Suez Canal

29 October–6 November 1956: Suez Crisis

14 July 1958: Overthrow of Iraqi monarchy

27 May 1960: Military coup in Turkey

19 June 1961: Kuwaiti independence

3 July 1962: Algerian independence

1962–1970: Yemen Civil War

8 February 1963: Ba'ath Party coup in Iraq

30 November 1967: South Yemeni independence

1 September 1969: Muammar Gaddhafi comes to power in Libya

15 September 1970–5 April 1971: Black September clashes in Jordan

12 March 1971: Military coup in Turkey

15 August 1971: Bahraini independence

3 September 1971: Qatari independence

2 December 1971: UAE independence

5 April 1971: PLO moves to Lebanon

1975–1990: Lebanese Civil War

10 June 1976: Syrian invasion of Lebanon

14 March 1978: First Israeli invasion of Lebanon

16 July 1979: Saddam Hussein becomes President of Iraq

24 December 1979: Soviet invasion of Afghanistan

12 September 1980: Military coup in Turkey

22 September 1980–20 August 1988: Iran–Iraq War

7 June 1981: Israeli attacks on Osiraq Facility

6 June 1982: Second Israeli invasion of Lebanon

18 April 1983: US Embassy bombing in Beirut

23 October 1983: Beirut Marine Barracks bombings

22 May 1990: Yemeni Unification

INTRODUCTION

The decades following World War II were critical in setting the main themes, controversies and political structures of the Middle East. This chapter will explore the Cold War period in the Middle East, with an emphasis on how global political dynamics interacted with local issues and forces. Here, a series of regional issues will be examined, notably the formation of the State of Israel, the Yemen Civil War, the Lebanese Civil War and the Iran–Iraq War, in order to explore how global political dynamics have impacted on regional affairs and how events in the Middle East have shaped global politics. In doing this, a series of assumptions about this period will be challenged. Specifically, a common theme of this period has been the efforts by the Cold War superpowers to manipulate the foreign policy of smaller states.

However, this chapter will outline how the regimes of the Middle East were able to act with a high degree of autonomy in pursuing their own interests. These interests were not always for the greater good of the people of the region, aimed primarily at perpetuating their rule. It was in this environment that resentment towards external powers amongst the people of the region became further entrenched, a theme that will be explored in subsequent chapters.

WORLD WAR II AND A NEW INTERNATIONAL RELATIONS OF THE MIDDLE EAST

In the lead-up to World War II, the European powers exerted more direct control over various parts of the Middle East. Ironically, this direct form of control came in the context of the obligations to prepare regional communities for independence under the League of Nations Mandate system. With the outbreak of war, the European powers vied for control of the region to control its strategic location and the importance of its oil resources. Local independence movements were largely inactive during this period, with large numbers of Algerians, Moroccans, Egyptians, Lebanese, Syrians and others participating in the war effort as part of British and Free French forces. The exception to this was the uprising in Iraq in 1942 that led to a British intervention and occupation.

During the war, the British and Free French troops along with a number of Commonwealth forces from Australia, New Zealand and Canada, occupied Egypt, Lebanon and Syria, whilst British and Soviet forces occupied the south and north of Iran respectively. This was a last glimpse of colonial might in the Middle East, with the end of World War II paving the way for a fundamentally new international system as well as a new regional political order.

This new international system came to be defined as a 'Cold War' between the United States and the Soviet Union. The Cold War was a confrontation between these two global powers, dominant after World War II. As such, the international environment was now a bipolar system, dominated by these states that operated

Figure 3.1 Australian troops in North Africa, January 1941

Source: Australian War Memorial

in confrontation with one another. It was a *cold* conflict in that it did not directly involve a conventional military confrontation between the two superpowers (Sayigh and Shlaim, 1997: 1).

In terms of the rhetorical and ideological confrontation, this broadly centred on the economic policies of capitalism and communism and, to a lesser extent, the

Figure 3.2 British troops in Iraq during the Anglo–Iraqi War of 1941

Source: Public domain

political systems of 'democratic localism and bureaucratic centralism' (Reynolds, 2000: 21). In other words, two poles of influence emerged around the US and its ideas of capitalism and democracy and the Soviet Union and its ideas of communism and state control, with each seen as the natural opposite of the other.

The immediate postwar environment was highly fluid. It was in this context that many of the key issues that have defined contemporary Middle Eastern politics were formed. For instance, the controversies surrounding the legitimacy of the state system, the role of ideologies and the military in politics would be issues formed in this period. In addition, the controversy over the status of the British Mandate in Palestine continued, and would be the defining issue of the postwar period in the Middle East.

THE ESTABLISHMENT OF ISRAEL

Figure 3.3 Israel's first Prime
Minister, David Ben
Gurion

Source: Public domain

As noted above, the Palestine Mandate was a site of conflict between Axis and Allied powers during World War II, as well as simmering tension between the Jewish and Palestinian Arab communities up to 1945. By the end of the war and with the emergence of independent states in the region, both communities sought to pursue their goals of an independent Jewish state, independent Arab state, or some form of union with one of the neighbouring states. Events between 1945 and the establishment of the State of Israel in 1948 are shrouded in controversy and remain sites of intense debate amongst historians. Whilst this section will outline this period as part of the discussion on the dynamics of the Cold War in the Middle East, it will also outline the origins of these controversies. Indeed, any interpretation of these events will be controversial. However, whilst readers are encouraged to engage with all particular interpretations, the purpose here is to examine these events to highlight the relative autonomy the key actors possessed during this conflict in order to illustrate how Cold War allegiances did not necessarily dictate the actions of regional states and other actors.

The name 'Israel' comes from the Old Testament book of Genesis (32:28) with the story of Jacob. The word itself means 'he who has striven with God'. The Hebrew *Yi* is the masculine pronoun 'he', *sra* means 'to strive and save' and *el* means 'God'.

The Jewish Revolt and the End of the Palestine Mandate

Whilst tension between Britain and the Zionist movement grew after the 1939 White Paper, they were mitigated somewhat with the election of a Labour government under Clement Attlee. However, whilst Labour had reiterated its support for the establishment of a Jewish state during the election campaign, it became increasingly clear that they would not abrogate the White Paper as the basis for British policy in Palestine. The British calculation was that its postwar reconstruction relied on access to Middle Eastern oil, access that increasingly relied on good relationships with the independent Arab states after World War II.

The Truman administration in the US took a different stance. Whilst seeking the return of displaced Jewish refugees to Europe after the war and the horrors of the Holocaust, Truman became increasingly sympathetic to the idea of the establishment of a Jewish state in Palestine, petitioning the Attlee government to sponsor the settlement of 100,000 Jewish refugees in the Mandate, a petition the British rejected (Fraser, 2008: 29). It was this move that led the Jewish Agency, the peak body pursuing Jewish statehood in Palestine, to move towards open rebellion against the British.

The three main Zionist armed groups, the Haganah (the 'official' armed wing of the Jewish Agency), the Irgun and the Lehi (both militias that had broken from the Haganah before 1945) formed a united command and launched attacks on British installations and infrastructure from October 1945. The Jewish community in Palestine rallied in support of these actions, making British

Figure 3.4 From left: US President Harry Truman and UK Prime Minister Clement Attlee

Sources: Public domain, Library of Congress

counter-insurgency operations virtually impossible, and seeing the revolt escalate through to April 1946.

As the Jewish Revolt continued, the British invited US participation to investigate a political settlement, launching the Anglo-American Commission of Inquiry in late 1945. The Commission's findings, handed down in May 1946, supported the settlement of 100,000 Jewish refugees in Palestine but also dismissed the notion of partition or the creation of ethnically based states, instead calling for an international trusteeship over all of the Palestine Mandate. Both the Jewish Agency and the Arab Higher Committee, who ostensibly represented the Palestinians, rejected the proposal. Wrangling in both London and Washington also saw this ultimately rejected by both governments.

With the collapse of this initiative, fighting broke out again between the Jewish forces and the British as well as between Jewish and Palestinian communities. In a sharp escalation, members of the Irgun bombed the British Mandate headquarters at the King David Hotel in Jerusalem on 22 July 1946, killing 91 people. Whilst

Figure 3.5 The bombing of the King David Hotel, Jerusalem on 22 July 1946

Source: Public domain

the Haganah officially condemned the attack, stating that the Irgun and its leader Menachim Begin (who would become Prime Minister of Israel between 1977 and 1983) had acted independently, it led the British to the conclusion that the costs of maintaining the Mandate were too high, and they should implement a settlement based on partition that would enable them to leave but still access regional oil supplies via the port in Haifa (Clarke, 1981: 26).

This was a seminal moment as the Arab Higher Committee rejected partition in principle whilst the Jewish Agency shifted their position in support of a partition plan. This coincided with an announcement by the Truman administration that they officially supported Jewish statehood with partition as the means to achieve this (Fraser, 2008: 33). For their part, the British referred the issue to the United Nations in early 1947 as they prepared to withdraw from the Mandate. This referral to the UN was important for two reasons. First, it reiterated partition as the official international position for settlement of the conflict and second, it also saw the clarification of the Soviet position, one also supportive of the establishment of a Jewish state. Therefore, both the US and

Figure 3.6 The United Nations Partition Plan for Palestine

Source: Public domain

Soviets supported the creation of an independent Jewish state prior to 1948, and would subsequently court the new Israeli government after its establishment.

The United Nations Special Committee on Palestine (UNSCOP) was charged with investigating a settlement, issuing findings that the British Mandate be terminated and that, on the basis of mutually exclusive interests, the territory be partitioned with Jerusalem as an international zone (UN, 1947). Territorially, both proposed entities would be roughly equal, a situation that favoured the Jewish community who made up an estimated 30% of the population of Palestine at the time. Indeed, the prospective Jewish state, by UNSCOP estimates, would have a slight Arab majority at the time of partition (Fraser, 2008: 37). The Jewish Agency supported the proposal whilst the Arab Higher Committee, along with the British, rejected it.

The **Arab Higher Committee** was established in April 1936 as the political organising committee for Arabs in the Palestine Mandate. It was formed in conjunction with the 1936 Arab Revolt, seeking to coordinate efforts against the British. It had representatives from the religious and tribal establishments, but did exclude some tribal groups and others. Whilst it was increasingly marginalised after 1945, it was given nominal authority to speak on behalf of the Palestinian Arab community, such as with the decision on partition, through to the events of 1948.

The 1947–8 War of Independence/*al-Nakhba*

From this point, the core narratives surrounding the establishment of the State of Israel were formed, many of which continue to define the parameters of the Arab–Israeli conflict. In particular, the issues of Palestinian statehood and territoriality, the use of violence as a political tool, Palestinian refugees, the perception of Israel facing existential threats and the status of Israel vis-à-vis its neighbours. This period is seen by Israelis as their War of Independence and by Palestinians (as well as the broader Arab community) as *al-nakhba*, or 'the disaster', covering the official recommendation by the UN on 29 November 1947 for partition of the Palestine Mandate along the lines of the UNSCOP report through to the Israeli Declaration of Independence on 14 May 1948.

Figure 3.7　David Ben Gurion reads the Israeli Declaration of Independence on 14 May 1948

Source: NSW Jewish Board of Deputies

At the UN, the General Assembly passed Resolution 181 in November for the partition of Palestine. In the wake of this, the violence that had simmered up to this point erupted between the two communities. The Palestinians were highly disorganised with no national military and lacking a command structure, particularly in the wake of the British prosecution of the community's leaders after the 1936–9 Arab Revolt. In contrast, the Zionist forces were well organised via the three main militia groups as well as auxiliaries of other militias. As with almost all events in this period, intense controversy surrounds interpretations of acts of violence against each community. However, the net result of these last months of 1947 was a spiralling of violence, and a complete breakdown of relations between the two communities whilst the remaining British forces stood aside.

Figure 3.8 Jewish refugees arrive in Israel during the war

Source: Public domain

Perhaps the most controversial issue during this period were allegations that the Zionist forces implemented a programme of forced removal of Palestinians in areas under their control. Here, a number of scholars, many of them Israeli revisionist historians, have argued that the Zionist forces either had a plan before the conflict for the removal of the Palestinian population or, in the words of Benny Morris, not a pre-ordained plan but 'transfer was inevitable and inbuilt into Zionism – because it sought to transform a land which was Arab into a Jewish state and a Jewish state could not have arisen without a major displacement of Arab population' (Morris, 2004: 60). Alternatively, others, including the official Israeli government position, argue that the majority of Palestinians left voluntarily. As will be discussed below, and in subsequent chapters, this led to the creation of the Palestinian refugee population that spread throughout the Middle East as well as across the globe. It also saw the origins of the calls for a 'right of return' for these refugees.

Upon the Declaration of Israeli Independence, in the midst of this fighting, on 14 May, the US, Soviet Union and a number of other states immediately recognised the new state. At the same time, armies from Egypt, Iraq, Jordan, Lebanon and Syria with auxiliaries from Saudi Arabia and Yemen invaded Israel. The combined invading Arab armies numbered roughly 25,000, with the Israeli forces numbering roughly 30,000 (a number that increased to over 40,000 by June). Despite some early gains by the Arab armies, it quickly became apparent that

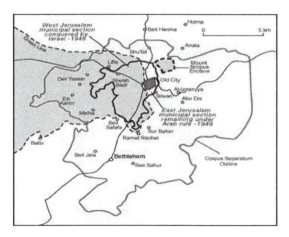

Figure 3.9   The status of Jerusalem from 1948 to 1967

Source: Embassy of the State of Palestine, Kuala Lumpur, Malaysia

they lacked common organisation and leadership, as well as, with the exception of the Jordanian army, modern weaponry. As a result, the Israeli forces were able to eventually push the armies back and claim both territory allocated under the UN Partition Plan as well as Galilee in the north, around Jerusalem including the western half of the city and the south that were areas to be part of the Palestinian state.

By early 1949, Israel had repelled all intervening Arab armies with the exception of Jordanian annexation of the West Bank of the Jordan River, including East Jerusalem as well as Egyptian annexation of the city of Gaza in the south and its immediate hinterland. Armistices were signed with Egypt in February, Lebanon in March, Jordan in April and Syria in July, leaving Israel in control of roughly three-quarters of the Palestine Mandate. Hundreds of thousands of Palestinians left the new state, however a number remained (estimated 10% of the total population). In addition, the large Jewish communities across the Arab world came under increased pressure, often direct government repression and violence, leading to the arrival of thousands of new Jewish migrants to Israel from the region as well as from across the world in the immediate aftermath of the war.

The **United Nations Relief and Works Agency for Palestine** (UNRWA) was created in 1948 as the peak international body providing 'assistance, protection and advocacy' for the Palestinian refugee community. UNRWA classifies these refugees as those who 'are people whose normal place of residence was Palestine between June 1946 and May 1948, who lost both their homes and means of livelihood as a result of the 1948 Arab–Israeli conflict' with descendants also eligible for UNRWA services.

According to UNRWA statistics, the Palestinian refugee population as of 1 January 2011 was 4,966,664 (registered with UNRWA). The largest community is in

Jordan (1,999,466), then Gaza (1,167,361), the West Bank (848,494), Syria (495,970) and Lebanon (455,373). In addition, many Palestinians arrived in states further afield in the Middle East, such as Kuwait and Saudi Arabia, as well as migrating to Europe, the United States, Canada and Australia.

Between 1947 and 1972, up to 900,000 Sephardi and Mizrahi Jews left the Arab states for Israel. Encouraging Jewish migration to Israel is an official part of the country's policy under the *aliyah* ('ascent' in Hebrew) programme. The Jewish communities in the Arab states either voluntarily migrated or were expelled, particularly in the period from 1948 to 1951.

Through this, both the US and the Soviet Union saw benefit in supporting the establishment of Israel, providing rhetorical and financial support as well as arms and intelligence during the conflicts. For the US, the Truman administration had both an ideological commitment to the establishment of Israel as well as a view to Israel as a potential bulwark against Soviet expansionism. For the Soviets, an ideological opposition to Zionism as a form of nationalism was put aside as Israel's confrontation with Britain, as well as the strong socialist roots of the Zionist doctrine, were seen as positive developments as well as potential building blocks for a future partnership. It was later, with the Suez Crisis and the emergence of radical Arab nationalist doctrine that the Soviet Union began to shift to a more hostile position towards Israel. This fluidity was something that benefited both Israel and its adversaries as they were able to manipulate both US and Soviet interests for their own benefit, particularly at times of crisis.

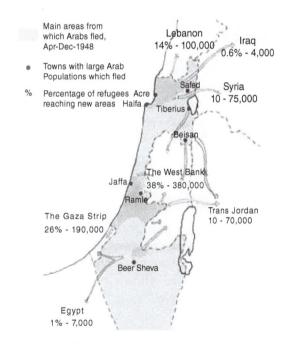

Figure 3.10 Palestinian refugee movements

Source: Jewish Virtual Library

THE COLD WAR IN THE MIDDLE EAST

The Dawn of the Cold War in the Middle East

The ordering principle of Cold War bipolarity defined global politics from the mid-1940s to the 1980s. Here, it has been a common view that through this period governments across the world, a number that increased dramatically after World War II with the waves of decolonisation, were not simply part of a superpower 'bloc', but operated in concert with their superpower patron. The Middle East is particularly interesting in this regard. The region was a logical site for Cold War competition for two reasons: first, its strategic location and second, the presence of two-thirds of the world's oil supply. As such, both the US and Soviet Union during the Cold War sought to exert control over the regimes of the region in a variety of ways.

US presidential advisor and businessman Bernard Baruch coined the term **Cold War** in April 1947 to describe the emerging geopolitical environment dominated by the United States and Soviet Union.

Whilst it is difficult to identify the origins of the term **bipolar** to describe the global environment during the Cold War, it became popularised by leading scholars and policy analysts such as Raymond Aron who defined it as an environment where 'two actors dominate their rivals to such a degree that both become the center of a coalition and the secondary actors are obliged to situate themselves in relation to the two "blocs", thus joining one or another, unless they have the opportunity to abstain' (1966: 128).

It may be argued that the first manifestation of the Cold War was in the Middle East in Iran and Turkey, as well as links to the conflict in Greece, reflecting a history of tension between Russia/Soviet Union and its southern neighbours. At the end of World War II, the Soviet Union began to pressure Iran for oil concessions in the northwest, continued to pressure Turkey over access through the Black Sea Straits as well as funnelling direct support to the Greek communist insurgency. In response, US President Truman announced the Truman Doctrine that called for the US to support 'free peoples who are resisting attempted subjugation by armed minorities or by outside pressures'.

US diplomat George F. Kennan developed the concept of **containment**, articulated in his 1947 article 'The Sources of Soviet Conduct' for the publication *Foreign Affairs*. Writing under the pseudonym 'X' to avoid implications for his diplomatic postings, Kennan argued that the Soviet Union, after World War II, had 'expansive tendencies' that must be met with 'patient but firm and vigilant containment' through the 'application of counterforce at a series of constantly shifting geographical and political points'. For Kennan, this was to be achieved through political and economic acts, particularly alliances, rather than direct military confrontation (1947: 575–6).

In other words, the US would actively assist in the prevention/suppression of communist uprisings and seek to curtail external (Soviet) assistance for these uprisings. The focus here was the prevention of communism spreading, at least initially, into Greece and Turkey. In relation to Iran, there was tension between the British and Soviets over the status of minority (Kurdish and Azeri) territories in the northwest, areas occupied by the Soviets during World War II. However, despite efforts on the part of the Soviets to pursue autonomy for these communities (that they hoped would translate into greater Soviet access to potential resources in the Caspian region), Soviet and pro-communist sympathisers were quickly marginalised by the pro-Western government in Tehran after the war.

Republics and Monarchies

The influence of the Cold War superpowers, in simple terms, can first be understood as a general trend towards the emergence of conservative monarchies that tended to establish close relations with the United States and often 'radical' nationalist republics that gravitated towards the Soviet Union. Here, the correspondence between regional regimes and superpower allies took place largely through bilateral relationships rather than, as outlined below, regional multilateral alliance frameworks. It was this period, from the mid-1950s through to the late 1970s, that the geopolitical order of the Middle East appeared to reflect the global bipolar system.

The gravitation of regimes towards either superpower gave the impression of direct superpower control. For some, the Middle East was 'deeply and ceaselessly caught up in Great Power politics' (Sayigh and Shlaim, 1997: 2). Central to this is the view that the lack of democratic development in the Middle East through the Cold War was a result of Cold War machinations. This is a crucial point, and one that continues to frame debate particularly on US foreign policy in the Middle East today. Namely, that the emergence and survival of military republican regimes in Egypt, Iraq, Syria, Algeria, South Yemen and Libya alongside closed monarchical regimes in Saudi Arabia, Oman, the United Arab Emirates (UAE), Bahrain, Qatar, Kuwait, Jordan and Morocco were facilitated by their alignments with one of the Cold War superpowers.

Table 3.1 Regime Types in the Middle East after World War II

State	Independence	Regime Type
Algeria	1962	Republic (since 1962)
Bahrain	1971	Monarchy (since 1971)
Egypt	1922	Monarchy (1922–52) Republic (since 1952)
Iran	No colonial rule*	Monarchy (1925–79) Islamic Republic (since 1979)
Iraq	1932	Monarchy (1932–58) Republic (since 1958)
Israel	1948	Republic (since 1948)
Jordan	1946	Monarchy (since 1946)
Kuwait	1961	Monarchy (since 1961)
Lebanon	1943	Republic (since 1943)
Libya	1951	Monarchy (1951–69) Republic (since 1969)
Morocco	1956	Monarchy (since 1666**)
Oman	No colonial rule	Monarchy (since 751)
Palestinian Territories	N/A	Status to be determined
Qatar	1971	Monarchy (since 1971)
Saudi Arabia	1932	Monarchy (since 1932)
Sudan		Republic (since 1956***)
Syria	1946	Republic (since 1946)
Tunisia	1956	Republic (since 1956)
Turkey	1923	Republic (since 1923)
United Arab Emirates	1971	Monarchy (since 1971)
United Arab Republic	1958–61	Republic****
Yemen (North)	1918–90	Monarchy (1918–62) Republic (1962–90)
Yemen (South)	1967–90	Communist Republic (1967–90)
Yemen	1990 (unification)	Republic (since 1990)

* Iran was occupied by the British and Soviet Union from 1941 to 1946.
** The Alaouite dynasty have ruled Morocco under Ottoman and French authority since 1666.
*** The southern regions of Sudan seceded via referendum in July 2011.
**** The United Arab Republic was a union between Egypt and Syria.

The Myth of Superpower Control

However, the influence of the Cold War, or, more specifically, the influence of super-powers over so-called client states has been inflated. Recent scholarship on the Cold War, now with access to previously closed archives, reveals regimes were certainly referential to the dominant logic of the Cold War, but were also able to operate with a good measure of autonomy, and to even manipulate the US and Soviets to their own advantage (Angrist, 2010: 56; Ashton, 2007; Barrett, 2007; Halliday, 2005; Khalidi, 2009; Sayigh and Shlaim, 1997). Therefore, the relationships between regional regimes and superpowers was one of interaction rather than direction, where local governments were able to pursue their own policy priorities, at times manipulating superpowers to their own ends (Halliday, 2005: 98–9; Sluglett in Fawcett, 2009: 52). These policy priorities related primarily to the security of the state in regional terms as well as the survival of regimes. In addition, it was not clear, at least until the 1960s, which states were aligned with which superpowers. As such, the view of a Middle East replicating a global pattern of superpower allegiance does not reflect the dynamics of the region, particularly during the early years of the Cold War.

The **Non-Aligned Movement** (NAM) was founded in the former Yugoslavia in 1961 as a loose association of states that sought to exert independence within the bipolar Cold War context. Made up primarily of states that achieved independence after World War II, the organisation aimed to extend principles of non-intervention and non-military solutions to conflicts. It was founded by Egypt's Nasser along with Yugoslav President Josip Tito, Indonesian President Sukarno, Indian Prime Minister Jawaharlal Nehru and Ghana's President Kwame Nkrumah. Limited in mandate, it currently has 120 member states and was chaired in 2012 by the Chair of the transitional Supreme Council for the Armed Forces of Egypt, Mohamed Hussein Tantawi.

Indeed, the interference of external powers in the Middle East was not limited to the Cold War period. It may be argued that this has increased since the end of the Cold War. Cold War interference was largely directed towards the maintenance and stabilisation of existing regimes rather than their overthrow. This was not a uniform process, of course, but efforts to overthrow regimes were more the exception than the rule. This has shaped much of the modern discourse on the interests of outside powers, particularly the US, in the Middle East.

In particular, they are criticised for acting ruthlessly in their own national interests in supporting regional dictatorships as a means to ensure regional stability at the expense of democracy in the Middle East. This rhetoric was pronounced in the controversy surrounding the lead-up to the US-led invasion and occupation of Iraq

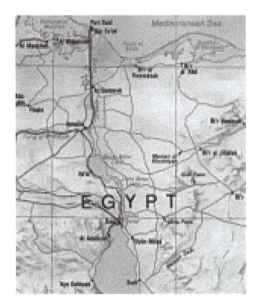

Figure 3.11 The Suez Canal Zone
Source: Public domain

Figure 3.12 Farouq I, King of Egypt (1936–52)
Source: Public domain

in 2003 (see Chapter 8) where the Bush administration, rhetorically at least, sought to highlight this as a reason for acts of aggression against the US, thus requiring a shift in US policy priorities to supporting the development of democracy. This logic was also clearly seen in the last years of colonial presence in the region, particularly in the 1956 Suez Crisis.

The Suez Crisis

The Suez Crisis is commonly presented as symbolising the transfer of power from the colonial powers to the new Cold War superpowers in the Middle East. Whilst this is certainly true, this event also captures how Middle Eastern states were able to use Cold War dynamics for their own interests. In particular, the contest for control over the vital waterway enabled a post-revolutionary regime in Egypt to not only challenge Britain, France and Israel, but to also extend its authority throughout the region.

British control over the Suez Canal zone had been an issue of great sensitivity in Egypt as it symbolised colonial domination and control. Even after Egyptian independence in 1922, the British remained in control of the canal as well as having a large British garrison near the city of Port Said. Despite a pro-British monarchy under King Farouq ruling in Cairo, popular sentiment calling for an end to the British presence grew. This also took root in the Egyptian military. As discussed in Chapter 2, this institution was highly influential in Egypt, with the middle ranking officer corps staffed by Egyptians from working-class backgrounds.

It was this group that became the most effective and organised opposition to the British through the late 1940s and early 1950s. This group was able to pressure the monarch into abrogating the 1936 Anglo–Egyptian Treaty in 1951 that ended the British lease on the Canal Zone (subsequent negotiations saw the British agree to withdraw their forces by 1956). However, continued support for the British presence by the Egyptian monarch saw this group remove him from power on 23 July 1952 in a bloodless coup. This became known as the Free Officers' Coup, after the Free Officers' movement who led the change in government under Muhammad Neguib and Gamal abd al-Nasser.

Neguib, Nasser and the Free Officers' movement abolished the monarchy, proclaimed Egypt as a republic and set about implementing a series of reforms aimed at economic centralisation, development and industrialisation as well as propagating a vision of Arab nationalism that questioned the legitimacy of the new state system in the region (i.e. that the newly independent Arab states represented an effort at colonial divide and rule, and the Arab people should unite into a single state; see Chapter 4), and was also confrontational with Israel.

Nasser succeeded Neguib in 1954, continuing the new policy of state-led economic development. The construction of the Aswan Dam was a central part of this (Baxter and Akbarzadeh, 2008: 47). Nasser sought funding from both the US and

Figure 3.13 The Egyptian 'Free Officers' (Nasser bottom left)

Source: Public domain

Figure 3.14   The signing of the Baghdad Pact in February 1955

Source: LookLex

UK for the building of the dam, who obliged in return for a pledge from Nasser that he would engage in negotiations with Israel. However, the UK remained apprehensive due to Nasser replacing the pro-British monarchy, with this apprehension leading Nasser to court the Soviets. By the mid-1950s, the US were increasingly concerned about a Soviet invasion of the region, but calculated that they lacked the resources to counter an intervention. As such, they sought to entice Nasser into the pro-Western Baghdad Pact. Nasser remained focussed on the British as the source of Egyptian insecurity, however, and thus did not respond to US overtures on the Soviet threat. Instead, Nasser saw this as an opportunity to play the US and Soviets against each other, hoping for US arms, as they would be more compatible with the largely British weaponry the Egyptians possessed. However, the Eisenhower administration could not convince the domestic audience to support this due to Egypt's increasingly confrontational stance vis-à-vis Israel.

As it emerged that arms from the US would not be forthcoming, Nasser negotiated an arms deal with communist Czechoslovakia in September 1955, the first substantial pro-Soviet agreement in the Arab world. For their part, the French were increasingly concerned about Nasser's support for the conflict in Algeria seeking to overthrow French rule. The US position was separate from the Anglo–French–Israeli view of Egypt as they sought to expand their influence in the Arab world primarily through their growing relationship with the Saudis, a government who were opposed to the Hashemite monarchies in Iraq and Jordan.

However, it was the Egyptian recognition of the People's Republic of China in May 1956 that saw the US withdraw funding for the Aswan Dam project in July, effectively ending efforts by the US to court Nasser. As funding for the Aswan Dam project fell through, Nasser nationalised the Suez Canal on 26 July, seized the assets of the Canal Company and blocked the canal to Israeli shipping as well as closing the Straits of Tiran and the Gulf of Aqaba to Israeli shipping. In response, Britain, France and Israel formulated a plan whereby Israel would invade the Sinai Peninsula, the UK and France would intervene to ostensibly separate the parties on either side of the canal. This would effectively give Israel possession of the Sinai, with the UK and France taking control of the Canal Zone in the interests of international stability.

Here, the use of superpower allegiances by regional regimes to pursue their goals was clear. Whilst not dictating events, Nasser's nationalisation of the Suez Canal saw him elevated to the status of regional hero in confronting the colonial powers whilst the nascent State of Israel saw cooperation as a means to spread their con-

Figure 3.15 From left: Egyptian President Nasser, Soviet Premier Nikita Khruschev, Iraqi President Abd as-Sallam Arif and North Yemeni President Abdullah as-Sallal at the opening of the Aswan Dam in 1964

Source: Public domain

trol as a territorial buffer against Egypt. In addition, this event also symbolised the transfer of power away from the European states to the Cold War powers as the key players in the region. In this regard, neither the British, French, nor Israelis consulted with the US on their plans for invasion, working under the assumption that the US would back it in a further push to remove the increasingly pro-Soviet Nasser from power.

This plan was launched with the Israeli invasion ('Operation Kadesh') of the Sinai on 29 October 1956, quickly pushing towards the Canal Zone. The British and French launched their campaign ('Operation Musketeer') on 31 October, shelling the Canal Zone and bombing Egyptian air force installations. The Egyptian army pulled out of the Canal

Figure 3.16 Nasser upon announcing the nationalisation of the Suez Canal on 26 July 1956

Source: Public domain

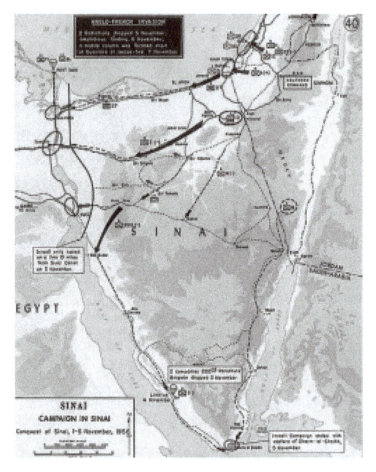

Figure 3.17 Military operations during the Suez Crisis
Source: Public domain

Zone by the start of November with British paratroopers taking Port Said at the mouth of the Canal by 5 November. However, whilst the military operation was successful, both the domestic response in Britain and the international response was highly critical.

Republican President Eisenhower and Secretary of State Dulles sought to apply sanctions to Israel, an action resisted by the Democrat-controlled Congress, particularly Lyndon Johnson who would become President in 1963. This is an important point to note in the shifting patterns of the US position vis-à-vis the Israeli–Palestinian conflict. Specifically, where the Republican Party positions itself as the closest ally of Israel, through to the 1980s the Democratic Party had

Figure 3.18 British Prime Minister Anthony Eden (1955–7) and French President René Coty (1954–9) and from left: US President Dwight Eisenhower (1952–60) with Secretary of State John Foster Dulles (1953–9)

Source: Public domain

been most vocal in their support of the Jewish state. This changed under the Reagan administration and the ascendancy of successive Likud governments in Israel from this point.

The US initiated negotiations in the UN to end the Suez Crisis via a request from Nasser. However, the Security Council remained deadlocked due to vetoes from the UK and France. Despite this, the UK and France agreed to withdraw from the Canal Zone with British Prime Minister Anthony Eden resigning in response. Israel initially refused to negotiate, with Israeli Prime Minister Ben Gurion announcing that the 1949 armistice with Egypt was now void before walking back from this and announcing an Israeli withdrawal by mid-November.

The Suez Crisis represented the transfer of dominant external interests from the European to the Cold War powers, particularly the US, in the Middle East. This was already a reality, but was now clearly demonstrated. In addition, it saw the rise of Nasser as the key player in Arab politics through the 1950s and 1960s. In the context of decolonisation and the rise of radical nationalist politics (see Chapter 4), including the 1958 Revolution in Iraq and the emergence of similar regimes in Syria and Algeria, Nasser's Egypt would become the most influential Arab state.

For the US, it saw their increasing focus on the Middle East, symbolised in the 1957 Eisenhower Doctrine that aimed at reassuring US allies in the region. The doctrine centred on funding for states who asked for assistance 'against covert armed aggression from any nation controlled by international communism'. Whilst they had supported Nasser during the crisis, the growing regional influence of his regime alongside the developing friendship between Egypt and the Soviet Union led the US to focus on efforts to counter the potential spread of Soviet influence through seeking to stem the flow of Soviet arms, advisors and funds to many states within the region.

Figure 3.19   From left: Syrian President Shukri al-Quwatli (1943–9, 1955–8), Iraqi President Abd al-Karim Qasim (1958–63) and Algerian President Houari Boumediene (1965–78)

Source: Public domain

GEOPOLITICS AND COLD WAR ALLEGIANCES IN THE MIDDLE EAST

The 'High' Cold War in the Middle East

Whilst the Cold War superpowers did not dictate the actions of states in the Middle East, there was an increasing division across the region between two loose blocs that had links to either the United States or the Soviet Union. This was not a concrete division. However, there was a group of regimes, largely monarchies, associated both formally and informally with the United States whilst a separate group, largely republics, had both formal and informal associations with the Soviet Union.

US Cold War Policy in the Middle East: Doctrines and Containment

During the Cold War, the United States pursued a policy of seeking to mitigate the expansion of communism globally. In the Middle East, the US used two mechanisms to pursue this. First was the setting of broad foreign policy priorities through presidential 'doctrines'. As stated above, the Truman and Eisenhower Doctrines set policy priorities for the US in the Middle East. This was followed by the 1961 Kennedy Doctrine, aimed at pre-empting revolutionary movements in Iran and Egypt; the 1969 Nixon Doctrine was aimed at US allies Iran and Saudi Arabia; the 1980 Carter Doctrine was aimed at protecting US interests in the Persian Gulf; and the 1985 Reagan Doctrine was aimed at rolling back Soviet expansionism, focussed on Afghanistan.

Many US presidents have issues foreign policy **doctrines**. Starting with President Monroe in 1823, 12 presidents have issued doctrines to set US foreign policy priorities. Several of these relate directly to US interests in the Middle East, including the Truman, Eisenhower, Carter, Reagan, Bush and Obama Doctrines.

The second tool was the policy of 'containment', the development of a network of alliances around the Soviet Union that would formally tie the security of these states to that of the US. That is, should the Soviets threaten the established regimes in these states, they would risk an armed response on the part of the US. The North Atlantic Treaty Organisation (NATO) formed the centrepiece of this system, and included the vital regional state of Turkey. However, despite the critical strategic importance of the Middle East, the expansion of the alliance system

Figure 3.20 From left: King Hassan II of Morocco (1961–99), King Hussein of Jordan (1952–99), King Saud of Saudi Arabia (1953–69) and President Habib Bourguiba of Tunisia (1957–87)

Source: Public domain

to this part of the world did not take root. The main attempt at this was the creation of the 'Baghdad Pact', or Middle East Treaty Organisation, in 1955. The Pact never formally included the US; instead it linked the then monarchies of Iraq and Iran as well as Turkey and Pakistan to the British.

The treaty itself provided for military cooperation and joint security, but did not result in large-scale cooperation between the states. This was further undermined in 1958 when the Iraqi monarchy was overthrown in a military coup, with the new regime of General Abd al-Karim Qasim seeking closer ties with the Soviet Union. Its replacement entity, the Central Treaty Organisation (CENTO), continued to exist but was largely ineffective at preventing the expansion of Soviet influence in Egypt, Syria and South Yemen through the 1960s and 1970s. The Islamic Revolution in Iran of 1979, which saw the country's withdrawal from the group, led to its dissolution in February of that year.

AN ARAB COLD WAR: EGYPT AND SAUDI ARABIA

As with the Suez Crisis, the Cold War logic continued to be exploited by regional states for their own benefit. In particular, from the 1950s to the 1970s, Egypt and Saudi Arabia vied for influence across the region. This confrontation replicated the logic of the Cold War, not in terms of Egypt being a communist state and Saudi Arabia championing liberal democracy, but in terms of two major powers competing for influence whilst exporting this conflict. A key example of a proxy of the 'Arab Cold War' was the Yemen Civil War.

The Yemen Civil War

Yemen was under Ottoman authority from 1872 to 1913, when authority reverted to the al-Qasimi dynasty under Imam Yahya Muhammad. The borders of the modern Yemeni state took form through the 19th and 20th centuries in confrontation with the emerging state of Saudi Arabia and British control over the port of Aden. In 1934, the British signed the Treaty of Sana`a with Imam Yahya, temporarily formalising the division between North and South Yemen.

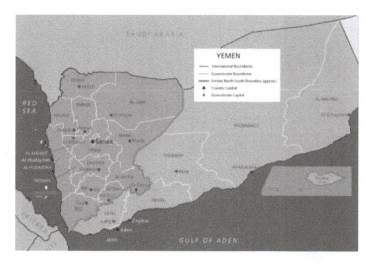

Figure 3.21 North and South Yemen

Source: Althistory

Imam Yahya Muhammad was assassinated in 1948, succeeded by his son Ahmad bin Yahya Hamidaddin. Ahmad bin Yahya drew Yemen closer to Egypt and Syria, joining the short-lived United Arab Republic between 1958 and 1961 as well as forging a close relationship with the Soviet Union and China. Ahmad's foreign policy was motivated by a desire to annex the British holdings in South Yemen. During the latter years of his rule, the imam survived a number of coup and assassination attempts from within the military whilst increasingly suffering from ill health. As a result, increasing authority was transferred to Ahmad's heir Muhammad al-Badr, who formally took the throne on Ahmad's death in September 1962.

Al-Badr assumed the throne as the military and tribal forces were developing a range of challenges to the central government. In addition, Egypt's President Nasser saw Yemen as a key part in his endeavour to spread his authority and

Figure 3.22 From left: Imam Ahmad bin Yahya, ruler of Yemen (1948–62) and Yahya's successor Muhammad al-Badr

Source: Public domain

nationalist ideology. As al-Badr took the throne, senior military officer Abdullah as-Sallal launched a coup that overthrew the monarchy and established a republic.

Figure 3.23 President of the Yemen Arab Republic, Abdullah as-Sallal (1962–7)

Source: Public domain

Nasser backed the coup whilst al-Badr called on the Saudis for assistance. This led to a rapid escalation in violence between republican and royalist forces, with an estimated 200,000 tribesmen mobilised against the republican government backed by Saudi and Jordanian aid. By 1965, Nasser had deployed over 70,000 Egyptian soldiers in support of Sallal's regime.

Whilst casualties were primarily on the royalist side, the conflict degenerated without a clear outcome. In addition, despite numerous negotiations, Nasser and Saudi King Faisal could not come to agreement, continuing their assistance of the warring parties. Egypt's focus on Yemen hindered its ability to respond to the Israeli attack of 1967 (see Chapter 4). Indeed, finding itself confronted by an overwhelming military defeat at the hands of Israel saw Nasser agree to withdraw his troops later in 1967.

This coincided with the British announcement that they would abandon their colony in the southern Yemeni port of Aden. British administration was replaced by the only communist government in the Middle East in South Yemen, a regime that immediately called for the overthrow of all monarchies in the region, with a focus on Saudi Arabia. As a result, the Saudis acquiesced to the demands of the republican government in North Yemen, seeing the civil war slowly wind down in the last years of the 1960s, as Riyadh turned its attention to countering the potential spread of challenges from the new South Yemeni government. Egypt, for its part, would retreat from a regional role after 1967 and particularly after the death of Nasser in 1970.

Whilst Yemen would reunite under the authority of the government in the north in 1990, this episode highlights the interconnectedness of regional affairs, particularly in terms of the efforts of larger states to exert their influence over smaller states. Whilst there was a mirroring of Cold War logic, with a pro-Soviet republican Egypt under Nasser confronting a pro-Western Saudi monarchy for regional dominance, this was not simply a replication of Soviet or US interests at the regional level. Cairo and Riyadh were pursuing their own regional ambitions, often exploiting superpower support for these ends. This would be a trend that would be replicated later in confrontation between Saudi Arabia and Saddam Hussein's Iraq through the 1980s, and in recent years between Saudi Arabia, in conjunction with increasingly assertive Gulf states such as Qatar, and the Islamic Republic of Iran in the context of the post-2003 US invasion of Iraq and the post-2010 Arab uprisings (see Chapters 8 and 10).

THE LEBANESE CIVIL WAR

Whilst the Arab–Israeli conflict has dominated global attention in relation to the Middle East since the end of World War II, a number of other conflicts have been more destructive. The conflict that captures the interconnection between internal and external dynamics perhaps better than any other is the Lebanese Civil War. From 1975 to 1990, the small state in the Levant descended into a violent conflict between its many sectarian communities, with invasions from both Israel and Syria that led to over 150,000 deaths and many more displaced.

The **Levant** refers to the area bordering the eastern Mediterranean encompassing modern-day Lebanon, Israel–Palestine, Syria and Jordan.

The Origins of the Lebanese Civil War

The Lebanese state is based on a political arrangement forged in the final decades of Ottoman rule. As outlined in Chapter 1, the Capitulations Treaties led to increasingly direct European intervention in various parts of the Empire. One example of this was in the area today known as Lebanon, a highly diverse region around Mount Lebanon on the eastern shore of the Mediterranean. Conflict between the Maronite Catholic and Druze communities in this area in 1860 led to French intervention on behalf of the Maronites, and the establishment of an autonomous zone that would form the nucleus of the modern Lebanese state (Khalifah, 2001).

Confessionalism in Lebanon

As explored in Chapter 2, Ottoman defeat in World War I led to the establishment of the League of Nations Mandates, with French authority over an expanded Lebanese territory. From the 1920s to the 1940s, the French sponsored the development of a political bargain to allay concerns of the Maronite and Muslim communities in this territory. This was formalised in 1926 with confessional identity to serve as the political organising principle in the country. That is, the Lebanese political system would be built around a person's religious identity, codified in one of 11 different 'official' communities.

> The **Maronites** are a Catholic community established in the region of Mount Lebanon in the 5th century CE. It is estimated that there are roughly 1 million Maronites in Lebanon (25% of the population) with 3–4 million worldwide.
>
> The **Druze** are a religious community found in Lebanon, Syria, Israel and Jordan. With roots in Shi`a Islam, theirs is a unique reformist vision of Islam. There are an estimated 500,000 Druze in Lebanon, predominantly in the Chouf region.

Here, the 1932 census, the last official census in Lebanon, claimed to show a Christian majority of 51.3% of the population. As a result, after independence in 1943, the Lebanese political system was organised 'confessionally'. Political posts and representation in the Lebanese parliament were allocated according to religious community, with a permanent Maronite President, Sunni Muslim Prime Minister and Shi`a Muslim Speaker of the House and a division of parliamentary seats according to six Christian members to five Muslim members. The elevation of Maronite and broader Christian positions was seen as a trade-off for their cooperation with the Muslim communities dominant in the north and south of the country (Traboulsi, 2007).

As a result, Lebanon was a democracy albeit with pre-determined limits of representation. In addition, it was from its founding a state that rested on fragile foundations. It required the participation of all designated groups, and in many ways the ability of the state itself to survive was dependent on the leaders of the confessional communities. This led to an early polarisation of Lebanese politics between broadly left-wing stances of the various Muslim communities and more conservative, right-wing politics from many within the Christian communities.

Lebanon's 'official' **confessional** communities are: (Christian) Maronite Catholic, Greek Orthodox, Greek Catholic, Armenian Orthodox, Armenian Catholic, Syrian Orthodox, Syrian Catholic, Protestant and (Muslim) Sunni, Shi`a, Druze, Alawi and Ismaili.

Lebanon and the Palestinian Question

Due to its weakness, and efforts by confessional groups to buttress their own strength via relations with foreign governments, Lebanon has consistently been at the mercy of regional affairs. This became apparent soon after independence and the outbreak of the first Arab–Israeli war. Whilst Lebanon participated in the invasion of what would become the State of Israel in 1948, it was the Palestinian refugee issue that would have immediate and lasting impact.

The Palestinian Liberation Organisation (PLO) had been active in Jordan since the mid-1960s. Tensions between the PLO and the Jordanian monarchy escalated, reaching their peak with the clashes of **Black September** in 1970. After a series of plane hijackings by the Popular Front for the Liberation of Palestine (PFLP) through 1970, Jordanian King Hussein declared martial law and attacked the headquarters of the PLO. After several thousand deaths, the PLO leadership left Jordan for Lebanon in 1971.

In particular, the arrival of over 100,000 largely Sunni Muslim Palestinian refugees from its southern neighbour through the late 1940s and early 1950s put immediate strain on the delicate sectarian balance in the country. As with all other Arab states with the exception of Jordan, the Lebanese government did not grant citizenship to the refugee community. This led to the founding of large Palestinian refugee camps throughout the country that existed largely separate from 'normal' political life in Lebanon (Fisk, 2001).

Whilst this was managed through the 1950s and 1960s, with the exception of a brief conflict in Lebanon in 1958, the 1967 War with Israel would have an inadvertently dramatic affect on stability in Lebanon. Specifically, with Israel's invasion and occupation of the West Bank territories in 1967, the PLO shifted its operations to Jordan then, after 1970, to Lebanon. From this new base, the PLO launched operations into Israel from the north. PLO operations in Lebanon were conducted under the guidelines established in the so-called 'Cairo Declaration' of 1969. The declaration effectively transferred authority within the 16 largest refugee camps in Lebanon from the Lebanese military to the PLO. Effectively, the Cairo Declaration enabled the establishment of a PLO-controlled state within a state in Lebanon, a base from which they would conduct a series of raids against Israel. These raids led to increasing Israeli reprisals against Lebanon, particularly the predominantly Shi`a communities in the south of the country.

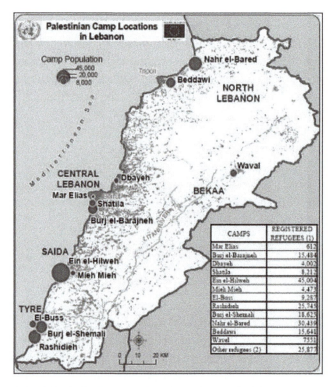

Figure 3.24 Palestinian refugee camps and numbers in Lebanon
Source: UNRWA

Civil War and External Involvement in Lebanon

The weakness of the Lebanese state and increasing rivalries between the leaders of the confessional communities, combined with the conflict between the PLO and Israel that spilled over the southern border, saw Lebanon drawn increasingly towards conflict. In this atmosphere, resistance to confessionalism became increasingly organised through the late 1960s and early 1970s, particularly amongst Sunni Muslim and Druze groups. These groups, now under the banner of the Lebanese

Figure 3.25 From left: PLO leader Yasser Arafat and Druze leader Kamal Jumblatt

Source: Pierre Tristam

National Movement (LNM) led by Druze leader Kamal Jumblatt, called for the replacement of the 1932 census and a restructuring of the political system to reflect what they alleged were new political and demographic realities.

The Maronite community labelled this as a threat to the National Pact, and therefore a reneging on the compromise that led to the establishment of the Lebanese state in 1943. In addition, tensions between the Maronite leadership and the Palestinian leadership began to escalate as the former saw the latter as emboldening the Muslim community in Lebanon to threaten to overturn the system that guaranteed them their privileged political position (Khalifah, 2001).

As a result, each community began to arm its own militias, each of which drawing manpower at the expense of the already weak Lebanese army. Effectively, the state lost control, with sectarian leaders, many backed by external partners such as Syria, threatening conflict. Remaining antagonistic to the idea of Lebanon being separated from what it saw as the natural Greater Syria, and hemmed in through the Israeli occupation of the Golan Heights in 1967, the Ba`athist regime of Hafiz al-Assad in Syria began actively campaigning to unsettle the Lebanese government as a means to extend its control into Lebanon as well as gain increasing control over the progressively more powerful PLO.

Tensions escalated into 1975 before a series of retributive killings between the Palestinian and Maronite communities in April ignited war between the now well-armed and organised militias across the country. One of the first manifestations of the war, and one of its enduring features, was the targeting of civilian populations by the militia organisations. Civilian identification cards in Lebanon

Figure 3.26   Beirut's Green Line

Source: Public domain

carried the confessional affiliation of each Lebanese citizen. As the fighting degenerated into 1976, neighbourhoods within Lebanon's larger cities and towns became strongholds for particular militia organisations. Civilians travelling through these areas were forcibly identified by these cards and removed and even killed when present in an 'enemy' area. As such, entire districts within Beirut and its surrounds were ethnically and confessionally cleansed. This was particularly so in Muslim West Beirut and Christian East Beirut, a division that became marked by the so-called 'Green Line' that divided the city in two (Khalaf, 2002).

Syria and Lebanon

It would not take long for external parties to become directly involved. In 1976, as the LNM and PLO looked likely to impose a total military victory over the Christian militias operating under the umbrella group the Lebanese Forces (LF), the Syrians responded to a request from Maronite President Suleiman Franjiyeh for intervention. Intervention by the Syrians on the side of the Christian militias, many of whom had sought to develop ties with Israel, appears, on the surface, counterintuitive. However,

Figure 3.27   Past and present political leaders of Lebanon's three main confessional groups (from left): Bashir Gemayel (Maronite), Nabih Berri (Shi`a) and Rafiq al-Hariri (Sunni)

Source: Public domain

Damascus saw this as an opportunity to gain a foothold in Lebanon with at least the appearance of legality. For the Christian militias, Syrian intervention prevented their defeat. However, the prevention of an LNM victory served to perpetuate the conflict as both sides found themselves closer to parity in terms of strength and proceeded to launch repeated operations against each other, with the civilian population suffering massive casualties. Fighting continued through the 1970s and 1980s, with confessionally based alliances breaking down and militias fighting one month, then forming makeshift allegiances the next.

Israel and Lebanon

The war intensified with the first of two Israeli invasions in 1978. The first engagement, 'Operation Litani', was limited to the southern portion of the country. Again, however, developments outside Lebanon would further unsettle the situation. The Camp David Peace Accords between Egypt and Israel (see Chapter 9) led Syria to fear Israel turning its full attention on them. Therefore, the continuation of a second front against Israel through Lebanon became increasingly important. As a result, Syria withdrew from its already cooling alliance with the Christian militias and began to openly support the PLO. This enabled an intensification of PLO actions on Israel's northern border.

As a result, Israeli Prime Minister Menachim Begin and Defence Minister Ariel Sharon began drawing up plans for a large-scale ground invasion of Lebanon that they hoped would destroy the PLO. In addition, the plan also aimed to remove

Figure 3.28 1982 Israeli bombardment of West Beirut
Source: Public domain

the Syrian army from Lebanon and sponsor the installation of a friendly Christian government in Beirut. Whilst the Israeli parliament (Knesset) was increasingly opposed to the idea, with Begin distancing himself from the plan through early 1982, Sharon continued with plans, leading to the launching of 'Operation Peace for Galilee' on 6 June 1982 (Schiff and Ya'ari, 1985)

Despite assurances to the Israeli Cabinet, this invasion was not limited to the south as Sharon led a push to Beirut, laying siege to the Muslim western half of the city to eliminate the PLO leadership stationed there. With the Israeli army in siege of Beirut, fierce fighting took place between the Israelis, the Christian militias, the PLO and the Syrians. International mediation efforts ensued with the PLO agreeing to withdraw from Beirut with a multinational escort headed by France and the United States. This was accompanied by the appointment of Bashir Gemayel as the new President of Lebanon on 23 August. With most of Israel's objectives apparently achieved, one of the most notorious episodes of the war took place.

Gemayel was assassinated on 14 September, throwing Israel's and the LF's plans into chaos. In response, the Israeli army violated the ceasefire and entered West Beirut with elements of the Phalange. Charging that those who had committed the assassination had sought refuge in the Palestinian refugee camps at Sabra and Shatilla in southern Beirut, the Israeli army barricaded the camps and allowed Phalange units to enter the camps. Whilst inside, the Phalange systematically executed

Figure 3.29   The Sabra and Shatilla Massacre
Source: UNRWA

over 1000 Palestinian civilians including women and children with no sign of any remaining PLO. The massacre shocked the world, including the Israeli public, and led to the resignations of both Begin and Sharon by 1983 and the complete loss of public support for the Israeli actions in Lebanon. Israeli forces steadily withdrew from Lebanon through 1983; however, they continued to occupy the southern strip along the border until 2000.

Iran and Lebanon

The 1982 Israeli invasion would have a side effect that would change the security landscape for all the states of the region.

The **Shi`a** are the largest single group in Lebanon, constituting an estimated 35–40% of the population. Historically marginalised, the Shi`a have become increasingly empowered since the civil war, particularly through their main party, Hezbollah.

After the 1979 Islamic Revolution in Iran (see Chapter 4), the new regime found itself in confrontation with the United States, isolated from the Soviets and in tension with the Arab states, particularly after the outbreak of war between Iraq and Iran in 1980. Therefore, Iran actively looked to expand its sphere of influence. Its solid relations with Syria proved to be beneficial in this respect, allowing them access to Lebanon's large Shi`a community.

Lebanon's Shi`a population have traditionally been marginalised, both politically and economically. This has been exacerbated by the growth of the community demographically, where they form the single largest confessional community in the country. Traditionally represented by the Amal Party, Iran sought to sponsor the creation of a new, more confrontational group that would also enable it to exert greater influence in the country and to confront Israel and by extension, the United States. Hezbollah (Party of God) emerged from the chaotic situation in southern Lebanon that stemmed from both the 1978 and 1982 Israeli invasions.

Whilst this will be discussed in more detail in Chapter 7, it is worth noting Hezbollah's role in the conflict here. In particular, they used the platform of the Lebanese Civil War to attack high-profile US and French targets, such as the April 1983 bombing of the heavily fortified US Embassy in Beirut that killed over 60, and the subsequent bombing of the multinational forces' barracks in October that year that killed 299 US and French service people.

Figure 3.30   1983 US Embassy bombing in Beirut
Source: Public domain

The attack on the US–French barracks was the single deadliest single-day death toll for US troops since the Vietnam War and shocked the US public. The US and France steadily wound down their operations in Lebanon through the 1980s despite some continued involvement in efforts to release US hostages held by Hezbollah in a bargain with Iran. These negotiations later emerged as the Iran–Contra scandal, further tarnishing the US reputation in Lebanon (see below).

An End to the War

From the mid-1980s, the conflict in Lebanon degenerated into a series of clashes and counter-clashes between the various militia organisations as various attempts at negotiation and peace failed. Finally, internal fighting within the Christian community and a series of peace initiatives assisted by the UN led to talks in the Saudi Arabian city of Taef. This resulted in the Taef Agreement, a document that re-set Lebanon's confessional balance with some minor adjustments. The biggest change was the formalisation of the Syrian military presence in Lebanon, a *de facto* military occupation that would last until 2005 as well as the formalisation of Hezbollah's status as a sub-state militia in confrontation with Israel (see Chapters 7 and 9). As such, Lebanon remained a highly fragile state, dependent on the acquiescence of all confessional leaders. The war did, however, herald the arrival of an increasingly assertive Shi`a community, position Lebanon more squarely in the conflict with Israel and allow Iran and Syria greater leverage in the region, all of which occurred despite the interests of the Cold War superpowers (MacQueen, 2009).

Selections from the Taef Agreement

First, General Principles and Reforms.

I. B. Lebanon is Arab in belonging and identity ... C. Lebanon is a democratic parliamentary republic ... II. G. Abolishing political sectarianism is a fundamental national objective.

Second, spreading the sovereignty of the State of Lebanon over all Lebanese territories.

A. Disbanding of all Lebanese and non-Lebanese militias ... D. the Syrian forces shall thankfully assist the forces of the legitimate Lebanese government to spread the authority of the State of Lebanon.

Third, liberating Lebanon from the Israeli occupation.

C. Taking all the steps necessary to liberate all Lebanese territories from the Israeli occupation, to spread state sovereignty over all the territories.

Fourth, Lebanese–Syrian Relations.

Between Lebanon and Syria there is a special relationship ... Lebanon should not be allowed to constitute a source of threat to Syria's security, ... Consequently, Lebanon should not allow itself to become a pathway or a base for any force, state, or organisation seeking to undermine its security or Syria's security.

THE IRAN–IRAQ WAR AND COLD WAR MACHINATIONS

Perhaps the clearest example of how the Cold War superpowers were able to affect state behaviour was their involvement in the war between Iran and Iraq from 1980 to 1988. More specifically, the United States sought to balance its tense but functional relationship with Saddam Hussein's Iraq and its open hostility with the Islamic Republic of Iran. However, in seeking to pursue a short-term goal of ensuring Iran was damaged by the war, whilst limiting the potential growing power of Saddam's Iraq, the US inadvertently locked itself into a course that would foster the growth of anti-American sentiment in the Middle East as well as see it engage in military operations in Iraq through the 1990s, culminating in the 2003 invasion and occupation of Iraq (see Chapter 8).

History of Iraq–Iran Tensions

Where Iraq was a relatively 'new' state, coming to independence in 1932, the Arab frontier had a tradition of confrontation with its Persian neighbour. Central to specific disputes between Iran and Iraq has been the issue of territory. The formation of the Iraqi state was done in such a way to ensure British control over access to the Persian Gulf. To do this, the British ceded territory to the future state of Kuwait that would have given Iraq full access to the Persian Gulf. As the British remained in control of Kuwait until their independence in 1961, Iraq remained largely a landlocked country, with its only maritime access through the Shatt al-Arab waterway.

Here, Iraq had consistently agitated for territorial claims against both Kuwait, a territory it considered to be part of its own claims, and Iran, particularly over the Shatt al-Arab waterway. The Shatt was traditionally shared between Iran and Iraq, with treaties through the 18th, 19th and 20th centuries establishing principles of either joint control or direct Iranian control. However, relations between the two countries deteriorated through the 1970s, with armed clashes over the Shatt in 1971 as well as Iranian military actions in the Gulf and Iraqi support of a Kurdish insurgency in Iran's northwest.

This led to negotiations between the Iraqi Ba`athist regime and the Iranian pro-Western monarch Shah Reza Pahlavi in Algiers in 1975. This agreement resulted in, amongst other things, a decision to share the waterway at its mid-point. Whilst

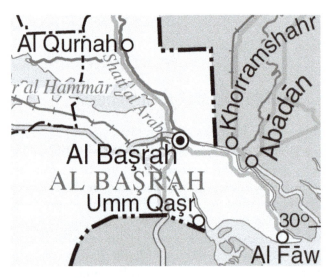

Figure 3.31 The Shatt al-Arab waterway
Source: Public domain

short-term stability resulted from this agreement, subsequent events would upset the balance. In particular, the 1979 Islamic Revolution in Iran, as well as Saddam Hussein formally taking hold of the regime in Baghdad, dramatically altered the regional order.

The fragile tenets of the Algiers Agreement soon began to buckle under the strain of renewed tensions between Iran and Iraq after this point. With 60% of Iraq's population Shi`a, the Shi`a character of the new Islamic Republic in Iran disturbed Saddam and his largely Sunni ruling elite. In response, Baghdad increasingly agitated for action against Iran, seeking financial support particularly from Saudi Arabia framed in terms of protecting the Arab world from revolutionary Iranian expansionism. The Saudis and other Gulf states had their own Shi`a communities, with Bahrain also a Sunni minority government ruling over a disadvantaged Shi`a minority.

The Role of the US

It was here that the United States became increasingly involved in the simmering tension. The new revolutionary government in Tehran and the United States were in open confrontation. This was based on a number of factors, including the US role in toppling the democratically elected government of Mohammad Mossadeq in 1953 and the intimate relationship between successive US administrations and the Iranian monarchy that was overthrown by the revolution. Mossadeq had become increasingly worrisome for both the US and Britain after his nationalisation of the Anglo-Iranian Oil Company (which would become British Petroleum, or BP) in 1951.

As a result, the US drew closer to Saddam's regime in Baghdad, seeing him as the most useful ally in confronting Iran. This was a relationship born out of mutual interest rather than ideological affinity, however. This would influence both US and Iraqi attitudes through the war, where the US sought to keep a measure of distance between themselves and Saddam. Indeed, as war became increasingly likely, the US saw their best outcome as supporting Saddam to the point of containing Iran whilst avoiding

Figure 3.32 Mohammad Mossadeq, Iranian Prime Minister (1951–3), was overthrown with assistance of the CIA

Source: Public domain

the possibility of seeing Iraq emerge as a regional power. The outcome of this, one that fit with this strategic aim, was the prolonging of the Iran–Iraq War so that it would become the longest conventional war, including both World War I and II, of the 20th century.

The Course of the War

With the support of the Gulf states and the US, Iraq invaded Iran on 22 September 1980. The immediate gains made by the Iraqi army appeared to vindicate the opinion that the new Iranian regime was vulnerable and would fall within months. However, despite initial Iraqi gains, as well as billions in funding from the Gulf states, the invasion appeared to consolidate the Iranian population behind the Ayatollah Khomeini's government. Indeed, by 1982, the Iraqi army had been pushed out of Iranian territory with the latter pushing into Iraq and threatening Baghdad itself.

> According to the US Energy Information Administration, the Gulf states (Iran, Iraq, Kuwait, Saudi Arabia, Bahrain, Qatar and the UAE) produce over 25% of the world's oil supplies whilst holding over 55% of the world's oil supplies. Saudi Arabia alone possesses 20% of the world's oil supplies.

Figure 3.33　President Jimmy Carter (1976–80)

Source: Public domain

From 1982 to 1988, the war became stuck in a stalemate with neither side gaining the upper hand. Iraq's superior firepower was countered by the weight of numbers on the Iranian side. Both sides targeted civilian populations, with rocket attacks on cities and supply lines. In addition, Iraq deployed chemical weapons against both Iranian troops and against Kurdish militias who rose in opposition to Saddam in the north of the country. This latter issue would form a core part of the argument for the need to 'forcibly disarm' Iraq in the lead-up to the 2003 US-led invasion.

US priorities here were articulated early. Prior to his electoral defeat by the Republican candidate Ronald Reagan, President Jimmy Carter defined his foreign policy position in 1980 as defined by ongoing instability in the Gulf. Responding to the Iran–Iraq War, the Iranian Revolution and the Soviet invasion of Afghanistan in 1979, the Carter Doctrine made explicit the centrality of Persian Gulf security and stability as part of US national interests. As a result, ongoing events in this vital strategic region would see the US drawn into a number of successive conflicts, often with negative consequences for the way they were perceived across the Middle East.

The Iran–Contra Affair

As the war raged, both the US and the Soviets supported Iraq, seeing Iran as a destabilising force. However, both superpowers were not adverse to the war continuing to sap the strength of both states. Here, the Soviets supplied limited assistance to the Iraqi army, but tentatively sought to court the regime in Tehran. Their limited role in the conflict, in retrospect, did highlight their decreasing power that would culminate in the collapse of the Soviet Union by the end of the 1980s.

On 7 June 1981, Israel launched 'Operation Opera', a surprise air attack on the **Osiraq** nuclear facility. Osiraq was built with French assistance. Whilst Iraq maintained that the facility was for peaceful energy purposes, Israel maintained that it would lead to Iraq gaining nuclear weapons capacity. The United Nations Security Council passed Resolution 487 in response, condemning the attack and allowed Iraq to claim compensation from Israel. In 2009, Iraqi Prime Minister Nouri al-Maliki raised the possibility of Iraq applying for compensation to begin construction of a new facility.

For the US, the situation became increasingly complicated. The Israeli attacks on the Iraqi nuclear facility at Osiraq in 1981 highlighted the conflicting interests at play. In addition, despite their funding for the war, the US allies in the Gulf were increasingly worried that Iraq would emerge from the war with a powerful military and ambitions of greater regional influence. In line with the Carter Doctrine, US concern centred on stable and reliable access to the Gulf, in terms of the extraction and transportation of its oil. An emboldened Iraq was seen to threaten this.

Strategic decision-making became increasingly complex for the Reagan Republican administration with renewed Cold War tensions. In particular, the rise of socialist regimes in Central and South America concerned the US greatly. The seizure of power by the socialist Sandanista administration in Nicaragua in 1979 was central to these worries as Washington feared it may lead to similar developments

Figure 3.34 President Ronald Reagan (1980–8)

Source: UPI/Bettman Newsphotos

in neighbouring states. As a result, the US began to actively support the overthrow of these regimes through funding insurgent movements, subsequently articulated under the 1985 Reagan Doctrine.

In Nicaragua, the Reagan administration covertly funded the far-right 'Contras', a group that engaged in guerrilla attacks against the Nicaraguan government as well as attacks on civilians supportive of the government. Revelation of this led Congress to pass the Boland Amendments that prohibited funding for the Contras and other like movements.

Figure 3.35 The Contras

Source: Public domain

In response, the Reagan administration made a decision that, for many, encapsulated their view that the continuation of the Iran–Iraq War served US strategic interest. To raise money, National Security Council advisor Lieutenant Colonel Oliver North led planning to circumvent the funding ban by selling arms to Iran and funnelling this money to the Contras. The US did not have direct contact with the Iranians, however, so dealt with them through Israel as the third party, with the trade-off being

Iran placing pressure on their Lebanese ally Hezbollah to release a number of hostages it had taken during the Lebanese Civil War. Iran was desperate for supplies, and US arms were welcome as the Iranian army was essentially built by the US under the Shah's regime.

This plan came undone when a plane carrying weapons for the Contras was shot down over Nicaragua in November 1986. Later the same month, the Lebanese newspaper *Ash-Shira`a* published information detailing the sale of arms to Iran and the US role in pressuring for the release of hostages. Whilst Reagan managed to avoid prosecution by denying direct involvement, North was convicted of receiving illegal funds and destroying documents relevant to the case, along with a number of other administration officials. In addition, the Nicaraguan government successfully sued the US government at the International Court of Justice for compensation that the US has refused to pay.

Figure 3.36 Oliver North after his arrest

Source: Public domain

The Legacy of the War

As the war continued through to 1988, the US became militarily involved after an Iranian sea mine destroyed the *USS Samuel Roberts* in April 1988. In response, the US launched a series of actions against Iranian oil platforms in the Gulf as well as sinking Iranian naval vessels. This engagement took a more unfortunate turn when the US shot down Iran Air Flight 655, killing 290 civilians. Whilst the US claimed this was a result of radar error, it led to a public backlash in the US and globally.

This event, and the sheer scale of destruction of the war, finally saw Iran and Iraq accept the provisions of United Nations Security Council Resolution 598 in July 1988. The resolution did not alter the territory of either state, and did not include a provision for Iraq to pay reparations, a key Iranian demand. The eight-year war claimed over 1 million Iranian lives, half a million Iraqi lives, as well as an estimated financial loss of over $500 billion for both states. These figures touch on the scale of destruction suffered by each country, leaving legacies that have been felt for decades.

In political terms, the war consolidated support for the Iranian revolutionary regime and also enabled Saddam's Iraq to develop one of the world's largest and most potent armed forces. However, Iraq remained in billions of dollars of debt to the Gulf states, particularly the Saudis and Kuwait. This would be an issue that would cause

Figure 3.37   Special Envoy to President Reagan Donald Rumsfeld meets Saddam
                 Hussein in Baghdad in 1983. Rumsfeld would later become US Defense
                 Secretary under President George W. Bush, and a major advocate for the
                 2003 US-led invasion and occupation of Iraq

Source: Public domain

increasing tensions up to 1990, contributing to Iraq's invasion of Kuwait that year. Finally, the perceived double-dealing of the US in this conflict, combined with their role in the subsequent war against Iraq after their invasion of Kuwait, would contribute greatly to a simmering sense of anti-American sentiment across the region. Indeed, this conflict would feed directly into the rhetoric of movements such as al-Qaeda, and their focus on the US as manipulating regional politics for their own benefit.

CONCLUSION

The Cold War was critical in shaping the political dynamics of the Middle East. However, as this chapter sought to highlight, this was not necessarily a dynamic of direct superpower control over regional allies. Instead, newly independent states were astute in their manipulation of Cold War dynamics in strengthening their rule and pursuing their regional interests. Whilst there was a reflection of the Cold War political dynamic in terms of emerging political issues, as shown by the civil war in Yemen, this was not always the case, as shown by external involvement in the Iran–Iraq War. This discussion is expanded in Chapter 4 where the key political ideologies shaping Middle Eastern politics, nationalism and Islamism, also represent this blend between the local, regional and global in Middle Eastern politics.

Study Questions

- How was the Middle East involved in World War II?
- What are the key controversies surrounding the establishment of the State of Israel?
- What was the significance of the 1956 Suez Crisis?
- What characterised superpower involvement in the Middle East during the Cold War?
- What were the major regime 'types' that emerged in the region upon independence?
- Was there an 'Arab Cold War' and what is the significance of the 1962–70 Yemen Civil War in relation to this?
- In what ways does the Lebanese Civil War highlight connections between local, regional and global political dynamics in the Middle East?

FURTHER READING

Karsh, Efraim (2002) *The Iran–Iraq War, 1980–1988*. London: Osprey.
A comprehensive examination of the longest conventional war of the 20th century, from an examination of local, regional and global forces.

Morris, Benny (2001) *Righteous Victims: A History of the Zionist–Arab Conflict, 1881–1999*. New York: Alfred A. Knopf.
A controversial work of revisionist history, this volume re-examines the origins of the State of Israel and the Israeli–Palestinian conflict to re-evaluate the parameters of the Peace Process.

Pappé, Ilan (2006) *The Israel–Palestine Question*. London: Routledge.
A reappraisal of the main parameters of the Arab–Israeli conflict in light of recent developments in both the Israeli and Palestinian communities.

Salibi, Kamal S. (1990) *A House of Many Mansions: The History of Lebanon Reconsidered*. Berkeley: University of California Press.
A seminal account of the cooperation and conflict between Lebanon's sectarian communities and how this political system has functioned and not functioned since the 1920s.

 Go to the companion website at www.sagepub.co.uk/macqueen for further material including free journal articles and links to other relevant documents.

REFERENCES

Angrist, Michele Penner (ed.) (2010) *Politics and Society in the Contemporary Middle East*. Boulder, CO: Lynne Rienner.

Aron, Raymond (1966) *Peace and War: A Theory of International Relations*. New York: Doubleday & Co.

Ashton, Nigel J. (ed.) (2007) *The Cold War in the Middle East: Regional Conflict and the Superpowers 1967–73*. London: Routledge.

Barrett, Roby C. (2007) *The Greater Middle East and the Cold War: US Foreign Policy Under Eisenhower and Kennedy*. London: I.B. Tauris.

Baxter, Kylie and Akbarzadeh, Shahram (2008) *US Foreign Policy in the Middle East: The Roots of Anti-Americanism*. London: Routledge.

Clarke, Thurston (1981) *By Blood and Fire: The Attack on the King David Hotel*. New York: Hutchinson.

Fawcett, Louise (ed.) (2009) *The International Relations of the Middle East*. Oxford: Oxford University Press.

Fisk, Robert (2001) *Pity the Nation: Lebanon at War*. Oxford: Oxford University Press.

Fraser, T.G. (2008) *The Arab–Israeli Conflict*, 3rd ed. New York: Palgrave Macmillan.

Halliday, Fred (2005) *The Middle East in International Relations*. Cambridge: Cambridge University Press.

Kennan, George (1947, originally published under the pseudonym of 'X' as an anonymous author) 'The Sources of Soviet Conduct', *Foreign Affairs*, July.

Khalaf, Samir (2002) *Civil and Uncivil Violence in Lebanon: A History of the Internationalization of Communal Conflict*. New York: Columbia University Press.

Khalidi, Rashid (2009) *Sowing Crisis: The Cold War and American Dominance in the Middle East*. Boston, MA: Beacon Press.

Khalifah, Bassem (2001) *The Rise and Fall of Christian Lebanon*. Toronto: York Press.

MacQueen, Benjamin (2009) *Political Culture and Conflict Resolution in the Arab World: Lebanon and Algeria*. Melbourne: Melbourne University Press.

Morris, Benny (2004) *The Birth of the Palestinian Refugee Problem Revisited*. Cambridge: Cambridge University Press.

Reynolds, David (2000) *One World Divisable: A Global History*. London: Allen Lane.

Sayigh, Yazid and Shlaim, Avi (1997) *The Cold War and the Middle East*. Oxford: Oxford University Press.

Schiff, Ze'ev and Ya'ari, Ehud (1985) *Israeli's Lebanon War*. New York: Simon & Schuster.

Traboulsi, Fawwaz (2007) *A History of Modern Lebanon*. London: Pluto Press.

United Nations (1947) *United Nations Special Committee on Palestine: Report to the General Assembly, Vol 1 (A/364)*. New York: United Nations.

4

Nationalism, Islamism and the Politics of Ideology

Learning Objectives

This chapter will enable a greater understanding of:

● The influence of ideologies on politics in the 20th century, with reference to the Middle East.
● The emergence of the ideology of Arab nationalism and its impacts on regional events.
● The emergence of the ideology of political Islamism and its impacts on regional events.
● How these ideologies took organisational form as well as being exploited by regional regimes.
● The role of these ideologies in perpetuating authoritarian rule and the difficulties faced by these ideologies in meeting popular expectations in the region.

TIMELINE

1928: Muslim Brotherhood founded in Egypt

22 March 1945: Arab League founded

7 April 1947: Ba'ath Party founded in Syria

1951: Iraqi branch of the Ba'ath Party founded

15 July–25 October 1958: Civil war in Lebanon

14 July 1958: Overthrow of the Iraqi monarchy

22 February 1958: Founding of the United Arab Republic

28 September 1961: Dissolution of the United Arab Republic

21–23 February 1966: Ba'ath Party coup in Syria, leading to the split between the Syrian and Iraqi branches of the Ba'ath Party

(Continued)

(Continued)

5–10 June 1967: The Six-Day War

17 July 1968: Baʿath Party comes to power in Iraq

28 September 1970: Gamal abd al-Nasser dies

15 October 1970: Anwar Sadat appointed President of Egypt

13 November 1970: Hafiz al-Assad comes to power in Syria

6–25 October 1973: October War

17 September 1978: Egyptian–Israeli Peace Treaty signed

1 April 1979: Islamic Republic of Iran proclaimed

16 July 1979: Saddam Hussein comes to power in Iraq

6 October 1981: Sadat assassinated by Islamic Jihad

14 October 1981: Hosni Mubarak appointed President of Egypt

INTRODUCTION

This chapter explores the influence of ideologies on the modern Middle East. Here, focus will be on the ideologies of nationalism, particularly Arab nationalism, and political Islam while similar ideologies, such as Zionism, are explored in Chapters 2 and 9. Certainly, many other ideological currents are present in the Middle East from liberalism to socialism and beyond. However, these two ideological streams have been the dominant discourses in the region since independence, and have shaped the way regimes have developed their policies and how the states of the region have engaged with the global community.

As such, this chapter will explore the foundations of these ideologies and their impact on both opposition movements and regimes. In addition, this chapter will outline how the potency of ideologies has changed over time, particularly in terms of how the popularity of Arab nationalism has declined in recent years, ostensibly replaced by political Islam. However, this common narrative will be presented in terms of how ideologies have been exploited for strategic legitimacy, often falling short of popular expectations.

IDEOLOGY AND POLITICS IN THE MIDDLE EAST

Ideology and Politics

The notion of ideology refers to a consistent set of ideas, beliefs and visions for social life held by an individual or a group. These ideas, beliefs and visions reflect needs or aspirations of the individual or group, and set priorities for how decisions should be made and what decisions should be of main concern. In this regard, ideologies have played a key role in political governance. A regime, party, social movement or other force will coalesce around an ideology as a set of prescriptions for how society should be governed. Here, ideologies often form all-encompassing sociopolitical programmes that dictate what a government will pursue as a matter of priority, what it sees as central to the greater social and political good. That is, a political ideology sets aspirations or goals for how society should ideally work as well as the means or methods for achieving this.

It can be argued that all politics is ideological. That is, all regimes and governments have to make decisions based on mutually exclusive interests. Deciding between competing interests is therefore guided by some ideological framework. As such, politics is often the result of a combination of ideology and self-interest. This is not always an either/or equation. Indeed, regimes and governments seek to hold on to power in both democratic and non-democratic societies. This often leads to decisions made in terms of political pragmatism (i.e. strengthening their rule) at the expense of ideological integrity, or the use of ideological rhetoric and symbols to pursue self-interest.

Ideology and Modernity in the Middle East

Political ideology is a modern phenomenon. Born out of the French Revolution, it was employed to understand how the new revolutionary regime articulated and sought to implement its vision for society. For the revolutionaries, the government should represent the interests of the national community (*la patrie*) rather than the Bourbon monarchy. This touches on an important point about ideologies in that they often form in times of crisis or rapid change. An ideology gives a new direction for a person or group of people to understand why a crisis has occurred (i.e. the failure of a previous way of doing things) and how to move beyond this (i.e. a plan for a 'correct' way of doing things in the future).

As will be discussed in Chapter 6, the economic development programmes implemented at this time, often in the form of state ownership and 'nationalisation' of key industries, was justified in terms of these notions of collective ownership. As we saw in Chapter 3, the Cold War impact on the Middle East was not uniform. However, the links between the Soviet Union as the global champion of communist ideology and regional allies was evident here. Whilst this will be discussed in detail below, particularly in relation to the development of so-called 'radical' Arab nationalist regimes, it is important to reiterate that the Cold War ideological contest of capitalism versus communism was not mirrored in the region. Whilst there were contests for influence often defined as ideological battles, this was heavily overlaid with strategic interest.

NATIONALISM

Before defining the ideology of nationalism, it will be useful to outline a working understanding of the concept of the nation. Nations are communities bound together by some combination of a common language, shared history, culture, ethnicity or descent. Whilst broad and fluid, this definition provides an important starting point.

Critically, this idea of a community bound by these forces is modern. That is, these communities have been constructed, with historical narratives being redefined, languages standardised and cultural practices homogenised to fit with the idea of a single, cohesive, standardised community. In this regard, whilst humans have always been part of communities and social systems, these are not the same as particular national communities. What sets this form of community apart, and highlights its contemporary nature, are the links to the ideology of nationalism. Put simply, nationalism is an ideology that claims supreme authority rests with the national community as a whole. As a result, each community, or nation, should have its own independent political system, or state, hence the concept of the *nation–state*.

The **Peace of Westphalia** refers to the treaties signed to end the 'Thirty Years War' in early 17th-century Europe. Briefly, the treaties established two principles, those of territoriality and the primacy of 'domestic' authority, or **sovereignty**.

That is, in order to prevent future conflict, it was agreed that a specified, clearly demarcated territory would have only one authority (a state). This was immediately concerned with the authority of the Catholic Church in various European empires.

The Peace of Westphalia restricted the authority all other actors than a state within its territory, giving it complete sovereign authority.

This is the base understanding for **state sovereignty**, the key organising principle of international politics. In this regard, a state has the so-called 'monopoly on the use of force' (i.e. the only entity with the power to rule and use coercive force) within a specified territory.

From key events in Europe in the 17th century, notably the Peace of Westphalia, this idea undermined the authority of alternative centres of power from religious to imperial authority. Eventually, the nationalist principle of the right to rule, or *sovereignty*, resting with the nation-state has come to define modern global politics. This has had significant implications. One of which is the notion of territoriality. That is, as each nation is to rule itself, and is separate from other nations, there needs to be clear and specific territorial separation. This resulted in the establishment of highly detailed borders between states. Within these borders, each state was the supreme authority over its people, who would belong to the relevant national community.

One useful way of understanding this is the notion of an 'imagined community' offered by Benedict Anderson. For Anderson, a nation is a community that exists in the *imagination* of its members as it is too large for all its members to meet face-to-face (Anderson, 1991). Without this personal contact, a national community still feels bound together through sharing common elements such as language, culture, history and symbols. The boundaries of these communities were established particularly through the growth of print media within a given territory that reiterated the common symbols and themes that each member, regardless of their physical position, could identify with.

In addition, the notion of 'national interest' should be the governing principle for how politics is organised. Whilst this point suggests that nationalist ideologies tend towards democratic systems (i.e. rule *by* the people), this has not always been so. Indeed, many authoritarian systems use nationalist rhetoric as a means to justify their rule and mobilise support. The call of nationalism, in this respect, has been particularly useful in consolidating popular opinion behind perceived 'enemies' to the nation. Inevitably, and often with great violence, nation-states forcibly sought to undermine or eliminate not only alternative claims to sovereignty, but challenges to the prescribed national identity. In states where ethnic identity was a key part of the national identity, the status of minority groups, including language and cultural rights, became a site of heated debate and contest. Many so-called civil wars have been fought over these matters, and many still rage today.

MIDDLE EASTERN NATIONALISMS

As we have seen in the previous chapters, the idea of the state arrived in the Middle East in controversial circumstances. The region was not alone in this, with the European powers establishing pseudo-state institutions across the globe during the period of colonisation. Often, these new creations established borders where none had previously existed. Across Africa, Asia, the Americas, as well as the Middle East, new states emerged into independence with only tentative links to cultural, linguistic or ethic realities on the ground.

As such, many of these new states lacked political legitimacy, with national identities fragile at best. The Middle East was no exception in this regard. However, there were a variety of tendencies at play. In Iran, for instance, the long history of Persian imperialism allowed for the development of a relatively cohesive sense of modern Iranian identity to emerge through the 20th century. However, the relationship of

Iran to its religious identity, particularly Shi`a Islam, remained fraught. This framed the uprising that eventually saw the toppling of the Pahlavi dynasty in 1979 and the establishment of the Islamic Republic.

In Israel, the ideology of Zionism was a conscious rearticulation of Jewish identity to fit with this idea of nationalism. As discussed in Chapter 1, Zionism was an expression of Jewish identity in nationalist terms, seeking to join the perceived cultural community with that of a territory, namely the then British Mandate of Palestine. Apart from the intense controversies surrounding the establishment of the state itself, there was also an intense internal struggle within this community as to how the new Israeli community, one drawn from all over the globe, would articulate its cultural, linguistic and historic identity, a debate that continues to the present day.

> The **Armenian genocide controversy** is a deeply divisive issue that still rages today. It is accepted that between 300,000 and 1.5 million Armenians died between 1915 and 1916. The deaths occurred at a time when the then Ottoman administration deported large numbers of Armenians from the east of Anatolia to southern Anatolia and northern Syria.
>
> The controversy centres on whether the deaths resulted from an orchestrated or systematic policy. This relates to the 1948 UN Convention on Genocide that defines genocide as a systematic programme to 'destroy, in whole or part, a national, ethnic, racial or religious group'.
>
> The Turkish government denies any systematic attempt, but the Armenian government, the Armenian community and many others continue to allege that the Ottomans were involved in a policy of genocide. The Young Turk movement, in control of the Ottoman government since 1908, were precursors to the government of the Republic of Turkey.

In addition, we saw in Chapter 1 how a conscious programme of articulating and consolidating a new Turkish identity with the decline of the Ottoman Empire led to the creation of the Republic of Turkey. However, this was a tumultuous process, with significant violence involving the new Turkish state as well as its considerable Kurdish and Armenian communities, involving allegations of organised violence and genocide.

Here, the story of Kurdish nationalism, along with that of other groups, has not resulted in achieving statehood. Fighting the governments of Turkey, Iran and Iraq as well as various factions fighting each other, the large Kurdish community has not been able to realise the establishment of a Kurdish state. However, the 2003 US-led invasion and occupation of Iraq has provided for the establishment of Kurdish

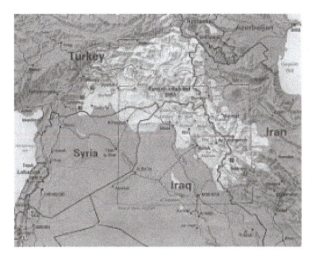

Figure 4.1 Areas with a Kurdish majority population
Source: Public domain

autonomy in the north of the country, a degree of freedom that operates as a virtual state within a state (see Chapter 10).

Arab Nationalism at a Glance

In relation to Arab identity, language is arguably the central feature. However, if we take Anderson's notion of how an imagined community develops, the apparent linguistic unity of the Arab people hides a great deal of diversity. For instance, in relation to the language itself, there are a large number of regional dialects that differ significantly from one another as well as the use of colloquial forms of Arabic and literary Arabic (often also referred to as *fusha*, or Modern Standard Arabic or MSA) (Versteegh, 2001).

Since the spread of the Arab people and their language from the Arabian Peninsula in the 7th century CE, the language has taken on a number of different colloquial forms across the region. As a result, colloquial, dialectic or spoken Arabic differs from

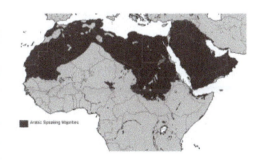

Figure 4.2 The Arabic-speaking community in the Middle East and North Africa

Source: San José State University

Morocco to Egypt, the Arabian Peninsula and the Levant. Traditionally, there have been five main groups of Arabic dialects: Arabian (Saudi Arabia and the Gulf), Mesopotamian (Iraq), Levantine (Syria, Lebanon, Jordan, Israel/Palestine and southern Turkey), Egyptian (Egypt) and Maghribi (North Africa). In addition, patterns of external interference have left legacies for the use of European terms, with strong evidence of this in countries such as Algeria and Lebanon as opposed to Saudi Arabia as well as the infusion of other languages, such as Berber/Amazigh, Persian and Turkish with Arabic.

> The **Berber** or **Amazigh** people are terms for the indigenous ethnic groups in North Africa. The Berber/Amazigh communities and their languages have mixed with the Arab community with the spread of the latter through the region since the 7th century CE.
> The name 'Berber' comes from Roman references to 'barbarian', relating to the Vandals and their invasions. Recently, the name 'Amazigh' (plural: Imazigen), or 'free men' has been adopted as an alternative.

Alternatively, MSA developed through the 19th and 20th centuries to standardise the formal written Arabic. Currently, it is in use across the majority of the Arab world in the production of newspapers and other formal writing. Thus, whilst language forms the core of Arab identity, it exists in a dual sense, in both local/dialectic form and formal/standardised form. Turning back to Anderson, the development of print media in the region occurred at the time of colonialism, when the boundaries of the current states were established. As a result, identities built around the mechanics of 'print capitalism', notably newspapers, were increasingly written in MSA but were referential to identities built around colonial and, later, state boundaries.

> It is difficult to acquire reliable statistics on religious affiliation. Indeed, identification with a particular religion does not capture other factors, such as levels of observance or the relationship of an individual to a religious establishment. However, tentative figures on religious affiliation show the Arab world today (roughly 350 million people) are 91% Muslim (80% of the total as Sunni Muslim and 11% of the total as Shi`a Muslim), 6% Christian (of many denominations) and 3% other religions (Jewish, Bahaïi and others).

There are also strong religious, cultural and historical elements underlying Arab identity. This is somewhat more problematic, as the Arab community, whilst majority Muslim, has a great variety of religious communities, both between religions (Islam, Christianity, Judaism, etc.) and within religions (Sunni and Shi`a Islam, Catholic and Orthodox Christianity, etc.). However, the links between Arab and Islamic history make the two almost inseparable in discussions of Arab identity, in particular, the history of Arab-Islamic empires and the articulation of Islam in the Arabic language. These links are important to remember when discussing the emergence of an Arab nationalist ideology in the late 19th and early 20th centuries. As with almost all aspects under discussion here, this discussion remains a point of historic debate today. The following will focus on the broad tension between the notion of Arab political unity and the consolidation of states that separated the community from the Atlantic Ocean to the Gulf (Barakat, 1993).

The Uniqueness of Arab Nationalism

The central tension in Arab nationalist discourse is the ideal of political unification for the Arabs and the reality of Arab political life divided amongst 22 states. In this regard, the doctrine of Arab nationalism is unique in that it challenges not just the existence of one or two states, but an entire regional state system. The idea of challenging state borders on the basis of ethnicity and nationalist claims is not unique. In this regard, irredentist movements have challenged established state borders across the globe often through armed conflict.

> **Irredentism** is a term referring to movements that advocate the division of two or more existing states or the annexation of territory of one or more states based on unifying common ethnic groups.

This has most often come in the form of one state making territorial claims on another, such as the conflict over the status of Northern Ireland (Ulster), Taiwan, Kashmir and many others. In addition, groups have also claimed for the division of existing states to create new entities, such as the various Kurdish movements in relation to Iraq, Turkey, Iran and Syria or members of the Pashtun population advocating for an independent state to be carved out of Afghanistan and Pakistan. However, the idea of Arab political unity is unique in two respects. First, the scale of the vision of Arab unity is unprecedented, calling for unity of the people from Morocco to Iraq and Syria to Yemen. A possible comparison is the creation of the European Union. However, this has been a move based on claims of political utility rather than nationalism and ethnic unity (Choueiri, 2000).

The second aspect relates to the status of the doctrine in relation to existing Arab regimes. Specifically, almost all Arab regimes give some measure of support to the idea of Arab political unity. Much of this does not move beyond the rhetorical level to be sure, but this is unique in that these regimes support an ideology that directly contradicts the existence of the states over which they rule. Again, it is important to reiterate that this may only exist at the rhetorical level, but it is an issue that has created a tension for the legitimacy of governments across the region.

> The **Arab League** was founded in Cairo in March 1945 as the peak multilateral body for Arab cooperation. It has 22 members (Algeria, Bahrain, the Comoros, Djibouti, Egypt, Iraq, Jordan, Kuwait, Lebanon, Libya, Mauritania, Morocco, Oman, the Palestinian Authority, Qatar, Saudi Arabia, Somalia, Sudan, Syria, Tunisia, the United Arab Emirates and Yemen).
>
> It has a variety of activities, but is often criticised for being able to do very little to address issues as it represents the interests of existing regimes rather than the people of the region.

In order to explore this in more detail, it is important to first explore the origins of the Arab nationalist doctrine. In particular, we shall outline here the early thinkers and organisations that championed this ideology, before exploring efforts at realising Arab unity by challenging the emerging state system. What will become evident is the centrality of Arab nationalist thought through the 20th century. Whilst its influence has declined since the late 1960s, the resilience of Arab identity continues to affect regional politics.

The Origins of Arab Nationalism

There were two streams of early nationalist sentiment amongst the Arab population. The first was amongst a sociopolitical elite, particularly the Hashemites who cooperated with the British against the Ottomans in World War I, and the second amongst a small group of urban intellectuals in Damascus, Beirut, Baghdad and Cairo. The role of the Hashemites, particularly Sherif Hussein, in the Arab Revolt during World War I was discussed in Chapter 2, particularly the efforts at the establishment of a unitary Arab state in the Levant. This may also be seen in the efforts of Muhammad `Ali in Egypt in the late 19th century.

> The **Hashemites**, or *Banu Hashim* (the clan of Hashim), are a family tracing their lineage to the Prophet Muhammad (via the Prophet's great grandfather and uncle Abu Talib). From the 10th century CE, the Hashemites were given custodianship of the Hijaz and, by extension, the Holy Cities of Mecca and Medina.

After their involvement in the Arab Revolt during World War I, members of the Hashemite family ruled in various parts of the Arab world (the Kingdom of the Hijaz, 1917–24; the Kingdom of Iraq, 1921–58 and the Kingdom of Jordan, 1946 to present).

What is critical to reiterate here is the sense of betrayal between the Arab leadership and Western powers that emerged out of the Arab Revolt and subsequent division of the region under the League of Nations Mandates. This became a feature of subsequent nationalist discourse in the Arab world, with suspicion of external parties whilst also looking to external parties for support. However, the articulation of Arab nationalism that had the most prominent impact through the 20th century originated amongst urban intellectuals, initially concerned primarily with a revival of the Arabic language (and involved in the development of MSA). Key figures in this early movement included Nasif al-Yaziji and Butrus al-Bustani, both Christian Arabs from current-day Lebanon writing in the mid- to late 19th century.

Here, the relationship between Arab nationalism and religion, particularly Islam, was already evident as many early nationalists were Arab Christians focussed on the linguistic component of Arab identity over that of Islam. Whilst nationalist sentiment spread amongst the Muslim community, the role of religion was often controversial. Despite this, a secular, or marginally religious version of Arab nationalist identity became the dominant theme through the 20th century.

Figure 4.3 From left: Butrus al-Bustani and Nasif al-Yaziji

Source: Gebhardt, Hans, *History, Space and Social Conflict in Beirut: The Quarter of Zokak el-Blat*. Beirut: Orient-Institut, 2005

The nationalist movement of the urban intellectuals failed to gain popular support up to World War I, where many of the key thinkers gave support to the Arab Revolt. However, the failure of this to gain its goals of an independent Arab state and the subsequent allocation of new states to Hashemite monarchs saw the movement increasingly politicised, and subsequently form new parties in the Levant and Egypt, often with anti-monarchical and leftist ideological leanings. Here, notions of Arab unity and nationalism oscillated between a variety of emphases. For instance, some writers focussed on more local or parochial loyalties (*wataniyya*) whilst others emphasised the notion of broader Arab unity (*qawmiyya*) beyond local allegiances. This latter sentiment became dominant in ideological terms; however, in practice, it was local parochialisms that increasingly asserted themselves. The history of the Ba`ath Party is a clear example of this (Barakat, 1993: 4).

The Baàth Party

The Ba`ath Party was founded in Syria in 1947 by Michel Aflaq and Salah al-Din al-Bitar. Meaning renaissance or resurrection, the Ba`ath was the first major Arab nationalist party. The initial party platform emphasised the secular nature of Arab identity, with Aflaq from the Greek Orthodox community and al-Bitar from the Sunni community. In addition, the party also focussed on elements of leftist, particularly socialist economic policies. However, it consciously distanced itself from direct identification with Marxism as the party was in direct competition with the Syrian Communist Party (SCP) at the time.

It was the split from the SCP in the mid-1940s that led directly to the formation of the Ba`ath. Specifically, the SCP supported French policies in the region,

Figure 4.4 From left: Michel Aflaq, Salah al-Din al-Bitar and Zaki al-Arsuzi
Source: Public domain

in conjunction with the French communists who were part of the government in Paris at the time. This helped sharpen the focus of the party to articulate the ideal of Arab independence and unity. At the same time, another French-educated middle-class Syrian, Zaki al-Arsuzi from the Alawi community, established the Arab Ba`ath with a similar doctrine. By the mid-1940s, Aflaq and al-Bitar's movement had started to eclipse that of al-Arsuzi, leading to a merger in 1947 and the formation of the Arab Ba`ath Party. Al-Arsuzi was marginalised in these early years of the party, with Aflaq elected leader of the group and al-Bitar as Secretary General (Devlin, 1976).

The party had two main platforms, that of Arab political union and socialism. Underlying this was a view that both the Ottomans and later the Europeans had directly undermined a 'natural' Arab unity. The best tool in pursuit of claiming this, for the Ba`athists, was the adoption of a socialist doctrine. The redistribution of wealth from the implementation of socialist policies would undermine traditional power structures that had facilitated this external dominance and give the Arabs a greater ability to resist further interference.

The **Alawi** are a Muslim community concentrated in the Latakia region of north-western Syria as well as southern Turkey and northern Lebanon and part of the Lebanese diaspora, particularly amongst the Lebanese-Australian community.

The community considers itself part of the Shi`a branch of Islam, however, despite many of the core tenets of the faith remaining secret, it is believed that there are a number of elements incorporated from Christianity.

Historically marginalised in Syria, where they constitute between 10% and 15% of the population, the Alawi were prominent in the Syrian armed forces. From here, they became increasingly prevalent in Syrian politics. This culminated with the rise of the Hafiz al-Assad, an Alawi, to the presidency in 1971 under the banner of the Ba`ath Party.

The party grew slowly through the late 1940s and early 1950s, struggling to grow a base within the large peasantry and working class in Syria. This was despite an official merger with the Arab Socialist Party in 1953 that saw a name change to the Arab Socialist Ba`ath Party. However, the rise to power in Egypt of Arab nationalist Nasser in 1954 and the success of the 1956 Suez Crisis (see Chapter 3) saw the party's ranks swell. Indeed, the party formed a formal alliance with the new Egyptian regime, helping it become an increasingly powerful force in post-independence Syrian politics and seeing it win a number of seats during the short-lived reintroduction of parliamentary democracy in 1954.

Nasserism and the United Arab Republic

With the Ba`ath espousing Arab unity on the basis of dismantling the post-independence states and implementing socialist policies of state-led economic development, Nasser moved to put this into practice. However, these first moves to realise the goal of Arab political unity would quickly run into problems, particularly over who should rule and how much control the new Arab leadership should have.

The Egyptian President's vision has been labelled 'Nasserism', a set of ideas based around the ideas of Arab political unity, socialism and confronting imperialism. Whilst not so much a coherent ideology, Nasserism was considered by some as an 'attitude [that] transferred, if only partially, to the Arab world itself, the center of decisions concerning the future of that world' (Khalidi cited in Podeh and Winckler, 2004: 2). That is, the ramifications of the Suez Crisis and the rollback of colonial rule alongside the emergence of Nasser calling for unity resonated across the region, and challenged the political status quo. For Nasser, this should include all means of challenge, including the use of armed force.

The appeal of Nasser's call for unity, alongside the growing threat of a communist coup, led the Syrian government of Shukri al-Quwatli, backed by the Ba`ath Party, to open negotiations with Egypt for a formal political union. This is important to note as this apparent first step towards the unification of the Arab world emerged as a result of a political manoeuvre on the part of the Syrian government to avoid collapse as much as it was an effort to pursue the goal of eventual region-wide unification; saying this, there were high levels of popular support for the idea of unification.

Figure 4.5   From left: Shukri al-Quwatli and Gamal abd al-Nasser sign the agreement to form the United Arab Republic and Nasser and al-Quwatli after the announcement of the founding of the United Arab Republic

Source: Public domain

Figure 4.6 Leaders of the 1958 Iraqi coup with Abd al-Karim Qasim (centre)
Source: Al-Ahram

On 22 February 1958, al-Quwatli and Nasser signed an agreement for formal uni-fication between Syria and Egypt, creating the United Arab Republic (UAR) with Nasser as President and Cairo as the capital. Nasser immediately banned all parties, a move that was aimed at undermining the Syrian communists, but also saw the official dissolution of the Ba`ath Party. Whilst the Ba`ath hoped it would be able to become the dominant organisation in Syria, Nasser quickly imposed a new consti-tution that gave more prominent positions to Egyptians.

Whilst the idea of the UAR resonated in Egypt, it quickly bred resentment in Syria. In particular, the UAR was increasingly perceived as a vehicle for extend-ing Nasser's power to Syria rather than an equal relationship. This led the Ba`ath to resign from the UAR government on 24 December 1959. In addition, other regional governments saw it as a threat to their interests. For its part, Saudi Arabia was worried about the growing power of Nasser and his calls for the overthrow of monarchies claiming that their pro-Western allegiances represented the continua-tion of imperial rule. Also, opposition to the Jordanian monarchy found refuge in Syria, agitating for the overthrow of King Hussein.

This instability spread to Iraq, with a military coup overthrowing the Hashemite King Faisal II on 14 July 1958. As discussed in Chapter 3, this greatly concerned the US, with Iraq as a key ally and founding member of the pro-Western Baghdad Pact. In Lebanon, Sunni and Druze advocates of Nasser's vision in Lebanon chal-lenged the government of Camille Chamoun. This led to the outbreak of civil war in 1958 (Salibi, 1990).

However, the internal tensions became too great for the union to bear. Whilst many within the new Iraqi government sought to join the UAR, this was resisted by the new Iraq President Abd al-Karim Qasim, undermining the momentum for unification. In this regard, the collapse of the UAR on 28 September 1961 has conventionally been put down to the inability of Nasser to share sufficient authority with his cohorts in Damascus. Nasser increasingly centralised power in Cairo through 1960 and 1961, marginalising the Ba`ath and appointing more reliable allies. This culminated in a military coup and a declaration of Syrian withdrawal from the union.

Syrian and Iraqi Ba`ath Party Split

The tension between a regional identity and formal political divisions continued to undermine the aspirations of Arab nationalism. This was evident in the collapse of the UAR as well as continuing tensions between the broader Arab community. Indeed, as the 20th century progressed, the strategic interests of each state became more entrenched, and the hopes of Arab union more distant. Even ideological similarity could not prevent this from happening. This was most evident with the split between the Syrian and Iraqi Ba`ath parties, an issue that is critical to understanding events up to the 2003 US-led invasion and occupation of Iraq that overthrew the Ba`ath regime of Saddam Hussein in Baghdad.

Figure 4.7 Hafiz al-Assad
Source: Public domain

The Iraqi branch of the Ba`ath was founded in the early 1950s, and had limited support through to the coup in July 1958. Qasim's reluctance to join the UAR saw the party, and its then leader Saddam Hussein, attempt to assassinate the President. Whilst this was unsuccessful, the still nascent Iraqi Ba`ath finally achieved power in 1963 when Qasim was overthrown by a group that included prominent Ba`athist Ahmed Hassan al-Bakr. The US actively supported the coup as they saw the Iraqi communists as too close to Qasim, effectively opening the way for Ba`ath Party rule in Iraq, an irony of history that would fully emerge in the 1990s (Devlin, 1976).

However, similar tensions would emerge as happened in the UAR. Through the 1960s, both the Syrian and Iraqi Ba`ath parties became embroiled in a series of factional disputes. In 1966, a faction of the Syrian Ba`ath led by Salah Jadid and Hafiz al-Assad took power leading to both Aflaq and al-Bitar being ostracised from the Syrian party in 1966. This led to a permanent split between the Syrian and Iraqi branches of the party, both in power. The enmity between the two parties was intense, with Syria actively supporting Iran during its war with Iraq in the 1980s (see Chapter 3) and nego-

Figure 4.8 From left: Saddam Hussein and Ahmed Hassan al-Bakr in the 1970s

Source: Public domain

tiating a bargain with the US where Syria would support their military action against the Iraqi invasion of Kuwait in exchange for tacit US support for the Syrian occupation of Lebanon with the end of the civil war in 1990.

The 1967 War and its Impacts on Arab Nationalism

As we saw in Chapter 3, the 1956 Suez Crisis is often pinpointed as symbolising both the end of colonial rule and the high watermark of power for Arab nationalist doctrine and influence. Here, the 1967 War is viewed as the event that saw the ultimate decline of Arab nationalism's influence. What we have seen is these things, such as the decline of Ottoman and colonial influence as well as other factors, change over a longer period.

Figure 4.9 Israel before the 1967 War

Source: MGFA

Lead-Up to the War

However, the war did highlight the weaknesses of the movement, particularly in terms of Nasser's claims in terms of confrontations with Israel. Saying this, was it the problem of nationalist doctrine that led to the defeat of Egypt, Syria and Jordan?

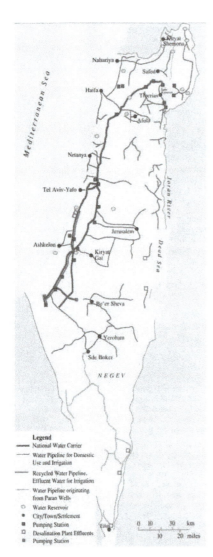

Figure 4.10   Israel's National Water Carrier programme

Source: American–Israeli Cooperative Enterprise

Regardless, this was the interpretation, and led to the change of focus amongst key Arab regimes, particularly Egypt, as well as a popular shift away from nationalist movements.

The origins of the war itself, again, are subject to intense debate. This largely centres around whether the war was an act of Israeli aggression against Egypt, Jordan or Syria, or, as the Israeli government claimed, an act of 'pre-emptive defence'. Whilst there had not been a major conflict between Israel and the Arab states since 1956, tension was high and Nasser in particular put Israel as a key symbol hindering the development of Arab nationalism. In addition, Israel was seen a representative of external influence and efforts to control the region. In other words, the confrontation with Israel was, for Nasser, a central part of the broader effort towards the realisation of the goals of Arab nationalism.

There were many basic strategic calculations at play here too, such as Israel's National Water Carrier (NWC) programme that was highly controversial in the Arab world. This came to a head in the early 1960s when Israel completed this project that diverted water from the River Jordan to irrigate agricultural projects and new settlements in the arid south of the country. This was another in a sequence of events that highlighted the apparent inability of the Arab states to prevent Israel from pursuing its aims at their expense (Zeitoun, 2011).

Israel began the programme in 1953, diverting the river from the demilitarised zone on the border with Syria. Whilst not often mentioned in relation to the lead-up to the 1967 War, this was a major issue for all parties at the time, leading to international mediation through the UN. Israel suspended diversion operations through the mid-1950s. The Arab states, particularly Egypt, argued that the water plan was tied to the broader issue of Palestinian rights, particularly the prospect for the return of Palestinian refugees and Israeli strategic strength, as the water plan would enable Israel to absorb large numbers of new refugees from Europe and Russia; this would further strengthen Israel in demographic and military terms. By 1964, the Arab states had agreed in principle to their own water diversion programme to counter Israel's plan.

Inter-Arab Tensions and Militarisation

As mentioned above, whilst pan-Arab nationalist ideology was dominant at this time, the leaders of the various Arab states were highly competitive in using this for their own specific interests, particularly in terms of using their claims to be a champion of the nationalist cause for domestic political consumption. In this regard, through the 1960s, the rhetoric of confronting Israel became increasingly radicalised where each leader sought to outdo the other as being at the forefront of this struggle (Shemesh, 2004: 5). This led to a great deal of confrontational rhetoric and a severe deterioration in already strained relations between the Arab states and Israel.

The two principal Arab players here were Jordan and Egypt, who took different paths. Jordan had formally annexed the West Bank in 1950, granting citizenship to all Palestinians in its territory with the exception of refugees from the Gaza Strip. Gaza was administered by Egypt under military authority, with the Egyptians seeking to organise Palestinian political institutions in the country as an alternative means of both challenging Israel and controlling the policy of the Arab states.

In terms of nationalist doctrine, this manifested in two trends. First, a group headed by Nasser that focussed on the creations of a formal, pan-Arab state. Second, a group headed by the Syrian Ba`athists that argued for a federal union that would retain the state structures. Here, relations between Egypt and Syria deteriorated markedly through the mid-1960s

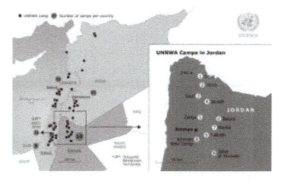

Figure 4.11 Palestinian refugee camps in the Gaza Strip, West Bank and Jordan

Source: UNRWA

using Israel, and particularly the water diversion issue, as the focus of conflict. That is, each claiming the other was inept at dealing with Israel's water plan, *ergo*, inept at dealing with Israel's growing strength in general.

> The **United Arab Command** was established in 1964 as an effort to coordinate Arab military activities through the Arab League. Whilst it represented a level of cooperation between the Arab states, it did not prove effective in response to Israeli military activity in Jordan in 1964 or in response to the 1967 War.

The clearest example of internecine Arab conflict was the tension between Nasser and Jordan's King Hussein. Egypt funded a number of groups, particularly Palestinian groups, that sought to topple the monarchy whilst also questioning the legitimacy of the Jordanian monarchy as well as the Jordanian state, arguing it was another colonial creation, and a particularly insidious one that divided the heart of the Arab world as well as illegally annexing the West Bank of the River Jordan. Thus, the Arab–Israeli conflict, through the 1960s, became increasingly entangled in the ideas of Arab nationalism itself. For the Jordanian government, this issue therefore become inextricably linked to its own survival. All this fed into the growing militarisation of all states in the Levant, particularly Israel, Egypt, Syria and Jordan as well as the Palestinians through the increasing military activity of the PLO. This latter fact was important as it started to transform the conflict to one not just between existing Arab states and Israel but one between an increasingly autonomous and organised Palestinian resistance.

What is clear is that through the 1960s, war became inevitable for Israel, Egypt and Syria. For the Arab states, they were in sharp disagreement as to strategy and goals, as well as being unsure of the military capacity of Israel. For Israel, they were unsure as to the behaviour of the Arab states, caught between the rhetoric of Cairo and Damascus calling for the destruction of Israel whilst also noting the divisions between the states. Here, the growing size of the Arab armies, particularly that of Egypt, was of concern, but this was mitigated by the lack of unity between the Arab governments.

There was some apparent cooperation between the Arab states, with the formation of the United Arab Command (UAC) in 1964, the Egyptian–Syrian mutual defence agreement in 1966 and the Egyptian–Jordanian mutual defence agreement in May 1967. In addition, the Egyptians and others continued to supply the Palestinians with aid whilst Israel and the PLO engaged in open conflict, including Israeli incursions into Jordan after PLO attacks in Israel.

The 'Six-Day' War

In the weeks leading up to the war, an estimated 100,000 Egyptian troops were massed in the Sinai, followed by a closing of the Straits of Tiran on 22 May and an expulsion of the United Nations peacekeeping force in place since the 1956 Suez Crisis. Alongside the heated rhetoric of the Egyptian regime, this was portrayed as a clear sign of Egypt's intent to invade Israel.

However, others have argued that Egyptian actions were an effort at 'brinkmanship' against Israel, as well as strengthening their hand vis-à-vis the other Arab states. Here, Israeli historian Benny Morris (2001: 301) points to fake Soviet intelligence passed to Egypt that Israeli troops were gathering on the Syrian border. In addition, Moshe Shemesh argues that the Egyptian troops were deployed in a defensive formation, back from the border, whilst the top Egyptian generals were left to continue the actions in the Yemeni Civil War. Shemesh goes on to point out that Israel was involved in a series of training exercises focussed on rapid offensive manoeuvres as well as gathering intelligence on Egyptian, Syrian and Jordanian troop placements. Indeed, Israeli intelligence had penetrated the upper levels of the Egyptian military. This was critical as the Israeli offensive was built around exploiting specific times where there was minimal security at Arab air bases. Israel had over a quarter of a million troops, but this number was inflated by a large number of reservists (Shemesh, 2004: 2–5).

Figure 4.12   Lands occupied by Israel after the 1967 War

Source: Public domain

Putting aside the contested interpretation of the lead-up to the conflict, the war itself broke out on 5 June when Israel launched a strike on Egyptian airfields. Nearly three-quarters of the entire Egyptian air force was destroyed without leaving the ground, as well as the destruction of air fields and air defences, giving Israel undisputed air control for the rest of the war. By 8 June, the Israelis had taken control of the entire Sinai Peninsula as well as the Gaza Strip suffering minimal casualties whilst routing the Egyptian forces.

The Arab–Israeli war is commonly known as the **'Six-Day War'** for the length of the conflict, from 5 to 10 June.

- 5 June: Israel launched air strikes against Egyptian, Jordanian and Syrian targets, destroying their air forces.
- 6 June: Israel takes the Gaza Strip, the eastern Sinai and territory in the West Bank with Egyptian and Jordanian retreats.
- 7 June: Israeli forces move through the Sinai and secure Jerusalem and the majority of the West Bank, Jordan accepts ceasefire, and fighting on the Syrian border.
- 8 June: Egypt accepts ceasefire and the rest of the West Bank is taken.
- 9 June: Israel moves into the Golan Heights.
- 10 June: Israel takes the Golan Heights and Syria accepts ceasefire.

News of the 5 June attack on Sinai saw fighting break out between Israel and the Jordanians around Jerusalem. The Israeli air force conducted operations across Jordan as well as in western Iraq that knocked out air defences and destroyed aircraft, extending their air superiority. By 7 June, after heavy fighting around the centre of Jerusalem, Israel had taken the old city and pushed further into the West Bank. Soon after, Jordanian troops withdrew to the other side of the Jordan River, allowing the Israelis to take the territory with minimal resistance.

In a similar dynamic to Jordan, Syria entered the war after the Israeli offensive of 5 June. Initial Syrian air strikes were repelled with the Israeli air force counterattacking and destroying the bulk of the Syrian air force. Syrian ground attacks were focussed on the facilities associated with the Israeli National Water Carrier programme, however these were quickly repelled. The Syrians then accepted a ceasefire early on 9 June; however, Israel pushed ahead with an offensive on the strategically important Golan Heights, taking it by the next day.

Legacies of the Six-Day War for the Ideological Trajectory of the Middle East

The immediate impacts of the war are evident. Israel more than tripled its size, secured key strategic areas and destroyed the military capacity of its adversaries. Whilst this is explored in detail in Chapter 9, there has been an emerging view that

Israel's victory may have been pyrrhic. In particular, the territory taken by Israel had large numbers of Palestinian refugees, dramatically altering the demographics of the country. It also solidified the permanent state of conflict for Israel, greatly affecting the political culture of the country through to the 21st century.

In addition, the war had two important symbolic impacts. First, it reiterated the idea that Israel was militarily unbeatable and second, it shattered the ideological hegemony of Arab nationalism and its claims of achieving regional unity. The collapse of the ideological potency of Arab nationalism in the wake of the Six-Day War was not unexpected. As detailed above, the divisions between the Arab states and the failure of projects to achieve political unity all point to the difficulties faced by nationalist doctrine. The war itself, it may be argued, merely exposed the inherent dysfunction of the nationalist vision. However, the sheer scale of the loss, and the fact that it impacted most on the two champion states of nationalism, Egypt and Syria, undermined its mass appeal.

As we shall explore below, this coincided with the development of new forms of Islamic political doctrine, particularly in the 1960s, that challenged not only the established international order, alongside Arab nationalism, but also regional regimes, many of whom prescribed to the nationalist doctrine.

POLITICAL ISLAM

Islam: A Snapshot

In Chapter 1, we briefly touched on the relationship between Islam and politics in a historical sense. Here, we shall expand on this through a brief outline of the tenets of the religion. This is not an exhaustive overview of Islam itself, but designed to sketch out those elements of the faith that are its defining features and the impacts of this on how ideologies seeking to explicitly combine Islam and politics have developed in recent years.

The Basic Tenets of Islam

Perhaps the key feature of Islam is its emphasis on the 'oneness' (*tawhid*) of God (*allah*). The indivisibility of God's unity and divinity supersedes all other aspects of the religion. For instance, Islam regards the notion of a Holy Trinity present in Christianity, particularly the claims to divinity on the part of Jesus Christ, as a dilution of God's absolute divinity. As such, at its core Islam is not a complicated religion in terms of tenets or models of adherence and practice. These revolve around five 'articles of faith' for belief and five 'pillars' of Islamic practice. The articles of faith, as outlined in the Muslim Holy Book the *Qur'an*, focus on a belief in God, a belief in the angels of God, a belief in the Prophets of God (from Adam to Muhammad, the last prophet), the belief in the divinely revealed Holy Books (the *Torah*, the Bible, and the *Qur`an*), and a belief in a Day of Judgement. As such, Islam positions itself as a continuation of the other two regional monotheistic faiths from the Middle East, Judaism and Christianity.

In terms of custom or ritual, there are five pillars (*arkan ad-din*) or duties (*faraidh*) of Islamic practice. These are a faith (*imān*) and belief in the oneness (*tawhīd*) of God, demonstrated through a profession of faith (*shahadah*). This profession is a statement declaring 'I bear witness that there is no God but Allah, and Muhammad is His messenger' (*ash hadu an la ilaha illa`llah, Muhammad ar-rasul Allah*). In addition, Muslims are required to perform prayer (*salah*) rituals five times daily, charity (*zakat*) through a minimum donation of 2.5% of one's net worth, fasting (*sawm*) during the month of Ramadan on the Islamic calendar and pilgrimage (*hajj*) of all able-bodied Muslims who can afford it to Mecca at least once in their lifetime (Armstrong, 2002).

The five pillars (*arkan ad-din* or *faraidh*) of Islam:

1. Faith (*imān*), testament (*shahadah*), and belief in the oneness (*tawhīd*) of God
2. Prayer (*salah*)
3. Charity (*zakat*)
4. Fasting (*sawm*)
5. Pilgrimage (*hajj*)

Qur`an and Hadith

From these core tenets, Islam draws from its central holy text, the *Qur`an* and the stories and accounts of the Prophet's life from others, the *hadith*. As outlined in Chapter 1, Muslims believe the text of the *Qur`an* itself to have been revealed to the Prophet Muhammad between 610 and 632 CE. As it was revealed directly, it is believed to contain the word of God. As with the other holy texts in Judaism and Christianity, it forms the core of spiritual guidance for Muslims.

There have been many critiques of particular *hadith*. The central component of these criticisms revolves around the authenticity of the particular saying of action as well as the way it has been applied in a legal context.

In particular, and in a criticism that is reminiscent of similar criticisms in relation to the formalisation of religious laws in Judaism and Christianity, there are charges that many *hadith* were developed to further particular political and social aims rather than being reflective of the actual narrative of the Prophet's deeds and sayings.

There are also differences between Sunni and Shi`a on the number of *hadith*. For the Sunni, only sayings and deeds attributable to the Prophet Muhammad are valid *hadith*. For the Shi`a, the narrations of Muhammad, his daughter Fatima and the 12 Imams are all valid *hadith*.

As the *hadith* are based on selected narratives and interpretations of the Prophet's actions, they are not without contest. In particular, in recent years, the interpretation of particular *hadith* has been used to justify violence by militant and terrorist groups. In addition, particular *hadith* are used to justify blocking the participation of women in positions of political leadership. The *hadith* are important supplements providing guidance for Muslims, particularly Muslim scholars, in areas that are not covered explicitly in the *Qur`an*. In this regard, the *hadith* provide details of the Prophet's Muhammad's life (*sunnah*) that were formally documented in the 8th and 9th centuries CE. The *hadith* therefore do not carry the same importance as the text of the *Qur`an*, but do provide important elements informing Islamic law, or *shari`ah* (Rahman, 1979).

Shari`ah

Shari`ah* is the legal code of Islam. The process of establishing *shari`atic principles varies, but generally revolves around the interpretation of principles in the *Qur`an*, the *hadith* and the *sunnah* by Islamic judges (*qadi*), religious leaders (*imam*) and religious scholars (*`ulama*) that would reflect the greatest level of consensus (*`ijma*) amongst the Muslim community. As is often highlighted, in the modern context, the application of the *shari`ah* as a state's legal code is often the goal of Islamist movements and organisations. This is often true, however there are also many instances, as we shall see below, of movements looking to combine elements of the *shari`ah* with civil or secular law codes. Despite this, the application of the *shari`ah* in both Muslim majority states and for Muslim minorities in other states remains a highly controversial issue (Rahman, 1979).

Sunni and Shi`a Islam

As touched on briefly in Chapter 1, the major division within the Muslim community is between the Sunni and Shi`a communities. This division arose over the contest of who should succeed the Prophet Muhammad after his death in 632 CE.

Simply put, the Sunni emerged from those who favoured popular selection of Muhammad's successor, whilst the Shi`a (the 'partisans of `Ali', *Shi`atu `Ali*) favoured authority passing to `Ali, the Prophet's son-in-law. Thus Shi`a have historically been marginalised, with the majority Muslims as well as the majority of Islamic empires being Sunni. Alongside numerical differences, there are important doctrinal differences. For instance, whilst the Sunni do not attribute any divine character to the Prophet, the Shi`a believe that the Prophet, his predecessors and successors, possessed a 'divine light' (*nur-e-elahi*) that enabled them to receive God's revelation. This is highly controversial for some, as it potentially dilutes the absolute oneness (*tawhīd*) of God.

In line with this, many Shi`a place special emphasis on the line of rulers (*imam*) that succeeded Muhammad and `Ali. The divine light that inspired Muhammad and the other Prophets gave his successors the right to rule the Muslim community (*ummah*). Here, there is contestation over the exact line of succession. However, the majority group are the 'Twelvers' (*ithna ashari*) who believe that the line of succession continued to Muhammad al-Mahdi who received 'occultation' by God (simply, was hidden by God), and will return with Jesus Christ (*Isa* in Islamic tradition) on the Day of Judgement.

The Twelver Shi`a Imams:

1. `Ali ibn abu Talib (Muhammad's son-in-law)
2. Hasan ibn `Ali
3. Husayn ibn `Ali
4. `Ali ibn Husayn
5. Muhammad ibn `Ali
6. Ja`far ibn Muhammad
7. Musa ibn Ja`far
8. `Ali ibn Musa
9. Muhammad ibn `Ali
10. `Ali ibn Muhammad
11. Hassan ibn `Ali
12. Muhammad ibn al-Hasan (al-Mahdi)

Legal Schools, the *`Ulama* and Religious Authority

The major division within Islam, as already discussed, is between the Sunni and Shi`a communities. However, issues relating to law and interpretation of Islamic doctrine give rise to further divisions. Amongst the Sunni, there are four major schools (*madhab*) of Islamic jurisprudence (*fiqh*): the Hanafis, Malikis, Shafi`is and Hanbalis.

The Hanafis are the largest of the four groups, and employed a liberal/rationalist interpretation of Islamic law dominant in both the `Abbasid and Ottoman Empires and remains dominant in Egypt and the Levant, Turkey and Central Asia. The second largest group, the Malikis, are prevalent in North Africa with smaller numbers in the Middle East. The Maliki school is notable for the greater emphasis it places on the role of the *hadith* as a source for Islamic law than the other *madhab*. The Shafi`i school, prominent in East Africa and Southeast Asia, is a highly rigorous approach to the sources of Islamic law, focussed on the process of interpretation, or *ijtihad*, to contextualise Islamic sources. Finally, the Hanbali school, prominent in the Arabian Peninsula, is focussed on a conservative interpretation of Islamic doctrine that centres on a literalist interpretation of Islamic sources (Armstrong, 2002).

There is also diversity in terms of approaches to law and legal authority. The power to interpret and arbitrate *shari`ah* rests with Islamic scholars (`*ulama*). `*Ulama* is a broad term referring to formally trained scholars who focus on all aspects of Islamic law and jurisprudence. This highlights the highly diverse nature of religious authority in Islam, with no strict hierarchy amongst `*ulama*. As a result, the sheer scope of those claiming the authority of being an Islamic scholar often leads to a great diversity of opinions, and a great deal of contradiction and misunderstanding.

Shi`a Islam does have a more formalised authority structure. Perhaps the most prominent example of this is the Ayatollah. The Ayatollah is part of a system of hierarchy amongst religious scholars in Shi`a Islam based on levels of learning achieved and position within a Shi`a religious school (*hawza*, as opposed to the Sunni *madrassah* school system). As we shall see below, the Islamic Republic of Iran has formalised this into their system of governance, the 'Rule of the Jurist' (*vilayet-e-faqih*). However, it is the diversity of opinion in Islamic doctrine that is its most defining feature. Here, there has been a constant effort on the part of political authorities to either contain or control the appeal and influence of Islam. The lack of a formal religious hierarchy has both facilitated the ability of states to do this as well as promoted a consistent pattern of dissenting voices. From the mid- to late 20th century, a definitively modern form of Islamic political doctrine has emerged to challenge established political authority as well as other ideologies such as Arab nationalism.

The Origins of Modern Political Islam

The notion of an Islamic political ideology is somewhat tautological, given the numerous references in Islamic doctrine to the notion of political authority. However, if we go back to our understanding of ideology outlined above, one can identify a set of ideologies around Islam and the modern political environment. In particular, from the late 19th century, there emerged a new set of ideas that sought to reconcile Islamic doctrine with the emerging reality of European (and, later, US) global domination, the nation-state system and other factors such as democracy.

> **Islam** is a term that refers to the religion and its practice whilst **Muslim** refers to an individual practitioner or community practising that religion.
>
> An important distinction is between an 'Islamic state' and a 'Muslim state'. An Islamic state is one that consciously seeks to define its legal and broader political system as defined by Islamic doctrine, particularly the *sharīah*. Examples of this include Iran and Saudi Arabia.
>
> A Muslim state is one that, conventionally, has a majority Muslim population, but has a civil law code or a non-religious political system. This is the far more common example, including states as diverse as Egypt, Turkey, Uzbekistan and Indonesia.

The emergence of this 'new' Islamic thought shall be outlined here. Particular attention is paid to the foundations of this thought from the late 19th century and how it changed through the 20th and early 21st centuries. Whilst most recent attention has been given to militant or terrorist movements who have sought to justify their actions in the language of Islam, this will be covered in greater detail in Chapter 7. However, these movements account only for a small part of the broader 'Islamist' movement. Instead, focus here will be on the mass political movements who consciously and explicitly identify themselves as 'Islamic' and who have participated in regional political issues and systems on this basis.

The Origins of Contemporary Islamist Political Discourse

Contemporary Islamist doctrine formed largely in response to the imposition of colonial authority. As we saw in Chapter 2, the colonial period presented not just a political challenge in the form of European strategic domination, but also a cultural challenge as captured by Said's notion of 'Orientalism'. It was the combination of these that shaped the response from a new generation of Islamic scholars. In this regard, the articulation of contemporary Islamist political discourse was as much about the 'external' challenge as it was about the 'internal' state of Islamic thought. Simply put, questions were asked as to how the Muslim world went from the dominant political and cultural force during the Middle Ages to one that could be so thoroughly dominated by outside forces by the modern era.

Colonialism and the Reform of Islamic Discourse

It was in the late Ottoman period that key debates that still define the modern Islamist political discourse emerged. Here, it is important to note that these discussions, whilst often separate from those of nationalist debate that emerged at the same time, also covered many of the same topics and involved some of the same thinkers. That is, nationalism and Islamism in the Middle East are not mutually exclusive despite the appearance of confrontation between the two streams of thought through the 20th century. Indeed, many of these debates, as we shall see below, were an effort to reconcile the ideas of nationalism with the place of Islam in the political life of the Middle East.

Central to these early debates was the tension between tradition and innovation in Islam. In particular, many reformist voices that emerged in the Middle East and South Asia (particularly the British colonial holdings in India) argued that the Islamic world had stagnated due to the dominance of religious leaders focussed on *taqlid* or emulation rather than *ijtihad*, or innovation. Of particular concern for reformist thinkers were `ulama who argued that the so-called 'gates of *ijtihad*' were 'closed' during the 10th century CE, prohibiting interpretation and adaptation of Islamic doctrine on the basis that this process would dilute the authority of the original message. This was criticised by thinkers such as the Iranian-born Jamal al-Din al-Afghani (1838–97) who argued that this attempt to 'forbid knowledge with a view of safeguarding the Islamic religion' was the source of Islamic decline (Rahman, 1979).

Figure 4.13   From left: Jamal al-Din al-Afghani, Muhammad Abduh and Muhammad Rashid Rida

Source: Public domain

Al-Afghani's student, the Egyptian scholar Muhammad Abduh (1849–1905) took this criticism further, arguing that the 'supposed superiority of the ancients was a mere pretext to keep intact the absurdities of the past, and such a pretext of infallibility must necessarily mean the thwarting of the human intellect' (for both of the last two quotes, see Husain, 2003: 109–11). This was a substantial challenge to the established religious authority in the Muslim world and, by extension, the colonial authorities who had largely co-opted these authorities. Indeed, many have argued that these challenges mirror those of the Protestant Reformation within Christianity.

> Reference to *ijtihad* is found in the *Qur'an* as a mode of interpretation over areas where there is no current source of law.
>
> The second of the 'Rashidun Caliphs' (immediate successors to the Prophet Muhammad), Umar, declared an opening of the 'gates of *ijtihad*' to clarify the stance of Islamic law on emerging areas.
>
> During the 10th century CE, a number of Islamic scholars declared the gates of *ijtihad* closed in a stated effort to stop Islamic discourse being diluted. This led to an emphasis on *taqlid* (emulation or traditionalism) dominating much Islamic scholarship up to the 19th century CE.

The tension between Islamist scholars and their secular contemporaries, notably the nationalists, soon emerged. For instance, Abduh's student Muhammad Rashid Rida (1865–1935) articulated the position that the greatest threat to Islamic society was not those supportive of *taqlid* over *ijtihad*, but those proposing secular ideologies that would more fundamentally marginalise the role of Islam in public life. For Rashid Rida, priority should be placed on a collective effort towards the articulation of a common *shari`ah* as the best buttress against secularisation.

Salafism and Islamic Reformism

Here, al-Afghani, Abduh and Rashid Rida were part of what was known at the time as the *salafiyya* movement. *Salafiyya*, or as is commonly known today, *salafi*, is a concept that has changed through the 20th century to mean something different today from its earlier incarnation. The term *salafiyya* comes from the term *as-salaf as-salih*, or the pious/venerable ancestors. The concept was developed in relation to the reformist thinkers outlined above as they sought to reconcile the core of the religion (that of the Prophet and his community, the pious ancestors) with contemporary circumstances (Armstrong, 2002).

> The term **fundamentalism** is often applied to religious movements who reject modernist philosophies and favour an emphasis on literal interpretations and implementation of religious doctrine.
>
> The phrase originated in relation to Protestant movements in the United States in the early 20th century, and has since been expanded, often controversially, to include similar movements in many religions, including Islam.
>
> It is a highly problematic term due to its pejorative use. It is also critiqued for not distinguishing between people who closely observe religious practice and those who may engage in acts of violence in pursuit of so-called religious aims.

Therefore, the origins of the *salafi* movement lie in an effort towards what could be termed an 'Islamic revival' in the face of colonial domination. This revival was, at its core, a reformist movement in seeking to reinterpret Islamic doctrine (*ijtihad*) in light of changed circumstances. However, in recent years, the connotations of *salafism* have changed significantly. In particular, the phrase has come to focus on movements focussed more on the purification element rather than the reformist element. That is, the term has been reified by observers and commentators on the Middle East as well as many movements themselves as an effort at resisting outside influences through a return to what may be seen as a mythical, pure, ideal past. It is here that the term 'fundamentalism' has been applied to a number of contemporary Islamist movements.

Islamist Organisations

Before examining specific movements, it is important to clarify what is meant by an 'Islamist organisation' and, by extension, an 'Islamist' in the contemporary political environment. As outlined above, this term is more than simply a Muslim involved in politics. Instead, these terms refer to an individual or group who seeks the political life of a state to reflect Islamic values, in one way or another.

The reference to the state does highlight the modern nature of this ideology, but still leaves a great deal of ambiguity. In particular, what are 'Islamic values' and how should they be translated into a political system? Is this simply the imposition of the *shari`ah* or something else? There are no single answers to these questions. As such, the term remains vague. However, it can be understood in ideological terms as a consciously identified set of ideals, principles or values held by an individual or group that shape their political priorities.

In this regard, there have been a number of movements that have self-identified as Islamist or Islamically oriented, whose aims revolve around a reorientation of political life along religious lines. The number of these movements in the Middle

East has grown in recent decades, particularly in the wake of the ideological vacuum left with the decline of Arab nationalism since the 1960s. As we shall see below, this occurred at the same time as many regional regimes sought to reorient their own claims for legitimacy in religious rather than nationalist terms. This has become a struggle for legitimacy between authoritarian governments and Islamist movements, a key feature of the contemporary politics of the modern Middle East.

The Muslim Brotherhood

Figure 4.14 Hassan al-Banna

Source: Public domain

Of the innumerable Islamist movements that emerged in the 20th century, the Muslim Brotherhood (*al-ikhwān al-muslimūn*) is the most prominent. The movement was founded in 1928 in Egypt by school teacher Hasan al-Banna in the city of Ismailia on the Suez Canal. Ismailia was home to a large number of workers on the canal, as well as part of the British military garrison system during their rule in Egypt. The proximity of British rule, and the growing resentment amongst the canal workers towards the British helped shape al-Banna's ideas of social resistance through emphasising the need to promote Islamic law and social values. In this regard, al-Banna drew from the work of al-Afghani, Abduh and Rashid Rida in highlighting the importance of Islam as a means of opposition and retaining what they saw as their own cultural heritage.

The organisation initially focussed primarily on education and social service, with the broader view that the modernisation of Egyptian society must be encouraged but not be at the expense of Egypt's Islamic identity. Therefore, focussing on efforts at ensuring the retention of Islamic identity amongst Egypt's working class was the best means of seeing the development of an independent, Islamically oriented Egypt.

However, this 'bottom-up' approach to Islamist activism soon blended with more overt challenges to the British-backed government in Cairo. After World War II, and as tensions with the British were simmering in the context of the conflict in the last years of the British Mandate in Palestine, the organisation began a programme of violence against the government.

The organisation was subsequently banned in late 1948. This led to open confrontation between Brotherhood members of the government, with then Egyptian Prime Minister Fahmi an-Nukrashi Pasha assassinated by a member of the organisation. This was followed in early 1949 with the death of al-Banna, allegedly at the hands of the government. As a result, through to the Free Officers' Coup of 1952 that removed the British-backed monarchy, the organisation engaged in a series of actions, particularly the burning of government buildings. Whilst the organisation supported the overthrow of the regime of Faisal II, they quickly drew the ire of the new regime, particularly after the ascension of Gamal abd al-Nasser to the presidency in 1954. As a result, the new regime and the organisation, which had grown to several hundred thousand members, became sharply critical of one another, a legacy that continued through to the end of the regime of Hosni Mubarak in 2011.

This was not always a policy of direct repression, however. As we shall see below, the shift of Nasser's successor, Anwar Sadat, towards an effort to rely more on the appeal of Islamist than nationalist ideology saw some relaxation of the activities of the movement. However, they remained formally banned, and the government's efforts at reconciliation were aimed more at attempting to harness and exploit the appeal of the widely popular movement than any form of genuine reconciliation.

Islam and Political Confrontation

The escalation of oppression by regimes contributed to the formation of a new, more confrontationalist form of Islamist ideology. This ideology drew from earlier articulations of Islamist thought, but diverged in terms of emphasis and method. Specifically, this new direction emphasised both the *taqlid* element of *salafi* ideology and prescribed the direct challenge of regimes as the best method of achieving their aims.

Sayyid Qutb's Ideology

This move towards an articulation of a more confrontationalist Islamist ideology was most famously captured by the work of Sayyid Qutb. Qutb was a member of the Muslim Brotherhood and a prolific author. His major work, *Milestones (Along the Way)* (*ma`alim fi al-Tariq*) is often cited as one of the most influential works of modern radical Islamist thought, cited by a variety of movements as central to their ideology.

Selections from *Milestones*

'anyone who serves someone other than God ... is outside God's religion, although he may claim to profess this religion'.

The *shariah* is 'of that universal law which governs the entire universe ... as accurate and true as any of the laws known as the "laws of nature" and is the only guarantee against any kind of discord in life'.

There is a necessity for 'physical power and *jihad* for abolishing the organisations and authorities of the *jahili* system'.

Qutb's ideology formed over several periods of his life. One of the most talked about was the time he spent as a student in the United States in the late 1940s. Here, Qutb wrote of what he saw as a society that had foregone religion, descending into indulgence. This propelled Qutb to seek out what he saw as an Islamic answer to the prospect of this lifestyle spreading to the Middle East.

The core of these new ideas formed around the concept of *jahiliyyah* (days of ignorance). This is a term in Islamic scholarship describing the period before Islam in the Arabian Peninsula. It is a pejorative term that Qutb used to describe the West (as influenced by his own experiences) and, increasingly, communities in the Middle East under the rule of secular republican governments or monarchies, the latter criticised as being subservient to Western powers (Khatab, 2006).

By 1954, Qutb had risen to the upper echelons of the Brotherhood's ranks, and regularly met with the new President Nasser. However, tension between the two quickly emerged, with an alleged assassination plot against Nasser in 1954 being pinned on the movement. This led to the arrest of the group's leadership, including Qutb. From this, Qutb's ideology was impacted most directly by his time in prison. It was here that he wrote the majority of his seminal text, *Milestones*. In *Milestones*, Qutb argued that all attempts by man to impose sovereignty were corrupt, and only God's sovereignty (*hakamiyyah*) was the just and appropriate form of rule. As such, the realisation of a 'true' Islamic society was hindered by many obstacles, the most prominent of which were the various un-Islamic regimes (*taghut*) across the Middle East.

In this regard, Qutb's ideology has been interpreted as the full extension of the *salafi* ideology where Islam forms a complete and inviolable ideology applicable to all aspects of life. This extends to the question not just of law, with the application of the *shari`ah*, but also to questioning the very claims of state sovereignty. Here, the model for political organisation can be taken from the example of the first Muslim community, one that should be emulated. As such, Qutb's writings saw an effort, counterintuitive as it may seem, to reconcile the previously reformist ideology of the early *salafis* with principles of *taqlid*, or emulation. However, there was a reformist element to Qutb's thought, one that has been influen-

Figure 4.15 Sayyid Qutb during his period of imprisonment

Source: Public domain

tial for many of the more confrontationalist or radical Islamist movements that have emerged through the late 20th and early 21st centuries. Central to this idea is the reinterpretation of the concept of *jihad* (Khatab, 2006).

Jihad

Jihad is the most contested concept of Islamist political discourse, with many different interpretations and applications. The term, loosely translated, means 'struggle', with its most common use in the *Qur'an* meaning to 'strive in the way of God' (*al-jihad fi sabil Allah*). This use refers to two of the four uses of the term dominant in Sunni Islam, to struggle against temptation and live as a virtuous Muslim (*jihad* of the heart/*jihad bil qalb*) as well as to spreading the word of Islam (*jihad* of the tongue/*jihad bil lisan*). The third usage of the term is in relation to social responsibility, or *jihad* of the hand (*jihad bil yad*). This links to the value of charity (*zakat*), one of the pillars of Islam, where Muslims are to struggle to build a virtuous society, one that fulfils the obligations towards social justice for the less fortunate. These first two interpretations are often referred to as the 'greater *jihad*', vital parts of living an Islamic life.

> The concepts of a **greater** and **lesser** *jihad* developed from a *hadith* where the Prophet Muhammad is claimed to have told the Muslim community that, upon returning from battle, that they have come from the lesser to the greater *jihad*. That is, they have returned from combat to help build the community.
>
> This distinction is still under debate amongst historians, with some arguing that there is insufficient evidence in Islamic history to give primacy to the inner/community struggle over the defensive/armed struggle.

The fourth usage is the most controversial, that of a requirement for the defence of the Muslim community if it is under threat (*jihad* of the sword/*jihad bis saif*). The *Qur'an* contains detailed examinations of the use of force, with a general theme of only allowing for its applicability in defence of the community. Whilst this has not always been the practice, with many Islamic empires expanding on the back of military conquest, there has been a relatively consistent effort to attempt to justify violence in religious terms. For Islamist movements, the use of force as a political tool emerged through the 20th century with the gradual radicalisation of parts of Islamist ideology, as we have seen with the writings of Qutb and others. Whilst we shall examine this in greater detail in Chapter 7 in relation to the activity of sub-state actors and terrorist organisations, it is worth looking at Qutb's use of the term as it was influential for many subsequent thinkers and movements (Khatab, 2006).

In particular, Qutb continuously justified the use of force as a defensive measure, however, his argument for where it should be applied changed in his later writings. For Qutb, the Muslim world was under threat from the secular nationalist or pro-Western regional regimes as well as the cultural challenge of Westernisation, the growth of *jahiliyyah*. Therefore, the religion needed a vanguard to protect its integrity. This protection needed to be proactive, to directly challenge regional regimes and their supporters to defend the 'true' values of Islam and pursue the implementation of an Islamic community that would adhere to Qutb's vision of God's laws and God's sovereignty (*hakamiyyah*).

In short, the trajectory of Islamist ideology through the 20th century went from one of social activism by the Muslim Brotherhood before World War II, an attempt to operate from the bottom-up, to one of more direct political and military confrontation to bring about change from the top-down. The vast majority of movements did not adhere to this radical trajectory, but an increasing number of movements took up this challenge, engaging in armed confrontation with regional regimes and, later, global powers such as the United States, Russia, the United Kingdom and others (see Chapter 7).

ISLAM AS A POLITICAL IDEOLOGY IN THE CONTEMPORARY MIDDLE EAST

Islam and Political Authority

Whilst Islamist opposition movements have been prominent proponents of this ideology, there was also a critical shift in terms of the use of Islam as a tool for regime legitimacy. In this regard, one may argue that, more than radical Islamist movements, the most important impacts of this shift came in the form of regimes increasingly using Islamic language, ideology and symbolism of Islam and Islamism to buttress their rule.

Wahhabism is a religious movement that emerged in the Arabian Peninsula in the 18th century. Led by conservative Muslim theologian Muhammad ibn'abd al-Wahhab, the movement emphasises the unity (*awhid*) of God as well as conforming to pre-scribed aspects of religious observance (*taqlid*).

Wahhab's followers joined with the Saud family during their conquests of the Arabian Peninsula in the 18th century, seeing this brand of Islam become the state-sponsored form of the religion in Saudi Arabia. In this regard, the Saudi state has been active is sponsoring the development of a similar form of Wahhabist Islam beyond its borders.

The Wahhabist doctrine is often criticised as legitimising the violation of the rights of women and minorities, particularly the Shia minority, in Saudi Arabia as well as playing a role in the emergence of radical movements in Saudi Arabia and across the Muslim world.

This was not a new process, with the Saudi regime employing their own form of Wahhabi Islam, alongside their claims as custodians of the Holy Cities of Mecca and Medina as key pillars of their claims to rule. In addition, the Hashemite monarchies as well as the Alaouite dynasty in Morocco emphasised their links to the Prophet Muhammad's family. However, the use of Islamic symbolism by republican, and often former radical nationalist, regimes, highlighted the changing ideological landscape in the Middle East. In addition, this also represented a broader geopolitical shift as conservative monarchies as well as increasingly conservative monarchies were key allies of the United States, also strengthening their hand in Middle Eastern affairs. Here, the reforms in Egypt under Anwar Sadat best encapsulate these changes.

Islam and Authority in Sadat's Egypt

This shift from a focus on Arab nationalism to the use of Islam as a political ideology can be seen starkly in post-Nasser Egypt under the presidency of Anwar Sadat. Sadat was part of the Free Officers' movement that came to power in 1952, later serving as Nasser's Vice President. Despite being perceived initially as seeking to continue Nasser's path, Sadat quickly broke with established patterns with a series of reforms to liberalise the Egyptian economy, purging the government and key agencies of potential rivals, and began planning to change Egypt's weak strategic position vis-à-vis Israel.

In relation to Israel, Sadat led planning for a war with Israel in 1973. On 6 October, the Jewish holy day of Yom Kippur, in 1973, Egypt and Syria launched a coordinated attack on Israeli positions in the Sinai and Golan Heights. Israel maintained its military supremacy; however Sadat's plan was more to demonstrate that Israel was not militarily invincible. This was achieved through the ability of the Egyptian army to cross the canal and push past the Israeli front line. Whilst the Israeli army subsequently pushed the Egyptian armed forces back, the early symbolic victory gave Sadat greater flexibility in future peace negotiations with Israel. This conflict also had significant global ramifications, with the oil-producing states of the Gulf imposing an oil embargo that threatened to push the global economy into recession (see Chapter 6).

This effort at strategic realignment was accompanied by an effort to push towards a permanent settlement of Egypt's conflict with Israel. Another part of this shift of Sadat's 'revolution of rectification' was the *infitah* or opening policy where previously nationalised Egyptian industries were deregulated and privatised. There reforms will be discussed later (see Chapter 6). However, it is important to note here that the eventual peace treaty signed between Egypt and Israel in 1978

Figure 4.16   The many guises of Anwar Sadat (from left): with nationalist leaders
Libya's Muammar Gaddhafi and Syria's Hafiz al-Assad, and with Israeli
Prime Minister Menachim Begin and US President Carter (centre)

Source: Public domain

that emerged from this conflict also saw Egypt reorienting its foreign policy away
from the Soviet Union and towards the United States. This came with the benefit
of Egypt becoming the second largest recipient of US aid, behind Israel, a factor
that was critical to Egyptian economic viability in the face of failing economic
reforms as well as feeding into growing discontent with Sadat's rule, particularly
from Islamic organisations who highlighted this as evidence of Sadat as simply
another Western proxy in the Middle East.

   This line of criticism was one that cut across both nationalist and Islamist rhetoric, drawing on the resentment of foreign interference born from the colonial
period. However, it was Islamist movements who were able to gain traction in their
criticism of the regime. The Muslim Brotherhood benefited from limited political
liberalisation under Sadat, and exploited this restricted room to expand its membership and lead the opposition to the regime.

   Opposition also emerged amongst radical Islamist organisations who advocated a violent overthrow of the regime and the imposition of a strict implementation of *shari`ah*. In this regard, the efforts by Sadat to shore up his own domestic
support through an ideological reorientation towards an emphasis on Islamic
legitimacy eventually proved too powerful for the regime to handle. With unrest
spreading throughout the general population, key government institutions were
increasingly infiltrated by members of radical organisations. This infiltration
was evidenced most starkly when Sadat was assassinated on 6 October 1981 by
members of the group Islamic Jihad, posing as military officers during an official
military parade.

Figure 4.17 The assassination of Anwar Sadat, 6 October 1981
Source: Public domain

Whilst Sadat was killed by Islamists, the reorientation of Egypt at this time represented a common trend across the region towards an emphasis on religious over nationalist ideology and legitimacy. Regimes sought to and often achieved control over this shift. However, momentous events in Shi`a Iran provide a different example, with revolution and the establishment of the Islamic Republic in 1979.

The Islamic Revolution in Iran

It is difficult to underestimate the importance of the Islamic Revolution in Iran. At an ideological level, it led to the creation of the first 'modern' form of Islamic state under the Ayatollah Khomeini's vision of the 'Governance of the Jurist' (*vilayat-e-faqih*). This was a challenge to republics and monarchies alike, a revolutionary model that the new government sought to export across the region. It also resonated at the geopolitical level, with the collapse of the Iranian monarchy depriving the US of a key ally in the region. Indeed, the new Islamic Republic introduced a third pole of influence in the Middle East outside the traditional dynamic of US-allied conservative monarchies and republics and Soviet-allied republics. The viability of the Islamic Republic has come under increasing question; however, the monumental change brought about by the revolution was a seminal moment in the history of the Middle East.

Iran, the US and the 'White Revolution'

The Iranian monarch Reza Shah abdicated his throne in 1941 under pressure from the British and Soviets, passing authority to his son, Mohammad Reza Shah. After the end of the war, Iran became a key ally of the United States during the Cold War. Here, the US assisted in the development of a nascent Iranian nuclear energy programme as well as training and arming the large Iranian army. As discussed in Chapter 3, the US also used clandestine means to support the monarchy through assisting in the overthrow of the democratically elected government of Mohammad Mossadeq in 1953.

Figure 4.18 From left: Reza Shah and his son and successor, Mohammad Reza Shah

Source: Public domain

In the wake of the 1953 coup, the tentative liberalisations implemented by Mohammad Reza Shah were drawn back. The Shi`a religious establishment alongside the new urban middle classes suffered the most from the imposition of these restrictions, particularly those who supported Mossadeq and his Tudeh Party. This repression also included the creation of a ruthless internal security organisation, the SAVAK (*sazeman-e ettela`at va amniyat-e keshvar*) in 1957 with support from the US and Israel (Keddie, 2006).

Opposition crystallised amongst the religious establishment as well as leftist intellectuals. These movements led a series of protests against the regime through the early 1960s led by the Ayatollah Ruhollah Khomeini that focussed on the corruption and repression of the regime as well as the efforts by the monarchy to marginalise the religious establishment and downplay the religious heritage of Iran. It is important to note here the more formal nature of the Shi`a religious establishment, as outlined above, and the ability of this structure to organise and mobilise oppositional support.

In response to these protests, the Shah did implement a series of reforms through his so-called

Figure 4.19 The 2,500 year anniversary celebration of 12–16 October 1971, was attended by a wide variety of world leaders and dignitaries. It was harshly criticised by the Iranian opposition for its lavish spending and emphasis on pre-Islamic Iranian heritage.

Source: Public domain

'White Revolution'. This involved a series of economic reforms, particularly rural land reform and literacy campaigns. In addition, the Shah also spent a great deal of state resources on campaigns to emphasise Iran's pre-Islamic history, linking the legitimacy of his regime to that of the ancient Persian empires of Cyrus and Darius. This process was encapsulated by the celebrations of the so-called 2500-year anniversary of Persian civilisation at the ancient capital of Persepolis in 1971. Whilst the Iranian economy was struggling, the regime spent $200 million on a lavish four-day celebration that focussed on Iran's pre-Islamic period and how the monarchy represented continuity between that period and the present (Keddie, 2006).

Islam and Revolutionary Ideology

By the mid-1970s, the monarchy gave the appearance of strength but this masked growing disillusionment in Iranian society. As is discussed above and in Chapter 6, the oil price shocks of 1973 that accompanied the Arab–Israeli war of that year saw a massive influx of funds into state coffers. Where some in Iran made massive fortunes, this set in train a cycle of inflation that impacted on both the lower and middle classes. At the same time, the regime perceived this as an opportunity to further restrict political freedoms that exacerbated tensions fed by the rapidly changing economic environment.

What emerged was a highly diverse opposition movement united by the common theme of opposition to the excesses of the monarchy. Representative of this diversity was perhaps the opposition's leading intellectual, `Ali Shariati. With a long history of

Figure 4.20   From left: Ayatollah Ruhollah Khomeini and `Ali Shariati
Source: Public domain

Figure 4.21 Iran

Source: Central Intelligence Agency

political activism and confrontation with the regime, Shariati articulated an ideology that combined Islamist reformism (particularly in terms of the role of the Shi`a political establishment) and revolutionary nationalism that echoed themes of Arab nationalists (Keddie, 2006).

Shariati's ideology proved immensely popular, particularly amongst Iran's large young urban population, and particularly through the blend of religious and revolutionary ideology. Whilst the details of this ideology were vague, particularly in terms of how a new government would look, Shariati's critique of the Shah's regime helped create a critical mass of opposition to royal rule. The death of Shariati in 1977, allegedly at the hands of the SAVAK, added further resentment and opposition momentum.

Despite this, the religious establishment remained divided over their stance to the regime. Cleveland and Bunton identify three positions amongst the religious establishment, with one group seeking to remain outside of politics, a second arguing for a re-establishment of the constitution that was suspended after the 1953 coup and a third group calling for an overthrow of the regime (2009: 426–7).

It was from exile in Iraq and France that the Ayatollah Khomeini took up the mantle of confronting the regime. Khomeini was able to influence the articulation of revolutionary sentiment through his writings and speeches which were smuggled into Iran. Apart from the articulation of opposition sentiment, Khomeini's most important contribution at this time was the volume *Government of the Islamic Jurist* (*vilayet-e-faqih: hukomat-e-Islami*). In this book, Khomeini not only argued for the removal of the Iranian regime, but also outlined how an Islamic regime should be structured and implemented.

The key features of this new arrangement would be rule by Islamic scholars (*faqih*) in conjunction with a political system. The applicability of this system to Islamic principles would be guided by decisions of the religious authorities who could veto government decisions and appointments should they deem them to be contrary to Islamic principles. This was particularly appropriate for Iranian Shi`a Islam with the presence of a religious hierarchy. Whilst this would help this ideology resonate in Iran, it would limit the spread of this ideology to the rest of the predominantly Sunni Middle East.

The Islamic Revolution and Structure of the Islamic Republic

Whilst opposition sentiment was increasingly articulated in Islamist terms by Khomeini, anti-regime sentiment still ran the gamut of opinion from revolutionary Marxist, nationalist and Islamist ideologies. However, the regime focussed on suppressing the religious establishment, with focus on subduing protests in the religious centre of Qom leading to the death of a number of protestors. Combined with Khomeini's increasingly prominent role, the opposition increasingly articulated its dissent in religious terms through 1978. This movement reached a critical mass through 1978 as the Iranian economy stagnated, drawing the powerful Iranian trade unions onto the streets. Confronted with mass protests, the lower ranks of the military broke to the opposition. In January 1979, the Shah left Iran, ostensibly for medical treatment. The power vacuum allowed for a return of Khomeini by February, declaring an end to the Iranian monarchy.

The toppling of the monarchy did not provide an immediate answer to the question of what would come next. The primary tension was between Khomeini and his supporters and those who supported the retention of the old constitution with a President to replace the monarchy. Supporters of the latter position, particularly the leftist organisations, threw their support behind the post-revolutionary Prime Minister Mehdi Bazargan. As a result, two branches of government

Figure 4.22 Khomeini in Tehran on 2 February 1979, the day after his return from exile

Source: Public domain

Figure 4.23 From left: Khomeini and Mehdi Bazargan at a joint
press conference in the months after the revolution

Source: Public domain

had formed, one under Bazargan and the other, modelled on Khomeini's ideas of government guided by Islamic jurists (*vilayat-e-faqih*). The dysfunctional relationship between the two led to Bazargan's resignation by the end of 1979 and a consolidation of power by Khomeini and his supporters.

The new regime faced a series of rolling crises, with challenges from groups, previously part of the revolutionary movement, who now openly challenged the authority of Khomeini. In addition, the invasion of Iraq in September 1980 (Chapter 8) and Iran's growing international isolation, and particularly the confrontation with their former ally, the US, led many to conclude the new regime would not survive.

Confrontation with the US

The confrontation between the Islamic Republic of Iran and the United States has been a key feature of regional affairs since the late 1970s. This was a tension rooted in the close relationship between the regime of the Shah and the US, including the American role in the toppling of the Mossadeq government in 1953 and the role of US aid and finance in the development of the SAVAK, the Shah's favoured tool for repression of the opposition. After the revolution, one of the most dramatic diplomatic stand-offs would solidify this confrontation, one that continues to define the relationship between Iran and the US. On 4 November 1979, a group of pro-revolutionary students, backed by elements of the regime, stormed the US Embassy compound taking 66 American citizens hostage. As embassies are considered part

Figure 4.24 From left: Iranian students storm the US Embassy in Tehran, and right, with some of the hostages taken. The hostages were held for 444 days, from 4 November 1979 to 20 January 1981

Source: Public domain

of the sovereign territory of a country, this was an audacious and provocative move that was tantamount to the invasion of US sovereign territory.

The hostage crisis helped buttress the new regime's popular legitimacy, portraying it as willing to follow up its rhetoric with action. For the US, this incident was critical to undermining domestic support for President Carter, who would be defeated in the 1980 presidential elections by Republican candidate Ronald Reagan. In addition, the confrontation would position the US as the Iranian's primary enemy or, in the words of Khomeini, the 'Great Satan'. For the US, and particularly the in-coming Republican administration, the inability of the US to rescue the hostages until the negotiated release in 1981, after 444 days, put Iran as their main antagonist in the Middle East. Here, the Islamic character of the Iranian regime was marginal to this antagonism. Instead, it was the loss of a key regional ally, coupled with the confrontational stance by both the US and the new government in Tehran that led to the tension that has characterised their relationship since.

The failure of the plan to rescue the US Embassy hostages, **'Operation Eagle Claw'**, was a disaster for the US. The operation was to involve the landing of US Special Forces in the embassy via helicopter, the freeing of the hostages and airlifting the hostages out.

However, the plan was aborted after the helicopters had left due to bad weather. The resulting confusion saw one of the six helicopters collide with a supply aircraft, resulting in the death of eight US servicemen.

The humiliation of the failed mission is seen by many as a key reason why President Carter lost the 1980 presidential elections to Ronald Reagan.

Structure of the Islamic Republic

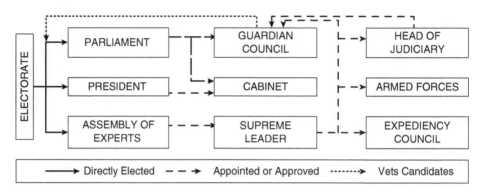

Figure 4.25 Structure of the Islamic Republic of Iran

The relative success of the hostage crisis did not end the series of dramatic events that marked the founding of the Islamic Republic. As was discussed in Chapter 3, the Iraqi invasion of Iran in 1980 saw Iran become mired in the longest conventional war of the 20th century, with an estimated 1 million Iranian deaths. In addition, various local insurgencies continued as well as geopolitical isolation as the US sought to pressure their new regional nemesis. Despite this, the new government pushed ahead with the implementation of its vision of how an 'Islamic Republic' should be structured. In this regard, it was an archetypically Shi`a version of Islamic governance, with an emphasis on the role of the religious hierarchy, particularly the Ayatollah's, and its role of overseeing temporal governance. This new model of governance was developed primarily by Khomeini, and was known as the 'Governance of the Jurist' (*vilayat-e-faqih*).

The central principle of the *vilayat-e-faqih* is the notion of governance or guardianship by Islamic jurists. The position of these jurists is enshrined in a number of key institutions, particularly the Supreme Leader, the Assembly of Experts and the Guardian Council. Codified in the 1979 Constitution, this system provides for a measure of civilian rule, but the decisions of a popularly elected parliament and president, including the selection of candidates for those running for seats in parliament or who runs for president, are vetted by the Guardian Council. In turn, the members of the Guardian Council are selected by the Supreme Leader.

In other words, the system of governance in Iran contains a series of checks and balances between the jurists and the popularly elected institutions. However, on balance the authority of the popularly elected positions is reliant on support by the

Figure 4.26   Presidents of the Islamic Republic of Iran (clockwise from top left): Abolhassan Banisadr (1980–1), Mohammad-Ali Rajai (1981), Ali Khamenei (1981–9), Akbar Rafsanjani (1989–97), Mohammad Khatami (1997–2005) and Mahmoud Ahmedinejad (2005–13)

Source: Public domain

Supreme Leader and, particularly the 12-member Guardian Council. The validity of this system has been bought into question in recent years, particularly in terms of the role of the Guardian Council in the vetting of candidates for the parliament and presidency. As such, the ultimate success and viability of the world's most visible example of Islamist governance remains in doubt.

CONCLUSION

Where the ideologies of nationalism and Islamism are often treated as exclusive, discrete concepts, this chapter has deliberately discussed them together. This is to highlight the interconnectedness of these ideologies. Whilst they focus on different priorities and themes, they also display similar trends primarily through their origins as responses to external interference in regional affairs. This has resulted in the formation of regimes across the region as an effort to achieve the goals of these ideologies, whether this is in the nationalist regimes in the Arab world or the Islamic Republic of Iran. Finally, where the ideology of political Islam came to dominate that of nationalist discourse, in recent years Islamist ideology has come under increasing scrutiny for its radicalisation and lack of clarity in terms of how its political vision is to be implemented. As is discussed in Chapter 10, this trend will continue with the rise to power of Islamist political parties in the wake of the post-2010 Arab uprisings.

Study Questions

- What have been the major ideological influences over the politics of the modern Middle East?
- What are the main features of Arab nationalism?
- What have been the main points of tension between pan-Arab ideology and local and parochial issues?
- What is the relationship between nationalism and Islamism?
- What are the main features of Islamist political discourse and how does this differ between Sunni and Shi`a communities?
- How have these ideologies taken organisational form?
- What role have they played in both opposition and in assisting authoritarian regimes to maintain their rule?

FURTHER READING

Dawisha, Adeed (2003) *Arab Nationalism in the Twentieth Century: From Triumph to Despair*. Princeton, NJ: Princeton University Press.
A comprehensive analysis of the origins, development and declining influence of Arab nationalist ideology, with a particular emphasis on its organisational manifestations and influence over key Arab regimes.

El Fadl, Khaled Abou (2004) *Islam and the Challenge of Democracy*. Princeton, NJ: Princeton University Press.
A short, but highly insightful analysis of the various elements of the debate surrounding Islam and democracy from a reformist perspective.

Esposito, John L. (1991) *Islam: The Straight Path*. Oxford: Oxford University Press.
A key work in outlining the tenets of Islam with a particular view to how the religion has developed its relationship with the political sphere.

Kepel, Gilles (2003) *Jihad: The Trail of Political Islam.* London: I.B. Tauris.
One of the first key works examining the development of radical Islamist discourse and its links to modern radical Islamist doctrine.

Go to the companion website at www.sagepub.co.uk/macqueen for further material including free journal articles and links to other relevant documents.

REFERENCES

Anderson, Benedict (1991) *Imagined Communities: Reflections on the Origin and Spread of Nationalism.* London: Verso.

Armstrong, Karen (2002) *Islam: A Short History.* New York: Modern Library.

Barakat, Halim (1993) *The Arab World: Society, Culture, and State.* Berkeley: University of California Press.

Choueiri, Youssef (2000) *Arab Nationalism: A History – Nation and State in the Arab World.* Oxford: Blackwell.

Cleveland, William L. and Bunton, Martin (2009) *A History of the Modern Middle East*, 4th ed. Boulder, CO: Westview Press.

Devlin, John F. (1976) *The Baath Party: A History from its Origins to 1966.* New York: Hoover Institution Press.

Husain, Mir Zohair (2003) *Global Islamic Politics.* New York: Longman.

Keddie, Nikki R. (2006) *Modern Iran: Roots and Results of Revolution.* New Haven, CT: Yale University Press.

Khatab, Sayed (2006) *The Power of Sovereignty: The Political and Ideological Philosophy of Sayyid Qutb.* London: Routledge.

Morris, Benny (2001) *Righteous Victims: A History of the Zionist–Arab Conflict, 1881–2001.* New York: Vintage.

Podeh, Elie and Winckler, Onn Nasserism (2004) *Revolution and Historical Memory in Modern Egypt.* Gainesville: University Press of Florida.

Rahman, Fazlur (1979) *Islam.* Chicago, IL: University of Chicago Press.

Salibi, Kamal S. (1990) *A House of Many Mansions: The History of Lebanon Reconsidered.* Berkeley: University of California Press.

Shemesh, Moshe (2004) 'Prelude to the Six Day War: The Arab–Israeli Struggle Over Water Relations', *Israel Studies*, 9 (3): 1–45.

Versteegh, Kees (2001) *The Arabic Language.* New York: Columbia University Press.

Zeitoun, Mark (2011) *Power and Water in the Middle East: The Hidden Politics of the Palestinian–Israeli Water Conflict.* London: I.B. Tauris.

PART II

Political Dynamics of the Modern Middle East

The preceding overview outlined a range of key factors that have defined the modern Middle East. In particular, the interplay between the imperial and colonial legacies laid the groundwork for both the political structures and political rhetoric that would characterise the Middle East through the 20th century. However, as this part outlines, the political actors of the Middle East and North Africa are not passive agents, simply responding to events beyond their control. Here, Part II of this volume outlines the key political dynamics of the modern Middle East. In particular, the issues of authoritarianism and democratisation, political economy and issues related to economic development, and key security concerns are discussed at length.

In relation to authoritarianism, Chapter 5 outlines debates on the persistence of authoritarianism in the region, particularly the arguments over a regional authoritarian 'exceptionalism', before discussing both the varieties of this form of rule and its mechanics of domination from direct coercion through to patron–client relationships and the rentier system. This is explored through the case studies of Syria from 1970 to 2000, Saudi Arabia from 1953 to 1982, Iraq from 1979 to 1990 and Turkey from 1950 to 1997. These cases highlight both consistencies and differences in terms of how political power was concentrated in the hands of a small group and the means by which this was achieved.

From this, Chapter 6 engages with the various issues related to the political economy of the region. Here, this chapter seeks to contextualise the dominant issue of resources, particularly oil, in terms of debates over the structural weaknesses of regional economies. This includes an outline of how regional economies exhibit great variety in terms of growth as well as different levels of influence of the informal sector. This discussion also seeks to gauge the broader impacts of economic stagnation, particularly in terms of discussions on 'human development' and 'human security'. From here, an obvious priority is placed on the politics of oil, with a focus on the impacts of an oil-based economy both in monetary and political terms. This is complemented with a discussion on how these economies have been increasingly impacted by the politics of economic liberalisation and globalisation.

Finally, key security themes are considered in Chapter 7. While security issues relating to terrorism and the threat of Weapons of Mass Destruction grab headlines, and are covered in this chapter, more 'conventional' security issues related to territory are covered at the beginning of the chapter. However, where an inter-state confrontation defines conflict such as that between Iran and the UAE over the Abu Musa and Tunb Islands, other examples such as the Moroccan occupation of the Western Sahara and allegations of genocide and crimes against humanity against the Sudanese government in Darfur highlight how these security themes are interrelated. This is expanded on through a discussion of the nuclear question in the Middle East, with a particular focus on nuclear programmes in Israel and Iran. Finally, this examination will consider the issues of terrorism, including a review of terrorist ideologies, terrorist organisations and the themes of the so-called War on Terror.

5

Authoritarianism in the Middle East

Learning Objectives

This chapter will enable a greater understanding of:

● How authoritarian regimes can be defined.
● The so-called 'exceptionalism' of authoritarianism in the Middle East since independence.
● The multiple forms of authoritarian rule in the region.
● The means of political participation for citizens under authoritarian regimes.
● Case studies (Syria, Saudi Arabia, Iraq and Turkey) highlighting the various mechanisms of authoritarian rule.

INTRODUCTION

The uprisings of the 'Arab Spring' have led to momentous change in the Middle East since 2010. However, this change has come at the end of a period where the Middle East was characterised by the stability of authoritarian regimes. Indeed, in the wake of these uprisings, authoritarian governments remain the dominant feature of the region. This chapter examines these regimes as the dominant form of rule in the Middle East since independence. Here, we will discuss the notion of the Middle East as an 'exceptional' region due to the persistence of these authoritarian regimes, particularly with the global spread of liberal democracy since the 1970s and 1980s. From this, discussion will move to understanding how authoritarian regimes display different forms and operate in different ways. This will be discussed through a closer examination of 'republican authoritarianism' in Syria from 1970 to 2000, the 'absolute monarchy' in Saudi Arabia from 1953 to 1982, a 'military-backed totalitarian regime' in Iraq from 1979 to 1990, and a 'hybrid regime' in Turkey from 1953 to 1997.

UNDERSTANDING AUTHORITARIANISM

Defining Authoritarianism

Authoritarianism can be defined as a political system in which a small group of individuals controls the state with minimal or no popular control. By contrast, liberal democratic systems contain institutions and mechanics that allow the population to exert control over those who are in positions of power through elections and what power they may exert through constitutions. Authoritarian states either lack these features or, where elections and constitutions exist, they are without power.

That is, in broad terms, authoritarianism is a particular type of rule that limits or prohibits direct and systematic input by the majority of the citizens in the affairs of governance. This is in contrast to liberal democracy that seeks to regulate and limit the authority of those in power. This is a definition that fits with that of Juan Linz, who focussed on authoritarianism as a system lacking alternative political voices, without genuine popular legitimacy, and with authority concentrated in the hands of a single person or small group of people (Linz, 2000).

Juan Linz's (2000: 159) definition of **authoritarianism**:

Political systems with limited, not responsible, political pluralism, without elaborate and guiding ideology, but with distinctive mentalities, without extensive nor [sic] intensive political mobilisation, except at some points in their development, and in which a leader or occasionally a small group exercises power within formally ill-defined limits but actually quite predictable ones.

However, this broad definition requires greater attention to the complexity of authoritarian rule. This complexity covers a range of factors that further define authoritarian governments. A useful starting point here is to clarify the difference between a state and a government. A state is the set of institutions that governs a territory. Looking back to the discussion in Chapter 4, the *state* is the political entity and the *nation* is the cultural community. In addition, the government is the group of people who control the institutions of the state. Therefore, governments can be classified by how they administer these institutions, how responsive they are to popular will and whether their behaviour is regulated by a set of formalised rules.

The presence of regulated institutions (i.e. constitutionalism and the rule of law) and the degree of responsiveness to popular will (i.e. democracy) are intimately linked. However, it is important to remember that the presence of regulatory institutions such as constitutions, and even elections and parliaments, does not necessarily denote the presence of a democratic system. Indeed, closed political systems often possess such institutions that serve to either reinforce the legitimacy of an authoritarian government ('electoral authoritarianism') or work in conjunction with extra-judicial constraints on popular control over the system ('liberalised autocracies', 'illiberal democracies', or 'hybrid regimes').

Daniel Brumberg's (2002: 56) definition of **liberalised autocracy**:

The trademark mixture of guided pluralism, controlled elections, and selective repression in Egypt, Jordan, Morocco, Algeria, and Kuwait is not just a 'survival strategy' adopted by authoritarian regimes, but rather a *type* of political system whose institutions, rules, and logic defy any linear model of democratisation.

Indeed, authoritarian rule employs a variety of means to ensure its power. This includes the use of coercive force often arbitrarily, a centralisation of power, the use of informal power such as 'personality cults', the arbitrary application of law without constitutional constraints, the lack of a separation of powers between the regime and the judiciary, no or minimal popular input in the selection of leaders, no peaceful rotation of power, the suppression of individual and group rights and a frequent use of privileging particular groups (ethnic or class groups) to divide potential opposition. These more negative inducements are combined with others, such as co-option, welfare programmes, employment programmes and populist politics as part of the authoritarian design.

Authoritarianism and Ideology

Authoritarian regimes need not necessarily be linked to any specific ideology. In conventional political terms, both 'left-wing' and 'right-wing' ideologies have produced many examples of authoritarian governments. In this regard, the presence of an ideology can often push regimes towards authoritarian governance. That is, the claims to be pursuing or defending certain ideological claims are employed to justify the closure of political participation for the majority of the citizenry.

This is not always the case, however, with many examples of authoritarian rule, including many in the Middle East, lacking a clear ideological motivation. As is outlined below, this is often the case with many of the monarchical governments, whose claims to absolute political power is based on the distribution of wealth (primarily oil wealth) or other factors such as claims to legitimacy based on the lineage of the royal family (such as the Hashemites).

AUTHORITARIAN RULE IN THE MIDDLE EAST

Even counting the uprisings that have swept the region since 2010, the Middle East and more specifically the Arab world has not experienced any region-wide democratic reforms since the independence period. In this regard, authoritarianism in the Middle East has been both resilient and diverse. For Mona el-Ghobashy, the Middle East contains examples of almost all forms of government we know, from democracy to authoritarian regimes with many sub-divisions (2010: 29–47). This has given rise to a number of debates seeking to explain this persistence as well as understand this diversity.

The 'Authoritarian Exception' in the Middle East

Before we examine the issue of diversity, the persistence and prevalence of authoritarianism in the region needs to be understood. This is a highly controversial debate, particularly those sections of the discussion that focus on the Middle East as an 'exceptional' region because of its apparent authoritarian character. Touching back on the themes discussed in Chapter 2, this has cultural overtones to it, particularly in terms of a view that the region and its culture is somehow more prone to authoritarian governance. This argument does not stand up to any analytical rigour as it could be used to explain any political phenomenon, such as the prevalence of wars in Western states through the 20th century (World War I and II as a starting point) as well as the presence of authoritarian governments across the world up to the 1970s and 1980s.

Freedom House and the Middle East

However, the presence of these regimes in the region and their longevity is an issue that is worth discussing. An illustration of this can be found in the statistics of Freedom House, the US-based analysis and advocacy group that releases its annual 'Freedom in the World' report that documents levels of political liberty. In these reports, levels of freedom or the lack of freedom are measured to give a state an aggregate score out of 10, positioning them in the categories or 'Free', 'Partly Free', or 'Not Free'. Based on statistics provided by Freedom House, from their inaugural 1973 report to the 2012 report, the number of 'Free' and 'Partly Free' states in the Middle East and North Africa (MENA) region not only remained static, but declined in the period between 1973 and 2011. This is in contrast to the rest of the world, particularly regions that were newly independent or exhibited similar rates of authoritarian rule from the mid-1970s.

The **Freedom in the World** reports from **Freedom House**, released annually since 1973, seek to measure political rights and civil liberties in all countries. Reports define political rights as 'electoral processes, political pluralism and participation, and functioning of government' and civil liberties as 'freedom of expression and belief, associational and organisational rights, rule of law, and personal autonomy and individual rights'.

Freedom House analysts use these categories to rate each country out of 10, aggregating the score from 1 (most free) to 7 (least free). This is then divided between three categories of a 'Free' state (1.0–2.5), a 'Partly Free' state (3.0–5.0) and a state that is 'Not Free' (5.5–7.0).

In 1973, MENA had two states (Israel and Lebanon) rated as 'Free', three states (Kuwait, Morocco and North Yemen) as 'Partly Free' and 14 states 'Not Free' (Turkey is classified in the Central/Eastern Europe and the former Soviet Union [CEE/FSU] by Freedom House). This was in line with other regions such as CEE/FSU that lacked any 'Free' or 'Partly Free' states and Sub-Saharan Africa (SSA)

Table 5.1 Freedom House Rankings of Middle Eastern and North African States (1973–2012)

	Free		Partly Free		Not Free	
Year	Number of Countries*	Percentage	Number of Countries	Percentage	Number of Countries	Percentage
2012	1	6.0	4	22.0	13	72.0
2002	1	5.0	3	17.0	14	78.0
1992	1	5.5	8	44.5	9	50.0
1982	1	5.0	8	42.0	10	53.0
1973	2	10.0	3	16.0	14	74.0

* Note, the number of states Freedom House incorporate in the Middle East and North Africa region decreased from 19 to 18 in 1990 with the unification of North and South Yemen.

that had three 'Free' and nine 'Partly Free' states. However, at each 10-year interval from 1973 to 2012, the number of 'Free' MENA states was reduced to one (Israel), with an intermittent increase of 'Partly Free' states to eight in 1982 (Bahrain, Egypt, Kuwait, Lebanon, Morocco, Qatar, Tunisia and the UAE) and 1992 (Algeria, Jordan and Tunisia replaced Kuwait, Qatar and the UAE), with this number decreasing to three in 2002 (Jordan, Kuwait and Morocco) and four in 2011 (Kuwait, Lebanon, Morocco and Tunisia).

This can be contrasted with the increase in 'Free' states in CEE/FSU, which increased to eight in 1992, 11 in 2002 and 13 in 2012, and SSA, which increased to eight in 1992 and nine in 2002 and 2012. In addition, the 'Partly Free' states in CEE/FSU peaked at 15 in 1992 and declined to 10 in 2002 and nine in 2012, largely due to the increase in 'Free States'. In SSA, there has been a greater cluster of 'Partly Free' states from 19 in 1992, to 25 in 2002 and 22 in 2012. In percentage terms, the MENA region has by far the greatest percentage of states in the 'Not Free' category in 2012, with 72%. CEE/FSU has 24% of states in this category (from 100% in 1973), SSA has 35% (from 70% in 1973), the Asia-Pacific region 21% (from 36% in 1973), the Americas 3% (from 15% in 1973) and Western Europe 0% (from 12% in 1973).

Beyond the Exceptionalist Debate?

Whilst this paints a bleak picture of political freedom and participation in the Middle East, these reports are not without criticism. For instance, the metrics employed have been criticised for their assigning of a numerical value to what may be argued is a subjective value of freedom. That is, freedom varies according to context and perception, and may not be linked to the categories of political rights and civil liberties used in the reports. In addition, the use of numerical scores hides the nuance of political life in these regimes. Indeed, it does not reflect the means by which people are active within authoritarian systems, or the way particular groups survive and even benefit under this form of governance.

In this regard, most recent scholarship has turned towards understanding not just *why* authoritarianism persists in the region, but *how* it functions. By doing this, we can gain a greater understanding of why citizens do not automatically rise up and challenge a government that denies or limits their political voice. Here, it is critical to examine the mechanics of authoritarian rule in the Middle East.

The Mechanics of Authoritarian Rule

The presence of authoritarian governments does not necessarily mean no political participation. As Holger Albrecht has argued, political participation 'exists in *every* political system, irrespective of whether it is democratic or authoritarian' (2008: 15). That is, an authoritarian system is not simply one of complete control by a regime over a passive population. In the Middle East, this has revolved around a number of key features, with some more prominent in states than others. Here, we shall explore a number of these, including republican and monarchical authoritarianism, formal and informal participation in this environment as well as the dynamics of the social contract in the Middle East.

Republics and Monarchies

Table 3.1 in Chapter 3 outlined the various regime 'types' in the region. Republics are the most common type of regime, with 12 of the 21 states falling into this category (13 counting the Palestinian Authority). During the Cold War, we have already seen how there was a tendency to group these regimes together as 'radical' or 'revolutionary'. This reflected an imposed view of regional dynamics designed to fit with global geopolitical trends and was not a label necessarily applicable to the way these regimes conducted their domestic policy.

That is, these regimes continued many of the practices and policies inherited from periods of Ottoman and colonial rule (see Chapters 1 and 2) that were designed, first and foremost, to ensure the continuation of their authority. There were some policies that aimed to change some existing social, political and economic systems such as policies of land redistribution or the nationalisation of large industries. However, as is outlined in the case studies below, these were not thoroughgoing reforms that altered the way their societies were fundamentally structured.

Indeed, as we shall see below, where certain regimes introduced new balances of power, such as the promotion of the interests and influence of the Alawi and Christian communities in Syria, this was a mechanism of regime survival rather than fundamental social restructuring. What was common to these regimes was the intermittent use of nationalist ideology that oscillated between calls to pan-Arab allegiance or (including the non-Arab case of Turkey) state-based allegiances.

In this regard, the governments of the region's republics were often drawn from non-traditional areas, whether this was geographic, ethnic or socioeconomic. As such, they tended to employ state-led development programmes and other mechanisms for developing allegiance amongst suspicious or hostile local populations. Saying this, such policies were not limited to these types of states, with monarchies also implementing these programmes as part of 'modernisation' processes.

In this regard, there were similarities between the types of policies pursued by both authoritarian republics and monarchies in the Middle East to ensure and legitimate their rule. The language of legitimation in monarchies did revolve more around claims to historic legitimacy, particularly in 'local' dynasties such as Morocco or Saudi Arabia and the Gulf. However, there were also 'new' dynastic regimes, such as the Hashemites in Jordan and Iraq (before 1958) who pursued similar paths as their counterparts in the republics.

On top of these broad trends, authoritarian regimes of all stripes have employed a range of tactics to ensure their hold on power as well as benefit their supporters. These have ranged from direct coercion to foreign policy, ideological claims, as well as the exploitation of traditional social structures through patron–client relationships and the effort to exploit the charisma of individuals through state propaganda.

Table 5.2 Political and Legal Structure in the Middle East

Country	Head of State	Parliament	Constitution	Parties	Suffrage	Legal System
Algeria	President	Yes: Bicameral, both elected	1976	Yes, Partially restricted	18y/o+, universal	Civil/ Islamic Law
Bahrain	King	Yes: Bicameral, upper house appointed, lower house elected	2002	Yes, Restricted	20y/o+, universal	Islamic/ Civil Law
Egypt	President	Yes: Bicameral, both elected	2011	Yes	18y/o+, universal	Civil/ Islamic Law
Iran	Supreme Leader	Yes: Unicameral, elected	1979	Yes, Restricted	18y/o+, universal	Islamic Law
Iraq	President	Yes: Unicameral, elected	2005	Yes	18y/o+, universal	Civil/ Islamic Law
Israel	President	Yes: Unicameral, elected	No	Yes	18y/o+, universal	Civil/ Religious Law
Jordan	King	Yes: Bicameral, upper house appointed, lower house elected	1952	Yes, Restricted	18y/o+, universal	Civil/ Islamic Law

Country	Head of State	Parliament	Constitution	Parties	Suffrage	Legal System
Kuwait	Emir	Yes: Unicameral, elected and appointed	1962	No	21y/o+, universal	Civil/ Islamic Law
Lebanon	President	Yes: Unicameral, elected (confessional quotas)	1926	Yes	21y/o+, universal	Civil/ Religious Law
Libya	N/A	Transitional	2011 (draft)	N/A	N/A	N/A
Morocco		Yes: Bicameral, upper house indirectly elected, lower house elected	1972	Yes, Partially restricted	18y/o+, universal	Civil/ Islamic Law
Oman	Sultan/ Prime Minister	Yes: Bicameral, upper house appointed, lower house elected	No	No	21y/o+, universal	Civil/ Islamic Law
Qatar	Emir	Yes: Unicameral, elected and appointed	2005	No	18y/o+, universal	Civil/ Islamic Law
Saudi Arabia	King/ Prime Minister	Yes: Unicameral, appointed	No	No	21y/ o+, male only	Islamic Law
Sudan	President	Yes: Bicameral, upper house indirectly elected, lower house elected	2005 (draft)	Yes, Partially restricted	17y/o+, universal	Islamic/ Civil Law
Syria	President	Yes: Unicameral, elected	1973	Yes, Restricted	18y/o+, universal	Civil/ Islamic Law

(Continued)

Table 5.2 (Continued)

Country	Head of State	Parliament	Constitution	Parties	Suffrage	Legal System
Tunisia	President	Yes: Unicameral, elected	1959	Yes	18y/o+, universal	Civil/ Islamic Law
Turkey	President	Yes: Unicameral, elected	1982	Yes, Partially restricted	18y/o+, universal	Civil Law
UAE	President/ Emir	Yes: Unicameral, appointed	1971	No	N/A	Islamic/ Civil Law
Yemen	President	Yes: Bicameral, upper house appointed, lower house elected	1991	Yes	18y/o+, universal	Islamic/ Civil Law

Formal and Informal Political Participation

As a result, whilst there is a degree of political participation in authoritarian regimes in the Middle East, this participation is only occasionally expressed through formal political institutions. This can be contrasted with liberal democracies where participation in the political process is almost always conducted through formal, regulated institutions such as political parties and elections through to trade unions and civil society organisations. As we shall discuss below, formal institutions are present in authoritarian systems across the Middle East, yet they are not 'as significant an influence on political participation in these regimes as they are in democracies' (Albrecht, 2008: 22).

Therefore, participation in authoritarian systems often occurs at the *informal* level. That is, formal participation has been conventionally understood as being conducted through institutions and organisations to directly shape or influence the decision-making of regimes. On the other hand, informal participation is less direct, serving a range of functions that may affect decision-making but also as a means for individuals and groups to 'extract resources from the state, to further personal interests, to voice and mobilise public opinion, to resist and oppose the status political quo, [or] to exchange ideas on political, economic, and social issues' (Alhamad in Lust-Okar and Zerhouni, 2008: 36).

Patron–Client Relationships

These 'informal networks' of political participation vary from region to region, and state to state. Indeed, this is not a process unique to the Middle East. However, the prevalence and persistence of authoritarianism in the region has made these forms of political activity particularly important. This importance is enhanced as they are ways of participation that are indigenous to the region, and most often pre-date the advent of the independent state.

One way of understanding these networks is through the concepts of clientelism and patronage. In this understanding, the majority of the population serve as *clients* whilst those in positions of power act as *patrons*. Individuals or groups act as clients by establishing relationships with patrons to extract specific things, whether this be employment, favourable treatment in terms of judicial or business matters, or other issues. As such, it is an asymmetric or imbalanced relationship that is not constrained by the normal rule of law that governs the behaviour of political leaders in liberal democracies.

For Nazih Ayubi, this is a dynamic that was entrenched in the Middle East over centuries, but particularly during the Ottoman period where intermediaries (*a'yan*) helped facilitate links between the public (*al-'amma*), or clients, and political patrons (*al-khassa*) (Ayubi, 1999: 165). This pattern has been repeated in the region upon independence, with regimes using state resources to create these informal relationships between individuals and social groups. Whilst this has generally been a one-way relationship where clients petitioned and patrons distributed largesse, there was also a dynamic whereby the political elite had to ensure that this largesse was distributed in such a way as to avoid unrest. Therefore, whilst there was not any direct input into decision-making by client groups, the patron–client relationship was an important part of the way non-democratic regimes ensured stability and the status quo.

The 'Social Contract' in the Middle East

Where patron–client relationships are a key part of understanding authoritarian dynamics in the Middle East, efforts at popular control and regulation of the political system have also been deflected and managed through what is often described as the Middle East 'social contract'. The notion of social contract relates to an implicit or explicit bargain that lays out the justification or source of legitimacy a government has over a people.

That is, depending on one's view, a government is required to fulfil basic functions to be considered legitimate, or to be deserving of the right to rule. These functions often include the respect of individual and/or group rights (however defined), the maintenance of order and security, the provision of a viable economy and economic freedom (such as the right to private property), and, in some instances, the pursuit of more specific ideological or religious aims. Often, these social contracts are articulated in the constitution of a state as well as in the actions of a state, such as through adherence to, for instance, international conventions on human rights, economic freedoms, or other issues.

In the post-independence Middle East, and particularly in the Arab states, there were particular features of a more implicit social contract that worked to limit popular political participation. These included a guarantee of security and a promise, rhetorically at least, to confront threats to stability both within and outside the state, state regulation of economic planning and development that included guarantees of state employment for citizens, and the use of state revenues, particularly in oil-producing states, for the provision of large-scale welfare programmes. The cost of these was a closed political system. In other words, the contract was a trading of political freedoms for economic and security guarantees.

This was not a static situation. As we shall see below, regional economic turmoil through the 1980s and 1990s led to widespread social unrest across the region, unrest similar to the unrest that broke out with the 'Arab Spring' towards the end of 2010 (see Chapter 10). This economic downturn forced many regional regimes to implement economic reform programmes that put the social contract under strain, particularly in the poorer regional states.

However, whilst there have been efforts at reforming or adapting authoritarian regimes in recent years, these types of regimes persist. In addition to the informal modes of control and managing political participation through patron–client relationships, regimes also employ a number of other mechanisms of ensuring rule. These include populist politics, the use of single-party systems, so-called 'rentier' politics, as well as the use of coercion and the state security apparatus.

Populist Politics and Single-Party Systems

Political populism is a common tool employed by authoritarian regimes, with those in the Middle East no exception. Populism can be broadly understood as a rhetorical tool to mobilise a population in support of a set of policies, a movement or a regime. It does not connote a specific set of ideas. Instead, populist politics revolves around broad, often ill-defined claims that a regime or movement is defending or pursuing the interests of 'the people' against an enemy.

As such, the content of populist politics differs from place to place. It can appeal to popular fears of 'outsiders', class tensions, historic antagonisms or even invoke conspiracy theories. By doing this, it aims to present 'the people', usually a national community, as a homogeneous group who require protection. In authoritarian settings, it is the regime that presents itself as the protector and champion of these interests and goals. Looking back to the ideological themes outlined in Chapter 4,

Figure 5.1 The headquarters of Egypt's former ruling party, the National Democratic Party, is burnt down during the uprisings in January 2011

Source: Al-Ahram

populist rhetoric has generally revolved around nationalism or religion, particularly Islam and, in relation to Israel, Judaism. Indeed, the controversy surrounding Israel in the Middle East has been a prominent feature of such political discourse, with regimes in Egypt, Syria, Iraq and elsewhere basing part of their claims to rule in terms of their confrontation with Israel. Similarly, populist rhetoric can resonate in democratic and semi-democratic systems as it does in Israeli, Lebanese, Turkish and Iranian politics.

Populist politics also extends to the realm of policy. In particular, this was linked to the particular ideological bent of the regime at the time. For instance, Nasser's nationalisation of the Suez Canal in 1956 or Mossadeq's nationalisation of the Iranian oil industry in 1951 are prime examples of 'showcase' populist moves. They generated massive popularity for the government of the day, as much for the economic benefit as for the symbolism of challenging the perceived foreign oppressor in the name of 'the people'.

Single-party regimes in the Middle East have included:

- National Liberation Front (FLN) in Algeria (1962–89)
- National Union and Arab Socialist Union in Egypt (1953–76)
- Rastakhiz Party and Islamic Republican Party in Iran (1975–87)
- Arab Socialist Union and Ba'ath Party in Iraq (1964–2003)

(Continued)

(Continued)

- Arab Socialist Union in Libya (1971–7)
- Yemeni Socialist Party in South Yemen (1978–90)
- Arab Liberation Movement and Ba'ath Party (National Progressive Front) in Syria (1952–2012)
- Neo-Destour Party, Socialist Destourian Party and Constitutional Democratic Rally in Tunisia (1957–89)
- Republican People's Party in Turkey (1923–46)

This also happened at the domestic level where nationalist regimes, influenced by socialist economic policies, implemented large land redistribution programmes through the 1950s and 1960s. Whilst the benefits of this for the poorer classes and the economy as a whole were questionable, they were a tool that was used to generate support for the regime. This was often done in conjunction with statements attacking economic elites and large landowners, often seeking to link them to the era of colonial and imperial exploitation.

Here, authoritarian governments have often employed political parties as mechanisms for both articulating and mobilising support for these populist politics. Below, we shall discuss the presence of elections and apparent democratic systems in authoritarian states (so-called 'hybrid regimes'), however it is useful to note here that authoritarian governments have often employed some of the symbols and practice of democracy in an attempt to boost their own legitimacy.

These symbols and practices are superficial, and do not challenge the ultimate authority of the authoritarian government. Instead, as is the case with single-party regimes, they are a tool to enhance the legitimacy of the government. Often, these are not strictly speaking single-party environments, with smaller parties allowed to function. However, these are often under close scrutiny by the government, or are small enough that they act as an outlet for marginal opposition, a tool of distributing patronage, or to deflect domestic or international criticism of the authoritarian nature of the regime. Many states across the region have had single-party systems under an authoritarian government. However, all former single-party systems have either collapsed altogether or, as is far more common, moved towards controlled multi-party systems. We shall explore a number of cases of the latter below, including the Ba'ath Party in Syria and Iraq.

The Rentier State

These forms of maintaining authoritarian rule outlined above are far more common amongst republics than monarchies in the Middle East. This is also due to economic and geographic concerns, particularly in terms of the presence of natural resources. The question of resources and particularly hydrocarbons (oil and natural gas) will be discussed in detail in Chapter 6. However, it is important to touch on how these factors have helped shape the way authoritarianism functions in the oil-producing states of the Middle East.

One of the most useful ways of understanding the relationship between oil and authoritarianism is through the concept of the 'rentier state'. In basic terms, a rentier state is one that receives 'on a regular basis substantial amounts of external economic rent' (Yates, 1996: 11). This 'external economic rent' comes in the form of revenues derived from the sale of natural resources. In the Middle East, this refers primarily to oil and, to a lesser extent, natural gas.

However, there are deeper implications of this beyond just the receipt of income from the extraction and sale of natural resources. For Hazem Beblawi, a rentier dynamic is established when the sale of this resource and thus its revenues flow directly to the state, the resource generates sufficient wealth so that the economy of the state relies on it to function, and the extraction and sale of the resource require only a small percentage of the domestic population to produce it. The net result of this is a state that possesses a source of income independent of reliance on the work of the domestic population (Beblawi and Luciani, 1987).

Therefore, states that produce and sell natural resources, as many states do, are not all rentier states. Instead, it is a concept that refers to states that are able to function without the need for other sources of revenue, particularly taxation. As a result, rentier states are able to use their wealth (resource *rents*) as a means to offset challenges to their rule through large state-sponsored employment programmes, welfare and other services. Here, one may invert the American Revolutionary maxim of 'no taxation without representation' where, for rentier states, there is 'no taxation therefore no representation'.

This has obvious consequences for the development of democratic or representative institutions as well as the economic functioning of these states. The latter factor will be explored in Chapter 6, but in terms of authoritarianism and democratisation, rentier systems use revenues to provide services and facilitate patron–client relationships that offset claims for democratic representation. The oil-producing states of the Gulf, particularly Saudi Arabia, Kuwait, Qatar, the UAE and, to a lesser extent, Bahrain and Oman alongside Libya and Algeria, have developed along these lines.

Coercion and the Security Apparatus

Apart from the mechanisms of maintaining authority outlined above, authoritarian states also employ more direct forms of oppression through state security services. Whilst all states possess internal security services in one form or another, authoritarian regimes use these agencies in direct oppression of opposition groups. This oppression is exacerbated by the lack of constitutional constraints on regime behaviour.

> *Mukhabarat* is the Arabic term for intelligence agency. It is the title often given to internal security and intelligence services in many Arab countries, and is often the focus of claims of excess on the part of authoritarian regimes.

Constitutional constraints and the rule of law serve as mechanisms for checking the power of the state to pursue policies such as detention without charge, torture, prevention of association and the suppression of public protest. However, as we can see in Table 5.2 above, many regional states have constitutions. Despite this, the weakness of these documents in terms of the powers of the head of state or the ease with which this rule of law can be suspended allows for the use of extra-judicial violence by authoritarian regimes. This has been one of the most visible features of authoritarian rule in the region. As we shall see below, the former Ba`athist regime of Saddam Hussein was notorious for its use of violence against its own citizens in the suppression of dissent, the maintenance of order and the effort to coerce support. Whilst other regimes may not have used these tools with such force as Hussein, almost all regimes across the region have resorted to violence outside the rule of law to maintain their authority. It is important to remember that this is not the only tool, or even the most useful tool, for the maintenance of authoritarian rule. It is a critical part to be sure, whether it is the use or mere threat of such acts. However, this is part of a broader matrix of tools used by such regimes to perpetuate their rule.

> In 1958, the new military-backed regime in Egypt introduced an **Emergency Law** (Law No. 162) that suspended constitutional rights, extended police and security services powers, legalised censorship and banned public demonstrations.
>
> Apart from a brief suspension in 1980 and early 1981, the assassination of President Sadat led to its reimposition and it has been in place ever since. Elements of the law have been suspended in the wake of the toppling of President Mubarak in 2011, but the law remains valid.

Personality 'Cults'

The importance of personality and charisma is one of the more difficult factors to gauge in understanding authoritarian rule. For Weber, the 'charismatic authority' was a central part of any authority structure. Indeed, those who visit these countries are often struck by the omnipresence of images of heads of state that dominate public spaces. However, as Lisa Wedeen has noted in relation to the 'personality cult' during Hafiz al-Assad's rule in Syria, 'the Syrian leadership considers the cult worthy of considerable expenditures of both time and money' even when efforts to 'create charisma and induce popular belief ... do not seem to be working' (1999: 4).

Therefore, whilst it is commonly thought that these personality cults are efforts to generate feelings of love or at least loyalty amongst the population towards the leadership, this is not always the case. In authoritarian regimes, the rituals and symbols that surround these personality cults often seek to make the leader the symbol of the nation's struggle. As was discussed in Chapter 4, this is particularly true of much of the imagery around many regional Arab leaders and their attempts to associate themselves with Palestinian rights or, more recently, with images of religiosity.

Figure 5.2   Images of state-sponsored propaganda (from left): Saddam Hussein and
                     Bashir al-Assad

Source: Sheldon Rampton

One result of this is the personification of the regime in one person. Whilst this is somewhat reflective of the highly centralised power of authoritarian governments, it has also led to situations where the toppling of an individual leader, the symbol of the old regime, leaves intact the mechanisms of authoritarian control. This has been an issue faced by many movements in the Middle East that seek to reshape the regional political order to one more politically open and inclusive.

EXAMPLES OF AUTHORITARIANISM IN THE MIDDLE EAST

The following case studies are not exhaustive histories of each regime. Instead, they offer a brief outline of the mechanisms of authoritarianism employed by each in the maintenance of their rule. This is designed to illustrate both the diversity of authoritarianism in the region as well as the various ways people participated within these systems.

Case Study: Republican Authoritarianism in Syria (1970–2000)

As Cleveland and Bunton argue, through the 1960s and 1970s both Syria and Iraq earned 'well-deserved reputations for political instability', with numerous coups and counter-coups (2009: 397). However, the regimes that emerged in the 1970s in both states led to durable authoritarian regimes. Whilst Iraq will be examined below, the authoritarian government established under Hafiz al-Assad between 1970 and his death in 2000 persists through to today, even in the face of two large-scale uprisings, one from 1976 to 1982 and one that broke out in 2011.

Here, the army and the *mukhabarat* were key elements of the regime's power. Coercion was an important part of the regime's strategy, employed when other means of maintaining order broke down. An example of this was the use of both the army and internal security services in the crushing of the Syrian Muslim Brotherhood's uprising in 1982, an event that culminated in the siege of the city of Hama in February when the government deployed the army against insurgents. The resulting fighting left the city levelled and between 10,000 and 20,000 people dead. Whilst the Syrian branch of the Brotherhood ceased to operate in any meaningful capacity, the city has persisted as a hotbed of anti-regime activity, being at the centre of the 2011 uprising in Syria.

Figure 5.3 From left: former Syrian President Hafiz al-Assad with his younger brother and head of the *mukhabarat* Rifaat al-Assad. Rifaat allegedly conducted the attacks against the Muslim Brotherhood in the city of Hama in February 1982 that led to an estimated 10,000–20,000 deaths

Source: Public domain

Aside from direct coercion, Assad also used sectarianism to his advantage. Syria is an immensely diverse country, but one with a majority Sunni Arab population. This community had traditionally dominated Syria's political and particularly economic life. Assad came from the traditionally marginalised Alawi community, and the most prominent positions in both the government and the various elements of the security services were given to those from the President's community with token positions going to Syrian Christians and Sunni.

Coercion and tactics of opposition division were more important to Syria as it lacked the oil wealth of many of the other Arab states in the region. There was a measure of economic development through Assad's reforms in the 1970s, including land redistribution, education and infrastructure development programmes. However, whilst the regime implemented a number of socialist-style economic reforms, it did not pursue a hardline socialist economic policy, allowing a measure of

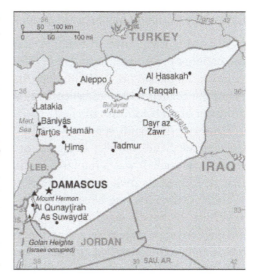

Figure 5.4 Syria

Source: Central Intelligence Agency

private ownership particularly amongst urban Sunni groups who were the most disenfranchised under the new regime. In addition, Syria was able to deflect some economic pressures after the end of the civil war in Lebanon in 1990 when their occupation of the country allowed them to export up to 1 million poor workers to Lebanon. This came on the back of an economic downturn in the late 1980s and early 1990s as well as the ramifications of the 1982 uprising.

Alongside many authoritarian regimes of the time, the Assad regime introduced a largely secular civil law code that led to the improvement for both women and minority groups in the areas of social mobility, inheritance law and other areas. These reforms often worked against the largely socially conservative social fabric, creating tension between society, particularly the Sunni religious establishment, and the regime.

At the regional level, the Syrian regime based its claims to legitimacy on its continued confrontationalist stance vis-à-vis Israel. This was a central platform of the regime's rhetoric, positioning itself as the champion of the Arab and Palestinian cause. However, efforts to control Palestinian organisations, ostensibly the rationale for the 1976 Syrian intervention in the Lebanese Civil War (see Chapter 3), created tension between the regime and the PLO as well as suspicion of the Syrian government's motives. This ultimately undermined Assad's goal of controlling the PLO and using it as an extension of Syria's aims to pressure Israel into returning the Golan Heights.

Case Study: Absolute Monarchy in Saudi Arabia (1953–82)

In discussing the politics of Saudi Arabia, there are three issues that dominate the discussion: oil, Islam and the Saudi–US relationship. Large-scale oil deposits were found in Saudi Arabia in 1938, deposits that are the second largest in the world behind Venezuela and would eventually see Saudi Arabia become the second largest producer of oil behind Russia.

However, the Saudi state was established prior to the influx oil wealth on the back of the Saudi family's conquest of the Arabian Peninsula in the early 20th century. As such, it was a monarchy indigenous to this part of the region, and one that developed its own form of religious ideology and legitimation through the Wahhabist doctrine (see Chapter 4).

Whilst the Saudis developed a state structure at least ostensibly along the lines of a modern state system, replacing the tribal confederations that existed before, the Saudi monarchy controlled almost all facets of government. This centralised power was established under the state's first king, Abd al-Aziz ibn Saud. Ibn Saud was succeeded by his son, Saud, after his death in 1953. The new monarch faced a series of challenges, particularly the influx of massive oil revenues into the country as well

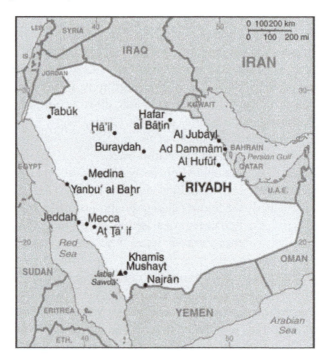

Figure 5.5 Saudi Arabia

Source: Central Intelligence Agency

as managing Saudi Arabia's regional role in the face of the rise of Arab nationalism in Egypt, Syria and Iraq (see Chapter 6).

King Saud's rule was characterised by a lack of innovation and adaptation. He continued with the lack of a constitution, a complete closure of the political system and an emphasis on the religious elements of legitimacy that the regime relied on for support. In addition, economic mismanagement drained the government's new-found wealth, leading to an internal coup in 1964 and replacement by his half-brother Faisal.

Faisal attempted to improve the functioning of government in Saudi society, through massive education, infrastructure and industrial programmes funded by the

Figure 5.6   King Faisal, who ruled Saudi Arabia from 1964 to 1975

Source: Public domain

state's oil wealth, wealth that increased dramatically after the 1973 oil embargo (see Chapter 6). However, this was a managed reform process that was not accompanied by a political reform process, with the state managing the process as a means to make their rule more effective, and less prone to instability and challenges.

For instance, education reforms were not aimed at developing critical skills but at training local technocrats and bureaucrats to staff the large new government departments. This would make the state more efficient, undercut the potential unrest that might stem from growing unemployment, as well as make people dependent on the state for their quality of life.

Therefore, even in the context of social and economic development programmes, the use of funds to deflect opposition and criticism was the centrepiece of Saudi governance. This was a tactic employed at the regional level also. Faced with growing criticism over their close alliance with the United States, the Saudi monarchy, particularly during and after the reign of Faisal, sent large amounts of money to the PLO as well as regional governments in exchange for a muting of their criticism of Saudi foreign policy.

Saudi Arabia's **Shià** community are believed to make up around 15% of the country's estimated 28 million people. They are concentrated in the oil-producing east of the country, but have been traditionally marginalised due to their religion and tension over alleged links to their religious cohorts in the Islamic Republic of Iran, a regional adversary of the Saudis.

However, the programme of attempting to implement modernising reforms 'without upsetting the conservative social structure and Islamic value system on which the regime's authority depended' came under increasing stress through the 1970s (Cleveland and Bunton, 2009: 459). The rentier-style system was struggling to accommodate the rapidly increasing population, leading to greater bureaucratic inefficiency, waste and evident corruption. This trajectory tied in with the emergence of Islamist ideology as a challenge to the regime. The seizure of the Grand Mosque in Mecca during the 1979 *hajj* and the 1979 Islamic Revolution in Iran presented challenges to both the domestic and international policy stances of the government. In the case of the former, the group that led the mosque seizure claimed to be leading an uprising against what was seen as a corrupt and un-Islamic monarchy, charges that grew from the regime's wealth, indulgence and ties to the US. In the case of the latter, it led to fears of an uprising amongst the substantial Shi`a population in the oil-rich east of Saudi Arabia, a community that had been long-oppressed by the regime.

This instability was also fuelled by the growing migrant worker population in Saudi Arabia, a situation mirrored in other oil-producing Gulf states such as Kuwait, Qatar and the UAE. In these states, citizens were employed by the state but rarely if ever in a production capacity, instead staffing the large state bureaucracies. Migrant workers from the poorer Middle East states (Yemen, Sudan and many Palestinians) as well as from poorer countries around the world swelled from the 1980s. In the case of the UAE, they now outnumber the resident population by an estimated 3 to 1 (Kamrava and Babar, 2012).

The **seizure of the Grand Mosque of Mecca** on 20 November 1979 was carried out by a group led by Juhaiman ibn Muhammad ibn Saif al Otaibi who claimed to be the Mahdi, or redeemer, and aimed to overthrow what he saw as the illegitimate and apostate Saudi regime. It is argued that this was the forerunner to the emergence of subsequent radical Islamist groups and preachers out of Saudi Arabia, including Osama bin Laden (see Chapter 9).

However, despite the growth of opposition, particularly through the articulation of radical Islamist ideology (see Chapters 4 and 7), the regime has been able to maintain a semblance of stability, even in the face of the events of the 'Arab Spring'. Greater delegation of authority to the religious establishment and amongst key members of the royal family have moved the country, partially at least, from an absolute dictatorship. However, the lack of any constitution, effective civil law code or official means of political participation remains the definitive feature of political life in the country.

Case Study: Military-Backed Totalitarian Regime in Iraq (1979–90)

During the 1980s and 1990s, two regional states were exemplars of closed political systems with leaders that divided international opinion, Iraq under Saddam Hussein and Libya under Muammar Gaddhafi. Both leaders would subsequently be overthrown, but in starkly different circumstances, with Hussein toppled at the hands of the US after the 2003 invasion and Gaddhafi by his own population after the 2011 uprising.

Figure 5.7 Iraq

Source: Central Intelligence Agency

Hussein came from the dominant Sunni minority in Iraq, but was from a family (al-Tikriti) that had been traditionally marginalised amongst the Sunni. However, Hussein's familial links to the leader of the Iraqi Ba`ath Party in the 1960s and future President, Ahmad Hassan al-Bakr, saw him elevated within the party structure and, finally, al-Bakr's deputy after 1969. Here we can see evidence of traditional structures surviving even within revolutionary reformist movements such as the Ba`ath. From his position as deputy of the powerful Revolutionary Command Council, Hussein extended his authority through the use of the state's internal security services and intelligence networks. In this regard, Iraq under al-Bakr and particularly Hussein from 1979 was a regime that maintained its authority primarily through the use of coercion and security measures (Cleveland and Bunton, 2009).

Other mechanisms were present, including the use of the Ba`ath as the single party as well as the implementation of large-scale industrialisation and development projects, particularly during the 1970s. In this regard, Iraq and Algeria shared the scenario of possessing large oil deposits. However, whilst this did lead to some rentier-style activity, the size of both countries' populations as well as the more established political structures made a Gulf-style rentier system untenable. Instead, the wealth was used in development projects and import-substitution industrialisation programmes (see Chapter 6).

During the Iran–Iraq War, various Kurdish militias in Iraq battled with Hussein's government for autonomy or independence. During this conflict, on 16 March 1988, Hussein's government deployed chemical weapons on the Kurdish village of **Halabja** killing an estimated 5000 people in one day (many more died after the attack as a result of the weapons used).

The Iraqi army used a number of lethal agents, including mustard gas and sarin gas indiscriminately on the almost exclusively civilian population.

This attack was a key part of the argument used by supporters of the 2003 invasion of Iraq as an example of the need to forcibly disarm and depose the Hussein regime (see Chapter 10).

In terms of organisations, the military played a critical role. Senior political posts were given to high-ranking military officials. However, this was framed by the control of the Ba`ath Party and, at its core, Hussein himself. Movement up the ranks within the military, or within the key unions and other important organisations was dependent on party membership. As such, all public servants in Iraq were Ba`ath Party members by necessity. This was a critical factor that contributed to the disintegration of the Iraqi state after 2003 when the US removed anyone with party affiliation from state employment after the toppling of the Hussein regime, effectively stripping the state of all trained professionals (see Chapter 8).

In this regard, state-funded employment served as a key tool of social control. For instance, al-Bakr nationalised the Iraqi oil industry in 1972 on the eve of the 1973 oil crisis, seeing a massive influx of funds into the regime's coffers. These funds were used to implement large-scale employment programmes. In addition, the regime also implemented reforms to personal status law similar to those in Syria during the 1970s and 1980s. However, in Iraq this was backed by the threat of violence should citizens challenge the authority of the party or the regime. In addition, the outbreak of war with Iran in 1980 and the ramifications of the failed invasion of Kuwait in 1990 led to the eventual decimation of the Iraqi economy.

This repression extended across all Iraqi society, from the use of security and intelligence services against the Kurdish and Shi`a communities as well as any suspected dissidents. Repression of Iraq's Shi`a, the majority community in the country, extended back to the Ottoman and Mandate period. However, it increased sharply under the Ba`ath, particularly after the 1979 Islamic Revolution in Iran and the Iraqi invasion of Iran a year later. The Iran–Iraq War also led to increased oppression of the Kurdish community in the north of the country, including the use of chemical weapons, with the Iranian government seeking to promote anti-government uprising (Dawisha, 2009).

A recurring theme here has been the ability of these regimes, at least during the Cold War period, to deflect international criticism. As discussed in Chapter 3, Hussein's Iraq was able to court both US and Soviet support in its war with Iran. This, ironically, would also sow the seeds of the future confrontation with the US, culminating with the 2003 invasion and occupation (see Chapter 8), as well as inadvertently contribute to the radicalisation of Islamist activism through the 1990s, forming a key part of Osama bin Laden and al-Qaeda's early rhetorical justification for militancy against the US and its regional allies such as Saudi Arabia (see Chapter 7).

Case Study: Hybrid Regime in Turkey (1950–97)

Outside the Arab world, authoritarianism has arguably not had as strong a hold in the Middle East. However, even in parliamentary democracies such as Turkey, there has been a tumultuous history of political participation, one that continues today. Indeed, the role of the military in Turkey, and the foundations of the Turkish government established by Kemal Atatürk in the early 20th century are still controversial and contested.

Figure 5.8 Turkey

Source: Central Intelligence Agency

During the pre-World War II period, both the Atatürk and Inönü governments implemented state-led development policies including control of the education system and the enforcement of the Kemalist principles (see Chapter 2). After the war, the hold of Atatürk and his successor Ismet Inönü's ruling party, the Republican People's Party (RPP), over government was broken in 1950 with the rise of the Democratic Party (DP), ending the single-party period of Turkish politics. This ushered in a new era of Turkish politics. For instance, where with the

RPP largely drew from Atatürk's cadres and former military officers, the DP was a party primarily of 'professionals and business people' (Cleveland and Bunton, 2009: 278).

The DP also deregulated the public environment, including privatisation programmes and publicly questioning Atatürk's secularisation programme. However, the faltering Turkish economy through the 1950s led the DP to respond with increasing repression. This led, in 1960, to the first of four military coups in Turkey. Justification for the intervention centred on allegations that the DP had both misused public funds and contravened the constitution, particularly the provisions relating to secularism (see Chapter 2).

Figure 5.9 Former Turkish Prime Minister Adnan Menderes, executed in 1961

Source: Public domain

As a result, former DP President Menderes as well as Foreign Minister Zorlu and Finance Minister Polatkan were executed in 1961 under the charges of high treason. Contrary to military coups elsewhere, the military honoured statements that they would not hold on to power, leaving office in 1961. However, their intervention, along with subsequent interventions in 1971, 1980 and 1997, all highlighted the limited strength of the civilian democratic leadership during this period. As such, Turkey operated more as a limited democracy than a full electoral democracy. During the subsequent decades, the instability of Turkey's parliamentary system led to the rise and fall of numerous coalition governments headed by the RPP and the successor to the DP, the Justice Party led by Suleiman Demirel. Unstable and changing governments mirrored the broader chaos in Turkish society at the time, with low-level violence between right-wing and left-wing groups engaging in bombings and kidnappings (Altunişik and Tür, 2005).

Some, such as Robert Naylor, argued that the military allowed this to happen as an excuse to intervene in the political system, particularly in 1980 (Naylor, 2004: 94). The 1980 coup was implemented, as with the other coups, as protecting the Kemalist principles of the constitution, in particular to protect the unity of the state and guarding against the increasing ideological influence of the left- and right-wing militias and parties. However, this coup was exceptional as it led to a suspension of the civilian government and the constitution as well as the temporary banning of all parties and unions and the imposition of martial law. In its stead, the military ruled for the next three years, after which it stepped aside for an elected government under the newly formed Motherland Party. Some have argued that the military only stepped aside with guarantees for control over the new constitution that was introduced during the military's rule (Özbudun, 2000: 117).

Foreign policy was not a major element in the issue of political openness in Turkey. The country remained neutral during World War II and whilst it became a close ally of the United States, including joining NATO in 1952 and seeking EU accession, it managed to maintain reasonably stable relations with all its neighbours. There was a flaring of tension between Turkey and Syria during the 1960s; however this did not dramatically affect its foreign policy nor domestic stability.

The **Kurdistan Workers' Party** (*Partiya Karkerên Kurdistan*, PKK), founded by Abdullah Öcalan in 1978, was a political and paramilitary organisation that fought the Turkish government for Kurdish autonomy and independence. During the period of military activity (1984–98), it not only confronted the Turkish government and military within the country, it also embarked on a series of bombings, assassinations and other activities against Turkish government officials around the world. As such, it became designated as a terrorist organisation by many governments.

Öcalan led the PKK from northern Syria until 1998, when the Syrian government ordered him to leave. He was captured by Turkish agents in Kenya in 1999. He was sentenced to death, with this being commuted to life imprisonment in 2002.

It was internal security matters that would become dominant. Whilst the political situation in the capital Ankara, the major cities including Istanbul, as well as the broader west and centre of the country improved, the situation in the Kurdish areas of the southeast worsened. Here, the constrictive nature of Turkish democracy again reasserted itself. This time, it was not the threat of religious conservatism or ideological radicalism but of ethnic separatism that provoked response. Unrest in the Kurdish region of southeast Anatolia led to the imposition of martial law in the region in 1987 primarily targeting Abdullah Öcalan's Kurdistan Workers' Party (PKK). Violence between the government and the PKK had broken out in 1984, and escalated to the point of insurgency by the late 1980s.

The military remained central to the functioning of Turkish politics, including another intervention in 1997 that led to the removal of the conservative Welfare Party (forerunner to the modern Justice and Development Party, AKP) for again seeking to violate the principle of secularism in the constitution; however, this role was scaled back after the 1980 coup, particularly in line with Turkish efforts to gain accession to the European Union; as such, the limited nature of Turkey's democracy has decreased to the point where the AKP government that came to power in 2002 and returned in elections in 2007 and 2011 now openly contests the core tenets of secularism and statism enshrined in the Kemalist vision.

CONCLUSION

Authoritarianism remains a key feature of regional politics. However, as this chapter has discussed, this does not necessarily mean standard political dynamics across the region. Whilst the lack of political freedoms is a constant, this is pursued in a variety of different ways, at different times, and through different means. For instance, this was shown through an examination of populist politics and single-party systems, the rentier state system, coercion and the security apparatus, and personality cults. Whilst measures such as those by Freedom House are not without controversy, they do highlight how the lack of political freedoms has been an undeniable feature of the political landscape of the Middle East and North Africa, one that has fed into the uprisings that have swept the region since late 2010.

Study Questions

- What is an authoritarian regime and how does it differ from other regimes?
- Is authoritarianism an endemic feature of Middle Eastern politics?
- What are the varieties of authoritarian governance?

- How do factors such as economy, social structure and history affect the functioning of authoritarian systems?
- How do citizens participate in the political life of authoritarian regimes?
- What is the difference between authoritarian republics and monarchies, if any?
- What has been the role of the military and security services in authoritarian governance in the Middle East?

FURTHER READING

Brynen, Rex, Korany, Baghat and Noble, Paul (eds) (1995) *Political Liberalization and Democratization in the Arab World*, Vols 1 and 2. Boulder, CO: Lynne Rienner.
A two-volume series that outlines the key conceptual debates over authoritarian governance and pressures towards democratisation combined with a series of case studies.

Cook, Steven (2007) *Ruling But Not Governing: The Military and Political Development in Egypt, Algeria, and Turkey*. Baltimore, MD: Johns Hopkins University Press.
This volume highlights the unique relationship between the military and political authority in these major regional states, with a particular focus on their modes of rule.

Elbadawi, Ibrahim and Makdisi, Samir (eds) (2011) *Democracy in the Arab World: Explaining the Deficit*. London: Routledge.
An effort at re-evaluating the trends that have mitigated the development of democracy in the region, with an emphasis on economic and institutional factors.

Posusney, Marsha Pripstein and Angrist, Michele Penner (eds) (2005) *Authoritarianism in the Middle East: Regimes and Resistance*. Boulder, CO: Lynne Rienner.
A useful volume in examining the persistence of authoritarian rule in the Middle East, exploring how authoritarian regimes adapt to changing circumstances.

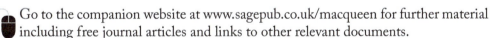 Go to the companion website at www.sagepub.co.uk/macqueen for further material including free journal articles and links to other relevant documents.

REFERENCES

Albrecht, Holger (2008) 'The Nature of Political Participation', in Lust-Okar, Ellen and Zerhouni, Saloua (eds) *Political Participation in the Middle East*. Boulder, CO: Lynne Rienner.

Altunişik, Meliha Benli and Tür, Özlem (2005) *Turkey: Challenges of Continuity and Change*. London: Routledge.

Ayubi, Nazih (1999) *Over-Stating the Arab State: Politics and Society in the Middle East*. London: I.B. Tauris.

Beblawi, Hazem and Luciani, Giacomo (1987) *The Rentier State*. Beckenham: Croom Helm.

Brumberg, Daniel (2002) 'Democratization in the Arab World: The Trap of Liberalized Autocracy', *Journal of Democracy*, 13 (4): 56–68.

Cleveland, William L. and Bunton, Martin (2009) *A History of the Modern Middle East*, 4th ed. Boulder, CO: Westview Press.

Dawisha, Adeed (2009) *Iraq: A Political History from Independence to Occupation*. Princeton, NJ: Princeton University Press.

el-Ghobashy, Mona (2010) 'The Liquidation of Egypt's Illiberal Experiment', *Middle Eastern Research and Information Project*, 29 December.

Kamrava, Mehran and Babar, Zahra (eds) (2012) *Migrant Labor in the Gulf*. New York: Columbia University Press.

Linz, Juan (2000) *Totalitarian and Authoritarian Regimes*. Boulder, CO: Lynne Rienner.

Lust-Okar, Ellen and Zerhouni, Saloua (eds) (2008) *Political Participation in the Middle East*. Boulder, CO: Lynne Rienner.

Naylor, Robert T. (2004) *Hot Money and the Politics of Debt*. Quebec City: McGill-Queen's University Press.

Özbudun, Ergun (2000) *Contemporary Turkish Politics: Challenges to Democracy Consolidation*. Boulder, CO: Lynne Rienner.

Wedeen, Lisa (1999) *Ambiguities of Domination: Politics, Rhetoric, and Symbols in Contemporary Syria*. Chicago, IL: The University of Chicago Press.

Yates, Douglas A. (1996) *The Rentier State in Africa: Oil Rent Dependency and Neocolonialism in the Republic of Gabon*. Trenton, NJ: Africa World Press.

6

Oil, Economy and Development in the Middle East

Learning Objectives

This chapter will enable a greater understanding of:

● The key economic dynamics in the Middle East.
● The relationship of the Middle East to the global economy.
● The structural weaknesses present within Middle Eastern economies.
● The role of oil in the economic dynamics of the Middle East.
● The impacts of economic liberalisation on both economic and political dynamics in the region.

INTRODUCTION

It is impossible to separate political and economic issues in the Middle East. Indeed, as Halliday has argued, the 'one pervasive and ultimately "Middle East crisis" [is] in inter- and intra-state political economy' with the roots of this crisis lying in 'the pattern of incorporation into the world market in regard both to the economies themselves … and also in the very pattern of formation of these modern states' (2005: 267). That is, regardless of the various political crises, all states across the region face critical economic issues. These range from the relationship of regional economies with the global economy to issues specific to each state. Overarching this are the impacts of oil on regional political dynamics.

As was discussed in Chapter 5, these issues have had immense impact on state and social development. To elaborate on this, this chapter will explore key issues in the region's economic landscape. Here, this discussion will outline an economic overview of the Middle East, including an outline of so-called structural weaknesses of the region's economies. This will cover both strictly economic measures as well as broader themes of human development. From here, the discussion will move to a detailed examination of the role of oil on regional economic dynamics. Finally, this chapter will explore efforts at regional economic reform, particularly the discourse around economic liberalisation.

AN ECONOMIC OVERVIEW OF THE MIDDLE EAST

The economies of the Middle East present a mixed picture. Rapid economic development in the Gulf continues alongside continuing economic stagnation in many other states in the region. Where development based on oil revenues has spurred stunning growth, there has also been economic development based on a range of service sectors in other states such as Turkey, Tunisia and Israel. Despite this, unemployment, inflation and corruption continue to undercut the economic potential of the region. As such, where there has been significant economic development in the Middle East in recent years, this has been combined with continued problems relating to broader issues of standards of living and human security. As such, this picture requires greater detail, one that sheds light on the structural weaknesses of the region's economies. These 'structural weaknesses' revolve around a number of issues, including the dependency of the region's economy on oil revenues, the 'multi-track' nature of the region's economies as well as the influence of the informal economy, or black market, in the region.

Figure 6.1 From left: Sheikh Zayed Road in Dubai, UAE in 1990 and 2010

Source: Ikatan Arsitek Indonesia, Public domain

Structural Weakness and Economies of the Middle East

The notion of structural weakness is contested. The debate centres on what one focuses upon as signs of economic development, therefore, dictating what one sees as an economic weakness. One sign of the structural weaknesses of the region's economies is the volatility of the Gross Domestic Product (GDP) of the region's states. This volatility is tied to the volatility of oil prices on the global market, showing the dependency on oil revenues on the part of the region's economies. As will be discussed below, it is important to note here that the reliance on oil revenues, by both oil-producing and non-oil-producing states, ties the region's economy to the volatility of oil price fluctuation. Here, there are myriad forces that affect the price of oil, from global demand and supply dynamics, to security and geopolitical issues, technological developments, labour issues, global regulatory mechanisms and environmental concerns, amongst others.

Figure 6.2 The largest cities in the Middle East (clockwise from left): Cairo, Egypt (14,450,000, 15th largest globally), Istanbul, Turkey (9,413,000, 25th largest globally), Tehran, Iran (7,380,000, 27th largest globally) and Baghdad, Iraq (4,796,000, 47th largest globally)

Source: bigskyline.com, AFP/Relaxnews, Henno Kruger, Public domain

It is this volatility that creates uncertainty within regional economies, making them unattractive to potential investors. That is, the likelihood of investment in regional projects is affected by the stability of the local economy and the perceived benefit to be gained. An unstable environment often undercuts investment momentum, preventing a diversification of regional economies and perpetuating a cycle of further dependency on oil production over other sectors.

Table 6.1 Regional Population (2011 estimates)

		Population			Population			Population
1	Egypt	83,688,164	8	Saudi Arabia	26,534,504	15	UAE	5,314,317
2	Turkey	79,749,461	9	Yemen	24,771,809	16	Lebanon	4,140,280
3	Iran	78,868,711	10	Syria	22,530,746	17	Oman	3,090,150
4	Algeria	35,406,303	11	Tunisia	10,732,900	18	Kuwait	2,646,314
5	Sudan	34,206,710	12	Israel	7,590,758	19	Palestine	2,622,544
6	Morocco	32,309,239	13	Libya	6,733,620	20	Qatar	1,951,591
7	Iraq	31,129,225	14	Jordan	6,508,887	21	Bahrain	1,248,348

Total regional population: 501,774,581.

This dependency also has also bred a boom and bust cycle, with periods of rapid economic growth at times when oil revenues are high (such as in the 1970s or in the 2000s) or times of austerity when the price of oil drops (such as in the 1980s). Both the volatility of this cycle, and the extremes it produces, create problems for states and societies. In particular, economic planning becomes difficult when there is no stability of revenue flows. In addition, an influx of funds can often lead to states using this to buttress often non-democratic means of rule (see Chapter 5) whilst struggling to manage discontent at times of economic downturn. This volatility has many flow-on effects, including for unemployment, bureaucratic and broader economic efficiency and social mobility within these societies.

As a result, most economies in the region are structurally weak. In particular, they are largely import-oriented and service-based, particularly after the privatisation and subsequent closure of many local industries. This is compounded by the types of services in many regional states that 'fall at the low end of the value chain, contribute little to local knowledge development, and lock countries into inferior positions in global markets. This trend, which has been at the expense of Arab agriculture, manufacturing and industrial production, is therefore of concern' (AHDR, 2009: 103). The consequence of this has seen Arab states less industrialised in 2007 than they were in 1970. Indeed, the only countries that increased their manufacturing sectors between 1970 and 2007 were, with the exceptions of Morocco and Tunisia, oil-producing states.

Multi-Track Economies

Whilst recognising these broad trends, there are various economic trends across the region. This can be illustrated by a variety of metrics, including GDP per capita (Table 6.2), unemployment rates (Table 6.3), inflation rates (Table 6.4) and poverty rates (Table 6.5). Table 6.2 highlights the variation in GDP per capita rates from a high of $102,700 in Qatar to a low of $2500 in Yemen. This table also shows a cluster of oil-producing states with lower populations as well as Israel at the top of the table followed by states with larger populations and fewer or no oil resources.

Table 6.2 GDP Per Capita (2011 estimates, US$)

	GDP Per Capita		*GDP Per Capita*		*GDP Per Capita*
1 Qatar	102,700	**8** Lebanon	15,600	**15** Jordan	5900
2 UAE	48,500	**9** Turkey	14,600	**16** Syria	5100
3 Kuwait	40,700	**10** Libya	14,100	**17** Morocco	5100
4 Israel	31,000	**11** Iran	12,200	**18** Iraq	3900
5 Bahrain	27,300	**12** Tunisia	9500	**19** Sudan	3000
6 Oman	26,200	**13** Algeria	7200	**20** Palestine	2900
7 Saudi Arabia	24,000	**14** Egypt	6500	**21** Yemen	2500

Table 6.3 Unemployment Rates (2011 estimates)

	Unemployment		*Unemployment*		*Unemployment*
1 Qatar	0.4%	**8** Turkey	10.3%	**15** Oman	15.0%
2 Kuwait	2.2%	**9** Saudi Arabia	10.9%	**16** Tunisia	16.0%
3 UAE	2.4%	**10** Egypt	12.2%	**17** Sudan	18.7%
4 Israel	5.6%	**11** Jordan	12.3%	**18** Palestine	23.5%
5 Syria	8.1%	**12** Bahrain	15.0%	**19** Libya	30.0%
6 Morocco	9.2%	**13** Iran	15.0%	**20** Yemen	35.0%
7 Algeria	9.7%	**14** Iraq	15.0%	**–** Lebanon	N/A

Unemployment figures roughly correspond to the GDP per capita rankings. The figures presented here are the 'official' rates, and therefore mask higher levels of unemployment as well as underemployment. In addition, the correlation with oil-producing states reflects the ability of these states to use oil revenues to provide employment for nationals. In this regard, whilst there are low unemployment numbers for oil-producing states, this also reflects a broader issue where the use of oil revenues to keep nationals employed leads to potential bureaucratic inefficiency.

Inflation is a critical measure of economic stability. When compared with the above tables, a slightly different picture emerges. Many of the states who were lower on the GDP per capita ranking in the region have lower levels of inflation. For instance, where Morocco ranks low on the regional GDP score, it is able to maintain a low level of inflation, helping offset potential unrest that often stems from low wages combined with rapidly rising prices on basic goods. By contrast, higher inflation rates affect oil-producing states such as Kuwait as well as non-oil-producing states such as Jordan.

Whilst official figures on poverty are also questionable with regard to their accuracy, they present another mixed picture. According to the World Bank, the global average of people living on less than US$1.25 per day was 22.4% by 2010, close to the regional average of 22%. Again, there is a mixed picture in terms of the economic make-up of the states where large oil producers, such as Kuwait and Qatar, have negligible poverty rates as well as lower poverty rates in non-oil producers Tunisia and Syria. In addition, oil producers such as Saudi Arabia, Algeria and Bahrain have mid-level poverty rates, a factor that can be accounted for by larger populations in these states.

Table 6.4 Inflation Rates (2011 estimates)

		Inflation			*Inflation*			*Inflation*
1	Bahrain	0.3%	8	Algeria	4.0%	15	Libya	6.1%
2	Morocco	1.9%	9	Palestine	5.0%	16	Jordan	6.4%
3	UAE	2.5%	10	Saudi Arabia	5.0%	17	Syria	7.0%
4	Qatar	2.8%	11	Lebanon	5.2%	18	Turkey	7.8%
5	Israel	3.2%	12	Kuwait	5.6%	19	Egypt	13.3%
6	Tunisia	3.7%	13	Iran	6.0%	20	Sudan	15.8%
7	Oman	4.0%	14	Iraq	6.0%	21	Yemen	20.0%

An additional measure of economic performance is the Global Competitive Index (GCI) developed by the World Economic Forum. Published since 1979, the GCI has developed a metric of economic performance based on 12 'pillars': institution, infrastructure, macroeconomic environment, health and primary education, higher education and training, goods market efficiency, labour market efficiency, financial market efficiency, technological readiness, market size, business sophistication, and innovation. This is an effort to focus on specific economic measures and the 'ability of countries to provide high levels of prosperity to their citizens' (World Economic Forum, 2011: 9).

Table 6.5 UNDP Poverty Rates* (World Bank 2011 estimates)

		Poverty			*Poverty*			*Poverty*
1	Kuwait	0%**	8	Turkey	17.1%	15	Iraq	25.0%
2	Qatar	0%**	9	Iran	18.0%	16	Lebanon	28.0%
3	Tunisia	7.6%	10	Morocco	19.0%	17	Libya	30.0%
4	Syria	11.9%	11	UAE	19.5%	18	Oman	32.0%
5	Jordan	14.2%	12	Bahrain	20.0%	19	Sudan	40.0%
6	Egypt	16.7%	13	Algeria	22.6%	20	Yemen	45.2%
7	Saudi Arabia	17.0%	14	Israel	23.6%	21	Palestine	50.0%

* Poverty rates are pegged at a daily income of US$1.25 per day.

** Figures for these states are not available, but are estimated as negligible.

Here, there is a clear correlation between oil production and economic performance. Qatar, Saudi Arabia, the UAE, Oman, Kuwait and Bahrain are all high on the GCI, alongside economies with strong service sectors in Israel, Tunisia and Turkey (see Table 6.6). In addition, most of the region's states are in the top half of the world's rankings, indicating that the states of the Middle East are in a reasonably strong position in terms of global economic competitiveness. However, there are a number of states, particularly those with relatively large populations, who are vulnerable to fluctuations in the regional and global economy. Indeed, those states who rank low on this list, or those where data are lacking, have suffered from the global financial crisis since 2007.

These basic figures provide a mixed picture of the economic landscape across the Middle East. Some consistencies are present, particularly the correlation between oil production and high GDP. These per capita levels are obviously mitigated by the size of the population in particular producing countries. In addition, Yemen and, to a lesser extent, the Palestinian Territories have consistently low scores on many indicators. However, beyond this there is greater variation in these indicators where oil revenues, for instance, have not offset high levels of poverty in states such as Libya and Oman. One factor that may account for this variation is the presence of conflict.

Table 6.6 Global Competitive Index* (2011)

		Rank	Score			Rank	Score			Rank	Score
1	Qatar	14	5.24	8	Tunisia	40	4.47	15	Egypt	94	3.88
2	Saudi Arabia	17	5.17	9	Turkey	59	4.28	16	Syria	98	3.85
3	Israel	22	5.07	10	Iran	62	4.26	17	Yemen	138	3.06
4	UAE	27	4.89	11	Jordan	71	4.19	18	Iraq	N/A	N/A
5	Oman	32	4.64	12	Morocco	73	4.16	19	Libya	N/A	N/A
6	Kuwait	34	4.62	13	Algeria	87	3.96	20	Palestine	N/A	N/A
7	Bahrain	37	4.54	14	Lebanon	89	3.95	21	Sudan	N/A	N/A

* The index, developed by the World Economic Forum, is based on 12 'pillars': institution, infrastructure, macroeconomic environment, health and primary education, higher education and training, goods market efficiency, labour market efficiency, financial market efficiency, technological readiness, market size, business sophistication and innovation.

Rank: out of 142 states, with 1/183 the highest rank and 183/183 as the lowest.

Score: out of 7, with 1 the least competitive and 7 the most competitive.

The links between conflict and economic turmoil are multifaceted. Apart from the tragedy of death and destruction during war, the ongoing violence and the destruction of infrastructure are among the many ways war, be it internal or inter-state, can undermine economic performance. This is borne out by these figures, where the importance of conflict and stability on economic performance becomes increasingly apparent. The instability associated with protracted violent conflict as has occurred in states such as Syria, Iraq, Sudan, Palestine and Yemen in recent years has undercut confidence in investment, stability in prices for basic food stuffs, with flow-on issues for economic viability.

The Formal and Informal Economy

The economies of the Middle East share another characteristic with other regions, that of an informal economy. The informal economy is often referred to in terms of the 'black market', however this neglects the full picture. The black market focuses on activity outside government control in terms of taxation and regulation whilst the informal economy includes this as well as the so-called 'grey economy' that uses government networks and channels outside taxation and regulation. Here, the informal economy has always been a part of the region's landscape. The weakness of state institutions partly explains this, with many states being unable to regulate all

Figure 6.3 Street vendors (clockwise from top left): Khartoum, Sudan; Esfahan, Iran; Gaziantep, Turkey; and Casablanca, Morocco

Source: Virtual Tourist, Incredipedia, Hassan Benmehdi

activities within their borders. However, this very weakness also facilitates the use of these networks by state officials themselves for their own benefit (i.e. through bribery and corruption).

Informal economies across the Middle East develop due to a range of factors, such as excessive labour market regulations, a lack of state capacity to manage and regulate employment and high taxes on manufactured goods. These informal activities range from activities such as smuggling, trade in illegal goods, to bribery and other criminal activities. However, the vast bulk of activity in this sector revolves around unregulated employment, the sale of legal goods outside state regulation and the provision of services. According to the World Bank, the informal sector may be understood in terms of two types of activities: first, 'coping strategies' or 'survival activities' such as casual employment and subsistence agriculture, and second, 'unofficial earning strategies' such as tax evasion, avoidance of government regulation and underground and criminal activities.

Estimates on the size of the informal sector vary from country to country across the Middle East (see Table 6.7). For instance, according to the International Labour Organisation, the largest informal sectors in the world are in Bolivia (67.3% of the total economy) and Georgia (65.9% of the total economy). Here, the informal sectors in the states of the Middle East with the exception of the Palestinian Territories are not as large as these, or other large informal sectors such as those in Thailand (53.3%), Chad (48%) or the Philippines (44.8%). Indeed, many of the region's states are close to the average of other states such as Vietnam (15.8%), Chile (20.1%) and

Table 6.7 Size of the Informal Sector (International Labour Organisation 2011 estimates)

		Poverty			Poverty			Poverty
1	Saudi Arabia	18.4%	8	Yemen	27.4%	15	Palestine	50.0%
2	Iran	18.9%	9	Turkey	32.1%	-	Iraq	N/A
3	Syria	19.3%	10	Algeria	34.1%	-	Kuwait	N/A
4	Jordan	19.4%	11	Lebanon	34.1%	-	Libya	N/A
5	Israel	21.9%	12	Egypt	35.1%	-	Oman	N/A
6	UAE	26.4%	13	Morocco	36.4%	-	Qatar	N/A
7	Bahrain	18.8%	14	Tunisia	38.4%	-	Sudan	N/A

India (23.9%). However, this is slightly above the rates in the United States (8.7%), Japan (11.2%) and Australia (14.7%).

Therefore, the informal sector is a critical part of most, if not all, regional economies but also one that is not larger, if not lower, than any other comparable regions. As shall be discussed below, international financial institutions such as the World Bank and International Monetary Fund (IMF) actively seek to pressure governments into shutting down the activities of the informal economy particularly in terms of its role in depriving the state of tax revenue. However, such pressures confront a variety of impediments including the lack of government capacity as well as the active involvement of governments themselves in the informal sector. In addition, efforts to regulate the activities of the informal economy can have detrimental effects for the many citizens who rely on this sector for their livelihood.

Aside from the clear benefits of the informal sector for many across the region, there are also downsides. In particular, workers within the informal sector operate outside regulation and protection offered by legal systems and international organisations such as the International Labour Organisation. In addition, the measures of the informal sector also include government corruption, a factor that has been critical in feeding into the ability of regimes to perpetuate undemocratic rule as well as the discontent behind the uprisings that engulfed the region since 2010.

Transparency International's Corruption Perceptions Index (see Table 6.8) highlights the troubling trend of corruption in the region. Here, 11 of the 21 regional states are in the top half of states globally with only four out of 21 regional states scoring higher than 5 out of 10 on the index. These figures are important to understanding how this particular structural weakness, alongside the persistence of political instability and conflict as well as regional inequalities greatly affect the economic functionality of the region.

Table 6.8 Corruption Perceptions Index* (Transparency International 2011 estimates)

		Rank	Score			Rank	Score			Rank	Score
1	Qatar	22	7.2	8	Jordan	56	4.5	15	Syria	129	2.6
2	UAE	28	6.8	9	Turkey	61	4.2/10	16	Lebanon	134	2.5
3	Israel	36	5.8	10	Tunisia	73	3.8	17	Yemen	164	2.1
4	Bahrain	46	5.1	11	Morocco	80	3.4/10	18	Libya	168	2
5	Oman	50	4.8	12	Egypt	112	2.9	19	Iraq	175	1.8
6	Kuwait	54	4.6	13	Algeria	112	2.9	20	Sudan	177	1.6
7	Saudi Arabia	57	4.4	14	Iran	120	2.7/10	21	Palestine	N/A	N/A

* The index, developed by Transparency International, is based on the perceived corruption of a country's public sector.
Rank: out of 183 states, with 1/183 least corrupt and 183/183 as most corrupt.
Score: out of 10, with 0/10 as most corrupt and 10/10 as least corrupt.

Alternative Economic Measurements and the Middle East

Whilst the above picture paints a reasonably clear picture of the regional economy, there are other ways of measuring economic development. The conventional measures of focussing on factors such as Gross Domestic Product (GDP) and Gross National Product (GNP) as well as data such as life expectancy, trade figures, income and other factors can be supplemented by new measures. These new measures have grown out of criticisms of particular models of development that have been seen as representative of an imposition of a neoliberal model of economic development with the centrality of economic growth. However, more recent understandings of development seek to focus on the welfare of humans within this system.

The Human Development Index and the Millennium Development Goals

This has been represented in a shift in focus on the part of international organisations towards alternative models of understanding economic development. The most prominent examples of this are the Human Development Index (HDI) and the Millennium Development Goals (MDG). The United Nations have been central here, particularly the United Nations Development Programme (UNDP), which produces reports measuring states according to the HDI in their annual Human Development Reports (HDR). The HDI and HDR employ a model of understanding of development first articulated by Harvard Professor and Nobel Laureate in Economics, Amartya Sen.

The original 1990 Human Development Report outlined how 'technical considerations of the means to achieve human development – and the use of statistical aggregates to measure national income and its growth – have at times obscured the fact that the primary objective of development is to benefit people' (UNDP, 1990: 9). As a result, new metrics should seek to include figures on 'better nutrition and health, greater access to knowledge, more secure livelihoods, better working conditions, security against crime and physical violence, satisfying leisure hours, and a sense of participating in the economic, cultural and political activities of these communities' (UNDP, 1990: 9). As such, the HDI was developed to try to measure the ability of people to make choices and have opportunities in all aspects of life. This broadens out from measuring income towards other key indicators (what the UNDP defines as key dimensions) such as life expectancy (health), knowledge (education) and living standards (income).

Table 6.9 Human Development Index* (2011)

		Rank	Score			Rank	Score			Rank	Score
1	Israel	17	0.888	8	Lebanon	71	0.739	15	Egypt	113	0.644
2	UAE	30	0.846	9	Iran	88	0.707	16	Palestine	114	0.641
3	Qatar	37	0.831	10	Oman	89	0.705	17	Syria	119	0.632
4	Bahrain	42	0.806	11	Turkey	92	0.699	18	Morocco	130	0.582
5	Saudi Arabia	56	0.770	12	Tunisia	94	0.698	19	Iraq	132	0.573
6	Kuwait	63	0.760	13	Jordan	95	0.698	20	Yemen	154	0.462
7	Libya	64	0.760	14	Algeria	96	0.698	21	Sudan	169	0.408

* The index, developed by the United Nations Development Programme, is based on three 'dimensions' (health, education and living standards) and four 'indicators' (life expectancy at birth, mean years of schooling, expected years of schooling and gross national income per capita).

Rank: out of 187 states, with 1/183 the highest rank and 183/183 as the lowest.

Score: out of 1, with 1 the highest and 0.000 the lowest.

This resulted in the development of metrics used by other groups, such as Freedom House (see Chapter 5), to measure and quantify standards relating to health, education and the standard of living to gauge new notions of 'development' outside previous emphases on, for instance, GDP or levels of debt. From this, countries are given a score of between 0 (lowest) and 1 (highest) on the HDI, then ranked out of 187 states' measures (see Table 6.9). As the statistics outlined in the previous section, there are a variety of conclusions that can be drawn from the HDI statistics in the Middle East.

Table 6.10 Human Development Rankings (2011)

Very High Human Development (1–47)	High Human Development (48–94)	Medium Human Development (95–141)	Low Human Development (142–187)
Israel (17)	Saudi Arabia (56)	Jordan (95)	Yemen (154)
UAE (30)	Kuwait (63)	Algeria (96)	Sudan (169)
Qatar (37)	Libya (64)	Egypt (113)	
Bahrain (42)	Lebanon (71)	Palestine (114)	
	Iran (88)	Syria (119)	
	Oman (89)	Morocco (130)	
	Turkey (92)	Iraq (132)	
	Tunisia (94)		

For instance, the states of the Middle East sit across the spectrum of rankings, with a number achieving what the UNDP refers to as 'very high human development' through to 'low human development' (see Table 6.10). The presence of oil revenues is a partial indicator of development here, with the UAE and Bahrain scoring 'very high' and Saudi Arabia, Kuwait, Libya, Iran and Oman scoring 'high', there are also oil-producing states scoring 'medium' (Algeria and Iraq) as well as 'low' (Sudan). Again, this does not paint the entire picture, with many regional states clustered at the lower end of the HDI. In addition, and as outlined below, this also illustrates problems with the HDI in that regional states towards the top of the list have been able to offset the lack of democratic freedoms in these states.

The United Nations Millennium Declaration, 18 September 2000

We consider certain fundamental values to be essential to international relations in the twenty-first century. These include: freedom ... , equality ... , solidarity ... , tolerance ... , respect for nature ... , shared responsibility ... . In order to translate these shared values into actions, we have identified key objectives to which we assign special significance: peace, security and disarmament ... , development and poverty eradication ... , protecting our common environment ... , human rights, democracy and good governance ... , protecting the vulnerable ... , meeting the special needs of Africa ... , strengthening the United Nations ... .

Another attempt to calibrate measures of economic development have been the Millennium Development Goals (MDG), delivered by the United Nations in September 2000. The MDG were an effort by the UN member states (all of whom endorsed General Assembly Resolution A/RES/55/2) and 23 international organisations to codify a set of development goals around eight priority areas to be achieved by 2015: eradicating extreme poverty and hunger; achieving universal primary education; promoting gender equality and empowering women; reducing child mortality rates; improving maternal health; combating HIV/AIDS, malaria and other diseases; ensuring environmental sustainability; and developing a global partnership for development.

In terms of regional statistics, the relationship between the MDG and the Middle East paints another varied picture (see Table 6.11). For instance, poverty rates in the region have risen across the region over the past 15 years, making the achievement of the 1.5% regional target by 2015 highly unlikely. This is a situation that has been compounded by the turmoil associated with the global financial crisis as well as the ramifications of the volatility associated with the 'Arab Spring'. However, this can be contrasted with the progress made on other indicators, such as efforts to expand primary education as well as the reduction of child mortality. Here, the region as a whole will come close to the forecast targets.

Table 6.11 Selected Millennium Development Goal Targets

Goal	1995 level	2010 level	2015 target
Eradicating extreme poverty and hunger	3.5%	4.5%	1.5%
Achieving universal primary education	84.5%	91.0%	100.0%
Reducing child mortality rates	73 per 1000	32 per 1000	28 per 1000

What these figures again indicate is a varied regional economic picture. In traditional economic terms, the region is again going through a period of intense turmoil, due in part to the fragility of the region's economic and political structures, the general fragility of the global economy as well as the momentous political change that has been sweeping the region since 2010. This varies across the states of the region, with solid economic growth, for instance, in Turkey and Morocco offset by the stagnation of economic development in Yemen and Iran. When this understanding of development is broadened out to include other factors, the future looks somewhat brighter, with improvements in the levels of education and health standards across the region. However, combined with the persistence of closed political systems and wealth inequality both within states and across the region, development of the economies of the Middle East will continue to be a defining feature in regional politics for decades to come.

THE POLITICS OF OIL

Views of the Middle East are most often seen, rightly or wrongly, in terms of the most definitive feature of the region's economic landscape, oil. Either directly or indirectly, oil is the central element of the economies of the Middle East whether this is through a state's production of oil, the use of oil revenue for economic assistance, or the ramifications of oil price fluctuations for the region's economy. In addition, the importance of oil to the global economy is a key factor shaping the way external powers have engaged with the states of the Middle East.

As such, the 'politics of oil' is as much about the logistics of extraction and production as it is about the power dynamics involved in controlling this most valuable of resources. Therefore, the politics of oil is a deeply controversial element in regional affairs. The impacts of oil on the region's economy are mixed. As stated by the 2002 Arab Human Development Report, the Arab world is seen as 'richer than it is developed' (AHDR, 2002: 7), a statement designed to highlight the 'disjunction between the region's material wealth and its real levels of human development' (2009: 99).

The Establishment of the Oil Economy in the Middle East

Oil was first discovered in Iran in 1908, an event that immediately gained the attention of the major European powers and culminated in a confrontation between the British, Germans and Ottomans for control of the new oil pipeline at the outbreak of World War I (Owen, 2008: 1). This was followed by the discovery of oil in 1927 around the city of Kirkuk in the then British Mandate of Iraq. Production on new discoveries began in Bahrain in 1932, Saudi Arabia in 1938 and the Persian Gulf by the early 1940s. This saw the Middle East become a focus of great power concern on the eve of World War II (Halliday, 2005: 270).

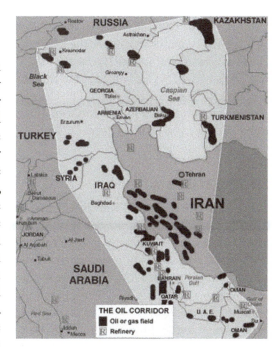

Figure 6.4 Major oil fields in the Middle East
Source: Online Opinion

The timing of the discovery of oil was important as it came at the same time as the formation of the state system in the region. As such, there was a 'symbiotic relationship' between the state system and the oil economy in the region 'that makes it virtually impossible to imagine one without the other' (Owen, 2008: 3). Therefore, in the oil-producing states, particularly the weaker, smaller states of the Gulf, domestic politics came to revolve almost exclusively around the generation and distribution of oil revenues rather than a diversified economy with a reliable and consistent source of tax revenue (Luciani, 1990: 65).

> An estimated 35 million people live in the states of the Gulf Cooperation Council (Bahrain, Kuwait, Oman, Qatar, Saudi Arabia and the UAE). Of these, around 13 million (37%) are **foreign-born workers** and their families.
> This is a demographic that varies from state to state in terms of proportions (with the largest number in the UAE, where an estimated 85% of the population are foreign-born) as well as origins (a larger proportion of Arab workers, particularly Yemenis and Palestinians, in Saudi Arabia and Kuwait, as opposed to South Asians in the UAE).

Oil income not only underwrites the economies of oil-producing states, the flow-on effects have ramifications for the entire region as well as for the global economy. Oil producers therefore operate within the context of global pressures (i.e. supply and demand), particularly in terms of meeting global demand with stable supply. It is within these parameters that oil producers make oil policy. As such, oil prices are affected by the policies of oil producers but also by global demand, oil speculation, global stability and other factors.

The 'Resources Curse'

Whilst the abundance of the world's most valuable resource would seem like a boon for any state, there is also a downside, often understood as the 'resources curse'. As discussed in Chapter 5, the wealth generated by oil revenues has enabled many states to buttress non-democratic forms of rule through the rentier state. In addition to the political impacts of oil revenues, there has also been 'an uneven and unsatisfactory process of economic development' (Owen, 2008: 2). For Mahdavy, the resources curse essentially revolves around the ability of states to rapidly fund development and industrialisation, however this comes along with a mitigation of the push for political reform (1970: 428). In addition, this development is often done without proper planning or done appropriate to the local context.

Table 6.12 World Oil Prices (US$ per barrel)

1945	$12.51	1958	$15.43	1971	$11.85	1984	$59.43	1997	$25.52
1946	$12.29	1959	$15.29	1972	$12.72	1985	$54.95	1998	$16.74
1947	$18.24	1960	$13.75	1973	$15.98	1986	$28.25	1999	$23.14
1948	$17.72	1961	$12.90	1974	$50.41	1987	$34.82	2000	$35.50
1949	$16.01	1962	$12.76	1975	$45.98	1988	$27.06	2001	$29.61
1950	$15.23	1963	$12.61	1976	$48.25	1989	$31.53	2002	$29.84
1951	$14.11	1964	$12.43	1977	$49.24	1990	$38.94	2003	$33.62
1952	$13.81	1965	$12.23	1978	$46.13	1991	$31.51	2004	$43.46
1953	$15.47	1966	$11.89	1979	$93.41	1992	$29.54	2005	$59.89
1954	$15.39	1967	$11.56	1980	$95.89	1993	$25.20	2006	$69.32
1955	$15.45	1968	$11.09	1981	$84.80	1994	$22.90	2007	$74.90
1956	$15.23	1969	$10.53	1982	$73.30	1995	$23.95	2008	$96.91
1957	$14.47	1970	$9.94	1983	$63.65	1996	$28.26	2009	$61.67

There is also an intra-regional dynamic to the resources curse where those in the non-oil-producing states have become increasingly resentful of their rich regional neighbours. Here, this is illustrated in the stark differences in the GDP from state to state, a situation that is illustrated clearly in the differences in per capita GDP (see Table 6.2).

Whilst the resources curse, or more generally the rentier dynamic, is a useful analytical tool for understanding the dynamics of oil economies, it does mask a level of complexity. For instance, Abu Dhabi and Dubai, the largest of the two Emirates in the UAE, have managed to develop reasonably diversified economies since the 1970s, including transport, tourism, investment, real estate and other service sectors outside oil production. However, the ability of the UAE government to provide the infrastructure for this diversification was initially provided by oil resources. It has also led to the UAE government, along with those in Qatar, Saudi Arabia and elsewhere, to maintain closed political systems as well as exclude the large migrant worker populations in these states from gaining citizenship.

The West and Middle East Oil

After the British–German–Ottoman confrontation in Iran on the outbreak of World War I, Britain became the dominant player in the exploitation of oil supplies in the Middle East. The British colonial presence in the Gulf, established as a security and trade measure vis-à-vis their colonial holdings in India, allowed them to exploit newly

Figure 6.5   From left: The Ghawar oil field in eastern Saudi Arabia, the largest proven
oil reserve in the world and the Saudi ARAMCO refinery at the Ghawar Field

Source: Swart, Peter K. et al. (2005) 'Origin of Dolomite in the Arab-D Reservoir from the
Ghawar Field, Saudi Arabia: Evidence from Petrographic and Geochemical Constraints', *Journal
of Sedimentary Research*, 75 (3): 477, ARAMCO.

discovered deposits in Iran, then the Gulf. British power was built on a series of treaties
established between 1820 and 1899 and a 1915 security treaty with the Saudi dynasty
whilst also dictating the formal political borders between Saudi Arabia, Iraq and Kuwait
with the 1922 Treaty of al-`Aqeer (Potter, 2008). Through this treaty, the British ena-
bled the Saudis to extend their authority over the peninsula by 1927. However, the
British presence in the Gulf was not a formal colonial relationship, but one administered through a series of relationships with the local tribal leaders, a dynamic that was
replicated with the establishment of the states in the region on their independence.

Unlike the rest of the Gulf and Iran, oil production in Saudi Arabia was linked
to the US from the very beginning. The first oil contract was won by Standard Oil
of California (Socal, now Chevron) in 1933, a concession that would become an
established oil field by 1938 (Bronson, 2006: 15). Standard Oil already had a presence in the region, running a profitable well in Bahrain since 1932. The relationship
between the US and Middle East oil is perhaps one of the most controversial aspects
of regional politics. It is an issue replete with uncertain intentions and controversial
strategic calculations. However, putting aside more conspiratorial allegations of US
intentions in the Middle East, that the US requires both access to and stability of

Table 6.13   Oil Production in the Middle East (2011)

		%WP*	BPD**			%WP*	BPD**			%WP*	BPD**
1	Saudi Arabia	10.0%	8.800	6	Libya	2.6%	2.210	11	Sudan	0.1%	0.112
2	Iran	4.8%	4.172	7	Saudi Arabia	2.5%	2.125	12	Tunisia	0.1%	0.091
3	UAE	3.3%	2.798	8	Egypt	0.8%	0.681	13	Turkey	0.06%	0.053
4	Kuwait	3.0%	2.494	9	Syria	0.5%	0.400	14	Bahrain	0.06%	0.049
5	Iraq	2.9%	2.399	10	Yemen	0.3%	0.288	15	Israel	0.01%	0.004

* %WP = percentage of world production.

** BPD = barrel per day (million, e.g. 8.800 = 8,800,000; 0.681 = 681,000).

Middle East oil is not a mystery. For instance, the Carter Doctrine of 1980 stated that 'an attempt by any outside force to gain control of the Persian Gulf region will be regarded as an assault on the vital interests of the United States of America'.

In this regard, US concern for control of regional oil, or at least reliable and stable access and pricing, does not stem from a strict 'reliance' on regional oil supplies. By the 1970s, the US moved from a net exporter to a net importer of oil. However, of the total 329,000 barrels per day imported by the US, around 81,000 barrels, or 25%, comes from the Middle East. This is not reliance *per se*. Instead, underwriting stability and maintenance of leverage over oil producers is perhaps more vital to US interests than the purchase of oil.

Oil Companies and Oil Politics

Central to the oil industry are the oil companies. Here, control over oil has often played itself out in control over these companies, often through the nationalisation of oil industries. In the Middle East, there were nationalisations in Iran in 1951, Iraq in 1961 and Egypt in 1962. However, a more common occurrence has been government intervention in controlling the distribution of oil leases, at times based on political rather than economic considerations. This was a feature of the Libyan oil market under the Gaddhafi regime from 1979 to 2011. Alternatively, governments have also established holdings in jointly owned oil companies, such as the Saudi Arabian Oil Company (ARAMCO).

Case Study: ARAMCO

Founded in 1933, soon after the establishment of the Saudi state, ARAMCO holds the largest proven reserves of crude oil of any company (including Ghawar Field, the largest proven oil field in the world) as well as the largest 'downstream' network of refining facilities globally. In 2010, ARAMCO made an estimated $182 billion dollar profit, with the company worth an estimated nearly $800 billion dollars, making it one of the largest companies in the world.

According to *Forbes* magazine, **oil companies** make up nine of the top 20 most valuable publicly listed companies in the world in 2012. This includes Exxon Mobil (US, No. 1), Royal Dutch Shell (Netherlands, No. 4), PetroChina (China, No. 7), Petrobras-Petróleo Brasil (Brazil, No. 10), BP (UK, No. 11), Chevron (US, No. 12), Gazprom (Russia, No. 15), Total (France, No. 18) and BNP Paribas (France, No. 20).

In addition, oil companies make up 10 of the top 20 leading companies by revenue. This includes Exxon Mobil (No. 1), Royal Dutch Shell (No. 2), BP (No. 4), Sinopec (China, No. 6), Chevron (No. 7), ConocoPhillips (US, No. 8), PetroChina (No. 11), Total (No. 12), ARAMCO (No. 16) and Gazprom (No. 17).

In the early 1930s, Standard Oil of California (Socal) and, later, the Texas Oil Company (Texaco), Standard Oil of New Jersey (Esso) and Socony Vacuum (Mobil) were granted concessions in eastern Saudi Arabia creating the California–Arabian Standard Oil Company (US ARAMCO). As the oil field became increasingly profitable through the 1940s, pressure from Saudi King Abdul Aziz ibn Saud saw an agreement struck where 50% of ARAMCO's profits would go to the Saudi regime.

Figure 6.6   The headquarters of Saudi ARAMCO in the city of Dhahran, eastern Saudi Arabia

Source: Virtual Tourist

As is outlined below, the 1973 oil price crisis saw the Saudi government acquire a 25% stake in US ARAMCO, taking a 100% stake in the company by 1980. Saudi ownership of the company was completed in 1988 through changing the name of the company to Saudi ARAMCO. Here, whilst the company is officially a privately owned enterprise, it has no shareholders and is essentially a state-owned oil company.

OPEC

The Organisation of Petroleum Exporting Countries (OPEC) emerged out of efforts by oil producers to coordinate production levels and take control of pricing. The original members of OPEC (Iran, Iraq, Kuwait, Saudi Arabia and Venezuela) were later joined by a number of other states, including Qatar, Libya, the UAE and Algeria. The rationale of the organisation was to ensure greater local control over production and pricing, and has also enabled OPEC members to not only affect global oil supplies but also impact on global economic stability. By the late 1960s, OPEC members became increasingly activist in the face of sustained low oil prices. As such, they began pressuring oil consumers as well as major oil companies by limiting supply as a means of increasing the price on the global market.

The 1973 Oil Price Crisis

As was discussed in Chapter 4, the 1973 October War involved not just military action by Egypt and Syria but also a broader coordination with Arab oil-producing states. The Arab oil-producing states, operating through OPEC and its associated network OAPEC (the Organisation of Arab Petroleum Exporting Countries), imposed an oil embargo on the US in response to President Nixon's announcement of his intent to send air supplies to Israel. This embargo was later extended to the Netherlands as the major port for oil to Europe.

> The **Organisation of Arab Petroleum Exporting Countries** (OAPEC) was founded in 1968 by Kuwait, Libya and Saudi Arabia joined later by Algeria, Libya, Egypt, Syria and Iraq.

By late October, the price of oil increased dramatically from $3 to $12 per barrel, causing oil shortages across the world and prompting both an inflationary spike in prices of related industries as well as triggering successive global recessions through the late 1970s and 1980s. More dramatically for the Middle East, the sharp rise in oil prices saw a massive influx of revenue into the oil-producing states.

This event was also seminal in shaping US engagement with the Middle East. As oil shortages swept across the country, there were flow-on effects throughout the US economy driving it into recession. This convinced many within the US government, particularly those within the Nixon administration such as then head of the Office of Economic Opportunity Donald Rumsfeld and his senior staffer Richard Cheney, both later key members of the Reagan, George H.W. Bush and George W. Bush administrations, of the need to avoid similar events happening in the future. As such, it was control over the supply of regional oil and the stabilisation of the price of oil rather than reliance on oil supply that have shaped US oil policy in the Middle East since this time.

LIBERALISATION AND REFORM

Framing these dynamics has been the pressure for economic reform in the Middle East. In particular, these pressures have centred on economic liberalisation, or the process of removing government regulation and restrictions on private ownership. The logic for this centres on the argument that 'public enterprises are less efficient that private ones' and more vulnerable to corruption (Ayubi, 1999: 329). The flip-side of this argument is that the private sector is the antithesis of this public inefficiency and corruption, providing the necessary competition to foster employment and economic development.

This is an ideological approach accompanied by a 'neoliberal' view of the global economic system. Neoliberal views of development focus on four categories that shape policy choices and priorities. These are the centrality of the individual as a rational actor, an unrestricted global market as the best mechanism for the distribution of wealth to these individuals, limiting the role of the state's potential to distort the logic of the market, and democratic systems that would, ideally, act to limit the potential for the state to interfere in the market (Dodge, 2009: 275). In simpler terms, neoliberalism focuses on unhindered individual choice in an unrestricted marketplace where the exercise of state power is to be minimised as much as possible, particularly in relation to economic activity.

Liberalisation and Globalisation

A common theme of globalisation has been the notion of the 'state in retreat'. That is, the globalising trends forcing the state to withdraw from previously held roles, with the privatisation of nationalised industries, for instance, as a key sign of this. However, for many there is another dynamic at work whereby the processes of globalisation, particularly the privatisation of state ownership, actually represents the resilience of the authoritarian state. That is, the state can 'still maintain its control over the economy and the accumulation and distribution of wealth through its informal patronage networks' (Guazzone and Pioppi, 2009: 6) (see Chapter 5).

As such, 'the restructuring of Arab states in response to neoliberal globalisation is characterised by the emergence and gradual consolidation of a new model of authoritarian political regime, in which the state increasingly represents the sum of the private interests of the members of the regime and is less and less accountable to its own citizens (i.e. privatisation of the state). This development is characterised by a fragmentation of the power structure and by an increase in informal modes of government (such as neo-patrimonialism and corruption), with a parallel political and economic marginalisation of large social sectors' (Guazzone and Pioppi, 2009: 7–8).

The Dynamics of Neoliberal Reforms in the Middle East

Therefore, this is a process of state restructuring along the lines of 'neoliberal' principles. From the 1990s, all states across the region implemented reforms ostensibly in pursuit of the goals that these liberalising reforms offered. This was in contrast to the expansion of state ownership, or what Nazih Ayubi has referred to as *étatisme*, from the 1950s to the 1970s (Ayubi, 1999: 329). These reforms were framed within the context of 'opening up' (*infitah*) policies where publicly owned enterprises were privatised. As previously outlined, state-owned industries, many of which were nationalised after independence, were sold. This occurred alongside reforms that were designed to remove state regulations over private ownership.

Where this was a process designed primarily around an economic logic, neoliberal doctrine also assumed that the removal of state regulations and diminishing state ownership of industry would lead to an opening up of the political system. That is, political liberalisation flowing from economic liberalisation. As such, these processes of moving control out of the state and into the private sphere were also one of diminishing control, *ergo* diminishing sovereignty.

For authoritarian states, loss of control presents a considerable challenge as this process may open up alternative avenues through which challenges to authority can be presented, whether this be through media and information technologies, professional exchanges, or a more complex process leading to the broadening of social awareness. Therefore, it has been a common assumption within both policy circles and the academy that this dynamic will inevitably lead to a challenge to the authoritarian structures such as those that have proven resilient in the Arab world.

However, as recent research has shown, apparent economic reforms across the Arab world have not only masked a lack of political liberalisation, but also the ability of states to retain control over sections of the economy. In terms of the persistence of authoritarianism, privatisation processes across the Middle East have 'represented a chance for ruling elites to reorganise or, better, shift patronage networks towards the private sector without undermining the power of the state as the ultimate source of rent' (Guazzone and Pioppi, 2009: 5). That is, whilst the formal mechanics of state control may be diminishing, these states are able to not only adapt but potentially thrive in a new environment where their control is outsourced through unofficial channels, the informal economy, whilst taking on the trappings of economic and political reform.

The Politics of 'Structural Adjustment'

Despite the persistence of authoritarianism under these reforms, they have guided the way in which global institutions, such as the World Bank and the IMF, judge economic development. These views impact regional economies and livelihoods through the imposition of structural adjustment programmes (SAPs). SAPs are a set of policies that states must follow in order to qualify for World Bank and IMF financing.

SAPs are framed in terms of the guiding principles of privatisation and economic liberalisation to promote export-led growth, requiring a devaluation of the local currency, deregulation of import and export restrictions (such as tariffs) and limits to governmental spending (including state subsidies and welfare programmes). Compliance with these measures, based on neoliberal views of economic development that emphasise production and global trade, enable states to qualify for lower interest rates on IMF loans. These reforms also emphasise privatisation of state-owned industries as well as deregulation of government oversight on the private sector.

Examples of Structural Adjustment Programmes (SAPs) and Pressures for Neoliberal Economic Reforms in Egypt, Yemen and Iraq

In the wake of the collapse of the Mubarak regime in 2011, the US Agency for International Aid and Development (USAID) contracted a $283 million reform project for the Egyptian agricultural sector. The release of these funds was conditional on the drafting of new laws to deregulate ownership of agricultural industries as well as the removal of food subsidies of basic foodstuffs. This has fed into a sharp inflationary trend on basic foodstuffs in the wake of the Tahrir uprising.

In 2007, the World Bank approved a $50 million loan to Yemen for economic reform. Key conditions of this finance included a new land registration law requiring citizens to hold legal titles for land ownership. However, many Yemenis did not possess formal land titles, having possession based on tribal modes of ownership. Thus, these reforms led to these communities effectively becoming dispossessed.

After the 2003 US-led invasion and occupation of Iraq, the Coalition Provisional Authority implemented 'General Order 39', officially as a response to UN Security Council Resolution 1483 (2003), that removed government controls and regulation on the Iraqi private sector, including the oil industry. These reforms facilitated unlimited foreign ownership of local industries as well as no regulation on sending funds generated by Iraqi industries overseas.

These programmes are deeply controversial. For instance, where currency devaluation is designed to promote spending on domestic goods to prompt greater demand, therefore greater employment, it also reduces the country's spending power. As many of these countries lack the infrastructure to meet local demand, they need to import either goods or the equipment necessary to produce these goods, necessitating loans that indebt the government even more (as they are paying it off in their local, and devalued, currency). Therefore, there is an inflationary trend, particularly on basic goods, thus, these policies tend to hurt poorer sections of society.

Spending cuts are the centrepiece of SAPs. With adjustment programmes often being implemented in countries with significant state spending programmes, they result in cuts to programmes such as health, education and welfare, thus, these cuts tend to hurt poorer citizens. This has been felt particularly in those states that pursued the largely failed state-led development programmes from the 1950s and 1960s such as Algeria, Egypt and Syria.

The **Washington Consensus** was a term coined by British economist John Williamson to define the bases for the way the IMF and the World Bank understood economic development. This revolved around a focus on the avoidance of GDP deficits, a removal of state subsidies, broadening the tax base, market-based (rather than state-regulated) interest rates, devaluation of currencies, trade liberalisation, deregulation of foreign direct investment, privatisation, broader deregulation and legal protection for private property.

Another detrimental effect of these reforms has been the focus on export-led growth. Here, countries receiving SAP funding are encouraged to export more goods in order to generate funds to pay off public debt. The increase in supply of these goods leads to a decrease in their price, forcing more production to keep money coming into the economy. As mentioned above, this leads to already fragile economies becoming more reliant on single commodities with the volatility associated with this. In addition, many states must take out loans to develop these industries, putting them further into debt and therefore reliant on SAP guidelines.

The Politics of US Aid in the Middle East

Alongside efforts towards breaking stagnant economic cycles has been direct state-to-state financial assistance. After the Cold War, this has been an area dominated by the United States, particularly through the United States Agency for International Development (USAID) and, more recently, the Middle East Partnership Initiative (MEPI), the Millennium Challenge Corporation (MCC), as well as smaller programmes through agencies such as the National Democratic Institute (NDI) and the International Republican Institute (IRI). Here, there have been links to the aforementioned pressures towards neoliberal economic reforms. However, this has also been overlaid with the even more controversial elements of military aid and its relationship to the broader strategic priorities of the United States in the Middle East.

The United States is the largest provider of financial assistance to the Middle East, with Middle Eastern states high on the list of global recipients of US financial assistance. For instance, of the estimated total of $25 billion of total aid, the states of the region receive around one-third. However, exact figures are hard to verify as financial assistance can include not only official aid programmes across both economic and military assistance as well as contributions from the private sector.

Here, US aid policy is ostensibly linked to development goals. The most recent articulation of this was the implementation of the US Global Development Policy at the 2010 Summit on the UN Millennium Development Goals. Here, President Obama outlined changes to the US approach to aid in line with those articulated in the MDG, particularly in terms of capacity building. In this regard, there has been a noticeable shift, rhetorically at least, from the Washington Consensus model towards one more oriented around ideas of human security and related concepts.

However, as Table 6.14 suggests, there are still clear strategic calculations to US aid. These have to do with the targets of US aid vis-à-vis need. That is, many of the top recipients of US aid in the Middle East (as well as globally) are not the most in need of assistance. For instance, the ratio of aid to GDP, as outlined in Table 6.2, shows that many states who receive aid already have relatively strong domestic economies, particularly when compared with the GDP of other regional states.

Table 6.14 US Aid to Middle Eastern States (2011, US$)

		Economic Aid	Military Aid	Total	Ratio of Aid to GDP
1	Israel	0	2,994,000,000	2,994,000,000	0.7%
2	Egypt	349,500,000	1,304,300,000	1,653,800,000	1.3%
3	Jordan	362,300,000	315,900,000	678,200,000	6.6%
4	Palestine	416,600,000	133,500,000	550,100,000	4.3%
5	Iraq	325,400,000	146,400,000	471,800,000	0.4%
6	Saudi Arabia	364,000,000	0	364,000,000	0.1%
7	Sudan	218,300,000	20,300,000	238,600,000	2.2%
8	Lebanon	101,600,000	84,800,000	186,400,000	1.2%
9	Yemen	56,300,000	26,600,000	82,900,000	3.1%
10	Morocco	19,000,000	15,100,000	35,100,000	1.3%
11	Tunisia	5,500,000	20,200,000	25,700,000	1.1%
12	Oman	16,100,000	0	16,100,000	0.2%
13	Algeria	8,200,000	1,600,000	9,800,000	0.3%
14	Libya	5,700,000	0	5,700,000	0.1%
15	Turkey	5,400,000	0	5,400,000	0.1%

In addition, the aid received by these states includes large amounts of military assistance. For instance, the top two recipients of US aid in the Middle East, Israel and Egypt, receive annually nearly $3 billion and over $1.3 billion worth of military assistance respectively. This figure is far in excess of the assistance provided for democracy promotion or civil society support schemes. As such, despite efforts to shape US aid priorities around altruistic goals such as those in the MDG, aid remains a political tool for external players in the Middle East.

CONCLUSION

This discussion has shown how economic development in the region cannot be captured in single indicators. Where some states exhibit rapid economic growth, others continue to stagnate. Where some have highly diversified economies, others draw their revenue primarily from single sources. However, in many respects, the issue of oil remains the dominant theme of regional economic development and stability. Indeed, this is an issue that tempers the way the world engages with the region. Overlaying this, this chapter has shown how oil has not ensured the economic independence of the region, but has instituted a pattern of economic instability and dependency – features that have been entrenched through efforts towards economic reforms and liberalisation. Indeed, the structural adjustment of regional economies has impacted disproportionately on the poorer members of regional states, exacerbating wealth inequalities and standards of living. This has fed into renewed calls for greater social justice and support for those ideologies and groups who pursue a populist cause.

Study Questions

- What are the key features of the economies of the Middle East?
- What do different understandings of economic 'development' tell us about the economies of the region?
- What are economic structural weaknesses and how are they reflected in the region?
- What is the impact of oil on the economies of the Middle East?
- How have economic liberalisation programmes been implemented in the Middle East?
- What are the political issues associated with aid and financial assistance to the Middle East?

FURTHER READING

Henry, Clement and Springborg, Robert (2001) *Globalization and the Politics of Development in the Middle East*. Cambridge: Cambridge University Press.
An insightful examination of how both governments and societies in the Middle East have responded to the pressures of globalisation.

Owen, Roger (1992) *The Middle East in the World Economy, 1800–1914*. London: I.B. Tauris.
A seminal study on the foundations of the region's economies, providing key explanations for the structural weaknesses that now plague them.

Richards, Alan and Waterbury, John (2007) *A Political Economy of the Middle East*. Boulder, CO: Westview Press.
Based on key approaches to political economy, this volume provides useful insights into the economic dynamics of the modern Middle East.

Yergin, Daniel (2009) *The Prize: The Epic Quest for Oil, Money and Power*. New York: Free Press.

A compelling account of the history of oil and its impacts on the global economy, helping provide insight into the vital role it plays in Middle Eastern affairs.

Go to the companion website at www.sagepub.co.uk/macqueen for further material including free journal articles and links to other relevant documents.

REFERENCES

AHDR (2002) *Arab Human Development Report 2002: Creating Opportunities for Future Generations.* New York: United Nations Development Programme.

AHDR (2009) *Arab Human Development Report 2009: Challenges to Human Security in the Arab Countries.* New York: United Nations Development Programme.

Ayubi, Nazih (1999) *Over-Stating the Arab State.* London: I.B. Tauris.

Bronson, Rachel (2006) *Thicker than Oil: America's Uneasy Partnership with Saudi Arabia.* Oxford: Oxford University Press.

Dodge, Toby (2009) 'Coming Face to Face with Bloody Reality: Liberal Common Sense and the Ideological Failure of the Bush Doctrine in Iraq', *International Politics*, 46 (2–3): 253–75.

Guazzone, Laura and Pioppi, Daniella (eds) (2009) *The Arab State and Neo-Liberal Globalization: The Restructuring of State Power in the Middle East.* Ithaca, NY: Cornell University Press.

Halliday, Fred (2005) *The Middle East in International Relations.* Cambridge: Cambridge University Press.

Luciani, Giacomo (ed.) (1990) *The Arab State.* Berkeley: University of California Press.

Mahdavy, Hussein (1970) 'The Patterns and Problems of Economic Development in Rentier States: The Case of Iran', in M.A. Cook (ed.) *Studies in the Economic History of the Middle East.* Oxford: Oxford University Press.

Owen, Roger (2008) 'One Hundred Years of Middle Eastern Oil', Crown Center for Middle East Studies (Brandeis University), January.

Potter, Lawrence G. (2008) *The Persian Gulf in History.* New York: Palgrave Macmillan.

UNDP (1990) *Human Development Report 1990.* New York: United Nations Development Programme.

World Economic Forum (2011) 'Global Competitiveness'; www.weforum.org/issues/global-competitiveness.

7

The Military, Security and Politics in the Middle East

Learning Objectives

This chapter will enable a greater understanding of:

- The size and relative power of military forces across the region.
- The impacts of ongoing territorial disputes in the Middle East and North Africa.
- The significance of nuclear proliferation and the impacts of Israeli and Iranian nuclear programmes.
- The development of sub-state and trans-state terrorism and political violence in the region and its global impacts.
- The ramifications of the 'War on Terror' in the Middle East and North Africa.

TIMELINE

November 1967: Opening of the Tehran Nuclear Research Centre

1968: Israel achieves nuclear weapons capacity

30 November 1971: Iran takes possession of the islands of Abu Musa and Greater and Lesser Tunb

10 May 1973: POLISARIO Front founded

31 October 1975: Morocco occupies positions in Western Sahara

7 June 1981: Israel destroys Iraqi nuclear facility at Osiraq

1982: Hezbollah founded

June 1983: Outbreak of Second Sudanese Civil War

1984: 'Office of Services' established by Abdullah Azzam and Osama bin Laden to coordinate foreign Islamist fighters in Afghanistan

September 1986: Mordechai Vananu's disclosure of Israel's

nuclear programme revealed in *The Sunday Times*

1989: Al-Qaeda formally established in Afghanistan

30 June 1990: Omar al-Bashir appointed President of Sudan

2 August 1990: Iraq invades Kuwait

8 August 1990: US-led 'Operation Desert Shield' launched

17 January 1991: 'Operation Desert Storm' is launched to remove Iraqi forces from Kuwait

28 February 1991: Iraq unconditionally accepts UN resolutions on Kuwait invasion

1992: Osama bin Laden and al-Qaeda arrive in Khartoum, Sudan

1992: Founding of the Armed Islamic Group (GIA) in Algeria out of members of the FIS

August–September 1992: First postwar elections in Lebanon

29 December 1992: First 'official' al-Qaeda attack targeting US servicemen in Yemen

26 February 1993: Al-Qaeda associates bomb the basement of the World Trade Center, New York City

April 1996: Israeli attacks on Hezbollah targets in Lebanon ('Operation Grapes of Wrath')

May 1996: Al-Qaeda expelled from Sudan, move to Taleban-ruled Afghanistan

25 June 1996: Al-Qaeda bombing of the Khobar Towers, Dhahran, Saudi Arabia

8 June 1998: Bin Laden formally indicted by the US for conspiracy to attack US forces

7 August 1998: Al-Qaeda bombs US embassies in Nairobi, Kenya and Dar-es-Salaam, Tanzania

20 August 1998: US aerial bombing of al-Shifa pharmaceutical factory in Sudan in response to the US Embassy bombings in Kenya and Tanzania

1999: Founding of the Salafist Group for Preaching and Combat (GSPC) in Algeria out of members of the GIA

7 July 2000: Israel withdraws from southern Lebanon

12 October 2000: Al-Qaeda attack on the *USS Cole* off the coast Yemen

11 September 2001: Al-Qaeda attacks on the United States

20 January 2002: Machakos Protocol ends the Second Sudanese Civil War

August 2002: Information revealing Iran's nuclear facilities at Natanz and Arak

2003: Al-Qaeda in Iraq founded

2003: Al-Qaeda in the Islamic Maghreb founded

February 2003: Outbreak of conflict in Darfur

15–20 November 2003: Al-Qaeda bombings in central Istanbul, Turkey

14 February 2005: Former Lebanese Prime Minister Rafiq al-Hariri killed in bomb-blast in central Beirut

12 July–14 August 2006: July war between Israel and Hezbollah

14 July 2008: ICC arrest warrant issued to Sudanese President Bashir for charges of war crimes and crimes against humanity

(Continued)

(Continued)

21 May 2008: Doha Agreement giving Hezbollah a veto over all government decision-making in Lebanon

January 2009: Al-Qaeda in the Arabian Peninsula founded

12 July 2010: ICC arrest warrant issued to Sudanese President Bashir for charges of genocide

9 July 2011: South Sudan formally secedes from Sudan after January 2011 referendum

INTRODUCTION

The Middle East is often understood as a region in crisis, one gripped by a series of rolling emergencies and critical security issues. In recent years, this dynamic has been understood primarily in terms of the danger posed by weapons of mass destruction or the threat of terrorism. This section will discuss how nuclear proliferation and the increase in sub-state and trans-state terrorism have interacted with 'conventional' security concerns. This will be aimed at understanding the changing security landscape of the region.

THE MILITARY AND POLITICS IN THE MIDDLE EAST

Whilst issues relating to nuclear proliferation and sub-state and trans-state terrorism are critical, this section explores the 'conventional' security landscape of the Middle East, with a focus on state-based military power. This discussion will outline the relative military strengths of each state, as well as touch on key security issues, notably ongoing territorial disputes across the region with a focus on the tension between Iran and the UAE over the islands of Abu Musa and Greater and Lesser Tunb, Morocco's ongoing occupation of the Western Sahara, as well as the conflict in Sudan's Darfur region.

The Military Landscape of the Middle East

The Middle East is a highly militarised region, both in terms of the size and capacity of military forces as well as the role of the military in politics. As was outlined in previous chapters, the military has been deeply involved in regional politics both through direct action, such as military coups, as well as acting as agents for ruling regimes to maintain their authority.

Table 7.1 Military Expenditures (2011)

	In Dollar (US$) Terms			As % of GDP	
1	Saudi Arabia	48,531,000,000	1	Saudi Arabia	10.1
2	Turkey	17,871,000,000	2	Oman	8.5
3	Israel	16,446,000,000	3	UAE	6.9
4	UAE	15,749,000,000	4	Israel	6.5
5	Algeria	8,665,000,000	5	Jordan	5.0
6	Iran	7,044,000,000	6	Lebanon	4.2
7	Iraq	5,845,000,000	7	Syria	4.1
8	Kuwait	5,640,000,000	8	Yemen	3.9
9	Qatar	4,468,000,000	9	Algeria	3.6
10	Oman	4,291,000,000	10	Kuwait	3.6
11	Egypt	4,285,000,000	11	Morocco	3.5
12	Morocco	3,342,000,000	12	Sudan	3.4
13	Syria	2,495,000,000	13	Bahrain	3.4
14	Sudan	1,991,000,000	14	Turkey	2.4
15	Lebanon	1,754,000,000	15	Iraq	2.4
16	Jordan	1,368,000,000	16	Qatar	2.4
17	Yemen	1,222,000,000	17	Egypt	2.0
18	Libya	1,100,000,000	18	Iran	1.8
19	Bahrain	878,000,000	19	Tunisia	1.4
20	Tunisia	614,000,000	20	Libya	1.2

In terms of relative military strength, Tables 7.1 and 7.2 highlight some interesting differentials between the relative military powers of each state. For instance, in terms of military expenditure, Table 7.1 shows large military expenditures by a number of states. This is particularly pronounced amongst oil-producing states in terms of military expenditure as a percentage of GDP. Here, Saudi Arabia has by far the largest expenditure both in dollar terms as well as a proportion of GDP, with the UAE also scoring highly on both accounts.

In addition, Turkey and Israel also spend heavily on their respective armed forces. For Israel, as was outlined in Chapter 6 (Table 6.14), their military expenditure is supplemented by substantial US military aid, including arms and technical assistance. Large US military aid contributions also supplement the military budgets of Egypt and, to a lesser extent, Jordan. However, US military assistance to Egypt,

Table 7.2 The Military of the States of the Middle East and North Africa (2011 estimates)

		Personnel	Conscription	Branches
1	Egypt	799,000	Yes	Army, Navy, Air Force
2	Turkey	617,000	Yes	Army, Navy, Air Force
3	Iran	585,000	Yes	Army, Navy, Air Force, Revolutionary Guard, Basij Force
4	Syria	416,000	Yes	Army, Navy, Air Force
5	Algeria	319,000	Yes	Army, Navy, Air Force
6	Morocco	251,000	Yes	Army, Navy, Air Force
7	Iraq	227,000	Yes	Army, Navy, Air Force
8	Saudi Arabia	216,000	No	Army, Navy, Air Force, National Guard
9	Israel	176,000	Yes	Defence Force, Navy, Air Force
10	Yemen	138,000	Yes	Army, Navy, Air Force, Republican Guards
11	Sudan	123,000	Yes	Army, Navy, Air Force, Defence Force
12	Jordan	111,000	Suspended	Army, Navy, Air Force, Public Security Directorate
13	Lebanon	85,000	Yes	Army, Air Force
14	Libya	76,000	Yes	Army, Navy, Air Force
15	UAE	51,000	No	Army, Navy, Air Force, National Coast Guard
16	Tunisia	47,000	Yes	Army, Navy, Air Force
17	Oman	46,000	No	Army, Navy, Air Force
18	Kuwait	23,000	Yes	Army, Navy, Air Force, National Guard
19	Bahrain	21,000	No	Defence Force, Ground Force, Navy, Air Force, National Guard
20	Qatar	12,000	No	Army, Navy, Air Force

an estimated $1.3 billion, has come under increasing scrutiny in Washington, and remains contingent on particular foreign policy choices, including the maintenance of the peace treaty with Israel as well as refusing support to the activities of Palestinian Hamas, particularly in the Gaza Strip (see Chapter 9).

However, military expenditures do not necessarily equate to military strength. Other factors, from the size of military forces, levels of training and expertise, types of weapons, as well as backing from powerful international players all impact on the strategic landscape of the region. Here, Israel's military, particularly the Israeli

Figure 7.1 Clockwise from top left: Turkish, Egyptian, Saudi and Algerian armies
Sources: Turkish Armed Forces, Public domain, AFP, Public domain

Defence Force (IDF), is considered to be one of the most effective military forces both in the Middle East and globally due to its military hardware, strategic knowledge and expertise, foreign assistance, battle-readiness and, as is outlined below, the impact of nuclear weapons. Indeed, the large military budgets of the Arab Gulf states do not equate to powerful militaries. In terms of sheer numbers, these states lack the human resources to fill the ranks of large standing armies, such as those in Egypt, Turkey, Iran, Syria and Algeria. In addition, despite possessing the latest military equipment, the lack of training or direct military experience leaves these states largely reliant on support from the US and UK to underwrite their security. This was seen with the international response to the 1990 Iraqi invasion of Kuwait (see below) through Operations 'Desert Shield' and 'Desert Storm'.

Regional Security Issues

Confrontations over territory and borders, whether this be between states or a state facing a separatist or irredentist movement, remain key features of the security landscape of the Middle East. Here, there is overlap between 'conventional' conflict and other, more damaging forms of conflict that have impacted on civilian populations. Here, we shall outline a range of these issues, from 'cold' confrontations over territory between Iran and the UAE, active separatist conflicts with Morocco's occupation of the Western Sahara, as well as wholesale military campaigns against civilian populations with Sudan's actions in its Darfur province.

Ongoing Territorial Disputes

Unresolved issues of borders are a central dynamic of regional security. Table 7.3 outlines how many regional states are currently involved in disputes over territorial frontiers with their neighbours. Most of these disputes remain 'passive', however, with claims under diplomatic negotiation or put aside for reasons of expediency, notably for the continuation of trade and other relations as well as for reasons of regional stability and security.

Table 7.3 Active Territorial Disputes Involving the States of the Middle East and North Africa

Claimants	Disputed Territories
Algeria and Libya	Algerian–Libyan border
Algeria and Morocco	Algerian–Moroccan border
Bahrain and Qatar	Fasht ad-Dibal, Qit'at Jaradeh
Egypt and Sudan	Bir Tawil, Halaïb Triangle, Wadi Halfa
Iran and the UAE	Abu Musa, Greater and Lesser Tunb Islands
Iraq and Iran	Shatt al-Arab
Israel, Lebanon and Syria	Sheba'a Farms
Israel and Palestinian Authority	East Jerusalem, West Bank, Gaza Strip
Israel and Syria	Golan Heights
Kuwait and Saudi Arabia	Qarooh and Umm al-Maradim
Lebanon and Syria	Aasal, al-Qaa, al-Qasr, Deir al-Aashayer, Kfar Kouq, Tufail
Morocco and Spain	Ceuta, Melilla, Peñón de Vélez de la Gomera, Perejil Island
Oman and Saudi Arabia	Omani–Saudi border
Oman and Yemen	Khuriya Muriya Islands
Sudan and South Sudan	Abyei, Heglig, Kafia Kingi, Kaka
Turkey and Cyprus	The Turkish Republic of Northern Cyprus
Turkey and Greece	Imia, Kardak, Aegean Sea
UAE and Saudi Arabia	UAE–Saudi border
Yemen and Saudi Arabia	Yemeni–Saudi border
Yemen and Somalia	Socotran Archipelago

However, there are also a number of active territorial disputes. For instance, as Chapter 9 outlines, the Israeli–Palestinian and broader Arab–Israeli conflicts revolve around contested issues of territoriality, overlaid with debates concerning legitimacy and competing norms and narratives of identity politics. Also, the secession of South Sudan from Sudan on 9 July 2011 came on the back of a civil war that had raged since 1983, with an estimated 150,000 civilian deaths and charges of mass human rights violations. Indeed, the end of the war has not fully resolved this issue, with the border continually contested and intermittent fighting between the government in Khartoum and the newly independent government in Juba.

Table 7.4 Active Separatist/Irredentist Disputes Involving the States of the Middle East and North Africa

State	Separatist Movement	Movement Type	Disputed Territories
Algeria	Mouvement pour l'Autonomie de la Kabylie	Separatist	Kabylie (northern Algeria)
Iran	Al-Ahwaz Arab People's Democratic Popular Front	Separatist	Khuzestan (southwestern Iran)
Iran	South Azerbaijan National Awakening Movement	Separatist	Azerbaijan (northwestern Iran)
Iran	Kurdish Democratic Party of Iran	Irredentist	Kurdistan (western Iran)
Iran	Baluchistan People's Party	Separatist	Baluchistan (southeastern Iran)
Iraq	Patriotic Union of Kurdistan	Irredentist	Kurdistan (northern Iraq)
Iraq	Kurdish Democratic Party of Iraq	Irredentist	Kurdistan (northern Iraq)
Iraq	Iraqi Turkmen Front	Separatist	Turkmenli (central-northern Iraq)
Morocco	POLISARIO Front	Separatist	Western Sahara
Sudan	Sudan Liberation Movement	Separatist	Darfur (western Sudan)
Sudan	Justice and Equality Movement	Separatist	Darfur (western Sudan)
Sudan	Darfur Liberation Front	Separatist	Darfur (western Sudan)
Syria	Kurdish Democratic Party of Syria	Irredentist	Kurdistan (northeastern Syria)
Yemen	South Yemen Movement	Separatist	South Yemen

In addition, as Table 7.4 outlines, there are a number of active separatist movements across the region, claiming territory for the establishment of independent states. Below, we shall outline an example of an inter-state territorial dispute between Iran and the UAE over control of strategically vital islands in the Gulf and a separatist movement involving Morocco and the POLISARIO Front over control of the former Spanish colony of the Western Sahara.

Iran and the UAE: Abu Musa and the Greater and Lesser Tunb Islands

The Gulf region has been one of the most hotly disputed areas in terms of borders involving a number of major wars, including the 1980–8 Iran–Iraq War, with Iraq seeking greater access to the Gulf through the Shatt al-Arab waterway (see Chapter 3) and the 1990 Iraqi invasion and attempted annexation of Kuwait. In addition, there are lingering territorial claims involving most of the regional states as well as broader tensions between Iran and the states with large Shi`a communities, particularly Bahrain, Iraq and Saudi Arabia.

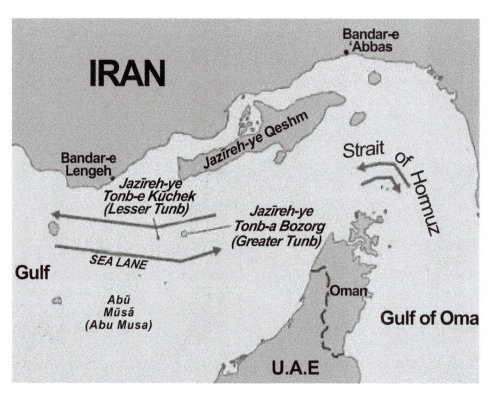

Figure 7.2 The islands of Abu Musa and Greater and Lesser Tunb

Source: Public domain

However, it is the Iranian occupation of the islands of Abu Musa and Greater and Lesser Tunb that is perhaps the most strategically consequential. Their importance lies in their strategic location, directly within the critical sea lanes through the Strait of Hormuz, the only maritime access point to the Gulf. As such, control of these islands essentially means control over access to the Gulf *ergo* control over the movement of oil and gas (see Chapter 6).

Iran had possession of the islands from the 17th century until their seizure by the British in 1921. The British withdrawal from the islands on 30 November 1971 saw the Shah's regime retake the islands despite the British formally passing control to the Emir of Sharjah, a member of the United Arab Emirates. Since this time, the UAE has pursued their claims over the islands, backed by the UK, US and Arab states, including formal legal action through the International Court of Justice. For their part, Iran maintains that the territory was illegally taken from it by the British in 1921, thus they have the valid claim over the region, including the completion of a military air base on Abu Musa in 1996. Whilst the issue remained dormant through the late 1990s and 2000s, the significance of the islands returned to the fore in 2012 when Iran threatened to forcibly close the Strait of Hormuz in response to efforts to place sanctions over their nuclear programme (Ahmadi, 2008).

Morocco and the POLISARIO Front: The Western Sahara Dispute

Whilst discussions of 'occupation' and 'security barriers' are dominated by the Israeli–Palestinian dispute (see Chapter 9), another continuing conflict has also witnessed these dynamics, that of the Moroccan occupation and attempted annexation of the Western Sahara. Under Spanish colonial rule from the 19th century, UN General Assembly Resolution 2072 of 1965 requested that a referendum on independence be held in the territory. This was contested by Morocco and Mauritania, with the former laying claim to the territory in 1957, soon after its own independence. Despite the resolution, the Spanish handed administration of the Western Sahara to Morocco on their withdrawal in 1975, leading to an ongoing conflict between Morocco and the *Frente Popular de Liberación de Saguía el Hamra y Río de Oro* (POLISARIO Front), who declared the independence of the Sahrawi Arab Democratic Republic on 27 February 1976.

Since this time, the conflict between the Moroccan government and the POLISARIO has taken a number of forms, and drawn in regional states. The POLISARIO, human rights organisations as well as the UN and EU, argue that the Moroccan occupation has resulted in numerous cases of human rights abuses inflicted on Sahrawi activists and the Sahrawi population. These have included arbitrary arrests, lengthy imprisonment without charge or trial, deaths in custody, exile and disappearances.

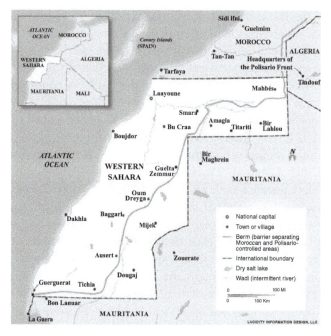

Figure 7.3 Western Sahara, including the 'Berm'

Source: Lucidity Information Designs/Carnegie Endowment for International Peace

A central mechanism of Morocco's control over the territory has been the construction of a 2700 kilometre-long wall that is bordered by landmine fields, army posts and razor wire, known as the 'Berm', which separates the interior of the country from the Moroccan-controlled central and coastal areas. The other area where Morocco has sought to impose itself on the Western Sahara has been through efforts to impose demographic change in the territory, displacing many hundreds of thousands of the Sahrawi and promoting the movement of Moroccan settlers southward.

The POLISARIO and their supporters argue that this programme of population transfer is an attempt to undercut the illegality of Morocco's occupation that rests on the Western Sahara's listing on the 1960 UN Declaration on the Granting of Independence to Colonial Countries and Peoples. This declaration requires the UN, under Chapter XI, to 'develop self-government, to take due account of the political aspirations of the peoples, and to assist them in the progressive development of their free political institutions'. This was reiterated in 1966 through Resolution 2229 that declared 'the inalienable right of the peoples of ... Spanish Sahara to self-determination'; similar resolutions at this time were passed in relation to Papua, the Trust Territory of New Guinea, East Timor and New Caledonia. In other

Figure 7.4 The 'Berm' including a Moroccan military outpost
Source: sommerwf

words, Resolution 2229 and multiple subsequent UN resolutions and rulings by the International Court of Justice have called for a referendum on independence for Western Sahara (Jensen, 2011).

However, as Spain and Morocco struck a deal for the transfer of power from the former to the latter in 1975, the chances of holding the referendum, one the UN openly admits will lead to Sahrawi independence, have slipped away. Since this time, several factors have hampered the ability of POLISARIO to press for the referendum, notably the inability of the movement to pursue its cause in the UN, the intransigence of Morocco vis-à-vis the referendum and the capacity of Morocco to resist its international obligations through the support of its key ally, the United States.

POLISARIO has relied on the Algerian government to campaign for it in the UN, a role that has been reliant on Algeria's fractured relationship with Morocco as well as the presence of the Tindouf refugee camp in southwestern Algeria, the *de facto* base of the POLISARIO and largest Sahrawi settlement outside the territory. Since a ceasefire between Morocco and POLISARIO in 1991, numerous peace plans have been tabled at the UN, the most notable being those led by former envoy James Baker in the late 1990s. However, the Moroccan government continually refused to engage the possibility of staging the referendum whilst POLISARIO reject incorporation into Morocco.

Despite the international rulings supporting the POLISARIO position, Morocco has been able to resist pressure, in large part through its strong relationship with the United States. The two states have forged a close alliance over many years, first with Morocco as a valuable Cold War ally, later as a key partner in the 'War on Terror' (see below). In addition, the US, as well as many other Western states, have continued to support the Moroccan government in favour of gaining access to the lucrative phosphate industry in the territory which is controlled by the government in Rabat (Zunes and Mundy, 2010).

Sudan and Darfur: Genocide and Separatism

Alongside inter-state conflicts and separatist uprisings, the regional security land-scape also features multilayered conflicts that involve mass humanitarian crises,

Figure 7.5 Sudan before the secession of South Sudan in July 2011
Source: Public domain

charges of genocide, and, according to some, the impacts of environmental changes. In this regard, perhaps no modern conflict exhibits all these trends as clearly as the crisis in the Darfur region in western Sudan.

Darfur is a large region, roughly the size of Spain, with an estimated population of about 6 million people divided between roughly 70 ethnic and tribal groups. From the late 1990s to the early 2000s, the region became the focus of inter-community tension and violence as a number of tribes with closer links to ethnically African communities in Chad formed two rebel movements, the Sudan Liberation Movement (SLM) and the Justice and Equality Movement (JEM), who launched attacks on government targets.

Figure 7.6 Sudanese President Omar al-Bashir

Source: PBS

The SLM and JEM accused the government of sponsoring ethnically Arab tribes and forcibly displacing indigenous peoples from the valuable arable land in the region. In response, the Sudanese government of Omar al-Bashir facilitated the transfer of arms and other supplies to a number of militia groups (known colloquially as the *janjaweed*) who embarked on a programme of ethnic cleansing across the region. *Janjaweed* raids on civilian communities were also directly supported by the Sudanese military through air strikes and the blocking of civilian escape routes.

A key tactic of the *janjaweed* was the destruction of villages and wholesale killing of communities as well as destruction of the vital economic infrastructure of the region such as livestock and water supplies. At its peak between 2003 and 2008, the UN has estimated that this conflict led to between 200,000 and 300,000 deaths as well as leaving roughly 2.7 million people displaced with a further 2 million directly affected through food shortages and a collapse of infrastructure.

This widespread humanitarian disaster, according to the United Nations Environment Programme (UNEP), has been worsened by environmental changes, including climate change. A 2007 UNEP report found that rainfall had decreased in the Darfur region by over 30% in the last 40 years in combination with the expansion of the Sahara into the remaining arable lands in western Sudan (UNEP, 2007). As a result, the scarcity of both arable land and water supplies has fostered regional tensions, driving the conflict.

Figure 7.7 Refugees from Darfur at a camp in Chad

Source: Mark Knobil

Whilst the international community has been largely unable to prevent ongoing violence in Darfur, the UN formed the United Nations African Union Peacekeeping Force (UNAMID) in conjunction with the African Union in order to deliver a measure of security and facilitate the delivery of humanitarian aid. However, it continues to struggle with the scale of the humanitarian and security disaster (Prunier, 2008). Another international response has been the indictment of President al-Bashir by the International Criminal Court (ICC) on charges of war crimes and crimes against humanity in 2008 and on charges of genocide in July 2010. Whilst Sudan is not a party to the ICC, thus technically not under its jurisdiction, UN Security Council Resolution 1593 of 2005 passed under Chapter VII makes it obligatory for Sudan to comply. This was the first arrest warrant for a standing president, however, the Sudanese government remains defiant in the face of international pressure.

THE MIDDLE EAST AND THE NUCLEAR QUESTION

Alongside these ongoing issues remains the concern over nuclear proliferation. A hallmark of Cold War tension, nuclear proliferation in the Middle East has re-emerged in recent years as a key security theme. The controversy surrounding Iran's nuclear programme after 2002 alongside the continued ambiguity around Israel's nuclear programme are key features of this controversy.

Nuclear Programmes in the Middle East

Nuclear proliferation in the Middle East has, by and large, focussed on three states, each adversaries of the other. Israel, Iraq and Iran have developed the most concerted programmes towards acquiring nuclear technology for both peaceful and weapons use. Whilst Egypt, Algeria and Saudi Arabia have all flirted with the idea of developing nuclear technology, these programmes have remained ineffectual.

In contrast, the three former regional powers have presented serious challenges to regional stability through their pursuit of nuclear technology (Bahgat, 2007: 26).

Iraq and Iran are signatories to the non-proliferation treaty (NPT) whereas Israel has never acceded to the treaty. This has raised a series of arguments and counter-arguments concerning the programmes of these respective states. Prior to the 2003 invasion of Iraq, both Iraq and Iran maintained that they were entitled to develop peaceful nuclear technology as specified under the NPT despite well-founded scepticism of the long-term intentions of the regimes in Baghdad and Tehran.

By contrast, they alleged that Israel's clandestine programme was illegal under international law, whether peaceful or not, as they were not signatories to the NPT. In contrast, Israel, despite never publicly acknowledging its programme, has maintained that it must have exceptional strategic resources such as nuclear technology, and a monopoly on these resources in the region, due to the constant threats it faces. Since 2003, Iraq has abandoned its nuclear programme, leaving Israel and Iran as the major players in this issue.

Israel's Nuclear Programme: 'Deliberate Ambiguity'

Israel's nuclear programme is unique amongst other states due to the ambiguity surrounding it. The US, UK, France, Russia, China, and in recent years India, Pakistan and North Korea were all at pains to publicise their crossing of the nuclear threshold. However, for Israel, it has consistently argued that it will not be the first state to introduce nuclear weapons to the region despite the unmistakable evidence that they are in possession of this weapons capacity. As former Israeli Prime Minister Shimon Peres has stated, the 'suspicion and fog' surrounding Israel's nuclear programme is 'constructive, because they strengthen our deterrent' (Peres, 1986).

Figure 7.8 Pictures of Israel's Dimona nuclear facility taken by dissident Mordechai Vananu in 1985

Source: Mordechai Vananu

Therefore, Israel's nuclear capability is difficult to assess despite general consensus that it achieved operational nuclear capability by the late 1960s. It has employed a strategy of deliberate ambiguity to maximise the strategic benefits of allegedly possessing nuclear weapons whilst avoiding the political consequences of this through remaining opaque about this possession. As such, it is able to avoid the obligations of declared nuclear powers under such articles as the NPT. It also helps the Israeli government avoid the questions about the legitimacy and efficacy of its nuclear programme that would arise both within Israel and through the region.

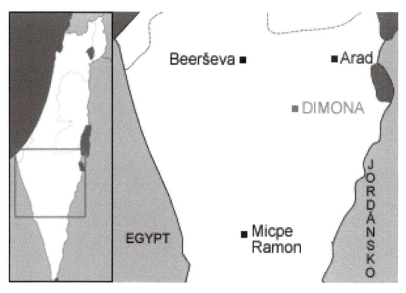

Figure 7.9 Site of the Dimona nuclear facility

Source: Public domain

According to reliable estimates, Israel's nuclear programme was developed with significant French help through the 1950s and 1960s with implicit US approval only fully emerging under the Nixon administration (Langford, 2004: 73). Previously, there had been tensions between the US and Israel over the latter's nuclear programme when President Johnson continued the pressure of his predecessor President Kennedy in seeking to compel Israel into allowing inspections of its nuclear facilities and signing the NPT (Bahgat, 2007: 36). In response, Israel allowed a small number of inspections but refused to sign the NPT. The US stance increasingly relaxed after 1967 and the defeat of what was seen as the Soviet Union's key ally in the Middle East, Nasser's Egypt. After this point, Israel's nuclear programme has largely been accepted by successive US administrations to the point where some observers have called it an 'off-limits subject for American foreign policy' (Cohen and Graham, 2004: 24).

Through the 1970s and 1980s, Israel developed their clandestine nuclear capacity at the Negev Nuclear Research Centre near the city of Dimona before the highly publicised outing of the programme by former nuclear technician Mordechai Vananu to the British media in 1986. Vananu became alienated from the rationale behind the nuclear programme after Israel's attacks on Iraq's Osiraq nuclear facility in 1981. This led Vananu to compile photographs and other evidence of Israel's nuclear programme, evidence that was published in 1986.

Figure 7.10   Mordechai Vananu after his release
Source: The Palestine Telegraph

The rationale for Israel's nuclear programme is much debated. Arguments range from the use of Israel's nuclear monopoly in the Middle East as a combination of deterrence, a negotiating tool and a means for giving Israel more strategic autonomy (Bahgat, 2007: 113). The combination of these factors strengthens Israel's bargaining position with its neighbours, particularly Syria, over potential future peace negotiations. Central to this has been the stance on the part of successive Israeli administrations since the 1960s that Israel should possess a nuclear monopoly in the Middle East, a policy supported by the US since 1979. As is outlined below, it actively supported the development of an Iranian nuclear programme under the regime of the Shah up to this point. In this regard, the discovery of the Iranian nuclear programme in 2002 has seen some change in the policy of 'deliberate ambiguity'.

Mordechai Vananu's report on Israel's nuclear programme was published by *The Sunday Times* in London in 1986, documenting the construction of thermonuclear weapons estimated today to consist of an arsenal of between 100 and 200 war heads with complementary short-, medium-, and long-range delivery capacity (Langford, 2004: 73). Vananu was subsequently kidnapped by Mossad in Rome in late 1986 and returned to Israel where he was convicted of treason in 1988. After 11 years in solitary confinement and six years in general confinement, Vananu was released in 2004 with strict limitations including a ban from leaving Israel and on talking to any media outlet.

Speaking on German television on 12 December 2006, former Israeli Prime Minister Olmert declared that Iran was a danger to regional security because of its assertion that Israel should be eliminated, and therefore should not be judged along with other nuclear states such as 'America, France, Israel, [and] Russia' (Verter, 2006). This was the first time an Israeli leader had declared Israel a nuclear state, and a move that was criticised by many within the country. In particular, critics argued that Olmert's statement, deliberate or not, overstepped the mark and potentially opened the door to give Iran and other regional states rationale for accelerating their nuclear programmes.

Iran's Nuclear Programme: Peaceful or Aggressive?

Abdul Qadeer (A.Q.) Khan is a Pakistani nuclear scientist who headed Pakistan's nuclear programme. From his position, Khan is alleged to have sold key nuclear technology and expertise to a number of states, including Iran, North Korea and Libya.

As mentioned above, Iran has a long history of seeking nuclear technology dating from the 1950s and 1967 as part of the US government's 'Atoms for Peace' programme. This led to the opening of Iran's first nuclear energy reactor, supplied by the US, in 1967 as well as Iran signing the NPT in 1968. As with recent controversies around Iran's nuclear programme, this early programme also courted options of upgrading from nuclear energy to a nuclear weapons programme, with the Shah's government seeking to acquire enrichment technology that would give it the option of moving in this direction in the future.

The 1979 Islamic Revolution saw Iran's nuclear programme put on a brief hiatus before resumption in the 1980s when Iraq's own nuclear programme was revealed. However, this programme was hindered due to the collapse of US–Iranian relations after

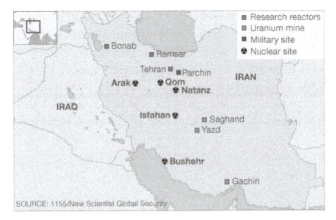

Figure 7.11 Iran's key nuclear sites
Source: Public domain

1979 where the bulk of existing nuclear technology in the country was US-supplied, with additional French and German assistance. As such, the Islamic Republic moved towards developing an indigenous nuclear programme as well as seeking assistance from Russia, China and Pakistan (Bahgat, 2007: 21–2).

Here, Russia became a key player in the Iranian nuclear programme, helping finish construction of the nuclear facility at Bushehr by the end of the 1990s, despite US pressure to halt all assistance to Iran. It was at this time that the key themes around the Iranian nuclear programme emerged that still define the debate today. Simply put, Iran has argued that its programme is legal under the NPT and International Atomic Energy Agency (IAEA) guidelines, whilst the US and others, particularly Israel, argue that Iran has no intention of limiting itself to peaceful nuclear technology, with the nuclear energy programme a stepping-stone to the eventual acquisition of nuclear weapons. For Israel, this is an unacceptable development as they see a nuclear-armed Iran as an existential threat to their state.

In order to be used for both peaceful (energy) and weapons purposes, **uranium** must be **enriched**. There are four grades of enrichment: reprocessed uranium (RepU), slightly enriched uranium (SEU, 0.9%–2%), low-enriched uranium (LEU, 2%–20%) and highly enriched uranium (HEU, greater than 20%). Most modern nuclear weapons require HEU of a grade of 85% or higher.

Enrichment is achieved through the separation of isotopes, a process that requires the use of **centrifuges**. Higher levels of enrichment can be achieved through the use of more powerful centrifuges.

Iranian claims to compliance with the NPT were undercut, however, in 2002 when it was revealed that they had secretly begun construction on a uranium enrichment facility at Natanz and a 'heavy water' facility at Arak (heavy water is used to stabilise the fission process during the production of nuclear energy). Whilst signatories to the NPT, like Iran, are required to allow the IAEA to access and inspect all nuclear sites in the country to ensure that they are not being used for the production of weapons-grade material, this only comes into effect after a plant has become active.

Israeli Prime Minister Netanyahu on the Iranian nuclear programme (9 March 2012):

The US is big and distant, Israel is smaller and closer to Iran, and – of course – we have different capabilities. ... So the American clock regarding preventing nuclearisation of Iran is not the Israeli one. The Israeli clock works, obviously, according to a different schedule. ... The result has to be that the threat of a nuclear weapon in Iran's hands is removed.

Since this time, the Iranian nuclear programme has been a key strategic issue in the Middle East, involving claims of clandestine nuclear enrichment, threats of unilateral military intervention to destroy the programme and arguments that Iran has a sovereign right to produce this technology under the NPT. This emerged particularly after the 10 November 2003 IAEA report that Iran was failing to meet its obligations in terms of the transparency of its programme and subsequent tension over the ability of IAEA inspectors to gain access and monitor facilities at Natanz and Arak.

As a result, Iran has found itself increasingly isolated, with the UN Security Council passing Resolution 1696 on 31 July 2006 that demanded a suspension of all uranium enrichment. This was a particularly important event as it was passed under Chapter VII of the UN Charter, making it legally binding on Iran and other states that were involved in the country's nuclear programme as well as facilitating sanctions under Resolution 1737 of 23 December 2006. Since this time, the IAEA has conducted a number of subsequent inspections, with a report in May 2012 revealing that there was increased enrichment activity for energy use whilst detecting traces of uranium enriched to 20%, well over the necessary limit for energy production but still short of weapons-grade levels.

This substantiated the statements made by Iranian President Mahmoud Ahmedinejad on 9 February 2010 that Iran had become a 'nuclear state', with reference to this enrichment ability for fuel production and for the use of enriched uranium for medical purposes. However, the continued ambiguity over the intent of this programme continues, with the US and Israel continuing to push for tighter sanctions, as well as leaving 'all options on the table' in terms of their warnings that any move towards weapons-grade enrichment would lead to unilateral military action.

TERRORISM AND POLITICAL VIOLENCE IN THE MIDDLE EAST

Terrorism is a contested concept, one with political implications for those who are the target of this designation. Indeed, most governments and international organisations have their own official definitions, not to mention those held by analysts and the broader community. This section will outline a brief definition of the concept, the changing nature of terrorist ideologies such as national liberation and jihadist/neo-jihadist ideologies, terrorist organisations in the Middle East, before examining the details of the so-called 'War on Terror' in the Middle East in the wake of al-Qaeda's attacks on the United States on 11 September 2001.

Defining Terrorism

For the United Nations, the lack of an agreed-upon definition has revolved around contest over what differentiates a terrorist organisation from, for instance, a national liberation movement. Here, the 2004 Secretary-General's High Level Panel Report defined terrorism as an action that 'is intended to cause death or serious bodily harm to civilians or non-combatants, when the purpose of such act is to intimidate a population, or to compel a government or an international organisation to do or to abstain from doing any act' (United Nations, 2004: 52). This is a comprehensive definition, but one that leaves a measure of ambiguity. This is particularly so in terms of clarification of whether a state can be deemed to have committed an act that falls in this definition, or so-called state terrorism.

It is on this issue that the United Nations as a whole has not officially adopted a definition such as that provided by the Secretary-General. Here, debate in the General Assembly has centred on whether or not to include a reference to state terrorism, particularly in relation to the Arab–Israeli conflict, and a reference to national self-determination. As a result, the UN is guided by 12 international treaties relating to various aspects of political violence such as financing, the movement of peoples and goods and the use of non-conventional weapons by non-state groups.

As such, much of the controversy and ambiguity surrounding the definition of terrorism extend from the question of legitimacy or, more specifically, legitimate force. This can be understood in the language around the use of violence by states and terrorist organisations. In particular, states employ legitimate violence, or force, through institutions such as the military, police force or intelligence services. By contrast, the violence employed by terrorist organisations is considered illegitimate as it is outside state-sanctioned bounds.

Understanding terrorism may be further enhanced by looking at it as a form of 'political altruism'. Whilst this may seem like a peculiar, even misplaced, phrase to use in relation to those who perpetrate political violence, it is a useful concept to differentiate these movements from other groups who use violence to achieve ends, such as criminal organisations. The altruistic element of these movements refers to their motivations where violence is used to achieve a greater aim that, in the minds of these organisations at least, will benefit a broader community. That is, these groups see themselves as working for a greater political good.

Definitions of terrorism

US Department of Defense: 'the calculated use of unlawful violence or threat of unlawful violence to inculcate fear; intended to coerce or to intimidate governments or societies in the pursuit of goals that are generally political, religious, or ideological'.

UK government: 'the use or threat, for the purpose of advancing a political, religious or ideological cause, of action which involves serious violence against any person or property'.

George Washington University Professor Walter Reich: 'a strategy of violence designed to promote desired outcomes by instilling fear in the public at large'.

Georgetown University Professor Bruce Hoffman: 'the deliberate creation and exploitation of fear through violence or the threat of violence in the pursuit of political change'.

ICJ Justice Rosalyn Higgins: 'a term without any legal significance. It is merely a convenient way of alluding to activities, whether of states or of individuals widely disapproved of and in which either the methods used are unlawful, or the targets protected or both.'

Violence is employed by organisations in different ways for specific ends. For instance, terrorist organisations can employ forms of 'mass terrorism' through acts of indiscriminate social violence, 'random terrorism' such as plane hijacking, or more 'focussed terrorism' such as attacks on military sites or targeted assassinations. Here, the violence itself is aimed at a number of targets, including those who are direct victims of the violence, the general public where groups seek to shift and polarise political views, the media where coverage of the violence is critical and governments who are the targets of terrorist demands.

As such, terrorism is a phenomenon that is broader than the act of violence itself. It requires the media for publicity in order to polarise opinion, pushing those not in support away from the movement and its ideology as well as consolidating a community of support around its message. As we shall see below, this polarisation also involves the implementation of harsh security measures by the state, further sharpening divisions and heightening tensions.

Terrorist Ideologies

Turning back to the discussion on defining terrorism, an important part of understanding these movements is that they do not operate in a vacuum. Putting aside judgements on how these groups rationalise their actions, it is important to recognise how they employ ideological justifications for their violence. In particular, these ideologies are critical in generating a community of support for these movements, communities that provide necessary legitimacy as well as the more practical elements of safe havens and supplies.

The trajectory of ideologies motivating terrorism and political violence in the Middle East has mirrored the broader shift in ideological forces in the Middle East as outlined in Chapter 5. Specifically, there has been a move from political violence employed for nationalist motivations to actions inspired by religious motivations. Here, we shall outline this shift in terms of the changing fortunes of the ideological foundations of 'national liberation' and 'Third Worldism' to that of 'jihadism' and 'neo-jihadism'.

Frantz Fanon, born in the French colony of Martinique in 1925, became a leading thinker of the anti-colonial movement through from the 1940s. He was active in the Algerian War of Independence against the French from 1954 to 1962. His most famous works include *Black Skin, White Masks* (1952), *A Dying Colonialism* (1959) and *The Wretched of the Earth* (1961). In *The Wretched of the Earth*, Fanon argued:

> The naked truth of decolonisation evokes for us the searing bullets and bloodstained knives which emanate from it. For if the last shall be first, this will only come to pass after a murderous and decisive struggle between the two protagonists. That affirmed intention to place the last at the head of things, and to make them climb at a pace (too quickly, some say) the well-known steps which characterize an organized society, can only triumph if we use all means to turn the scale, including, of course, that of violence. ... The violence which has ruled over the ordering of the colonial world, which has ceaselessly drummed the rhythm for the destruction of native social forms and broken up without reserve the systems of reference of the economy, the customs of dress and external life, that same violence will be claimed and taken over by the native at the moment when, deciding to embody history in his own person, he surges into the forbidden quarters. To wreck the colonial world is henceforward a mental picture of action. (1961: 37–9)

National Liberation

National liberation movements are those that justify actions based on claims to national self-determination. Whilst the goal of these movements has been one of independence, through the period of decolonisation there was an ideological gravitation towards particular critiques of imperialism and models of what the state should represent upon independence. This ideology was one heavily influenced by Marxist ideology, often with the active support of the Soviet Union during the Cold War. Soviet support was important, but there are important distinctions in terms of ideology. Robert Malley defines this as an ideology of 'Third Worldism ... the belief in the revolutionary aspirations of the Third World masses, in the inevitability of their fulfilment, and in the role of strong, centralised states in this undertaking' (Malley, 1996: 2). This was an all-encompassing worldview that tied national independence to a throwing off of the shackles of imperialism, hence national *liberation*.

This was an ideology that was global in scope, with movements from Central and South America, Asia, Sub-Saharan Africa and the Middle East and North Africa. Perhaps the clearest example of a national liberation movement in the region was the National Liberation Front (*Front de Libération Nationale*, FLN) that fought the French in Algeria from 1954 to 1962 as well as liberation movements amongst the Zionist movements, then the Palestinians as well as the Western Sahara (outlined above).

National liberation movements have employed a range of tactics from guerrilla warfare and attacks on military facilities through to the targeting of civilian populations through bombings and other actions. Here, these different tactics were designed to cause different reactions, whether as an effort to display the vulnerability of the colonial or state authority such as the 1946 bombing of the headquarters of the British Mandate authority in Palestine at the King David Hotel in Jerusalem by the Zionist Irgun organisation (see Chapter 3), or attacks on civilian targets such as the Palestine Liberation Front's 1985 hijacking of the *Achille Lauro*.

These movements have also traditionally been organised to avoid counter-terrorism and counter-insurgency policies. Here, movements were structured in a hierarchy where a member of a 'cell' would only be in contact with members immediately above and below. This was designed to prevent military authorities from being able to uncover all members of the organisation should one of them fall into custody. However, such 'cellular hierarchy' structures were able to be deconstructed by state intelligence agencies through the use of torture and other coercive means.

However, there have been numerous instances of success of these movements, particularly through their infiltration of key government institutions, notably the military. This was a prominent theme through the 1950s and 1960s in the Arab states where national liberation ideologies and movements were able to topple pro-Western monarchies as well as colonial authorities through military coups, leading to the installation of so-called 'radical' nationalist regimes (see Chapter 5).

Jihadism and Neo-Jihadism

As was previously mentioned, the broader ideological shifts across the region from nationalist to Islamist ideologies have been reflected in the influence and prevalence of militant organisations based on Islamist ideologies. This particular manifestation of Islamist ideology as justification for political violence can perhaps be better understood as 'jihadism' or 'neo-jihadism'.

Chapter 4 provided an outline of *jihad*, including the controversial element of *jihad bis saif* (*jihad* of the sword) as part of other understandings and applications of the concept (*jihad* of the heart/*jihad bil qalb*, *jihad* of the tongue/*jihad bil lisan*, and *jihad* of the hand/*jihad bil yad*). In addition, this discussion of *jihad* found its articulation through the work of thinkers such as Sayyid Qutb, particularly as an attempt to justify the use of violence as a defensive measure.

This ideology influenced earlier jihadist movements such as Egypt's Islamic Jihad, the group responsible for the assassination of President Anwar Sadat in 1981 led by prominent al-Qaeda member Ayman al-Zawahiri. Here, jihadist movements active in the Middle East through the 1980s were focussed primarily on attacking regional regimes as symbolic of defending local Muslim communities from abuses of power and what they saw as deviations from the path towards a realisation of a 'true' Islamic society.

The more recent manifestations have exhibited trends towards a more simplistic application of the concept, yet a more complex manifestation in terms of organisation and structure. According to Lentini, this new manifestation is something different from previous ideological motivations, and can be understood as neo-jihadism (Lentini, 2008). This form is distinct in terms of its 'multi-dimensional and syncretic' nature where violence is justified 'through highly selective and literalist (often incorrect) interpretations of sacred texts' (Lentini, 2008: 3). It has political aims in seeking to establish an

Figure 7.12 A still shot from an al-Qaeda video featuring Osama bin Laden (left) and Ayman al-Zawahiri, likely to have been taken in the border region between Afghanistan and Pakistan

Islamic community governed by the understanding of Islamic law advocated by the various spokespeople active within neo-jihadist movements.

The core religious concept within neo-jihadist movements is jihad. Here, this interpretation reinterprets the concept in a very literal sense to emphasise and elevate the notion of violence as a means to defend Muslim communities against what they see as a host of global and local threats. This understanding is grand in scope in that it rejects distinctions between direct action and complicity on the part of those it sees as its enemies. That is, citizens of countries deemed viable targets for neo-jihadi violence are complicit in the policy choices of that country's government, therefore, viable targets themselves.

Its other main theological tenet is that of martyrdom, also reinterpreted, again literally, to mean sacrificing one's life for the cause of the global *jihad*. It removes any reference to the idea of martyrdom and, indeed, *jihad*, as giving a life of service to the faith. Instead, it is focussed on the sacrifice of the physical self for the political cause.

As is discussed below, the clearest manifestation of this ideology can be found in the various writings and proclamations associated with al-Qaeda and its affiliates. Here, Betts highlights four key points that characterise this worldview: (1) Islam is under an unjust attack from the West led by the United States working through proxies such as Israel and regional (i.e. friendly Arab/Muslim) regimes; (2) the neo-jihadis are defending the Muslim world from these attacks; (3) the actions taken by neo-jihadis are defensive and, therefore, proportionally and religiously justified; and (4) it is the duty of all Muslims to support these attacks (2008: 520).

Middle Eastern Terrorist Organisations

Sub-state and trans-state terrorist organisations have been key features of the security landscape of the Middle East and North Africa for many decades. Indeed, the independence of many states, from Israel to Algeria, was achieved through the actions of such movements. This section will outline a number of these movements, with a particular focus on the Irgun during Israel's War for Independence and the Lebanese movement Hezbollah. This discussion is designed to outline the history of these movements as well as highlight the varying interpretations of these movements' actions, depending on the communities that either support or oppose their actions.

The Irgun

During the discussion of the establishment of the State of Israel in Chapter 3, there was a brief discussion of the various militant groups involved in challenging British rule. A key organisation involved in this was the *Irgun Zevaui Leumi*, or the Irgun. This organisation drew heavily from the work of Ze`ev Jabotinsky and 'revisionist

Zionism'. Central to this ideology was the belief that not only should there be a Jewish state, but that 'every Jew had the right to enter Palestine; only active retaliation would deter the Arabs; only Jewish armed force would ensure the Jewish state' (Sachar, 2003: 265–6).

The cornerstone of the Irgun's aims was the creation of a Jewish state in the original boundaries of the British Mandate of Palestine from 1920 to 1923 that covered the lands both west and east of the Jordan River (the latter forming the future state of Jordan). In pursuit of this, the organisation argued that all means, including violence against both the British and the Arab population, were both valid and necessary. This included the policy of 'active defence' of Jewish communities during the 1936–9 Arab Revolt as well as the bombing of the King David Hotel in Jerusalem in 1946. In addition, the organisation employed a public relations arm to enlist popular support for their cause.

After the establishment of the State of Israel in 1948, the new government sought to absorb all former militias into the new security structure of the state. Whilst an initial agreement was reached, the movement continued its operations independently of the new government's authority, resulting in armed clashes between members of the Irgun and the IDF. This peaked with an effort by the Irgun to import arms aboard the ship the *Altalena* in June 1948. The IDF sank the ship off the Israeli coast and arrested the bulk of the movement's fighters, seeing the leadership of the movement acquiesce to Israeli government authority.

Figure 7.13 The sinking of the *Altalena* on 20 June 1948
Source: Public domain

However, whilst this might have seen the end of the movement, its members and its ideology not only continued to be present within the Israeli political scene, but have in many ways become dominant themes. In particular, the leadership of the Irgun, including future Prime Minister Menachem Begin, founded the Herut Party in 1948, the forerunner to the Likud Party that has dominated Israeli politics since the 1990s.

Hezbollah

Along with the discussion of political violence amongst early Zionist groups, Chapter 3 also outlined the founding of Lebanon's Hezbollah in 1982. Established after the Israeli invasion of Lebanon in 1982 in the context of the Lebanese Civil War and with active support from the Islamic Republic of Iran, the movement's initial aim was both the removal of Israeli forces followed by the establishment of a Shi`a Islamic Republic in Lebanon.

From its establishment, the movement conducted large-scale terrorist attacks against IDF forces in Lebanon as well as against US targets, including the bombing of the US Embassy and the US Marines barracks in Beirut in 1983. A key tactic employed by the movement in these and other attacks was the use of suicide bombings as well as kidnappings and rocket attacks. As with the Irgun, after the end of the civil war the movement took on a more explicitly political role. However, unlike the Irgun, it has managed to maintain its militia, which is used in confrontation with

Figure 7.14   Posters in the Shi`a town of Bint Jbeil in southern Lebanon showing Hezbollah leader Hassan Nasrallah at front with Hezbollah 'martyrs'

Source: Views from the Occident

Israel as well as domestically. As outlined in Chapter 3, Lebanon has an electoral system based on confessional quotas. Here, Hezbollah became an active participant in the Lebanese electoral system as early as 1992, successfully challenging the Amal Party that had previously monopolised the Shiʾa vote.

Importantly, Lebanon's postwar settlement, the Taeif Agreement, contained explicit provisions that have facilitated the ability of Hezbollah to act in its dual role as political participant in Lebanon, forming coalition governments and supplying social services, as well as maintaining an armed wing separate to the Lebanese state. Specifically, whilst the Taeif Agreement calls for the disarming of all militias, it contains provisions relating to the necessity of 'liberating Lebanon from Israeli occupation'. Israeli withdrawal from Lebanon was further enshrined in UN Security Council Resolutions 425 (1978), 508 (1982) and 509 (1982).

Whilst Israel formally withdrew from southern Lebanon in May 2000, it continues to occupy the 25 square-kilometre Shebaʾa farms district in southeastern Lebanon. This territory, internationally recognised as part of Syria, was occupied by Israel after the June 1967 war along with the Golan Heights. The Lebanese government's claim to sovereignty over the farms district with Syrian compliance can be seen as a way to assert that Israel has not fully complied with Security Council Resolutions 425, 508 and 509 even after their withdrawal from the south of the country. This gives Hezbollah tacit exemption from disarmament called for in the Taeif Agreement as they can claim to be acting to remove Israeli occupation.

The continued confrontation between Hezbollah and Israel peaked in July 2006 when the movement attacked an Israeli border patrol, killing three IDF soldiers and taking two hostages. In response, the Olmert administration launched large-scale air strikes and artillery bombardments across Lebanon leading to over 1300 Lebanese casualties and wholesale destruction of Lebanon's infrastructure. Whilst Israel did not achieve its stated aims of destroying the movement, the Lebanese government under Prime Minister Fouad Siniora approved the adoption of UN Security Council Resolution 1701 that included, amongst other tenets, the full disarmament of all militias including Hezbollah (Norton, 2007).

After this, domestic tensions in Lebanon saw political deadlock emerge through 2007 and 2008, resulting in suspension of the government

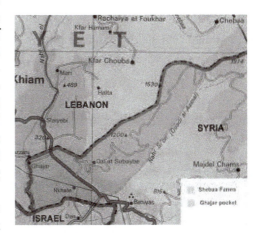

Figure 7.15 The Shebaʾa farms

Source: Crethi Plethi

Figure 7.16 From left: 8 March 2005 pro-Syrian Protests and anti-Syrian
14 March 2005 protests in Beirut's Martyr's Square

Source: Views from the Occident, Reuters/Damir Sagoli

and eventual fighting on the streets of Beirut involving Hezbollah fighters by May 2008. These tensions were based on the split within the Lebanese political system that emerged after the February 2005 assassination of former Prime Minister Rafiq al-Hariri. Al-Hariri's assassination led to massive international pressure for the withdrawal of Syrian troops that had remained in Lebanon from their initial intervention in the country in 1976. The violence of May 2008 saw all major groups sign the so-called Doha Agreement that ended the political deadlock. Whilst Hezbollah and their 'March 8 coalition' remained in opposition, they gained a veto over all major government decision-making. As such, despite the Lebanese government being bound by the provisions of Security Council Resolution 1701 for the disarmament of all militias, including Hezbollah, the movement can veto any move to that end, leaving them as a virtual 'state within a state'.

The Middle East and the 'War on Terror'

As we can see, the issue of sub-state and trans-state political violence has been an important feature of the Middle Eastern security landscape since the period of independence. However, it was the attacks on the United States on 11 September 2001 that saw the issue of terrorism take centre stage. Whilst the major impact of this has arguably been the 2003 US-led invasion and occupation of Iraq (see Chapter 8), there have been a variety of other impacts on the region.

In particular, the US has been active in providing funding, training and intelligence to a number of regional states under the banner of the 'War on Terror'. Here, US support for what were labelled as 'counter-terrorism' programmes in states such as Egypt, Saudi Arabia, Yemen, Jordan, Morocco and elsewhere has had contradictory outcomes, with a rolling back of the capacity of many militant organisations in these states but also a sharpening of tensions between Arab populations and their governments over exploitation of this environment. This will be explored below in relation to Algeria, however, it is important to first discuss the links between the perpetrators of the 11 September attacks, al-Qaeda, and the Middle East.

Al-Qaeda

The name 'al-Qaeda' literally means 'the base', a name given to the movement after it conducted the 1998 bombings against the US embassies in Kenya and Tanzania. The organisation emerged from the so-called 'Services Office', an agency active in recruiting Muslims across the world to fight against the Soviet Union after their invasion of Afghanistan in 1979. The key figures in the founding of the movement were Saudi Osama bin Laden and Palestinian Abdullah Azzam. Bin Laden was the chief financier whilst Azzam provided the ideology for the movement's *jihad* against the Soviet army.

Osama bin Laden, former leader of **al-Qaeda**, came from the wealthy bin Laden family of Saudi Arabia. The bin Laden family are owners of the Saudi Binladin Group, a conglomerate company that includes oil and finance wings as well as comprising the world's largest construction company, with a total net worth of over $5 billion.

Here, there were early links between the organisation and the US as, first, the Carter then Reagan administrations supplied funding, intelligence and, later, arms to the anti-Soviet *mujahedin* forces that included those who would form al-Qaeda. It is important to recognise here the diversity of opposition to the Soviets in Afghanistan in the 1980s, with those rallying around bin Laden and Azzam predominantly from outside Afghanistan. By the time of the Soviet withdrawal from Afghanistan in 1988–9, bin Laden formalised his control over the organisation under the banner of the 'International Front for Jihad against the Jews and Crusaders'. This new organisation began to expand its operations into Indian-controlled Kashmir and other areas. However, it was events in the Middle East that would see the organisation fully articulate its jihadist ideology as well as direct the focus of its operations against regimes in the region as well as the US.

'Operation Desert Storm' was the multinational military operation based on UN Security Council Resolution 678 (1990) authorising the use of force to remove Iraq from Kuwait.

In total, 956,600 troops were stationed in Saudi Arabia during the conflict, with the largest numbers being from the United States (697,000), Saudi Arabia (100,000), the United Kingdom (45,400), Egypt (33,600), France (14,600), Syria (14,500) and Morocco (13,000).

On 2 August 1990 Iraq invaded its neighbour Kuwait, based on Iraqi territorial claims over Kuwait that stretched back to the founding of the Iraqi state in 1932. Iraq's invasion came on the back of their devastating war with Iran from 1980 to 1988 (see Chapter 3) that involved Iraq becoming heavily indebted to the oil-producing states of the Gulf. The Iraqi regime was not looked on kindly by bin Laden and his organisation, seen as part of the broader 'infidel' socialist movement that had weakened the Islamist cause across the Middle East.

Figure 7.17   From left: the 11 September 2001 attacks on the World Trade Center Buildings in New York City, the Pentagon in Washington, DC and the crash site of United Airlines Flight 93 in Shanksville, Pennsylvania

Source: Public domain, Public domain, Public domain

In addition, bin Laden saw the Iraqi invasion as a threat to the security of the Holy Cities of Mecca and Medina within Saudi Arabia. In response, bin Laden offered to the Saudi regime the deployment of the *mujahedin* in protection of the Holy Cities and, by extension, the Saudi state. However, the Saudis refused, opting instead for the deployment of over 500,000 US and other troops first in defence of Saudi Arabia then, in 1991, the removal of the Iraqi army from Kuwait. In response, bin Laden openly called for the overthrow of the Saudi regime and increasingly turned his attention to the US as the key supporters of what he now called 'apostate regimes' (Riedel, 2010).

From 1992 to 1996, bin Laden and the leadership core of al-Qaeda operated with relative freedom from their base in Sudan's capital Khartoum. The organisation had come onto the radar of US intelligence as a terrorist organisation as well as being targeted by Egyptian, Saudi and allegedly US intelligence services for assassination. This led to bin Laden returning to Afghanistan in 1996 under the protection of the Taleban regime that had seized power earlier that year, where he planned and sought financing for a range of terrorist operations, including the attacks on the United States on 11 September 2001 (Soufan, 2011).

The Al-Qaeda 'Franchise' Dynamic
Whilst the ramifications of these attacks, the 'War on Terror', on regional politics are outlined below, events since 2001 have also seen a dramatic change in the way

this form of trans-state terrorism and political violence has manifested. In particular, there has been what some have called a 'franchising' dynamic whereby the al-Qaeda ideology has been taken up by existing organisations or led to the creation of new organisations across the region.

Al-Qaeda affiliates include:

- Egyptian Islamic Jihad (Egypt), active since the late 1970s, merged with al-Qaeda in 2001
- Al-Qaeda in Iraq (Iraq), affiliated with al-Qaeda from 2003
- Al-Qaeda in the Islamic Maghreb (Algeria, Mali, Mauritania, Morocco, Niger and Tunisia), affiliated with al-Qaeda from 2003
- East Turkestan Islamic Movement (Xinjiang, China), affiliated with al-Qaeda from 2006
- Libyan Islamic Fighting Group (Libya), active since the early 1990s, affiliated with al-Qaeda from 2007 to 2009
- Al-Qaeda in the Arabian Peninsula (Yemen and Saudi Arabia), affiliated with al-Qaeda from 2009

For instance, after the US-led invasion and occupation of Iraq in 2003 (see Chapter 8), ostensibly as part of the War on Terror, an organisation calling itself al-Qaeda in Iraq (or *tanzim qaidat al-jihad fi bilad al rafidayn*, 'Organisation of Jihad's Base in the Country of the Two Rivers') was founded by Jordanian militant Abu Musab al-Zarqawi. Whilst never being a popular movement, thus lacking the critical domestic community of support, this organisation conducted a range of attacks against both US and Coalition forces in Iraq as well as against Shi`a and other communities in the country under the broad al-Qaeda banner.

In addition, a new group emerged in 2003 out of the various Islamist groups that had been active during Algeria's long-running civil war, a conflict that had claimed over 200,000 lives since 1990. Calling itself al-Qaeda in the Islamic Maghreb (*tanzim al-qa`idah fi bilad al-maghrib al-Islami*), this group formed around so-called 'rejectionist' elements of previous groups such as the Salafist Group for Preaching and Combat as well as the Armed Islamic Group, themselves derivatives of the earlier Islamic Salvation Front (FIS). The FIS had won municipal and legislative elections in Algeria in the late 1980s, victories that were cancelled by a military coup leading to the outbreak of conflict. By the early 2000s, the new al-Qaeda-linked organisation had broadened its attacks across the borders to target government sites in Mali, Mauritania, Morocco, Niger and Tunisia as well as in Algeria.

Osama bin Laden was killed in Pakistan on 2 May 2011 by members of a US Naval Special Warfare Development Group (Navy SEALs). He was found in a residential compound in the city of Abbottabad, a garrison city 100 kilometres from the capital Islamabad. Whilst the Pakistani government denied sheltering bin Laden, intense controversy remains as to the connections between Pakistan and organisations such as al-Qaeda, the Taleban in Afghanistan, Lashkar-e-Toiba in Kashmir and other groups.

Finally, many within Western intelligence and analyst circles have turned their attention to al-Qaeda in the Arabian Peninsula (*al-qa`idah fi jazirat al`arab*) as the most active and potentially dangerous contemporary trans-state terrorist organisation. Formed by American-born Yemeni Anwar al-Awlaki in 2009, the organisation has undertaken a string of attacks against Yemeni, Saudi and US targets, leading the US, particularly under the Obama administration, to introduce drone strikes on the bases of these groups, a highly controversial policy that some allege has increased the militancy of this group and alienated Yemeni civilians due to the civilian casualties associated with this tactic (Soufan, 2011).

US Counter-Terrorism Policy in the Middle East

Response to al-Qaeda and al-Qaeda-inspired groups has been multifaceted. Alongside direct military interventions, the US has also been active in supporting regional regimes in their own security operations. However, this has drawn much criticism in terms of allowing states to increase their control over opposition forces at the expense of political liberalisation. Despite this, both the US and regional beneficiaries of US support maintain that these activities are necessary in combating these forms of militant Islamism. Here, we shall outline one example of this in Algeria, where the US has actively supported the Algerian counter-terrorism campaign in the wake of a brutal civil war in the country.

The US and the Algerian Civil War

The Algerian Civil War broke out in 1992 after the cancellation of the nascent electoral process in January of that year. The conflict emerged at the end of a tumultuous period of civil unrest followed by hasty, ill-defined political reform. The domination of Algerian politics by the single-party regime of the National Liberation Front (FLN), since the end of French rule in 1962, laid the foundations of an increasingly unrepresentative and dysfunctional political and economic system.

Figure 7.18 The October 1988 'Bread Riots' that prompted the opening of the political system in Algeria between 1988 and 1992

Source: Public domain

The fragility of the Algerian state was fully exposed when anti-government 'bread riots' broke out in October 1988 in scenes strikingly similar to those that would emerge with the 'Arab Spring' after 2010 (see Chapter 10). Initially disorganised, these protests turned violent, leading to government forces killing 159 people by the end of the month. Popular criticism of this heavy-handed approach led the regime to announce a series of political reforms, including an opening of the political system for municipal, national legislative and presidential elections from 1989 to 1991.

By the time the first round of municipal elections were held in June 1989, a new political force had emerged on the Algerian political scene. The Islamic Salvation Front (*Front Islamique du Salut*, FIS) had come to the fore, taking 55% of the vote. This was replicated in the first round of legislative elections held in December 1991, with the FIS claiming 188 of the 231 seats on offer. In response, the military intervened,

Figure 7.19 Habib Souaïdia

Source: Public domain

cancelling the elections and annulling the election results, dismissing the government, and installing a military-backed transitional government in January 1992 (Kouaouci, 2004: 32).

After the events of 1992, the security situation in Algeria rapidly deteriorated where the FIS and the regime engaged in a series of violent confrontations. This would mark the start of a spiral of violence that would consume all elements of Algerian political, social and economic life by the mid-1990s where the violence would move outside limited engagements to direct violence and the targeting of citizens, allegedly by both sides (Slisli, 2000: 44; Joffé, 2002: 4). This violence would lead to an estimated 200,000 civilian deaths between 1992 and 2000 as well as allegations of government involvement in a number of atrocities (Souaïdia, 2001).

Allegations of government involvement in the violence against civilians were particularly controversial. These centred on events through 1996 and 1997 where the government claimed the Armed Islamic Group (GIA) conducted a number of massacres in villages south of the capital Algiers. However, according to a number of accounts, the government was active in either allowing these attacks to take place or were involved in the violence itself as a means to justify the continued closure of the political system.

The US, alongside the majority of the international community, paid little attention to the ongoing violence in Algeria as it raged through the 1990s. When statements were made, they oscillated between condemnations of the violence and arguments that this was a domestic security issue to be handled by the Algerian authorities. However, after 11 September 2001, the US–Algerian security relationship became much closer (MacQueen, 2006). This was based on joint security initiatives, such as the 2002 Pan-Sahel Initiative (PSI) and the 2005 Trans-Sahara Counterterrorism Initiative (TSCTI).

The core of these initiatives involved both security training as well as funding for the Algerian security services. In addition, the broader context of the War on Terror allowed the government to increase the intensity of those operations. For some, this has led to a worsening of the security situation that has prompted the perpetuation of political violence in Algeria, and seeing this violence spill over the border into neighbouring states, particularly Mauritania (Testas, 2004: 97). Indeed, this is a situation mirrored in many regional states, including the controversy over drone strikes in Yemen and Somalia, support for government security measures in Egypt, Morocco, Jordan and elsewhere. Alongside economic deterioration and general social malaise, this harder line by regional regimes, an exploitation of a global environment defined by the War on Terror, contributed to the tensions and discontent expressed after 2010 through the 'Arab Spring'.

CONCLUSION

This chapter has demonstrated how security issues in the Middle East, as with most issues in the region, are interrelated in complex ways. Where 'conventional' security issues remain, particularly in terms of inter-state conflict, they also spill over into controversies surrounding war crimes, humanitarian concerns and non-conventional weapons. Indeed, as the cases of Darfur and Western Sahara highlight, territorial concerns are overlaid with issues of war crimes and accusations of sub-state and trans-state political violence. Indeed, questions over nuclear proliferation feed into instability at the local, regional and global level, a trend mirrored by the development of trans-state terrorist organisations, such as al-Qaeda.

Study Questions

- What are the main 'conventional' security issue in the contemporary Middle East?
- How important are territorial disputes in the regional security landscape?
- Why is nuclear proliferation a particularly important issue in the Middle East?
- How do Israel and Iran justify their respective nuclear programmes?
- What is 'terrorism' and how has it manifested itself in the Middle East?
- Are historic and contemporary forms of terrorism in the Middle East the same phenomenon?
- What have been the impacts of the 'War on Terror' on the Middle East and North Africa?

FURTHER READING

Burke, Jason (2004) *Al-Qaeda: The True Story of Radical Islam*. New York: I.B. Tauris.
A compelling and detailed account of the emergence of al-Qaeda, highlighting the origins of the movement and its ideology.

Chaliand, Gérard and Blin, Arnaud (2007) *The History of Terrorism: From Antiquity to al-Qaeda*. Berkeley: University of California Press.
A detailed and sharply analytical examination of the development of terrorism and political violence, allowing the contextualisation of modern terrorist tactics and ideology.

Palmer Harik, Judith (2005) *Hezbollah: The Changing Face of Terrorism*. New York: I.B. Tauris.

Palmer Harik's volume provides a detailed examination of Lebanon's Hezbollah through examining the question of how to understand the various roles the movement plays.

Roberts, Hugh (2003) *The Battlefield, Algeria 1988–2002: Studies in a Broken Polity.* London: Verso.
One of the leading scholars on Algerian politics provides a compilation of the key events in this country's troubled history, allowing for a thorough overview of key events in modern Algerian politics.

 Go to the companion website at www.sagepub.co.uk/macqueen for further material including free journal articles and links to other relevant documents.

REFERENCES

Ahmadi, Kouroush (2008) *Islands and International Politics in the Persian Gulf: The Abu Musa and Tunbs in Strategic Context.* London: Routledge.

Bahgat, Gawdat (2007) *Proliferation of Nuclear Weapons in the Middle East.* Gainesville: University of Florida Press.

Betz, David (2008) 'The Virtual Dimension of Contemporary Insurgency and Counter Insurgency', *Small Wars and Insurgencies*, 19(4): 510–40.

Cohen, Avner and Graham, Thomas Jr (2004) 'WMD in the Middle East: A Diminishing Currency', *Disarmament Diplomacy*, 76.

Fanon, Frantz (1961) *The Wretched of the Earth.* New York: Grove Press.

Jensen, Erik (2011) *Western Sahara: Anatomy of a Stalemate?* Boulder, CO: Lynne Rienner.

Joffé, George (2002) 'The Role of Violence within the Algerian Economy', *Journal of North African Studies*, 7 (1): 1–20.

Kouaouci, Ali (2004) 'Population Transitions, Youth Unemployment, Postponement of Marriage and Violence in Algeria', *Journal of North African Studies*, 9 (2): 28–45.

Langford, R. Everett (2004) *Introduction to Weapons of Mass Destruction: Radiological, Chemical, and Biological.* Hoboken, NJ: Wiley-Interscience.

Lentini, Peter (2008) 'The Transference of Neojihadism: Towards a Process Theory of Transnational Radicalisation', in Sayed Khatab, Muhammad Bakashmar and Ela Orgu (eds) *Radicalisation Crossing Borders: New Direction in Islamist and Jihadist Political, Intellectual, and Theological Thought in Practice*, International Conference, Melbourne, Victoria, Australia.

MacQueen, Benjamin (2006) 'Islamism in Algeria and America's Global Campaign', in Fethi Mansouri and Shahram Akbarzadeh (eds) *Political Islam and Human Security.* Newcastle: Cambridge Scholars Publishing, pp. 181–200.

Malley, Robert (1996) *The Call from Algeria: Third Worldism, Revolution, and the Turn to Islam*. Berkeley: University of California Press.

Norton, Augustus Richard (2007) *Hezbollah: A Short History*. Princeton, NJ: Princeton University Press.

Peres, Shimon (1986) 'Testimony at the Trial of Mordechai Vananu'.

Prunier, Gérard (2008) *Darfur: A 21st Century Genocide*. Ithaca, NY: Cornell University Press.

Riedel, Bruce O. (2010) *The Search for Al Qaeda: Its Leadership, Ideology, and Future*. Washington, DC: Brookings Institution Press.

Sachar, Howard M. (2003) *A History of Israel: From the Rise of Zionism to Our Time*. New York: Knopf.

Slisli, Fouzi (2000) 'The Western Media and the Algerian Crisis', *Race and Class*, 41 (3): 43–57.

Soufan, Ali H. (2011) *The Black Banners: The Inside Story of 9/11 and the War Against al-Qaeda*. London: W.W. Norton and Company.

Souaïdia, Habib (2001) *La Sale Guerre*. Paris: Éditions La Découverte.

Testas, Abdelaziz (2004) 'The United States' Approach to Algeria's Civil Conflict: Implications for Democratization, Internal Peace and Anti-American Violence', *Democratization*, 11 (2): 87–120.

Verter, Yossi (2006) 'Olmert: Iran Seeking to Develop Nuclear Bomb, "like America, France and Israel"', *Haaretz*, 12 December.

UNEP (2007) 'Environmental Degradation Triggering Tensions and Conflict in Sudan'; www.unep.org/Documents.Multilingual/Default.asp?ArticleID=5621&DocumentID=512&l=en.

United Nations (2004) *A More Secure World: Our Shared Responsibility*. New York: United Nations.

Zunes, Stephen and Mundy, Jacob (2010) *Western Sahara: War, Nationalism and Conflict Irresolution*. Syracuse, NY: Syracuse University Press.

PART III

Continuing Crises in the Middle East

Building on the discussions of the formation of the state system in the region and the key political dynamics of regional affairs, Part III will outline three key continuing crises confronting the Middle East and North Africa. Where this will facilitate a detailed examination of the issues of US military intervention, the Israeli–Palestinian conflict and the so-called 'Arab Spring', it also enables one to see how the previous themes either continue to influence regional affairs or have been downgraded in importance.

As both Parts I and II outlined, the role of external powers in modern Middle Eastern affairs has been a constant and highly controversial theme. As such, Chapter 8 discusses patterns of contemporary US interventionism in the region with a view to understanding the ongoing debates around how the world, and particularly its great powers, engage with the Middle East. Through a detailed discussion of the US-led invasion and occupation of Iraq from 2003 as well as US operations in Afghanistan from 2001 and the issues of US security operations in Yemen and Somalia, all ostensibly under the banner of the so-called 'War on Terror', this chapter enables a greater understanding of how external intervention remains a key theme of regional politics, and how this discussion has changed since the colonial and Cold War periods.

External involvement is one of a number of issues that defines what many see as the definitive security issue in the region, if not globally, the Israeli– Palestinian conflict. Chapter 9 builds a discussion of this most contentious of issues focussed on the ongoing 'Peace Process' between the Israelis and the Palestinians. This is done through an outline of the specific parameters debated in negotiations between the two parties, particularly those of the Israeli occupation of the West Bank and settlement construction and growth in this territory, the question of Palestinian refugees and the 'Right of Return', and the broader issue of territory. This is then expanded through consideration of competing norms between the two parties, particularly the Israeli claim to 'self-defence' and the Palestinian claim to 'self-determination' as well as the ongoing debates over the questions of national identity amongst both the Israeli and Palestinian communities. Turning back to the question of external involvement, this chapter delves into the various factors around the US role in negotiations and the relationship between the US and Israel and the US and the Palestinians.

Where the Israeli–Palestinian conflict, for many, has been a defining feature of regional affairs, this has increasingly been overtaken by the instability around the US-led invasion and occupation of Iraq as well as the outbreak of uprisings across the Arab world since late 2010. The so-called 'Arab Spring' is the focus of Chapter 10, with a particular emphasis on the question of whether this signifies a democratising trend in the region. Drawing on those elements covered in Part II, this discussion will outline the key features of the democratisation debate in the Middle East and North Africa, from the controversies surrounding Islam and democracy through to the US and its 'democracy promotion' programmes of the last decade, before turning to the events that have seen world attention captivated yet again by the region. First focusing on the key themes of catalysts for the unrest and discussions on the role of information technology, this chapter will then outline the cases of Tunisia, Libya, Egypt, Yemen, Bahrain and Syria in order to consider whether this is a fundamental turning point in the history of the region. Whilst it appears that it is so, it is less clear whether this means a new democratic spring for the Middle East and North Africa, or a new period of instability.

8

US Military Intervention in the Middle East

Learning Objectives

This chapter will enable a greater understanding of:

- The controversial background to the US intervention in Iraq.
- The impacts of the Iraq War on the Iraqi people.
- The continuing crises confronting the political system in Iraq.
- The impacts of counter-terrorism policy on the perception of the US in the Middle East.
- The dilemmas resulting from US counter-terrorism efforts in Iraq, Afghanistan, Pakistan and Somalia.

TIMELINE

3 April 1991: UN Security Council Resolution 687

5 December 1992–4 May 1993: 'Operation Restore Hope'

1994: Beginning of Taleban military operations

27 September 1996: The Taleban take Kabul

16–19 December 1998: UNSCOM inspectors withdraw from Iraq

16–19 December 1998: 'Operation Desert Fox'

7 October 2001: 'Operation Enduring Freedom' launched

5 December 2001: Bonn Agreement signed

19 January 2002: President Bush's 'Axis of Evil' State of the Union Address

13 June 2002: Hamid Karzai appointed President of the Afghan Transitional Administration

16 October 2002: Passing of 'Authorisation for Use of Military

(Continued)

(Continued)

Force against Iraq Resolution' through the US Congress

8 November 2002: UN Security Council Resolution 1441

19 March 2003: 'Operation Iraqi Freedom' launched

9 April 2003: Baghdad falls to Coalition forces

21 April 2003: Establishment of the Coalition Provisional Authority

1 May 2003: Formal removal of Ba'ath Party from power

22 May 2003: UN Security Council Resolution 1483

16 May 2003: CPA issues General Order Number 1 ('De-Ba'athification')

4 April–1 May 2004: First Battle of Fallujah

8 May 2004: Transitional Administrative Law

9 October 2004: Karzai elected Afghan President

7 November–23 December 2004: Second Battle of Fallujah

30 January 2005: First post-invasion elections in Iraq

15 October 2005: Iraq's post-Ba'ath constitution adopted

5 December 2005: Iraqi parliamentary elections

2006: Emergence of Islamic Courts Union in Somalia

20 July 2006: Ethiopian invasion of Somalia

25 December 2006: ICU driven from Mogadishu

25–31 March 2008: Battle of Basra

20 August 2009: Karzai re-elected President of Afghanistan

2010: Emergence of *al-shabaab*

31 August 2010: Last US troops leave Iraq

30 September 2011: Leader of al-Qaeda in the Arabian Peninsula Anwar al-Awlaki killed by drone strike

26 February 2012: Ali Abdullah Saleh replaced by Abd al-Rab Mansur al-Hadi as President of Yemen

INTRODUCTION

As has been discussed at length, the US has been the dominant player in the Middle East since the end of World War II. This engagement with the region has been controversial, with allegations of hypocrisy and self-interest being highlighted by many as the source of anti-American sentiment. Whilst previous chapters have discussed numerous aspects of this engagement, this chapter will focus on US military intervention in the Middle East, particularly Iraq and Yemen, as well as military intervention on the 'periphery' of the region, particularly Afghanistan and Somalia.

This discussion will outline in detail the dynamics and scope of these US military interventions as well as engage with the various legal and ethical debates around them. In this regard, there will be particular focus on how the perceptions of the US in the Middle East have been profoundly affected, both positively and negatively, by these events. In addition, this discussion will outline how these interventions have shaped the emergence of new political and security dynamics across the region.

US INTERVENTION IN IRAQ

Alongside the 11 September terrorist attacks and the subsequent 'War on Terror', the war in Iraq was the defining global political issue of the first decade of the 21st century. Indeed, it may be argued that the war in Iraq has been the single most significant event in the Middle East in modern history. This importance relates as much to the scale of destruction brought by this conflict as it does to the controversy over the motivations and the justifications for the US-led invasion and occupation. This section will outline the war in Iraq, with a focus on the debate over the lead-up to the conflict as well as detailed examination of the impacts of the conflict.

The Road to War in Iraq

The roots of the 2003 US-led invasion and occupation of Iraq lie in the build-up of tension between Washington and Baghdad through the 1990s. The 2003 intervention itself stemmed from US efforts to develop a legal and a moral argument that Iraq represented a threat to international peace and security serious enough to warrant armed intervention and forceful regime change. These arguments took on added significance in the wake of al-Qaeda's terrorist attacks on the US on 11 September 2001 (see Chapter 7) where the Bush administration sought to both implicitly and explicitly link the Hussein regime to al-Qaeda. As we shall see, in the wake of the invasion and occupation, no credible evidence has emerged that revealed an active nuclear, chemical or biological weapons programme in Iraq or links between Iraq and al-Qaeda.

Lead-Up to the War

The legal argument surrounding this is rooted in the ramifications of Iraq's 1990 invasion of Kuwait. Iraq's defeat in this conflict required compliance with a range of UN Security Council Resolutions, including Resolution 687 of 3 April 1991 that required Iraq to destroy all stockpiles of chemical, biological and nuclear weapons ('Weapons of Mass Destruction', or WMD) as well as any medium- or long-range delivery (missile) capacity.

United Nations Security Council Resolution 687 (1991):

Decides that Iraq shall unconditionally accept the destruction, removal, or rendering harmless, under international supervision of: all chemical and biological weapons and all stocks of agents.

Figure 8.1   No-fly zones over Iraq (1991–2003)

Source: Public domain

Iraq's compliance was to be monitored by the UN Special Commission (UNSCOM) from 1991 to 1999 then by the UN Monitoring, Verification and Inspection Commission (UNMOVIC). During this period there were allegations of Iraqi non-compliance with Resolution 687. This reached its peak in 1998 when UNSCOM inspectors withdrew from Iraq, followed by a four-day bombing campaign led by the US and UK in December ('Operation Desert Fox') designed to destroy Iraq's security infrastructure. This intensification came on the back of a series of rolling crises in Iraq through the 1990s where the US enforced no-fly zones in the north and south of the country as well as an economic sanctions regime.

The Sanctions and the 'Oil for Food' Controversy

In addition, UN Security Council Resolution 661 of 1990 imposed a wide range of sanctions on Iraq that impacted all sectors of the Iraqi economy. Whilst they were ostensibly designed to lead to the destruction of Iraq's WMD programme and stockpiles, they were also designed to pressure Iraq to pay reparations to Kuwait as part of Resolution 687. However, the impacts of the sanctions on the Iraqi civilian population came under greater international scrutiny. In particular, the UN Children's Fund (UNICEF) documented figures relating to sharp increases in infant mortality rates and child malnutrition in Iraq under the sanctions regime. This occurred alongside deaths as a result of the shortages of medicine, polluted water supplies, starvation and a range of other impacts. This period also saw the collapse of the education system as well as Iraq's entire domestic infrastructure (UNICEF, 2000).

According to the UN Children's Fund (UNICEF), by 1997 the **sanctions** regime on Iraq contributed to malnutrition rates of 32% of children under five years old, a rise of 72% between 1991 and 1997.

In response to increasing international pressure over the effects of sanctions, the UN implemented the 'Oil for Food' programme to allow for greater access to food and other necessities as well as funding reparations payments to Kuwait. The parameters of the programme allowed for the sale of $1.6 billion in oil for the purchase of non-embargoed items with the funds to be managed by a third-party bank. Between 1997 and 2000, the programme raised an estimated $46 billion, with an estimated 60% of Iraqis dependent on food rations bought under the programme in these years. However, this programme was mired in controversy revolving around accusations that the Iraqi government, UN officials, Western government officials and Western corporations were diverting funds for their own benefit. The UN Independent Inquiry Committee estimated that the Hussein regime diverted $1.8 billion up to 2000 whilst nearly half of the 4500 foreign companies were alleged to have been involved in fraud and paying bribes to the regime.

In the wake of allegations of corruption under the **'Oil for Food' Programme**, the UN announced an official investigation on 19 March 2004, whose report highlighted widespread fraud and involvement in paying bribes.

This led to similar inquiries to be held in the US (Government Accountability Office audit) and Australia (Cole Inquiry). Despite controversy around the scope of the Australian inquiry, no charges were laid against government officials or members of the Australian Wheat Board who were implicated in the scandal.

Iraq and Disarmament

However, it was the argument surrounding Iraq's alleged non-compliance with disarmament obligations and possession of WMD stockpiles that formed the core of the legal rationale for the 2003 invasion. As discussed in previous chapters, Iraq had a history of both developing and using WMDs against external and internal enemies. Through the 1990s, there was great controversy over whether Iraq continued to retain its WMD stockpiles. However, by 1999, former UNSCOM Chief Inspector Scott Ritter declared that 'Iraq today possesses no meaningful weapons of mass destruction capability' (Arons, 1999).

Whilst this situation continued through 2001, the events of 11 September changed the landscape completely. In particular, it led to allegations that Iraq had links to al-Qaeda and their potential capacity to transfer WMDs to the terrorist network constituted a threat to international peace and security. As a result, it saw the crystallisation of the 'moral' argument around intervention in Iraq where the Bush administration formulated the plan that Iraq must be forcibly disarmed, and the Hussein regime forcibly removed.

Figure 8.2 Signatories of the Project for the New American Century 1998 open letter to President Clinton (clockwise from top left): John Bolton, Paul Wolfowitz, Elliott Abrams and Richard Armitage

Sources: Public domain, Public domain, Gage Skidmore

This was not, however, an argument that emerged as a direct response to the 11 September attacks. Planning for a full-scale invasion of Iraq to replace the Hussein regime had been in place through the 1990s. In January 1998, a US conservative 'think-tank' called the Project for the New American Century (PNAC) sent an open letter to President Clinton claiming that 'removing Saddam Hussein and his regime from power' should 'become the aim of American foreign policy' (Abrams et al., 1998). What made this letter significant was that it was signed by former Republican government officials, including many future members of the George W. Bush administration, including Secretary of Defense from 2001 to 2008 Donald Rumsfeld, US Ambassador to the UN from 2001 to 2005 John R. Bolton, Deputy Secretary for Defense from 2001 to 2005 Paul Wolfowitz, Deputy Secretary of State from 2001 to 2005 Richard Armitage, National Security Council Senior Director for Near East and North African Affairs from 2002 to 2005 Elliott Abrams, US Ambassador to Afghanistan from 2003 to 2005 and Iraq from 2005 to 2007 Zalmay Khalilzad, as well as scholars Francis Fukuyama and Robert Kagan.

As such, by 2001 there was an attempt to bring together a legal and a moral argument for the removal of the Saddam Hussein regime particularly amongst senior Republican figures. This gained momentum in the US as well as in the UK under the Blair Labour government. In the wake of the 11 September attacks, the newly elected Republican Bush administration pushed the case for war on two fronts. First, it launched an effort in the UN to pass a Chapter VII resolution to authorise the use of force to remove the Hussein regime. Second, it launched a campaign to find links between Iraq and the al-Qaeda network.

In terms of domestic US politics, the push for a response to 11 September directed at Iraq was immediate. Indeed, as has been subsequently reported, Secretary of Defense Donald Rumsfeld requested all intelligence 'related or not' that could link Iraq to the attacks (Summers and Swan, 2012). More explicit efforts were made in President Bush's January 2002 State of the Union address that focussed on Iraq, Iran and North Korea as a so-called 'Axis of Evil' that were 'seeking weapons of mass destruction' and 'arming to threaten the peace of the world', with these threats including alleged links with 'terrorist allies' (The White House, 2002).

Selections from President Bush's 19 January **2002 State of the Union Address**:

Iraq continues to flaunt its hostility toward America and to support terror. The Iraqi regime has plotted to develop anthrax and nerve gas and nuclear weapons for over a decade.

This is a regime that has already used poison gas to murder thousands of its own citizens, leaving the bodies of mothers huddled over their dead children. This is a regime that agreed to international inspections then kicked out the inspectors. This is a regime that has something to hide from the civilized world.

States like these, and their terrorist allies, constitute an axis of evil, arming to threaten the peace of the world. By seeking weapons of mass destruction, these regimes pose a grave and growing danger. They could provide these

(Continued)

(Continued)

> arms to terrorists, giving them the means to match their hatred. They could attack our allies or attempt to blackmail the United States. In any of these cases, the price of indifference would be catastrophic.
>
> We will work closely with our coalition to deny terrorists and their state sponsors the materials, technology and expertise to make and deliver weapons of mass destruction.

This was reiterated in the 2002 US National Security Strategy that explicitly highlighted Iraq as symbolic of 'rogue states' who were focussed on developing chemical, biological and nuclear weapons capability. Here, an explicit link was made between such states and 'their terrorist clients' with the potential dangers of arms transfers between them. No concrete links between Iraq and al-Qaeda were given in spite of this assertion. Instead, the statement went on to argue that this potential threat requires 'proactive counterproliferation efforts' at both the doctrinal and enforcement level (The White House, 2006: 18).

The move towards unilateral action against Iraq developed in response to disagreements within the UN Security Council, with the US and UK on one side and France, Russia and China on the other, over the veracity of allegations of Iraqi possession of WMDs. This confrontation reached its peak through late 2002 as the US pushed for the passage of a Chapter VII resolution that would authorise the use of force against Iraq. Here, President Bush addressed the UN General Assembly on 12 September 2002 outlining a case that Iraq was in league with al-Qaeda and that it continued to pursue an active WMD programme. This debate led to two outcomes. First was an effort to sanction the use of force under US law with the 'Authorisation for Use of Military Force against Iraq Resolution' of 16 October 2002. This Bill was designed as an authorisation for the use of force to remove the Hussein regime based broadly on the charges of Iraqi WMD possession and links with al-Qaeda, drawing on the 1998 Iraq Liberation Act to pursue regime change in Baghdad.

The **Bush Doctrine** was largely a response to the 11 September 2001 terrorist attacks, and focussed on the increasing prevalence of unilateral US actions targeting states alleged to support terrorist organisations through what the regime labelled 'preventative war'. That is, the Bush administration argued that it had both the legal and moral right to impose forced **regime change** in states that posed a threat, as determined by the regime, to US national peace and security.

The second was Security Council Resolution 1441 on 8 November 2002, passed under Chapter VII, that declared Iraq 'has been and remains in material breach of its obligations' under previous disarmament resolutions. However, this was not an automatic trigger for war, with the resolution allowing Iraq 'a final opportunity to comply with its disarmament obligations' through facilitating UNMOVIC and IAEA inspections.

For the US, this was inadequate as it did not provide an immediate authorisation for the removal of the Hussein regime. In addition to continued obfuscation on the part of the Hussein regime, the US pressed ahead with Secretary of State Colin Powell presenting the US case before the Security Council on 6 February 2003. The core of Powell's presentation centred on a claim that Iraq was in 'material breach' of Resolution 1441. Therefore, a new Chapter VII resolution should be passed to authorise the use of force.

According to Powell, the purpose of Resolution 1441 was to 'disarm Iraq of its weapons of mass destruction' with its failure to do this raising the possibility of 'serious consequences' (*The Guardian*, 2003). Indeed, Powell raised the possibility of the UN's 'irrelevance' if it failed to enforce these 'serious consequences' against Iraq. In addition, Powell sought to link the danger of the Hussein regime's alleged maintenance of a WMD programme to the 'terrorist' threat to the United States. He declared that al-Qaeda could potentially turn to Iraq for acquiring weapons of mass destruction (UN News Centre, 2003). Whilst Powell asserted that Hussein had 'terrorist associations', no specific evidence was given as to these associations. Instead, Powell's argument was built around the inference that Saddam had 'grandiose plans' to 'exact revenge on those who oppose him', thus, it was too much of a risk for the US and the world community generally to continue without directly confronting his intransigent stance. Despite these claims,

Figure 8.3 The looming invasion of Iraq in early 2003 led to demonstrations across the world, such as the protest in London pictured here. Estimates put the total number of those involved at up to 20 million worldwide, with the largest protests in Rome, Madrid and London, each in excess of 700,000 protestors. Other large protests occurred in the cities of Melbourne, New York, Los Angeles and Montreal

Source: Simon Rutherford

Powell subsequently argued that there was little debate in the White House as to whether or not to plan for an invasion of Iraq, with Vice President Richard Cheney in particular pressuring the State Department to pursue the case at the UN, an act he describes as 'one of my most momentous failures' (Powell, 2012).

'Operation Iraqi Freedom'

On 19 March 2003 the United States, in cooperation with the United Kingdom and the so-called 'Coalition of the Willing' launched 'Operation Iraqi Freedom'. The operation was launched outside of UN authorisation, creating a great deal of international controversy and criticism of the US and its Coalition partners both inside and outside the region. Indeed, the lead-up to the war and the subversion of UN authority would take on added controversy with the revelation by the Iraq Study Group that Iraq had discontinued all WMD programmes in 1991 and there were no links between Iraq and al-Qaeda.

'Shock and Awe'

The **Coalition of the Willing** refers to states that supported the military intervention in Iraq.

By the end of 2003, this included: US (150,000), UK (46,000), South Korea (3600), Italy (3200), Poland (2500), Australia (2000), Georgia (2000), Ukraine (1650), the Netherlands (1345), Spain (1300), Romania (730), Denmark (545), Bulgaria (485), Thailand (423), El Salvador (380), Honduras (368), Dominican Republic (302), Czech Republic (300), Hungary (300), Azerbaijan (250), Albania (240), Nicaragua (230), Mongolia (180), Singapore (175), Norway (150), Latvia (136), Portugal (128), Lithuania (120), Slovakia (110), Macedonia (77), New Zealand (61), Philippines (51), Kazakhstan (29), Moldova (24) and Iceland (2).

The initial military operation was quick, leading to the fall of Baghdad on 9 April and the formal removal of Ba`ath Party rule on 1 May 2003. The 21-day military operation commenced with a massive aerial bombardment of Iraqi military sites across the country as well as the targeting of other key government facilities. This so-called 'Shock and Awe' strategy was designed to paralyse Iraqi military capacity before the arrival of the initial ground forces comprising 148,000 US soldiers, 45,000 British soldiers, 2000 Australian soldiers and 194 Polish soldiers. This would be supplemented by troops from a range of countries during and after 2003.

Figure 8.4 From left: 9 April 2003 toppling of a statue of Saddam Hussein in Firdus Square in central Baghdad and 1 May 2003 speech by President Bush on the *USS Abraham Lincoln* declaring an 'end of major combat operations' in Iraq

Sources: Public domain, History Commons

In the wake of the bombing campaign, the ground force invasion saw the rapid disintegration of the Iraqi army. This led to quick proclamations of victory, with President Bush appearing on the deck of aircraft carrier the *USS Abraham Lincoln* on 1 May to proclaim the end of major combat operations. However, even with the capture of Saddam Hussein on 13 December 2003 the occupation forces faced an ongoing resistance in the form of Ba'ath Party loyalists, Islamist insurgents and other armed groups that continued to challenge the foreign military occupation of Iraq.

The Looting of Baghdad and the Disintegration of the Iraqi State

The **Grand Bargain** refers to an approach made by the Iranian regime to the US, via the Swiss Ambassador in Tehran, for a full peace treaty between the two states. Allegedly, the bargain involved full Iranian acceptance of the two-state solution in the Israeli–Palestinian conflict, an end to support for terrorist organisations, cooperation with the US in Iraq and Afghanistan, a comprehensive security agreement with the Arab Gulf states, and the suspension of Iran's nuclear programme.

In exchange, the US and Iran would establish full mutual diplomatic recognition as well as a halt to calls for regime change in Tehran. The US never replied to the approach, and it was withdrawn after the deterioration of the security situation in Iraq after 2004.

Before the outbreak of widespread insurgency in Iraq, there were signs of the rapid deterioration of the political and security environment. One indication of this was the widespread looting that swept the country, particularly Baghdad, including the stripping of Iraq's rich cultural heritage as well as the looting of the country's government departments.

This was important in a number of respects. First, the cultural heritage of Iraq, one that dates back thousands of years, was not protected by the invasion forces as lawlessness gripped Iraq in the weeks and months following the invasion. In contrast, Iraq's oil ministry was immediately placed under direct US control, leading to allegations that the invasion force was not one of liberation but exploitation. Regardless of the validity of these claims, they began to undercut the legitimacy of the US presence in Iraq. Second, the stripping of Iraq's physical infrastructure, from ministerial records to hospital and other equipment, handicapped the capacity of the local administration to function after the invasion. This was a process that was compounded by the so-called 'de-Ba`athification' programme that saw the dismissal of the Iraqi army as well as the entire management of the Iraqi public sector.

The Coalition Provisional Authority and 'Operation Iraqi Prosperity'

Figure 8.5 The Grand Ayatollah 'Ali as-Sistani is the most senior Shi'a religious figure in Iraq

Source: Public domain

The de-Baàthification policy was the first act of the post-invasion political authority established by the US, the Coalition Provisional Authority (CPA). The CPA was established under Security Council Resolution 1483 (2003) that terminated all sanctions on Iraq and passed authority to the US and UK as the legal governing authorities in Iraq. In this regard, the US and UK were charged with implementing a transitional administration, an administration that came with the CPA.

Created on 21 April 2003, the CPA quickly courted controversy. Resolution 1483 called for a rapid transfer of authority to Iraqi authority, something backed by key local figures such as Shià leader Ayatollah Àli as-Sistani and the first head of the CPA, General Jay Garner. However, disagreement over this issue led to the dismissal of Garner and his replacement by L. Paul Bremer on 11 May. Bremer then quickly implemented the de-Baàthification policy, the CPA's General Order Number 1, on 16 May.

Figure 8.6   From left: first director Ret. LT Gen. Jay Garner (21 April–11 May 2003) and
second director L. Paul Bremer III (11 May 2003–28 May 2004) of the CPA

Source: Public domain, Public domain

Alongside this trend was an effort to fully restructure the future economy of Iraq under the CPA's General Order Number 39 of 21 September 2003. As was discussed in Chapter 6, economic reforms have moved towards the implementation of neoliberal models. The Bush administration saw in Iraq the opportunity to create the ideal model of such reforms, with Order 39 providing for 'complete foreign ownership of Iraqi companies and assets (apart from natural resources), total overseas remittance of profits and some of the lowest taxes in the world' (Coalition Provisional Authority, 2003). The reforms contained here were dubbed 'Operation Iraqi Prosperity', an effort to remake the normative landscape of the region.

The pressure for a transition of authority increasingly came to bear on the CPA with their drafting and introduction of the Transitional Administrative Law (TAL) on 8 March 2004. The TAL was implemented after domestic pressures in Iraq for reform

Figure 8.7   The first post-CPA
Prime Minister
Ayad Allawi

Source: Public domain

and the growing evidence of insurgent unrest. From this, elections for a local transitional administration were held, despite protests from the CPA, on 30 January 2005.

These elections were boycotted by the major Sunni parties, with the Shi`a United Iraqi Alliance gaining a majority in both the new parliament and the committee that would draft Iraq's new constitution that was formalised on 15 October 2005.

The Iraqi Insurgency and the Ramifications of the Invasion 2003–2008

Despite these political changes, by June 2003, the presumption that the invasion of Iraq would be over by the end of the year started to unravel, with the emergence of a variety of insurgent groups across the country. Throughout the conflict, there was not one single militant movement that dominated the security landscape. In addition, the violence was not only directed towards the US, with attacks between the groups as well as attacks on civilian groups.

Whilst estimates on the number and size of groups vary dramatically, one can identify three main groups involved in violence alongside the Coalition forces. First, a group of nationalist and former regime loyalists including Ba`ath militants as well as self-defined nationalists; second, a range of Shi`a militias including members of the Badr Organisation as well as followers of Muqtada as-Sadr, particularly the Mahdi Army; and third, a range of Islamist militias including the newly formed al-Qaeda in Iraq under the leadership of Jordanian militant Abu Musab al-Zarqawi (see Chapter 7).

Figure 8.8 The so-called 'Sunni Triangle'
Source: Public domain

Through the last half of 2003, the power vacuum in the country combined with the presence of a large foreign military saw sporadic, largely uncoordinated violence emerge throughout the country. This violence took more definable shape through 2004 as a result of the de-Ba`athification programme, full political control wielded by the CPA and the arrival of foreign militants.

Ba`athists and Nationalists

Cited in Chebab, Zaki, *Iraq Ablaze: Inside the Insurgency* (London: I.B. Tauris, 2006: 7):
   Author's conversation with an Iraqi 'nationalist' insurgent June 2003: 'We started this national front with ten people. We then opened it up to more people, and with the help of the faithful and those who believe in our cause, we have expanded to the extent that we have bases or cells all over Iraq. People join us from all walks of life. Those who cannot fight support us financially. We don't have any connections at all with Saddam's regime. We are all trained, as most of us took part in the Iran–Iraq War, but occasionally young recruits ask us for training. We tend to hold training sessions when we get together as a group so that each one of us knows how to use the weapons of other members in case something happens to them. We have bases in Basra, Mosul, Baghdad, and in five towns in al-Anbar Province: al-Qaem, Haditha, Anah, Hit, Fallujah, and al-Ramadi. There is plenty of coordination going on between these different groups and bases.'

Here, the Ba`athists and Iraqi nationalists began implementing a number of attacks in the Sunni heartland of Iraq north of Baghdad. Many of those active in these groups drew primarily from former members of the military and others displaced from the government after 2003. This saw the US focus on the so-called 'Sunni Triangle' as the base of insurgent activity from 2004. This area included the major cities of Fallujah, Samarra and Ramadi as well as Tikrit, the home of Saddam Hussein.

The deterioration of the situation through the end of 2003 and the start of 2004 saw the US implement a range of counter-insurgency operations that saw further militarisation of the Iraqi environment. Indeed, according to reports from inside Iraq, these operations pushed many Iraqis towards either passive support for or active involvement in the insurgency. As one senior member in the Sunni village of Samarra put it, attacks on the Americans increased at this time as their operations 'all lead to bitterness and hatred, and so people resort to violence to take revenge' (cited in Chebab, 2006: 12).

Perhaps the best example of this deterioration was the US occupation of Fallujah after April 2003. The US troop presence sparked immediate protests,

Figure 8.9 Clockwise from top: Iraqi nationalist militants, members of the Mahdi Army
and members of al-Qaeda in Iraq

Sources: AP, AP, Areeb Hasni

with one such protest on 28 April leading to US troops firing on crowds in
an effort to disperse them. Seventeen deaths resulted, leading to successive
rounds of confrontation between locals and US troops. Throughout the rest of
2003 and early 2004, attacks on US forces and civilian contractors increased.
By April 2004, Fallujah had become a hotbed of unrest, with the US surrounding and laying siege to the city. Attempts at a negotiated settlement
proved unsuccessful, with allegations of US use of snipers and cluster bombs
and insurgent use of rockets and bombings. By May, US forces withdrew to
the outskirts of the city leaving the insurgents in control of the city and claiming
victory.

This situation continued through to 8 November when a combined force of
US and newly trained Iraqi soldiers stormed the city with the estimated 6000
insurgents fleeing. However, this offensive drew international debate for the use
of cluster bombs and white phosphorus during the offensive. This was particularly
controversial as white phosphorus is an incendiary weapon, whose use in civilian
areas is considered illegal under international law.

Figure 8.10 US troops during the November 2004 Fallujah offensive
Source: AP

Shi`a Militias

Whilst the Ba`athists and nationalists were a key part of the insurgency, the first attack on US forces came from the Shi`a militants, namely the 'Mahdi Army' led by Muqtada as-Sadr. This attack came on 18 April 2004, sparking confrontations between the US and the Mahdi Army through to June, then again from August 2004 until 2008. During this time, as-Sadr was intermittently involved in the political process as well as in militant activities.

As-Sadr's core of support is drawn from the predominantly Shi`a districts of Baghdad's 'Sadr City'. This group took control of this area after the fall of Hussein's regime in early 2003 as well as in a number of Shi`a-majority

Figure 8.11 Muqtada as-Sadr
Source: Public domain

cities south of Baghdad. Alongside its militant activities, the group has been involved in providing food and health services to the communities in its areas of control, helping establish a large community of support. This support also grew from as-Sadr remaining in Iraq under Saddam Hussein's rule with many other Shi`a leaders seeking refuge in Iran. In this regard, there has been much written about the apparent influence of Iran over the now dominant Shi`a parties and movements in Iraq. However, whilst there are links between Iran and other leaders, such as Sayyed Ammar al-Hakim and Ayatollah `Ali as-Sistani, as-Sadr has publicly rejected calls for an Iranian-style Islamic Republic in Iraq (Arato, 2009).

> Three hundred and eleven **foreign fighters** associated with **al-Qaeda in Iraq** were captured in Iraq from 2003 to 2005, coming from 27 countries. Their countries of origin were: Egypt (78), Syria (66), Sudan (41), Saudi Arabia (32), Jordan (17), Iran (13), Palestinian Territories (12), Tunisia (10), Algeria (8), Libya (7), Turkey (6), Lebanon (3), Qatar (2), UAE (2), India (2), Macedonia (1), Morocco (1), Somalia (1), Yemen (1), Israel (1), Indonesia (1), Kuwait (1), UK (2), Denmark (1), Ireland (1) and France (1).
> from: Krueger, Alan B., 'The National Origins of Foreign Fighters in Iraq', *American Economic Association Annual Meeting*, 2007

In addition to the Mahdi Army, other Shi`a groups have been active in the fighting. However, these groups, such as the Badr Brigades, exist between being part of the official security apparatus and part of the insurgency. This has been a particular feature of Shi`a militias in Iraq as many were active in opposing the regime of Saddam Hussein, thus seen as natural allies of the US and Coalition forces after 2003. However, whilst members of these groups were incorporated into the new Iraqi security services, they also conducted insurgent attacks on Sunni militias as well as being part of alleged ethnic cleansing programmes across the country.

Sunni Islamist Militants

In terms of Sunni Islamist militants, this group was dominated by the emergence of 'Al-Qaeda in Iraq' (or *tanzim qaidat al-jihad fi bilad al rafidayn*, 'Organisation of Jihad's Base in the Country of the Two Rivers') after 2003. This group, and their links to the broader al-Qaeda organisation, were discussed in Chapter 7. Mirroring the earlier development of al-Qaeda in Afghanistan through the 1980s, this organisation drew on militants from across the Middle East and the broader Muslim world who had travelled to Iraq to take up this particular vision of *jihad*.

Whilst this organisation was the smallest of the three insurgent groupings, it conducted the most high-profile attacks during the peak of insurgent activity between 2004 and 2008. These included kidnappings and executions of Coalition service personnel, the use of improvised explosive devices (IEDs) against both military and civilian targets, as well as direct involvement in the targeting of non-Sunni and non-Muslim communities across the country. Indeed, focus on this movement was made more intense due to the ongoing controversy over the alleged links between the Hussein regime and al-Qaeda as well as the effort to enfold the Iraq War into the broader logic of the War on Terror (see Chapter 7).

The Human and Material Costs of the Conflict

Understanding the costs of any war is difficult, particularly in terms of how to measure the impacts of violence on the lives of people living in a war zone. However, by any measurement, the war in Iraq has had a profound and devastating impact on the country as well as on the US and Coalition forces. Whilst debate continues over the relative merits of the arguments justifying the invasion, these remain conjecture in the face of the scale of the damage that the conflict wrought on this already war-weary country.

Table 8.1 Major al-Qaeda in Iraq Bombings (2003–8)

	Attack	Casualties		Attack	Casualties
7 Aug. 2003	Jordanian Embassy, Baghdad	17 killed, 40 injured	5 Jan. 2006	Public squares, Karbala and Ramadi	120+ killed, 120+ injured
19 Aug. 2003	UN HQ, Baghdad	22 killed, 100 injured	7 Apr. 2006	Buratha mosque, Baghdad	85 killed, 160 injured
29 Aug. 2003	Imam Ali mosque, Najaf	83 killed, 500+ injured	1 Jul. 2006	Public square, Sadr City, Baghdad	62 killed, 114 injured
27 Oct. 2003	Red Cross HQ, Baghdad	35 killed, 244 injured	23 Nov. 2006	Public squares, Sadr City, Baghdad	215+ killed, 250+ injured
12 Nov. 2003	Italian Military Police HQ, Nasiriyah	28 killed, 103 injured	22 Jan. 2007	Bab al-Sharqi market, Baghdad	88 killed, 160 injured
27 Dec. 2003	Coalition military barracks, Karbala	20 killed, 200+ injured	3 Feb. 2007	Public market, Baghdad	135 killed, 339 injured
2 Feb. 2004	PUK HQ, Irbil	117 killed, 133 injured	18 Feb. 2007	Public squares, Baghdad	63 killed, 120+ injured
2 Mar. 2004	Day of Ashura, Karbala and Baghdad	180+ killed, 500+ injured	6 Mar. 2007	Religious festival, Al-Hillah	115 killed, 250+ injured

(Continued)

Table 8.1 (Continued)

	Attack	Casualties		Attack	Casualties
21 Apr. 2004	Iraqi Police HQ, Basra	74 killed, 100+ injured	27 Mar. 2007	Public square, Tal Afar	152 killed, 347 injured
24 Jun. 2004	Iraqi Police HQ, Mosul	60+ killed, 220+ injured	29 Mar. 2007	Public market, Baghdad	82 killed, 138 injured
28 Jul. 2004	Public market, Baquba	68 killed, 30+ injured	18 Apr. 2007	Public squares, Baghdad	198 killed, 251 injured
14 Sep. 2004	Iraqi Police HQ, Baghdad	47 killed, 114 injured	28 Apr. 2007	Imam Abbas mosque, Karbala	68 killed, 162 injured
30 Sep. 2004	Water treatment plant, Baghdad	40+ killed, 130+ injured	19 Jun. 2007	Al-Khilani mosque, Baghdad	87 killed, 218 injured
19 Dec. 2004	Shîa mosques, Karbala and Najaf	70+ killed, 100+ injured	26 Jul. 2007	Public market, Baghdad	92 killed, 127 injured
28 Feb. 2005	Iraqi Police HQ, al-Hillah	127 killed, 300+ injured	14 Aug. 2007	Yazidi targets, Mosul	796 killed, 1562 injured
16 Jul. 2005	Public market, Musayyib	100+ killed, 150+ injured	6 Mar. 2008	Public market, Baghdad	68 killed, 120 injured
17 Aug. 2005	Bus stations, Baghdad	43 killed, 76 injured	17 Mar. 2008	Public square, Karbala	58 killed, 100+ injured
14 Sep. 2005	Public square, Baghdad	160 killed, 570 injured	17 Jun. 2008	Bus station, Baghdad	51 killed, 75 injured
18 Nov. 2005	Shi`a mosques, Khanaqin	75+ killed, 100+ injured	12 Sep. 2008	Police station, Dujail	31 killed, 60 injured

Impacts on Iraqi Civilians

Efforts to quantify the costs of war have been highly controversial due to the intense political debates that have surrounded this conflict. This controversy first erupted in 2004 when the British medical journal *The Lancet* published an article that claimed close to 100,000 Iraqi civilians had died in the first year of the conflict. Criticisms of this centred on questions over the ability to gain accurate data or that this was part of a political effort to discredit the war effort. The authors of the report defended its findings, arguing that the death toll of the war should include both direct combat-related casualties as well as deaths that occurred as a result of the general impacts of the conflict. As such, deaths that occurred as a result of deteriorating health conditions, starvation and malnutrition and other related issues should be included as casualties occurring from the conflict (Roberts et al., 2004).

Table 8.2 Estimated Iraqi Civilian Deaths (2003–11, Brookings Institution estimates*)

	Civilian Casualties	*Annual % Change*
2003	7300	–
2004	16,800	+130.1%
2005	20,200	+20.2%
2006	34,500	+70.8%
2007	23,600	−31.6%
2008	6400	−72.9%
2009	3000	−53.1%
2010	2500	−16.7%
2011	1578	−36.9%
Cumulative Total	115,878	

* Figures include only casualties reported by the CPA and Iraqi government.

Smaller, yet still considerable estimates are given by the group Iraq Body Count (IBC), who have compiled a list of reported casualties as a result of the violence. From 2003 to 2012, IBC puts this at 115,367 civilian casualties. Similar figures are given by Brown University's 'Costs of War' Project, who has estimated over 126,000 civilian deaths as a result of violence since 2003 (see also Table 8.2).

As mentioned above, the physical destruction of the country has had a range of impacts on the Iraqi population. The Costs of War Project puts the

Figure 8.12 An Iraqi refugee camp in Syria
Source: UNHCR

number of total refugees as a result of the conflict at over 3 million people, including an estimated 1.5 million internally displaced persons. In addition, roughly 1 million refugees fled to Syria, 500,000 to Jordan, 150,000 to Europe, 48,000 to Iran, 30,000 to Lebanon, 6600 to Turkey and 5400 to the US.

The human cost of the war was also felt in terms of excesses by both the US and new Iraqi forces. Here, Iraqi security forces were implicated in a range of alleged human rights violations, including torture, coercion, arrest without charge and extortion. US forces were also implicated in a number of these issues, including the infamous Abu Ghraib prisoner abuse scandal. This scandal involved the torture and ritual humiliation of Iraqi prisoners in the former Ba'ath Party prison, and came to light when photos of the abuse were leaked to the *60 Minutes* programme, sparking widespread condemnation across the globe, and perpetuating the increasing suspicion of US motives by Iraqis.

Figure 8.13　Images from the Abu Ghraib prison abuse scandal
Source: Public domain

In addition, the issue of public health in Iraq remains critical. The Iraqi health system had suffered from massive shortages through the 1990s, a situation that worsened dramatically after the 2003 invasion. Here, there are widespread shortages of vaccinations against diseases such as polio, diphtheria, whooping cough, tetanus and measles. There has also been a trend of medical professionals fleeing the country in the face of a deterioration of the security situation. As such, shortages of both supplies and skilled personnel have impacted primarily on the vulnerable members of Iraqi society, particularly children and the elderly.

Table 8.3 Troop Deployments in Iraq* (2003–10)

	US	Other	Total	Annual % Change
2003	132,000	25,605	157,605	–
2004	142,000	23,306	165,306	+4.9%
2005	155,000	20,560	175,560	+6.2%
2006	160,000	19,500	179,500	+2.2%
2007	163,245	11,755	175,000	-2.5%
2008	150,000	840	150,000	-14.3%
2009	120,000	0	120,000	-20.0%
2010	49,700	0	49,700	-58.6%

* Figures calculated at year's end.

This question of population movements reveals a further disturbing result of the violence. In particular, there have been allegations of mass population movements akin to ethnic cleansing across the country, particularly in Baghdad and the strategically important city of Kirkuk in the north. The broader implications of this in terms of the levels of violence in the country are explored below. However, this process had a profound effect on Iraq's minority groups, particularly the Turkmen, Assyrian Christian and Yazidi communities.

As with all demographic figures in contemporary Iraq, it is difficult to gain accurate statistics on numbers. However, these groups constitute an estimated 5%, or 1.5 million of Iraq's roughly 30 million citizens. Other estimates put this number higher, particularly for the Turkmen population. As is discussed below, this is important in discussions of the political future of Iraq, where demographics will have a critical impact on the future of Kirkuk and its valuable oil resources.

Impacts on the US

Where the brunt of violence has been felt by the Iraqi population, the US and Coalition forces also suffered tremendous losses in this conflict. By the start of 2012, 4486 US service personnel (see Table 8.4) and 318 service personnel from the other Coalition countries as well as 1537 civilian contractors had been killed in Iraq. In addition, it is estimated that 99,065 US service personnel and 51,031 US civilian contractors (150,096 total) were injured during this period.

Table 8.4 Casualties of US Service Personnel in Iraq (2003–11)

	Casualties	Annual % Change
2003	486	–
2004	849	+74.7%
2005	846	–0.4%
2006	823	–2.7%
2007	904	+9.8%
2008	314	–65.3%
2009	149	–52.5%
2010	60	–59.7%
2011	54	–10.0%
Cumulative Total	4486	

Figure 8.14 A protest by US veterans against the conflicts in Iraq and Afghanistan

Source: Public domain

However, as with the broader impacts on the Iraqi population outlined above, the impacts on US and other Coalition personnel is broader. In particular, the scope of US troop numbers in Iraq (see Table 8.3) saw large numbers of US service personnel return from duty suffering post-traumatic stress disorder and a variety of undiagnosed injuries, including mental illness. These legacies of the conflict are also felt by those who were wounded, many now living with significant physical injuries after their service. These impacts also extend to the economic realm. In the lead-up to the war, the Bush administration estimated that the total war effort would not exceed $60 billion. Here, former Secretary of Defense Donald Rumsfeld claimed, on 2 October 2003, that Iraqi reconstruction would 'come from Iraqis – from oil revenues, recovered assets, international trade, direct foreign investment – as well as some contributions we've already received and hope to receive from the international community' (cited in Murphy, 2011).

As is outlined above, part of this programme was to be funded by the liberalisation of the Iraqi economy. However, the failure of this programme to generate resources, alongside the collapse of the state and the continuing violence, saw the financial burden for the war and reconstruction effort fall back on the

US tax payers. Here, estimates put the total cost of the war at over $3 trillion across the US economy. This has had profound impacts on both the US and global economies and helped facilitate the global financial crisis from 2007. The financial cost (see Table 8.5) also includes estimates of over $9 billion in reconstruction financing as well as over $500 million in parts and munitions, including several hundred thousand firearms that went missing between 2003 and 2004.

Table 8.5 Estimated US Expenditures on the Iraq Conflict (2003–12, Congressional Research Service estimates*)

	Expenditures ($USD billions)	Annual % Change
2003	53.0	–
2004	75.9	+43.2%
2005	85.5	+12.6%
2006	101.6	+18.8%
2007	131.2	+29.1%
2008	142.1	+8.3%
2009	95.5	–32.8%
2010	71.3	–25.3%
2011	49.3	–30.9%
2012	17.7	–64.1%
Cumulative Total	823.2	

* Figures include only funds requested through the US Congress during these financial years.

Declining Violence

As violence peaked in 2007 and 2008, a variety of factors contributed to a drop-off in these levels from this point through to the formal withdrawal of US troops on 31 December 2011. At the time, President Bush's so-called 'troop surge' of 2007, the commitment of 20,000 additional troops on top of the existing deployment of over 150,000 service personnel, was highlighted as the key to the decrease in attacks. However, three other factors were more important in halting the violence: the post-2005 'National Council for the Awakening of Iraq' (*al-majlis al-watani li-inqadh al'Iraq*), the March 2008 offensive against the Mahdi Army in Basra and the movement of populations including ethnic cleansing across Iraq.

The 'National Council for the Awakening of Iraq'

As is discussed above, two of the three main insurgent clusters, the Ba`athists/ Nationalists and the Islamist radicals, were based in Iraq's Sunni community. Here, the US and Coalition forces found their counter-insurgency operations against the former groups the most difficult due largely to the levels of popular support they enjoyed as opposed to the actions of the Islamist organisations. Where counter-insurgency operations met with some success, this was limited. A change of direction came in 2005 when middle ranking US army officers opened discussions with tribal elders in the Sunni-majority areas of Iraq's central-north. These discussions came as a result of common antagonism towards the radical Islamist movements, who both saw as counter to their own interests.

In exchange for arms, money, training and the promise of badly needed jobs, many of the large Sunni tribes who had previously fought the US agreed to stop targeting US and Coalition forces and direct their attention towards combating the Islamist movements as well as maintaining law and order in their respective regions. By 2008, it was estimated that over 50,000 Sunnis had joined one of the many ad hoc 'Awakening' councils. However, whilst this development, probably more than any other, contributed to the sharp decrease in violence from 2006 and 2007, it led to other problems where the Iraqi government became increasingly reliant on these groups for general security matters. This was problematic where the leaders of these groups were largely unmonitored, often using their control over vast regions

Figure 8.15 US soldiers with Sunnis recruited as part of the 'Awakening' movement in 2008

Source: Public domain

to engage in criminal activities and to extort funds from residents. As of 2012, the Iraqi government continued to rely on these forces for the maintenance of order in many regions across the country.

The Basra Offensive

With many of the Sunni insurgent movements halting attacks, the 25 March 2008 offensive on Basra helped offset attacks from the largest Shi`a militia, the Mahdi Army. Ceasefires had been implemented with intermittent success between the US and the Mahdi Army from 2004 to 2008. However, this situation broke down by early 2008. In the first major offensive led by the new Iraqi security forces, the Mahdi Army stronghold in the southern city of Basra was attacked over the last week of March. After intense fighting, including an estimated 300 casualties, the Iraqi, US and coalition forces subdued the militias and secured Basra. This led to the Mahdi Army ceasing military operations, and committing instead to involvement in the nascent political system in the country.

Ethnic Cleansing and a New Demographic Map in Iraq

Whilst strategic and tactical initiatives such as the 'Awakening' councils and the Basra offensive were important to the decrease in violence, the effects of what may be defined as ethnic cleansing were also significant, if not central. Indeed, the violence from 2004 became increasingly defined in terms of sectarian conflict rather than attacks on US and Coalition forces. This exhibited various trends in different parts across the country.

For instance, in Baghdad, neighbourhoods that were previously mixed between Sunni and Shi`a communities had become almost exclusively populated by one or the other of these sects by the end of 2007. Here, the city became increasingly 'cantonised' between sectarian neighbourhoods, such as the Shi`a in Sadr City and Zafaraniyah and Sunni neighbourhoods of al-Mansour and Dora. The neighbourhoods also became increasingly closed, with local militias guarding access in and out of the areas.

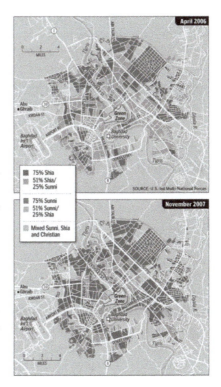

Figure 8.16 The separation of sectarian communities in Baghdad

Source: Thorp, Gene and Smith, Dita, 'Changing Baghdad', *The Washington Post*, 15 December 2007

As mentioned above, the conflict also saw large numbers of the smaller ethnic and religious groups either flee the country or become displaced within Iraq. This was a situation particularly pronounced in the northern city of Kirkuk. Here, the status of Kirkuk remains unresolved in terms of the federal system in the country, a point of contest between the Kurdish, Sunni Arab, Turkmen and Christian populations in terms of control over this oil-rich region.

US Withdrawal and the Future of Iraq

From 2007, debate over the future of the US troop presence in Iraq increasingly centred on debates of questions of if, how and when this deployment would end. For the Bush administration, pressure for the withdrawal of troops on various fronts was met with repeated statements refusing to outline a withdrawal plan arguing that this was a 'white flag of surrender'. Despite this, plans were in place as early as 2008 for a draw-down of troops, a plan given increasing impetus in light of the worsening security situation in America's other major deployment, Afghanistan.

This plan manifested in the 2008 Status of Forces Agreement (SOFA), the blueprint for the future withdrawal implemented by President Obama up to 2010. Approved by the Iraqi parliament, SOFA's main element focussed on a withdrawal of all US forces from Iraqi cities by the end of June 2009. This was extended after Obama took office to 31 August 2010, when the last US troops were withdrawn.

The New Iraqi Political System

In the wake of this massive military enterprise, including widespread casualties and the virtual destruction of the physical infrastructure of the country, efforts have been made to rebuild the political system in the country. This included a transfer of power from the CPA to a new Iraqi government in 2005, the drafting of a new constitution and the resolution of questions over the political structure of the country. The first elections, boycotted by the major Sunni parties, saw the election of the Shi`a-based United Iraqi Alliance under Prime Minister Ibrahim al-Jafaari. However, Jafaari was replaced by Nouri al-Maliki in May 2006 due to the continuing violence and lack of government services. Both Jaafari and Maliki sought to create representative governments, with selected members of the largest sectarian communities in key posts. However, the dominance of the Shi`a parties was resented by many Sunnis whilst the Kurdish parties were engaged in the federal system but also acted with increasing autonomy in the north and through the Kurdish Regional Government.

Here, the Kurdish region had become, since 2003, a virtual state within a state, seeing minimal violence on the back of security efforts by Kurdish security forces with the exception of the contested city of Kirkuk. In addition, the Kurdish parliament, or *Perleman*, administers most day-to-day affairs of the region under a coalition of the Kurdish Democratic Party (KDP) and the Patriotic Union of Kurdistan (PUK).

Figure 8.17   From left: the Iraqi Kurdish parliament building and the Kurdish Regional Government in session, in the northern Iraqi city of Irbil. The Kurdish parliament controls a variety of critical policy areas with the Kurdish-controlled regions in the north of the country operating as a virtual 'state within a state'

Sources: AP, Reuters/Caren Firouz

This dysfunctional nature of the Iraqi political system is a key source of domestic unrest, with an inability to provide regular essential government services such as electricity, sanitation, health, in addition to the ongoing security issue. This has been compounded by the ongoing controversy over the remaining ambiguities in the Iraqi constitution. The March 2010 parliamentary elections reflected this instability, with the banning of candidates before the poll and allegations of massive voter fraud.

The results of the election led to a deadlock between Ayad Allawi's al-Iraqiyya Party and Nouri al-Maliki's State of Law Coalition. This led to the paralysis of the government through 2010 as neither side could form a majority government, with Maliki finally forming a new government by 22 December. However, this did not lead to the stabilisation of the situation, with Sunni parties continuing to voice scepticism of the Shi`a dominated system whilst others saw the sectarian-based appointments as a portent of Iraq moving towards a Lebanese-style confessional system, with the instability of this model sowing the seeds of perpetual crises in Iraq.

US INTERVENTION IN AFGHANISTAN

Whilst not part of the purview of this volume, the ongoing conflict in Afghanistan has impacted on the Middle East in a variety of ways. As was discussed in Chapter 7, the origins of the al-Qaeda terrorist movement can be traced to resistance to the

Soviet forces that had invaded Afghanistan in 1979. In addition, the conflict in Afghanistan alongside the US-led invasion and occupation of Iraq has worked to gradually undermine the legitimacy and influence of the US since 2001.

This section will briefly outline the conflict in Afghanistan since the US-led actions in response to the terrorist attacks of 11 September 2001. Here, essential context is given around the origins and emergence of the Taleban, the troubled deployment of the International Assistance and Reconstruction Force (ISAF) in Afghanistan, as well as the influence of Pakistan in this conflict. This is not designed to provide a comprehensive overview of Afghan politics, but as a supplement to concurrent events in the Middle East since 2001 that have shaped the US engagement with the region, particularly in terms of security issues and the so-called 'War on Terror'.

The Taleban, Pakistan and al-Qaeda in Afghanistan

The first response to the 11 September 2001 attacks on the United States came through 'Operation Enduring Freedom', a US-led military operation launched on 7 October 2001 to remove the Taleban regime from power. Now active more than a decade, this conflict has become the longest conventional war the United States has been involved with in its history. It has also led to questions over regional stability, particularly in terms of the role of Pakistan, and has contributed to the changing role of the US in the Middle East.

The Taleban and al-Qaeda

The Taleban regime had harboured al-Qaeda since their flight from Sudan in 1996 (see Chapter 7), providing a safe haven from which the organisation planned and conducted its terrorist operations. The Taleban has its roots in the collapse of central government authority in Afghanistan after the Soviet withdrawal in 1989 and the ensuing civil war that erupted in 1992. This conflict was a result of the breakdown of the tenuous links between the various *mujahedin* anti-Soviet forces as they competed for control over the country. This saw the emergence of a variety of militias operating independently across the country, with widespread lawlessness and destruction. In addition, many Afghans become involved in a flourishing trade in opium production with the collapse of the Afghan economy (Tomsen, 2011).

This conflict dynamic changed in 1994 with the arrival of the Taleban. This movement developed out of Afghan refugee camps in northwestern Pakistan, particularly those under the influence of staunchly conservative religious groups such as Pakistan's *Jami`at `Ulama-e-Islam* (Assembly of Islamic Clergy, JUI) with funding from Pakistan's Directorate for Inter-Services Intelligence (ISI) who saw this as an opportunity for Islamabad to extend its influence over its

Figure 8.18 Taleban fighters in Afghanistan
Source: The Heritage Foundation

northern neighbour. Its origins in the *madrassah* (religious schools) of Pakistan and, later, southern Afghanistan led to the use of the name Taleban, the Pashto word for 'students' (Rashid, 2010).

This movement began to consolidate from 1991, before establishing itself within Afghanistan, in the southern city of Kandahar, by 1993. It espoused a hardline conservative religious vision for combating the chaos that plagued

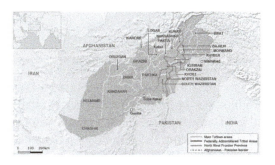

Figure 8.19 The Pakistan–Afghanistan border
Source: Central Intelligence Agency

Afghan society that combined literalist interpretations of *shari`ah* with tribal law codes and the jihadist worldview that had emerged with radical Islamist groups through the 1980s and 1990s (see Chapter 4). In this regard, it vigorously attacked any deviation from its vision for Afghan society. Its military activities began in 1994 when the group took the city of Kandahar, securing a base of operations and controlling the critical border regions with Pakistan. Here, the strict form of rule imposed by the movement was offset for many Afghans by the relative order they brought, seeing popular support drain away from the warlords and allowing the movement to take control of most of the country and the capital by the end of 1996 (Rashid, 2010).

Table 8.6 Casualties of US Service Personnel in Afghanistan (2001–11)

	Casualties	Annual % Change
2001	12	–
2002	49	+308.3%
2003	48	–2.0%
2004	52	+8.3%
2005	99	+90.4%
2006	98	–1.0%
2007	117	+19.4%
2008	155	+32.3%
2009	317	+104.5%
2010	499	+57.4%
2011	418	–16.2%
Cumulative Total	2022	

Pre-existing links between senior Taleban figures and al-Qaeda members who had fought in Afghanistan during the 1980s saw the organisation move back to Afghanistan in 1996 under the newly established Islamic Emirate of Afghanistan. It was from this base that al-Qaeda planned a number of high-profile attacks on the US, including the bombing of US embassies in Kenya and Tanzania in 1998, the attack on the *USS Cole* off the coast of Yemen in 2000 and the 11 September 2001 attacks.

'Operation Enduring Freedom'

Taleban support for al-Qaeda saw Afghanistan become the first target of the US response with the launching of 'Operation Enduring Freedom' on 7 October 2001. The initial rationale of the intervention was for the removal of the al-Qaeda safe haven in Afghanistan including the removal of the Taleban from power, to locate and prosecute those directly responsible for the 11 September attacks and to destroy the al-Qaeda organisation.

Table 8.7 Casualties of Service Personnel by Country in Afghanistan (2001–11)

Origin	Casualties	Origin	Casualties	Origin	Casualties
Albania	1	Georgia	10	Poland	35
Australia	32	Germany	53	Portugal	2
Belgium	1	Hungary	7	Romania	19
Canada	158	Italy	47	South Korea	1
Czech Republic	5	Jordan	2	Spain	34
Denmark	42	Latvia	3	Sweden	5
Estonia	9	Lithuania	25	Turkey	14
Finland	2	New Zealand	6	UK	419
France	86	Norway	10	US	2022

As is discussed above with the war in Iraq, the initial US operation in Afghanistan was not authorised by the UN Security Council. However, the George W. Bush administration argued that this intervention was legal under Article 51 of the UN Charter that allowed states to act in self-defence. In addition, the US never formally declared war on Afghanistan, arguing that the Taleban, alongside al-Qaeda, were terrorists or supporters of terrorist organisations rather than a state army. This was a critical factor in the latter stages of the conflict where detainees from this conflict were refused rights under the Geneva Protocol, instead incarcerated as 'unlawful combatants' in prisons such as the Guantanamo Bay facility on the island of Cuba.

In terms of the conflict itself, this also mirrored the trajectory of the conflict in Iraq where the initial military intervention saw the quick collapse of the regime followed by the emergence of an insurgency. Here, the al-Qaeda network in Afghanistan was largely dismantled and the Taleban forces pushed into remote pockets of Afghan territory or over the border into Pakistan by December 2001. However, the Taleban was able to re-establish itself and re-commence operations in Afghanistan by 2003.

The Ramifications of Continued Conflict in Afghanistan

Here, the US-led presence in Afghanistan struggled to make progress in terms of political development and, from 2003, also saw the re-emergence of the Taleban from both southern Afghanistan and from across the border in Pakistan leading to a deteriorating security situation and an increase in casualties for both US service personnel (see Table 8.7). This was a situation that was linked to the conflict in Iraq where the initial US deployment and its increase through 2007 as part of the so-called troop 'surge' undermined the ability of the US and its allies to conduct the war on this front with sufficient force (see Table 8.3 and discussion above).

The New Afghan Political System

The re-emergence of insurgent fighting alongside the often dysfunctional new political system bought into question the rationale for continued Western involvement in Afghanistan, an argument exploited by both the Taleban in Afghanistan and militant movements in the Middle East and elsewhere to justify further attacks on US forces and their allies. Indeed, the US-led presence in Afghanistan has been heavily exploited in the rhetoric of radical neo-jihadist movements as another instance of Western attacks on the Muslim world (see Chapters 4 and 7).

In terms of the new Afghan political system, this stemmed from an effort to draw together key factions in Afghan society, including those who had fought alongside the US-led forces from 2001. The first steps towards this came in the December 2001 Bonn Agreement under the authority of senior figure within the Pashtun community Hamid Karzai. The Bonn Agreement also set in place the structure for the drafting of a new constitution and the convening of a *loya jirga* (Grand Assembly) that met in June–July 2002, formally appointing Karzai as the President of the Afghan Transitional Administration (Maley, 2006: 33).

The **Pashtun** are an ethnic group that live on the Afghan–Pakistan border, and form the largest ethnic group in Afghanistan. The links between the Pashtun populations on either side of the border are strong, making this border region highly porous and difficult to control for either government.

In addition there is the political structure on the Pakistani side of the border, where there is minimal Pakistani government authority in the North-West Frontier Province (NWFP) and the Federally-Administered Tribal Areas (FATA), with authority wielded primarily by local notables and tribal leaders. It is estimated that 30 million Pashtun live in Pakistan and 13 million in Afghanistan.

However, despite being re-elected in 2004 and 2009, the Karzai administration has struggled to restore law and order, economic viability, or curb corruption and government excesses. In addition, the government remains vulnerable to Taleban attacks with the Afghan security services vulnerable to Taleban infiltration. The Afghan government as well as the US-led forces have also been unable to curb opium production that has boomed since 2001 with the continued stagnation of the Afghan economy.

Drone Strikes, US Security and its Legacy

The original intent of the US intervention in Afghanistan was the destruction of the al-Qaeda network and depriving it, or other militant organisations, of any future potential safe havens. In pursuit of this, the US government has employed a number of highly controversial tactics alongside the ground invasions of two countries. Together with allegations of human rights abuses through torture and other activities, the use of unmanned 'Predator' drones has been increasingly controversial. These drones conduct air strikes against suspected insurgent targets often resulting in heavy collateral

Figure 8.20 An unmanned US 'Predator' drone in action over Afghanistan

Source: Public domain

damage. Here, these attacks are increasingly highlighted as reasons why the people of Afghanistan and, increasingly, Pakistan have continued to support the Taleban. As is discussed above, the use of controversial tactics ostensibly in the prosecution of the War on Terror has fed into a cycle of further violence and instability not only in Afghanistan and Pakistan, but in the Middle East and elsewhere (Schmitt and Shanker, 2011).

POST-IRAQ US INTERVENTIONISM IN THE MIDDLE EAST

Alongside the major interventions, including the commitment of large numbers of ground troops as well as engagement in 'state-building' in Iraq and Afghanistan, the US has also been involved in security activities in Yemen and Somalia. As with the recent emerging patterns in Afghanistan, the interventions in Yemen and Somalia have focussed on the use of unmanned drone strikes aimed at suspected militant strongholds of al-Qaeda in the Arabian Peninsula in Yemen and *al-shabaab* in Somalia.

The Politics of Drone Strikes

Unmanned drones were used under previous administrations, but have been used with increasing frequency by the Obama administration. Here, the administration has sought to justify the use of this tactic in terms strikingly similar to those used to sanction the US-led invasion and occupation of Iraq. Specifically, this has focussed on the logic of 'pre-emptive defence', or the elimination of threats deemed imminent.

Figure 8.21   US Secretary of Defense since July 2011, former Director of the CIA from 2009 to 2011 and Chief of Staff for President Clinton from 1994 to 1997, Leon Panetta. Panetta has been central in speaheading the use of unmanned drones in Afghanistan, Pakistan and Yemen

Source: Public domain

The controversy surrounding this tactic stems from the civilian casualties associated with its use. This has gained added controversy in terms of the identification of those targeted through the use of so-called 'signature' strikes. This activity involves deploying drone strikes against targets based on signature patterns. These patterns are drawn from intelligence reports on probability of behaviour. That is, an estimate of where a target is likely to be. However, this has proven an inexact mode of operation, increasing the risk of civilian casualties and thus feeding into the broader antagonism generated by these tactics.

This is a controversy that has resonated not only at the local level, with a number of international non-government organisations, human rights associations and even the UN releasing reports sharply critical of the practice. On 21 June 2012, UN Special Rapporteur on Extrajudicial, Summary or Arbitrary Executions Christof Heyns stated that signature strike practices 'weaken the rule of law' and where these they 'may be lawful in an armed conflict … many target[ed] killings take place far from areas where it's recognised as being an armed conflict' (cited in Glaser, 2012). This is significant as it has called into question the legality of US government actions vis-à-vis drone strikes, leaving open the possibility for legal action to be taken against the US government through the International Court of Justice.

US Interventions in Yemen

The focus of recent US interventions in Yemen has been an effort to target the activities of al-Qaeda in the Arabian Peninsula after their formation in 2009 (see Chapter 7). However, US engagement with the Yemeni government had been active since 2001, as had been similar relationships between the US and other regional regimes such as the US and Algeria, the US and Egypt and many other bilateral connections. However, US intervention in Yemen has taken on a more direct and controversial role with the increasing reliance on drone strikes since 2011.

Unlike many other states in the region, Yemen confronts a range of other conflicts alongside the presence of Islamist militancy. These include a Shi`a insurgency in the north, ongoing tribal conflict across the country, the re-emergence of a separatist movement in the south of the country, continued problems associated with the low levels of economic development in the country (see Chapter 6) and unrest associated with the 'Arab Spring' (see Chapter 10). Each of these factors has complicated the security situation not just in the southern Arabian Peninsula, but throughout the Middle East and even into eastern Africa.

Figure 8.22 From left: Ali Abdullah Saleh, former President of Yemen Arab Republic (North Yemen) from 18 July 1978 to 22 May 1990 and the Republic of Yemen from 22 May 1990 to 26 February 2012 and Abd al-Rab Mansur al-Hadi, President since 26 February 2012

Sources: Public domain, Yemen Fox

Alongside the increased use of drones, since 2012 the US, and more specifically the CIA, has been increasingly active in training senior Yemeni military officials. There are also unconfirmed reports of the use of Special Operations groups in conjunction with Yemeni government forces in targeting alleged al-Qaeda in the Arabian Peninsula strongholds. However, as with other US military interventions, there have been strong criticisms that insufficient attention is being paid to the broader issues related to human security and development in Yemen (Phillips, 2010). As outlined in Chapter 6, Yemen lags behind in almost all indicators of development, a situation that has worsened since 2010 to the point that international humanitarian agencies now estimate that over 40% of the population had insufficient access to food, adequate sanitation and potable water, with over 1 million children suffering from malnutrition and over 500,000 people internally displaced.

The collapse of the government of Ali Abdullah Saleh and his replacement by Abd al-Rab Mansur al-Hadi on 26 February 2012 has seen a reiteration of the security focus of the US government. Here, the US has implemented new plans for training Yemeni counter-terrorism forces to weaken al-Qaeda in the Arabian

Peninsula, particularly after the successful targeting of former leader Anwar al-Awlaki by drone strike on 30 September 2011.

US Interventions in Somalia

US activities in Somalia have been more difficult to quantify than even those in Yemen. This is largely due to the complete lack of governance in Somalia and the controversial nature of previous US interventions in the Horn of Africa between 1992 and 1994. This intervention followed the collapse of the central government in Mogadishu and the outbreak of civil war in the country. There were 25,000 US troops deployed in December 1992 ('Operation Restore Hope') in support of the UN Operation in Somalia (UNOSOM) to assist in the delivery of humanitarian relief. The deteriorating security situation resulted in a failed security operation leading to the deaths of 18 US service personnel as well as 84 wounded (Harper, 2012).

Figure 8.23   Leader of the Islamic Courts Union, Sheikh Hassan Dehir Aweys (on right)

Source: Reuters/Ismail Taxta

The subsequent withdrawal of US troops came alongside the descent of Somalia into a state of lawlessness for the next decade and a half, with the country divided between competing factions and warlords combined with a humanitarian crisis that has led to over 1 million deaths from starvation and similar numbers displaced both internally and externally. Despite repeated efforts towards the establishment of rule by the Transitional Federal Government (TFG), the country remains largely lawless.

US re-engagement with Somalia came on the back of the rise of the Islamic Courts Union (ICU) in Somalia through 2006. Similar to the rise of the Taleban in Afghanistan, the ICU emerged as a strictly conservative Islamist movement that was able to generate support and extend its authority through establishing relative levels of security and stability in the areas under its control. Here, it was able to displace established 'warlords' in the southern portion of Somalia and take control of Mogadishu.

The rise of the ICU led the TFG to request international intervention. This prompted an invasion by neighbouring Ethiopia in July 2006 who feared the spread of ICU influence over its own Muslim population. By the end of 2006, the Ethiopian government had defeated the ICU forces, seeing them withdraw from

Mogadishu. However, the disbanding of the ICU saw a splinter group calling itself *harakat al-shabaab al-mujahedin* ('Movement of the Striving Youth', or simply *al-shabaab*/the youth) emerge on the Somali scene in 2010, who announced their affiliation with al-Qaeda in June 2012 (Harper, 2012).

Central to US interests here have been the reprised statement that Somalia, like Yemen and Afghanistan before it, provides a potential terrorist safe haven where attacks can be planned and implemented. Again like Yemen and Afghanistan, the US have responded with a number of policies that have increasingly centred on the use of unmanned drone strikes as well as clandestine counter-terrorist activities aimed at eliminating key members of these organisations. And again, the dilemma in terms of implementing security priorities that lead to greater resentment and insecurity has become a dominant theme of US intervention in the region.

CONCLUSION

In many ways, US military intervention in the Middle East has mirrored earlier interventions by the British and French. In particular, each of these countries occupied key regional states with public declarations that this was for the betterment of the local population. Indeed, these interventions led to widespread local unrest and resistance, further straining the relations between local actors and regional states. Whilst new forms of intervention, such as the use of drone strikes, have raised new controversies they continue to echo themes on how regional actors relate to global powers.

Study Questions

- What were the main controversies surrounding the US-led invasion and occupation of Iraq?
- What defines the patterns of insurgency in Iraq after 2003?
- What have been the main impacts of the war on the Iraqi people?
- What has characterised US military interventionism since the invasion and occupation of Iraq?
- What is the political legacy of the Iraq War within Iraq, across the Middle East and globally?
- What controversies surround the use of unmanned drone strikes as part of US counter-terrorism efforts?
- What dilemmas have resulted from US counter-terrorism operations in Iraq, Afghanistan, Pakistan and Somalia?

FURTHER READING

Akbarzadeh, Shahram, Piscatori, James, MacQueen, Benjamin and Saikal, Amin (eds) (2012) *American Democracy Promotion in the Changing Middle East: From Bush to Obama.* London: Routledge.
This volume brings together key thinkers on the issues of conflict and reconstruction that have stemmed from key US interventions in Afghanistan and Iraq.

Maley, William (2009) *The Afghanistan Wars*, 2nd ed. London: Palgrave Macmillan. An examination from perhaps the leading scholar on Afghan politics, providing a thorough overview of the various factors that continue to feed instability in Afghanistan.

Ricks, Thomas E. (2006) *Fiasco: The American Military Adventure in Iraq.* New York: Penguin.
A much publicised and critical account of the US invasion and occupation of Iraq, providing particular insights into the lack of pre-war planning on the part of the Bush administration.

Special Inspector General for Iraq Reconstruction (2009) *Hard Lessons: The Iraq Reconstruction Experience.* Arlington, VA: Special Inspector General for Iraq Reconstruction.
A highly detailed account from those involved in the troubled reconstruction process in Iraq.

 Go to the companion website at www.sagepub.co.uk/macqueen for further material including free journal articles and links to other relevant documents.

REFERENCES

Abrams, Elliott et al. (1998) 'Letter to President Clinton', 26 January; www.newamericancentury.org/iraqclintonletter.htm.
Arato, Andrew (2009) *Constitution Making Under Occupation: The Politics of Imposed Revolution in Iraq.* New York: Columbia University Press.
Arons, Nicholas (1999) 'Interview with Scott Ritter', *Federation of American Scientists*, 24 June.
Chebab, Zaki (2006) *Iraq Ablaze: Inside the Insurgency.* London: I.B. Tauris.
Coalition Provisional Authority (2003) 'Coalition Provisional Authority Order Number 39: Foreign Investment', 20 December; www.iraqcoalition.org/regulations/20031220_CPAORD_39_Foreign_Investment_.pdf.

Glaser, John (2012) 'US Drone Strike in Pakistan Kills Five People', Antiwar.com, 18 August; news.antiwar.com/2012/08/18/us-drone-strike-in-pakistan-kills-five-people/.

Harper, Mary Jane (2012) *Getting Somalia Wrong? Faith, War, and Hope in a Shattered State*. London: Zed Books.

Krueger, Alan B. (2007) 'The National Origins of Foreign Fighters in Iraq', *American Economic Association Annual Meeting*.

Maley, William (2006) *Rescuing Afghanistan*. Sydney: UNSW Press.

Murphy, Dan (2011) 'Iraq War: Predictions Made, and Results', *Christian Science Monitor*, 22 December; www.csmonitor.com/World/Backchannels/2011/1222/Iraq-war-Predictions-made-and-results.

Phillips, Sarah (2010) *Yemen: The Politics of Permanent Crisis*. London: Routledge.

Powell, Colin (2012) *It Worked for Me: In Life and Leadership*. New York: Harper.

Rashid, Ahmed (2010) *Taliban: Militant Islam, Oil and Fundamentalism in Central Asia*. New Haven, CT: Yale University Press.

Roberts, Les, Lafta, Riyadh, Garfield, Richard, Khudhairi, Jamal and Murnham, Gilbert (2004) 'Mortality Before and After the 2003 Invasion of Iraq: Cluster Sample Survey', *The Lancet*, 364 (9448): 1857–64.

Schmitt, Eric and Shanker, Thom (2011) *Counterstrike: The Untold Story of America's Secret Campaign Against Al Qaeda*. New York: Times Books.

Summers, Anthony and Swan, Robbyn (2012) *The Eleventh Day: The Full Story of 9/11*. New York: Ballantine Books.

The Guardian (2003) 'Full Text of Colin Powell's Speech: US Secretary of State's Address to the United Nations Security Council', 5 February; www.guardian.co.uk/world/2003/feb/05/iraq.usa.

The White House (2002) 'President Bush Delivers State of the Union Address', 29 January; georgewbush-whitehouse.archives.gov/news/releases/2002/01/20020129-11.html.

The White House (2006) 'The National Security Strategy of the United States of America', 16 March; www.comw.org/qdr/fulltext/nss2006.pdf.

Tomsen, Peter (2011) *The Wars of Afghanistan: Messianic Terrorism, Tribal Conflicts, and the Failures of Great Powers*. Ann Arbor, MI: Public Affairs.

UNICEF (2000) *Joint Government of Iraq–UNICEF Programme Review*. New York: United Nations.

UN News Centre (2003) 'Powell Presents US Case to Security Council of Iraq's Failure to Disarm', 5 February; www.un.org/apps/news/storyAr.asp?NewsID=6079&Cr=iraq&Cr1=inspect.

9

Israel, the Palestinians and the Peace Process

Learning Objectives

This chapter will enable a greater understanding of:

- The dynamics of the Israeli–Palestinian Peace Process.
- The key controversies surrounding specific issues in the Peace Process and the various arguments associated with these views.
- The influence of competing norms, particularly Israeli claims to self-defence and Palestinian claims to self-determination, over the conflict.
- The influence of Israeli and Palestinian narratives, particularly those relating to identity and politics.
- The impacts of the US–Israeli relationship on the conflict as well as its impacts on both Israeli and US domestic politics.

TIMELINE

29 November 1947: UNGA Resolution 181

11 December 1948: UNGA Resolution 194

22 November 1967: UNSC Resolution 242

15 December 1969: Golda Meir elected Prime Minister of Israel (Labour-led coalition)

22 October 1973: UNSC Resolution 338

3 June 1974: Yitzhak Rabin elected Prime Minister of Israel (Labour-led coalition)

20 June 1977: Menachim Begin elected Prime Minister of Israel (Likud-led coalition)

10 October 1983: Yitzhak Shamir appointed Prime Minister of Israel (Likud-led coalition)

13 September 1984: Shimon Peres elected Prime Minister of Israel (Labour-led coalition)

20 October 1986: Yitzhak Shamir elected Prime Minister of Israel (Likud-led coalition)

March 1987: Founding of Hamas

December 1987–December 1993: First *intifada*

15 November 1988: Palestinian Declaration of Independence

30 October 1991: Madrid Peace Conference

13 July 1992: Yitzhak Rabin elected Prime Minister of Israel (Labour-led coalition)

20 August 1993: Signing of the Declaration of Principles from the Oslo Negotiations

25 February 1994: Settler Baruch Goldstein kills 29 Palestinians in Hebron

4 May 1994: Palestinian Authority formed

4 November 1995: Assassination of Israeli Prime Minister Yitzhak Rabin by Israeli citizen Yigal Amir

22 November 1995: Shimon Peres appointed Prime Minister of Israel (Labour-led coalition)

18 June 1996: Benjamin Netanyahu elected Prime Minister of Israel (Likud-led coalition)

17 January 1997: Signing of the Hebron Protocol

23 October 1998: Signing of the Wye River Memorandum

6 July 1999: Ehud Barak elected Prime Minister of Israel (Labour-led coalition)

11–25 July 2000: Camp David Negotiations

28 September 2000: Ariel Sharon's visit to Haram ash-Sharif

September 2000–May 2005: Second (al-Aqsa) *intifada*

21–27 January 2001: Taba Peace Summit

7 March 2001: Ariel Sharon elected Prime Minister of Israel (Likud-led coalition)

27 March 2002: Arab League Peace Proposal

16 June 2002: Construction commences on Israeli security barrier

24 June 2002: Road Map Peace Plan announced

11 November 2004: Yasser Arafat dies

9 January 2005: Mahmoud Abbas elected head of the PA

15 August 2005: Gaza withdrawal

23 November 2005: Ariel Sharon forms the Kadima Party

4 January 2006: Ehud Olmert appointed Prime Minister of Israel (Kadima-led coalition) after Ariel Sharon suffers a stroke

25 January 2006: Hamas wins Palestinian legislative elections

12 July–14 August 2006: Israel–Hezbollah war

15 December 2006–14 June 2007: Fatah–Hamas conflict

14 June 2007: Dissolution of the Palestinian Unity Government

27 December 2008–18 January 2009: Israeli invasion of Gaza ('Operation Cast Lead')

31 March 2009: Benjamin Netanyahu elected Prime Minister of Israel (Likud-led coalition)

27 April 2011: Fatah–Hamas rapprochement (Cairo Agreement)

24 September 2011: PA submits request for full membership of the United Nations

INTRODUCTION

This chapter moves from an overview of key historic events and Israel's regional role to explore the ongoing controversies around the Israeli–Palestinian conflict. In particular, discussion here is framed around the key controversies that have hindered the development of the 'Peace Process' since 1991. In particular, detailed discussion of the process itself will be outlined in conjunction with a discussion of the issue of Israeli settlements, Palestinian refugees and the 'right of return', and the question of territory and Palestinian statehood.

In addition to these specific issues, this chapter will also discuss factors that have framed the conflict, particularly in terms of the competing norms of self-defence and self-determination alongside the competing narratives of Israeli and Palestinian identity. Finally, this chapter will also discuss the influence of the US–Israeli relationship, including the various dynamics that affect the US role in the ongoing conflict.

THE ISRAELI–PALESTINIAN PEACE PROCESS

The Israeli–Palestinian Peace Process was initiated in 1991 in Madrid and has continued with minimal success. The initiation of the process occurred as a result of the 1987 Palestinian *intifada* pressuring the Israeli government and the PLO support for Iraq during the 1990–1 Gulf War and pressuring the Palestinians towards negotiations. It was also facilitated by the thaw in Cold War tensions by the end of the 1980s. Below is an outline of the major stages of the Peace Process.

The *Intifada* and the Impacts of the Gulf War

On 9 December 1987 a wave of violent protests spread across the Occupied Territories. Characterised by organic civic unrest against both the Israeli occupation since 1967 and the ineffective leadership amongst the Palestinians, the uprising, or *intifada*, fundamentally changed the dynamics between the Israelis and the Palestinians. In particular, the 'rallies, boycotts, and protests' raised the costs of occupation for Israel as well as symbolising a challenge to the established Palestinian leadership (Baxter and Akbarzadeh, 2008: 140).

In terms of the 'internal' aspect of the *intifada*, the PLO leadership, exiled in Tunis since the 1982 Israeli invasion of Lebanon (see Chapter 3), tried desperately to gain control over events that were quickly spiralling beyond control. In terms of the 'external' aspect, the conventional military power of the Israeli army struggled to respond to this form of civil unrest, drawing heavy international criticism for armed responses to unarmed Palestinian protests. As such, the Likud government

Figure 9.1 Confrontations between Palestinian protestors and IDF personnel became a common scene from the 1987 *intifada* broadcast on the global media, seeing Israel become an increasing target of international criticism

Source: Public domain

of Yitzhak Shamir felt increasingly pressured to engage in a political process of negotiation with the Palestinians.

As the PLO leadership under Arafat struggled to respond, as well as counter the growing influence of newer Palestinian movements such as Hamas (see below), a strategic miscalculation was made that would contribute to the push towards negotiations. The Iraqi invasion of Kuwait on 2 August 1990 led to UN Security Council Resolutions 661 and 662 authorising the use of force to expel Iraqi forces from Kuwait. In response, the Arab League was divided in their response, with the Syrian regime supporting armed action as leverage for their position in Lebanon. For their part, the PLO rejected armed action, hoping to preserve the valuable funding received from Hussein's regime.

However, the oil-rich Kuwaiti regime reacted strongly to Arafat's position, labelling Arafat a traitor and calling for a cessation of all Arab funding to the PLO. They also expelled the tens of thousands of Palestinian workers from the country. This loss of funding and regional support combined with a lack of control over the *intifada* led Arafat to also consider the path of negotiation.

The Peace Process

Despite this momentum, the initial process did not result in direct talks between Israel and the Palestinians. Instead, this happened through back channels alongside a new regional initiative for regional peace negotiations. These back channel negotiations would eventually manifest into the faltering Peace Process that has become a mainstay of regional affairs.

The Madrid Conference (1991–3)

The Peace Process commenced with Madrid Conference in October–November 1991. Ostensibly, it was a conference to kick-start negotiations between Israel and its regional neighbours, with the conference attended by Israel, the Palestinians and representatives from Syria, Lebanon and Jordan. However, Israel refused to participate if the PLO served as the Palestinian representatives resulting in the Palestinians attending in a joint committee with the Jordanians.

Whilst these negotiations did not result in an official agreement between the PLO and the then-Likud Shamir government, they did lead to unofficial talks between the Palestinians and the new Labour government of Yitzhak Rabin after 1992 as well as laying the groundwork for the 1994 Israeli–Jordanian Peace Treaty. Indeed, it was the symbolism of the negotiations that was the most important outcome of the Madrid process, allowing both the Israelis and the Palestinians to outline the parameters they saw as a prerequisite for peace.

The Oslo Process and the Declaration of Principles

These developments would make their most significant progress in the Oslo Process. These negotiations began with secret negotiations between Israeli government representative Yossi Beilin, PLO representative Ahmed Qurei and Norwegian facilitator Terje Rød-Larsen during the Madrid process. This resulted in a series of meetings between high-ranking officials from both sides in Norway through 1992 and 1993, facilitating an initial agreement on negotiation parameters and, critically, recognition from both sides of each other as legitimate representatives. This was important as it established Israeli recognition of the PLO as the legitimate representatives of the Palestinians (*ergo* recognition of the Palestinians as a community) and Palestinian recognition of the State of Israel. The US became an increasingly central part of the negotiations as they took on a more official tone. By September 1993, both parties had agreed on a Declaration of Principles for future negotiations codified in a signing ceremony on the front lawn of the White House, and also leading to Nobel Peace Prizes in 1994 for Arafat, Prime Minister Rabin and Foreign Minister Shimon Peres.

The Declaration of Principles laid out aspirational goals including Palestinian self-government to be achieved through the establishment of a new Palestinian political authority that would later become the Palestinian Authority (PA). This new authority would assist in a transfer of governance during a five-year interim period during which negotiations over key issues would take place. This would culminate in so-called 'final status' negotiations resulting in a peace treaty. This final status would be

Figure 9.2 The signing of the Declaration of Principles, 13 September 1993 (from left): Yitzhak Rabin, Bill Clinton and Yasser Arafat

Source: Public domain

full mutual recognition and security assurances with a settlement based on the 1967 borders and the principles of Security Council Resolutions 242 (1967) and 338 (1973). In order for this transfer to take place, a Palestinian security force would be established and an elected parliament formed that would extend its authority over the West Bank and the Gaza Strip. This authority would also ensure Israeli security (Milton-Edwards, 2009).

However, as is discussed below, the lack of detail in the Declaration of Principles led to the process faltering almost immediately. Questions over the future of Israeli settlements, the issue of Palestinian refugees, security assurances, control of territory and many other issues remained unresolved. As such, the lack of progress through the mid-1990s saw the Peace Process stall, with a hardening of positions on both sides as they sought to strengthen their bargaining position.

The Camp David Summit

In addition to the lack of concrete progress, there was an escalation of violence between the two parties, both in terms of conflict between the IDF and the PA as well as more consequential conflict between various groups on both sides, from settlers, militant groups, to the broader civilian population. This was increasingly reflected in the growing influence of right-wing and religious parties in the Israeli political scene as well as the increasingly violent tactics amongst a number of Palestinian groups.

Figure 9.3　From left: Ehud Barak, Bill Clinton and Yasser Arafat at the　Camp David
　　　　　　Summit, 11–25 July 2000

Source: Public domain

The deterioration of the situation and the ongoing stagnation of progress over
the phased reciprocal negotiation style of the Oslo Process saw a new initiative
launched by the US in 2000. As President Clinton neared the end of his second
term, he proposed a summit between Arafat and Labour Prime Minister Barak
designed to address all the key issues in a single high-level meeting. Convened at
Camp David, the same location as the negotiations that led to the Israeli–Egyptian
Peace Treaty, this summit had ambitious aims, and failed to meet its objectives.
This failure was as much about the problematic nature of the goals of the negotiations as it was about the levels of distrust between the two parties, particularly
in terms of the increasing lack of control Arafat exerted over the Palestinians as a
result of the growing influence of Hamas (Baxter and Akbarzadeh, 2008: 147). In
addition, the Israeli political scene was increasingly polarised in terms of how to
respond to Palestinian violence through the 1990s as well as the growing radicalism of many religious parties and those in the settler movement.

Malley, Robert and Agha, Hussein (2001) 'Camp David: The Tragedy of Errors', *The
New York Review of Books*, 9 August:

In accounts of what happened at the July 2000 Camp David summit and the
following months of Israeli–Palestinian negotiations, we often hear about Ehud

Barak's unprecedented offer and Yasser Arafat's uncompromising no. Israel is said to have made a historic, generous proposal, which the Palestinians, once again seizing the opportunity to miss an opportunity, turned down. In short, the failure to reach a final agreement is attributed, without notable dissent, to Yasser Arafat.

As orthodoxies go, this is a dangerous one. For it has larger ripple effects. Broader conclusions take hold. That there is no peace partner is one. That there is no possible end to the conflict with Arafat is another.

For a process of such complexity, the diagnosis is remarkably shallow. It ignores history, the dynamics of the negotiations and the relationships among the three parties. In so doing, it fails to capture why what so many viewed as a generous Israeli offer, the Palestinians viewed as neither generous, nor Israeli, nor, indeed, as an offer. Worse, it acts as a harmful constraint on American policy by offering up a single, convenient culprit – Arafat – rather than a more nuanced and realistic analysis.

Ross, Dennis and Grinstein, Gidi (2001) 'Camp David: An Exchange', *The New York Review of Books*, 20 September:

... their [Malley and Agha's] account of 'the tragedy of errors' of Camp David – though correct in many aspects – is glaring in its omission of Chairman Arafat's mistakes. One is left with the impression that only Barak did not fulfill commitments. But that is both wrong and unfair, particularly given Arafat's poor record on compliance. Moreover, while striving to prove that the reality was far more complicated than Israel offering and Palestinians rejecting, they equate tactical mistakes with strategic errors. Did Prime Minister Barak make mistakes in his tactics, his negotiating priorities and his treatment of Arafat? Absolutely. Did the American side make mistakes in its packaging and presentation of ideas? Absolutely. Are Prime Minister Barak and President Clinton responsible for the failure to conclude a deal? Absolutely not.

On the surface, the failure of the negotiations themselves was put down to a refusal on the part of Arafat to accept an unprecedented offer on the part of the Israelis. However, this is hotly contested. For instance, Robert Malley (Special Assistant to President Clinton for Arab–Israeli Affairs and member of the Camp David negotiating team) and Hussein Agha (Palestinian participant at Camp David) have argued that this is misleading in that the Israelis never presented a specific plan to the Palestinians as well as not addressing key issues such as the question of Palestinian refugees (Malley and Agha, 2001).

In response, Bill Clinton's Middle East envoy Ambassador Dennis Ross has argued that this view ignores what he calls 'Arafat's poor record on compliance' with previous negotiations where both the US and the Israelis were prepared to

Figure 9.4 Ariel Sharon visits
Haram ash-Sharif on
28 September 2000, a
visit that sparked the
outbreak of the second,
or al-Aqsa, *intifada*

Source: Public domain

reach a deal (Ross and Grinstein, 2001). For Ross, these negotiations were to be set in a broader context of Palestinian intransigence whilst, for Malley and Agha, this was a moot point as the Palestinians did not have an agreement to consent to.

The failure of these negotiations, and the arguments over responsibility, led to a significant degeneration of the conflict and polarisation of both sides. This was symbolised in the outbreak of violence in 2000. On 28 September of that year, the leader of the Likud Party Ariel Sharon visited the Haram ash-Sharif in Jerusalem's Old City, including the al-Aqsa mosque. This visit proved provocative, sparking protests across the territories, protests that led to organised violence that would become known as the *al-Aqsa intifada*.

Government posts formerly held by **Ariel Sharon**:

- Commander, IDF (1948–74)

    o Active: 1948 War of Independence
    o 1956 Suez Crisis
    o 1967 War
    o 1973 War

- Special Aide to Prime Minister Rabin (1975–6)
- Agriculture Minister (1977–81)
- Defence Minister (1981–3)
- Industry, Trade and Labour Minister (1984–90)
- Housing and Construction Minister (1996–98)
- Foreign Minister (1998–9)
- Prime Minister (2001–6)

Sharon broke from Likud on 24 November 2005 forming the Kadima Party. He suffered a stroke on 4 January 2006, and was succeeded as Prime Minister by former Mayor of Jerusalem, Ehud Olmert.

As violence spiralled out of control again, the provisions of all previous negotiations were suspended. This sharpening of tensions was fostered by a hardening of attitudes on both sides, including the furthering of the influence of Hamas, the election of Sharon's Likud in February 2001 and the global context influenced by the events of 11 September 2001. These divisions and the general hopelessness of the situation were also reflected in the back-and-forth allegations over responsibility for the violence.

Arab League Initiatives, the 'Road Map' and Unilateral Actions

From this point, the Peace Process became sidelined by the ongoing violence as well as the global tensions post-9/11 and the subsequent US-led invasions of Afghanistan in 2001 and Iraq in 2003 (see Chapter 8). In this context, in 2002 the Arab League proposed a broad settlement that revolved around a full normalisation of relations between Israel and its neighbours, withdrawal from territories occupied after 1967 (including East Jerusalem) and a 'just settlement' of the refugee issue. The Palestinian Authority fully supported the plan, whilst it was officially rejected by the Israelis (Quandt, 2005).

Israeli rejection of this came alongside their support of the so-called 'Road Map for Peace' proposed by US President George W. Bush with the support of the UN, the EU and Russia in 2002. In many ways, the Road Map was a return to the phased negotiations process of Oslo, with a staged transition to a final settlement based around the establishment of a Palestinian state. Again, the lack of progress on key issues and reciprocal allegations of violation of the tenets of the agreement saw it essentially become redundant by the end of Bush's second term in 2008.

There was one significant change to the political landscape when Prime Minister Sharon instigated a unilateral withdrawal of settlements from the Gaza Strip, an area increasingly dominated by Hamas. For their part, the growing power of this movement was codified in 2006 when they defeated the dominant Fatah faction in the elections for the Palestinian parliament. Whilst this is detailed below, this has led to a situation that resembled the pre-Madrid scenario where key factions on both sides refused to recognise the other as legitimate.

Indeed, this was reinforced by a successful effort on the part of Sharon and President Bush to marginalise Arafat, seeing him confined in his compound in Ramallah after 2002 under allegations of instigating the violence associated with the al-Aqsa *intifada*. By late 2004, Arafat had fallen ill, passing away on 11 November of that year. His old combatant Sharon suffered a stroke in 2006, leaving him incapacitated. As such, even the most basic building blocks of the Peace Process lay in tatters.

THE PARAMETERS OF NEGOTIATIONS

From exploring the dynamics of the negotiation process, it is important to now unpack the key parameters of negotiations. In particular, this section will outline the key elements that continue to define the conflict between the Israelis and the Palestinians. These include the issue of Israeli settlements, Palestinian refugees, the occupation, borders and territory and Palestinian statehood. In addition, competing norms relating to violence and self-determination and competing narratives relating to the character of both the Israeli and Palestinian communities remain hotly contested.

Israeli Settlements

Settlement construction and expansion are perhaps the most inflammatory issue defining this conflict. For many Palestinians, they represent the efforts to control and divide the territory they hope will be the basis for a future Palestinian state. For many Israelis, they represent the fulfilment of the goal of Israeli control, ensuring Israeli security and an expression of the desire for control over the historic areas of Judea and Samaria.

Under international law, the construction of **settlements** is considered illegal. For the United Nations, this is based on an interpretation of the Fourth Protocol of the Geneva Convention relating to the 'Protection of Civilian Persons in Time of War' and enshrined in Security Council Resolution 465 of 1980. The resolution states, in Article 5, that 'all measures taken by Israel to change the physical character, demographic composition, institutional structure or status of the Palestinian and other Arab territories occupied since 1967, including Jerusalem, or any part thereof, have no legal validity and that Israel's policy and practices of settling parts of its population and new immigrants in those territories constitute a flagrant violation of the Fourth Geneva Convention relative to the Protection of Civilian Persons in Time of War and also constitute a serious obstruction to achieving a comprehensive, just and lasting peace in the Middle East'.

Settlements are Jewish districts built on land occupied after the 1967 War, including the formerly Jordanian-held territories in the West Bank and East Jerusalem, Syrian-held territories in the Golan Heights, until 1982, Egyptian-held territories in the Sinai Peninsula and, until 2005, Egyptian-held territories in the Gaza Strip. The construction and growth of these settlements is a critical part of the ongoing conflict, particularly in terms of the issue of territoriality and the establishment of a territorially contiguous state.

For the United Nations, and many within the international community, the construction and maintenance of settlements are illegal. For the UN, this stems from a view that settlements are an effort to change the physical and demographic character of the Occupied Territories, an act in contravention of the Fourth Geneva Protocol. The Israeli position counters that this provision in the protocol relates to the legal status, not physical status, and that the construction of settlements has not affected final status negotiations.

In addition, there is greater ambiguity around the construction of settlements in East Jerusalem and the rest of the West Bank. After the 1967 War, Israel extended the municipal boundaries of East Jerusalem and formally annexed this area. As a result, Israel considers this to be a separate issue to both the status of settlements as well as broader negotiations to the rest of the West Bank territory.

According to the Israeli Information Centre for Human Rights in the Occupied Territories (B'Tselem), Israel has constructed 124 'official' settlements in the West Bank as of 2011 with over 100 more 'unofficial' settlements

Figure 9.5 Israeli settlement construction in the West Bank up to 2010

Source: UN-OCHA

or outposts. In addition, there are 12 large settler communities in East Jerusalem alongside 'settler enclaves' in Palestinian neighbourhoods through East Jerusalem (B'Tselem, 2011a). These settlements, outposts, enclaves and other communities house an estimates 516,569 people (see Table 9.3). In addition, the growth rate of the settler population is more than double that of the non-settler Israeli population. Here, settlements range in size from around 50,000 people such as Beitar Illit south of Jerusalem and 20,000 people in Ma`ale Adumin east of Jerusalem to smaller communities. Indeed, the majority of the settlements in the West Bank are small communities. In this regard, it is often argued that it is not the size of the settlements but their strategic location that is of most controversy, in enabling Israeli control over strategically important and agriculturally rich areas of the territory.

Controversy over settlements has moved from one of new settlement construction (at its peak through the 1980s, 1990s and mid-2000s) to the expansion of existing settlements. This relates to the provisions of the various stages of the Peace Process that have sought to prohibit settlement construction outside 'natural growth'. This reflects the ambiguity of the provisions of the Oslo Accords on this issue where there was no explicit reference to the prohibition of settlement expansion. However, on the other hand, there was reference to efforts to preserve the

Figure 9.6   East Jerusalem,
including municipal
boundaries,
settlements and
major population
centres

Source: Palestinian Academic
Society for the Study of
International Affairs

'integrity' of the West Bank as a basis for a future, territorially contiguous Palestinian state. Equally important in this regard are the issues of access and mobility between the settlements and the connections between settlements and pre-1967 Israel. Here, all the major arterial roads are controlled by the IDF with the broader infrastructure network throughout the West Bank being connected to the broader system of IDF-controlled checkpoints.

As such, Israeli settlements now form an indelible part of the demographic, geographic and socio-economic landscape of the West Bank. However, many Palestinians and indeed many Israelis argue that there can be no final resolution to the ongoing crisis without the withdrawal from some, if not all, of the settlements across this territory. This has caused a major division within Israeli society. On the one hand, there are those that argue that the abandonment of support for the settlements puts at risk the security of Israel, shows weakness in the face of Palestinian aggression, or forfeits a final goal of establishing permanent and official control over all of Mandate era Palestine. On the other hand, Palestinians argue that settlements are designed to create new 'facts on the ground', dispossessing Palestinians of legally held land and undermining the possibility of a viable Palestinian state in the future. In addition, Israeli opponents of the settlements argue that they also strip the Israeli state of valuable resources and create unnecessary tension and conflict.

Palestinian Refugees and the Right of Return

As was outlined in Chapter 3, the issue of Palestinian refugees was one of the earliest and most controversial elements surrounding this conflict. According to the UN Relief and Works Agency for Palestine (UNRWA), the peak international body assigned to this issue, over 700,000 Palestinians left the newly created state of Israel between 1947 and 1948. These communities settled largely in Jordan as well as the territories to be occupied after 1967 (the West Bank and the Gaza Strip), and in Syria, Lebanon as well as across the region and globally. Here, there are an estimated 5 million descendants of this original community. The status of this community and their rights continue to be a central feature in the conflict and negotiations over a settlement.

The Origins of the Refugee Crisis

One aspect of this controversy centres on the causes of the flight of Palestinians during 1947–8. In simple terms, the Israeli government position has been to argue that, by and large, the Palestinian population left of their own accord after ignoring offers to stay and accept Israeli citizenship. Those that fled did so in response to deliberate scare campaigns on the part of invading Arab governments. Alternatively, the Palestinian position is one where the various Zionist groups of then the new Israeli state forcibly expelled the Palestinians in line with the broader vision of 'ethnically cleansing' the former British Mandate.

An alternative view to this is presented by Israeli revisionist historians, such as Benny Morris, who have not discounted the forced removal of Palestinians during 1947–8, but argue that it was 'born of war, not by design, Jewish or Arab' (Morris, 1987: 286). This is a perspective that is not an echo of the official Arab stance. Indeed, for Morris, the Arab invasions were the primary factor in sparking a broader crisis.

The 'Right of Return'

UNRWA has a mandate over 'people whose normal place of residence was Palestine between June 1946 and May 1948, who lost both their homes and means of livelihood as a result of the 1948 Arab–Israeli Conflict'. Here, the activities of the organisation are guided by United Nations General Assembly Resolution 194 of December 1948, that 'refugees wishing to return to their homes and live at peace with their neighbour should be permitted to at the earliest practicable date' with the choice of 'returning to their homes now in Israel … or receiving compensation for the lost property'. As such, the controversy surrounding this issue stems not just from the flight of Palestinians but controversy over a claimed 'right of return' and compensation.

> **Resolutions** passed through the General Assembly that do not relate to the internal workings of the organisation are considered **non-binding** on members.
>
> Those passed through the Security Council can be both **binding** and non-binding depending on the Chapter that it is issued under. Binding resolutions are passed under Chapter VII, 'Action with Respect to Threats to the Peace, Breaches of the Peace, and Acts of Aggression'.
>
> Chapter VII resolutions can also authorise the use of force against a member state.

Officially, the Israeli government position on the right of return refers back to the stance of the Jewish Agency during the 1947–8 war, the tenets of United Nations General Assembly Resolution 181 (the Partition Plan), as well as the Israeli

Declaration of Independence that state Arab inhabitants of the proposed Jewish state would be entitled to full citizenship. However, this is conditioned by the premise that those who left during the 1947–8 period are not entitled to this citizenship. Therefore, there is no basis for accepting Palestinian refugees back into Israel and their claims for citizenship and, hence, evidence of land ownership prior to 1947–8 is void. In addition, Israel also discounts the provisions of General Assembly Resolution 194 as it is a non-binding resolution.

Mahmoud Abbas, head of the Palestinian Authority (15 May 2010): 'The return of the Palestinian refugee to his or her home is a constant right that can never be debated and a solution to the refugees issue would never be fair as long as it doesn't include all their historic rights.'

Benjamin Netanyahu, Prime Minister of Israel (28 June 2011): 'The solution to the refugee problem, both in a practical sense and in the question of justice has to be addressed in the Palestinian state and not at the expense of the solitary, the one and only Jewish state.'

Overlaying this is a view that the return of Palestinian refugees to Israel would destroy the Jewish character of the state. With an estimated 7.5 million people living in Israel, the return of even a portion of the refugee population under the UNRWA mandate would significantly alter the demographics of the country. In addition, the provision for compensation is countered by charges that should this be paid, the Arab states should compensate the loss of property for those Jewish communities who were expelled across the Arab world during 1947–8.

There are a variety of 'official' Arab views on this. For the Arab League, the official stance is one of confrontation with Israel that entails a refusal to grant citizenship to Palestinian refugees outside the Occupied Territories. In this regard, Arab states, with the exception of Jordan in 1967, have avoided granting citizenship to Palestinian refugees as a means to keep this issue on the global agenda, as well as maintain their confrontational stance vis-à-vis Israel.

This is a position also rooted in the unique legal position of the Palestinian refugees. The 1951 Refugee Convention did not include reference to the Palestinian refugee community as Arab states sought to avoid 'submerging Palestinian refugees within the 1951 Convention' as well as avoiding the direct responsibility for their welfare (Knudsen, 2009: 12). As such, the rights of Palestinian refugees are not covered by the 1951 Convention, only by the provisions of the UNRWA mandate. Here, the protections afforded refugees under the Convention do not cover Palestinian refugee communities, and even then Palestinian refugees must be resident in one of the operation areas of the UNRWA mandate (the Occupied Territories, Jordan, Syria and Lebanon).

This legal ambiguity extends to the official Palestinian position, claiming the right of return based on Article 13 of the Universal Declaration of Human Rights that states 'everyone has the right to leave any country including his own, and to return to his country' as well as the tenets of Resolution 194. This is not without controversy also, where the Israeli government claims that this provision of the Declaration of Human Rights applies only to those with citizenship of said 'country', therefore, the Palestinian communities who left during 1947–8 have no binding claim.

The Occupation, Borders and Territory

The issue of territory and demographics extends through to the broader question of territory and control. In particular, the possibility of the creation of a Palestinian state on some or all of the territory occupied by Israel after 1967 (with the exception of the Golan Heights) is central here.

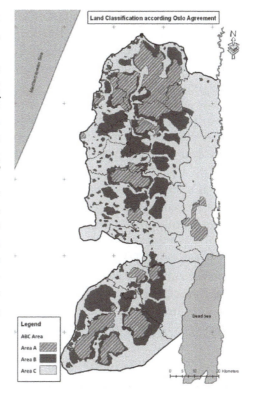

Figure 9.7 The division of the West Bank into Areas A, B and C under the Oslo Accords: Area A (18% of the West Bank) has full PA control; Area B (21%) has PA civil and joint security control; Area C (61%) has Israeli civil and security control

Source: Public domain

Alongside the issue of settlements, this is an issue that deals with Israeli military control, land appropriation, control over resources (particularly water) and infrastructure, and Palestinian movement.

The Two-State Solution and Palestinian Statehood

The 'Two-State Solution' is perhaps the central premise of negotiations, based on the vision of the creation of a Palestinian state in the West Bank and the Gaza

Strip. It is based on the principles of General Assembly Resolution 181 (1947) for the partition of the former British Mandate of Palestine. Whilst there was rejection of this proposal by the Arab states (see Chapter 2), it did establish the principle of two independent states within the territory as the default international position on the crisis.

As with any state, achievement of *de jure* independence requires a number of factors. The two most important of these are recognition by the international community and control over a clearly defined territory. This control requires clear, demarcated borders over which a state can extend its sovereignty. This principle was a core part of the Oslo Negotiations as well as subsequent negotiations. At Oslo, agreement was reached over a gradual transfer of authority from Israel to the Palestinian authority, based on three areas (A, B and C).

However, this process received sharp criticism due to the division of the West Bank into pockets of territory under direct PA authority, divided by areas still under Israeli control. Here, allegations are made that Israel has a view of a future Palestinian 'entity' that would be disarmed, only semi-independent and without territorial contiguity (i.e. territory in contact or viable proximity). Here, Israel would maintain control of the major arterial roads in the territory, incorporate major settlements into Israel-proper, and prevent the Palestinian state or entity from sharing a border with its neighbour Jordan. For Israelis supportive of this view, it is necessary to prevent the Palestinian state emerging as a future security threat. For Palestinians, it is an attempt to create a Palestinian community dependent on Israel for its economic viability and security.

East Jerusalem and the Old City

In addition to the aforementioned issues, there is also no consensus on the status of East Jerusalem. As was mentioned previously, Israel had expanded the municipal boundaries of the city and formally annexed the territory after the 1967 War. Here, Israel claims both the western and eastern portions of the city as its formal capital, a move not recognised by the majority of states in the international community. The Palestinian desire is for the establishment of East Jerusalem as the capital of a future Palestinian state.

In many ways, the struggle for control over East Jerusalem is a microcosm of the entire conflict. The city holds a significant place for all communities in religious and historic terms. Here, struggles for territory often come down to control over residential neighbourhoods, controversies over housing demolitions and the legal status of land ownership, as well as custodianship over the core of the Old City of Jerusalem, the Temple Mount/Haram ash-Sharif. Official custodianship over the Temple Mount/Haram ash-Sharif had been part of an Islamic *waqf* (religious

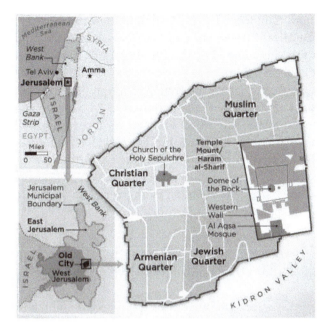

Figure 9.8 The Old City of Jerusalem

Source: Public domain

endowment) since 1187 CE, after the Muslim reconquest of the city during the Crusader period. After 1967, the Israeli government passed the 'Preservation of the Holy Places Law' that preserved the *waqf*. Here, the IDF controls access to the site, whilst PA representatives control security inside the site.

Perhaps the most contested piece of territory in Israel/Palestine is what Israelis call the **Temple Mount (Har haBayith)** and the Palestinians call the **Noble Sanctuary (Haram ash-Sharif)**. It is a site of critical importance for Judaism and Islam.

In Jewish tradition, it is the site of creation and the historic centre of governance, including the last remnants of the second Jewish Temple destroyed by the Romans in 70 CE. For Muslims, it is the site of the Prophet Muhammad's ascension to heaven (Dome of the Rock) and the al-Aqsa mosque, one of the oldest mosques in the world.

The Palestinian Declaration of Statehood

Along with a range of unilateral actions, including Sharon's 2005 Gaza withdrawal, there have been efforts by the Palestinians to circumvent stalled negotiations through declarations of independence. The first of these came in 1988, with a proclamation that included the designation of East Jerusalem as the capital of the state. However, whilst this was adopted by the PA after 1993, it was never implemented or used as a tool in negotiations.

Despite this, a new effort at a unilateral declaration of statehood came in 2011 in the wake of the string of failed negotiations. On 24 September 2011, the head of the PA Mahmoud Abbas submitted a request for recognition of Palestine as an independent state in the UN based on the 1967 borders, with East Jerusalem as its capital. Whilst rejected by Israel as well as the US, UK and a number of other states, this move had significant implications in that, should Palestine gain full UN membership it would redefine the conflict as an inter-state conflict, drawing implications for Israel in its occupation of territory.

COMPETING NORMS AND COMPETING NARRATIVES

Framing these specific issues are broader issues of norms and narratives that have worked to perpetuate this conflict, hardening attitudes on both sides and rationalising the use of violence. This section will unpack these broad issues, articulated in terms of the competing norms of Israeli self-defence versus Palestinian self-determination as well as the evolving and contested nature of both Israeli and Palestinian identity.

Whilst the discussion of norms may seem superficial, their influence on efforts to end the Israeli–Palestinian conflict is important, with real-world impacts. In particular, the competing norms of self-determination on the part of the Palestinians and self-defence on the part of the Israelis play a key role in the perpetuation of violence, instability and mistrust (Rane, 2009: 41). That is, Palestinian claims for independence and self-determination are used to validate various actions, whether they be labelled as resistance to occupation, struggles for independence, or terrorism. On the other hand, Israeli claims for security and self-defence are also used to justify actions that are variously understood as necessary protection of a community from an existential threat, a sovereign right, violation of international law, or state-sponsored terrorism.

In this way, one may say that these issues of 'identity and insecurity' are 'mutually reinforcing processes' (Peleg, 2004: 11; Smith in Fawcett, 2009: 234). This section will explore the issue of violence through this question of competing norms by examining the actions of the highly controversial Palestinian organisation Hamas, and the equally controversial Israeli programmes of the 'security barrier' and control of Palestinian movement in the West Bank.

National Security and the Question of Violence

Hamas

Central to this discourse have been the activities of Hamas. Founded in 1987 as a branch of the Muslim Brotherhood (see Chapter 4), a core tenet of the movement was the establishment of an Islamic state in all of the Mandate of Palestine. This goal is enshrined in the 1988 Hamas Charter, a factor highlighted as evidence that this organisation is focussed on the destruction of the State of Israel. Indeed, the movement continues to be classified as a terrorist organisation by Israel as well as the US, UK, the EU, Australia and many other states.

Table 9.1 Israeli–Palestinian Casualties (B'Tselem 2000–12 estimates)

Palestinians killed by IDF	6473
Palestinians killed by Israeli civilians	50
Palestinians killed by Palestinians	669
Israeli civilians killed by Palestinian civilians	254
IDF personnel killed by Palestinian civilians	252

The movement was marginal in influence compared to the dominant Fatah faction in the PLO and, later, PA. However, it was an important element in the first *intifada* before rising to prominence through the 1990s on the back of a range of violent activities. From 1993 to 2005, the organisation instigated a campaign of suicide bombing of civilian targets within Israel, resulting in hundreds of civilian deaths (see Table 9.1). In addition, it continues to carry out rocket attacks on civilian targets from its stronghold in the Gaza Strip (see Table 9.2).

The Hamas presence in the Gaza Strip was magnified by two interrelated events. The first of these was the so-called 'Disengagement Plan' implemented by Israeli Prime Minister Ariel Sharon in 2005. First announced the previous year, Sharon's plan involved the withdrawal of the 21 Israeli settlements from the Gaza Strip (as well as four smaller settlements in the West Bank). A number of settlers refused, prompting controversy as the IDF were employed to remove these settlers from the Gaza region. In addition, the plan involved military withdrawal from the Strip, with Israel to maintain control of access in and out of the territory (Levitt and Ross, 2006). Both of these actions prompted dissent among the pro-settler lobbyists, who opposed any withdrawal, and among pro-Palestinian lobbyists, who characterised

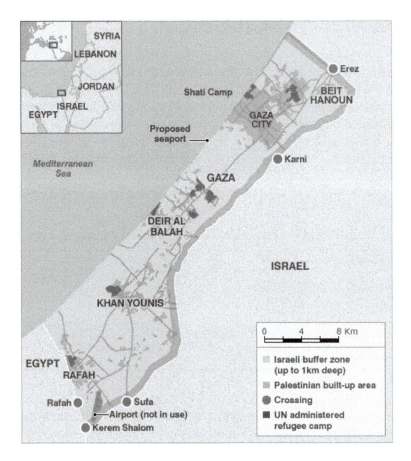

Figure 9.9 The Gaza Strip
Source: UN-OCHA

the closure of Gaza's borders as a form of mass imprisonment of the estimated 1.7 million people who live within the 365 square-kilometre territory.

Table 9.2 Palestinian Attacks in Israel

Attack Type	Number of Attacks	Casualties
Suicide bombings in Israel (2000–7 estimates)	140	542
Rocket and mortar attacks from the Gaza Strip (2005–11 estimates)	11,138	33

The second decisive event happened in 2006 when Hamas defeated the previously dominant Fatah faction for control over the Palestinian Legislative Council, claiming 76 of the 132 seats in the Palestinian parliament. This led to a great deal of consternation amongst the Palestinians and Israelis as well as within the international community, as Hamas, who maintained a confrontational stance with Israel, received a democratic mandate. As a result, the US led calls for Hamas to announce adherence to all previous negotiations between the PA and Israel, including a renunciation of violence and recognition of Israel. Hamas countered with an offer of a ceasefire coupled with an Israeli withdrawal to the pre-1967 borders. This led to a stalemate and subsequent freeze on international aid to the Palestinian Territories.

This tension was not limited to the regional and global level, with hostilities between Hamas and Fatah quickly erupting into open violence through 2007. The fighting left over 600 Palestinians dead and PA authority in disarray. By the end of 2007, Palestinian political authority became split with Fatah loyalists fleeing Gaza and Hamas loyalists fleeing the West Bank, essentially creating two Palestinian entities. However, by 2012 signs of a rapprochement were evident when Hamas and Fatah signed an agreement for a new national unity government, a move that was coupled with efforts at the UN for an application for international recognition of the Palestinian unilateral declaration of statehood (see above).

Checkpoints and the 'Security Barrier'

This trend towards unilateral actions in the wake of the stalled Peace Process continued in 2002 with the initiation of construction of the Israeli 'security barrier'. The barrier policy was implemented by the Sharon government ostensibly to guard against Palestinian suicide bombings that accompanied the al-Aqsa *intifada*. However, the barrier has courted controversy, where its construction and planned route have deviated from the 1967 Green Line. Here, there have been allegations that the barrier is being used as part of a 'land grab' policy, alongside settlements, to create new facts on the ground in terms of territorial demarcations.

In this regard, the Israeli government frames the construction of the barrier strictly in terms of the 'fundamental right of self-defence' in the protection of citizens inside the 1967 borders as well as in East Jerusalem and the larger West Bank settlements. Here, the Israeli government highlights the sharp decline in suicide attacks since the construction of the wall, from 17 attacks between April and December 2002 to five in all of 2003 (Israeli Ministry of Foreign Affairs, 2007). In addition, the Israeli government has claimed that the fence is a temporary measure, not a permanent fixture.

Figure 9.10   The security barrier is a highly controversial element of the occupation. Critics argue it is part of a 'land grab' and plan for permanent occupation whilst supporters argue it is a legitimate response to violence and has resulted in a sharp decline in Palestinian suicide bombings in Israel

Source: Electronic Intifadah, Reuters/Reinhard Krause

For others, the barrier is a clear example of an effort to concretise Israeli territorial gains, particularly in relation to the hotly contested issue of East Jerusalem. In total, roughly 12% of the West Bank falls on the western, or Israeli, side of the barrier, a move that includes 60 settlements, including roughly 380,000 settlers or 87% of the total settler population (B'Tselem, 2011b). This figure includes all of East Jerusalem, including the settlements and Jewish communities there. In addition, the barrier directly affects roughly 500,000 Palestinians with a number of communities now on the western side of the barrier or either fully or partially surrounded by the barrier, cut off from other Palestinian territories. As such, it is also alleged that the barrier works alongside the series of checkpoints and security stations in the West Bank. For instance, Palestinians on the west of the barrier require permits to leave their communities whilst those fully or partially enclosed by the barrier have to pass through IDF-administered checkpoints.

These checkpoints are another highly controversial element of the occupation, and again court differing views. For the Israeli government, they are a key part of ensuring security to monitor the movement of people to guarantee that no potential attacker may pass into Israel proper or target Israeli settlements. In contrast, it is argued that these checkpoints are a violation of Palestinian human rights in terms of freedom of movement and transportation relating to the viability of the economy in the Occupied Territories. In addition, many have argued that the checkpoints, along with the security barrier and other features are designed for a permanent state of occupation rather than temporary measures designed for general security.

Identity Politics in Israel

As discussed in Chapter 2, the State of Israel is the culmination of the Zionist vision of rearticulating Jewish life on a national basis. As such, perhaps the central premise of the Israeli stance on all elements of the ongoing conflict is the establishment, maintenance and preservation of Israel as a Jewish state. Here, there is ambiguity around the relationship between Judaism and Israel in terms of how this relates to citizenship, inclusion and the attitude towards the ongoing conflict with the Palestinians.

Israel as a Jewish State

This notion of Israel as a Jewish state differs from that of, for instance, the nature of post-revolutionary Iran as an Islamic state (see Chapter 4). In particular, the structure of the Israeli political system is one of a unicameral parliamentary democracy similar to those found in many parts of the world. It does not have an official religious element defining how political institutions are structured. However, the founding principle of Zionism is focussed first and foremost on the role of Israel as a homeland for the Jewish people. Whilst Israel has no formal

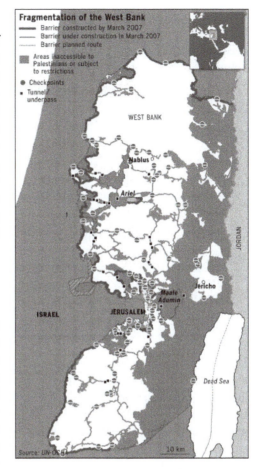

Figure 9.11 The 'security barrier', checkpoints and areas under IDF control throughout the West Bank

Source: UN-OCHA

constitution, this position is expressed in the Declaration of Independence that opens with the statement that 'The Land of Israel was the birthplace of the Jewish people' where 'their spiritual, religious and political identity was shaped'.

Israel has no formal written **constitution**, but, like Britain and many other states, has a constitutional framework based on a number of documents. These include the 1948 Declaration of Independence, the 1950 Law of Return and the 1952 World Zionist Organisation Law.

In addition, this Jewish character would be strengthened with Israel being 'open for Jewish immigration' as well as an 'appeal to the Jewish people throughout the diaspora to rally round the Jews of *Eretz*-Israel in the tasks of immigration and upbuilding' (State of Israel, 1948). Finally, the centrality of the Holocaust in the narrative of the Israeli state is central, emphasising the need for a national home to protect the community after the horrors of World War II.

In broad terms, the Jewish community can be divided between **Ashkenazi** and **Sephardi** communities. The Ashkenazi are Jewish communities from Europe (excluding southern Europe), particularly those who migrated from Germany and Eastern Europe from the 19th century.

The Sephardi are communities from southern Europe (Spain and Portugal), North Africa and the Middle East. Those from North Africa and the Middle East are sometimes referred to as Mizrahi Jews.

In Israel today, it is estimated that half of the population are descendants from the Mizrahi communities and the other from Ashkenazi communities, particularly recent migrants from Eastern Europe.

Here, there are controversies surrounding the relationship between Judaism and Jewish statehood. These are reflective of the similar tensions in Islam in reconciling temporal or earthly sovereignty with divine sovereignty (see Chapter 5). Unlike Iran, where the political system was shaped around particular conceptions of how religious authority should be structured (*vilayet-e-faqih*), Israel has opted for a formal division between the parliamentary system and areas of civil law where religious law is employed, a response mirrored in many other societies across the Middle East such as Egypt, Iraq and Turkey.

Whilst this is a critical question for Israel itself, it has also become a key feature of negotiations with the Palestinians. Since 2011, Israeli Prime Minister Netanyahu has focussed on explicit recognition of Israel as a 'Jewish state' by both Fatah and Hamas as a prerequisite for further negotiations. Here, this is seen to undercut the recognition of the *state* of Israel, without reference to the religious element, made by Fatah and the broader PLO during the Oslo Negotiations in 1993. Further, critics argue that this position does not have a basis in any of the earlier documents or positions on the conflict (Shlaim, 2011). For instance, as was discussed in Chapter 2, the Balfour Declaration and the Anglo-American Commission of Inquiry both argued for the establishment of a Jewish homeland without explicit references to a Jewish state.

Yisrael Beiteinu ('Israel is Our Home') was formed in 1999 by former Likud member Avigdor Lieberman. Based largely on support from the large Russian migrant population in Israel, the party holds a hardline position on the Peace Process as well as advocating the removal of citizenship from Arab–Israeli citizens if they do not publicly proclaim allegiance to the State of Israel. In addition, the party advocates a prioritisation of an official Orthodox Judaism over other streams within the religion.

In the 2010 legislative elections, the party won 15 seats, making it the third largest party in the Knesset (Israeli parliament) and a key coalition partner in the government headed by Likud Prime Minister Benjamin Netanyahu.

In addition, this has significant ramifications for the political scene inside Israel where there is heated debate over the current and future character of the state. This question of the country's Jewish character has become an increasingly central question in Israeli political discourse, reflected in the increasing representation of explicitly religious parties in the Israeli parliament. Since the 1970s, focus on the Jewish identity of Israel was led by the Likud Party, whose victory in the 1977 general election under Menachim Begin was a key turning point in Israeli politics and that saw Likud dominate conservative politics with victories seeing them in power from 1977 to 1991, 1996 to 1999, 2001 to 2005 and then again from 2009.

From this point, a number of newer parties have emerged that have sought to frame Israel in terms of religious identity. This is a problem for the founding documents of the State of Israel that do not classify the country as a religious state. Indeed, should this notion of an explicitly Jewish state be followed through, it raises questions over the status of civil versus religious law, allegations that the country is moving towards theocracy, and the status of non-Jewish citizens in the country.

Table 9.3 Israel and the Palestinian Territories Population Statistics (2011 estimates)

Population Totals	
Israel: Total	*7,590,758*
Palestinians (Arab–Israeli Citizens): Total	*1,713,500*
Settlers: Total	*516,569*
Settlers: East Jerusalem	192,202
Settlers: West Bank	304,201

(Continued)

Table 9.3 (Continued)

Population Totals	
Settlers: Golan Heights	20,166
*Palestinian Territories: Total**	*4,225,710*
West Bank (excluding East Jerusalem)*	2,568,555
East Jerusalem*	192,800
Gaza Strip*	1,657,155
Total	*11,816,468*

Demographic Changes per Annum	
Israel 1967 borders: Total	*1.9%*
Jewish population	1.7%
Arab population	2.6%
Settler population: Total	*4.9%*
*Palestinian Territories: Total**	*2.7%*
West Bank (including East Jerusalem)	2.1%
Gaza Strip	3.4%

* Not including Israeli settler population.

Moreover, the debate about the place of religion in Israel is unique in that it is as much about demographics as it is about religious-political doctrine. This is not to discount these important debates, particularly in terms of religious opinions on statehood, refugees, the ongoing occupation and other matters. However, the question of numbers, and what this means for the future of Israel as a Jewish state, is a defining feature of the contemporary debate.

Table 9.4 Israeli Demographics* (2011 estimates)

Ethnic and Religious Groups	*Percentage*	*Total*
Jewish: Total	*75.6%*	*5,738,613*
Palestinians (Arab–Israeli Citizens): Total	*22.6%*	*1,713,500*
Palestinian Sunni	18.1%	1,374,229

Table 9.4 (Continued)

Ethnic and Religious Groups	Percentage	Total
Palestinian Christian	2.3%	175,290
Palestinian Druze	2.2%	163,981
Other**	1.8%	138,645
Total		7,590,758

* Not including population outside the 1967 borders.
** Include non-Arab Christians, African refugees, Armenians, Assyrians, Circassians, Roma and others.

As is shown in Tables 9.3 and 9.4, the Jewish population is a clear majority within the pre-1967 borders of Israel. However, the growth of the Arab Israeli population outpaces that of the Jewish Israeli population by 1% per year. Currently more than 20% of the population, this shift is gradual but consequential. In a parliamentary system such as Israel, this has raised concerns over the growing proportion of Arab voting power. However, this is a situation that is more worrisome for Israeli policy makers with regard to the total population of both Israel proper as well as the Occupied Territories. Here, the Palestinian population is in a majority, and growing at a quicker rate.

Table 9.5 Regions of Origin of Jewish Migrants to Palestine/Israel 1882–2010 (2010 estimates)

	Region of Origin	Total
1	Asia (including the Middle East and former Soviet Asian Republics)	3,620,586
2	Europe (including former Soviet European Republics)	2,217,632
3	Africa	540,507
4	Americas	203,073
5	Asia/Pacific	4991
6	Unknown	5746

In addition, as mentioned above, there are questions over the notion of Jewish identity in Israel itself. This is a question that often occurs in so-called settler societies, countries such as the US, Australia, Canada, New Zealand and others where the majority of the population are migrants from across the globe who have arrived relatively recently. In Israel, as Table 9.5 highlights, there is great diversity even amongst the Jewish population. These divergent heritages, including differences over notions of Jewish identity that relate to differing historic experiences, have crystallised into political divisions between older and newer communities as well as communities from different regions on the questions of the Peace Process, the character of the State of Israel and other issues.

Palestinian Nationalism and Identity

As was discussed in Chapter 4, nationalist ideologies have formed a key part of Arab political discourse from the 20th century onwards. Whilst the influence of nationalist ideologies has waned in recent decades, it remains a key part of Palestinian discourse. In particular, as outlined above, the key normative claim outlined by the Palestinian movement is that of the right to self-determination.

Underlying this, however, is a persistent controversy over the conflicting narrative of how identity relates to political claims. Specifically, debate rests on Palestinian normative claims to self-determination in terms of the existence of a discernible Palestinian national community prior to the establishment of the State of Israel. That is, defenders of Israeli sovereignty have often argued that Palestinian identity, as separate from broader Arab identity, developed only in response to the founding of Israel. As such, their claims to territory based on the British Mandate and the notion of self-determination are not valid (Sayegh, 1998).

For Palestinians, this is a deeply controversial claim. As was discussed in Chapter 4, all national identities are in one way or another 'constructed'. That is, there is nothing organic in one's national community, they are constructed or invented communities that require a constant re-establishment of how they are defined. This can be seen in the debates over the Jewish character of the Israeli state outlined above. However, in terms of the Palestinians, it has a deeper legal significance in that it challenges the very existence of the community vis-à-vis their political claims.

THE ISRAELI–US RELATIONSHIP

The relationship between the US and Israel is often seen as the most controversial element of this conflict. As has been outlined in previous chapters, Arab political discourse draws heavily on historic experiences, including the narratives around external interference and great power machinations. Here, Israel is the largest recipient of US aid as well as the US serving as a key defender of Israel when the latter's actions are bought before the United Nations Security Council. This 'special relationship' is multifaceted, resting on arguments relating to the strategic value of Israel as a military ally, ideological arguments about cultural and political affinity between the two states, overlaid by political concerns in terms of the domestic political influence of Israel within the US.

Towards the 'Special Relationship'

The US–Israeli relationship was not always exceptional. Indeed, as outlined in Chapter 3, there were clear trends towards the gravitation of Israel to the Soviet Union during the late 1940s and early 1950s, particularly due to the affinity between Zionist and socialist economic doctrines as well as the role of the US in the 1956 Suez Crisis. Here, France was a key early backer of Israel, including playing a vital role in the development of Israel's nuclear programme through the 1950s and 1960s (see Chapter 7).

This dynamic continued through the 1950s and early 1960s, with Presidents Eisenhower and Kennedy both giving qualified support to Israel, but also seeking to maintain strong ties with Arab states. However, this would change with the response of President Johnson to the 1967 Six-Day War, including the use of the US 6th Fleet in protection of Israel in the face of Soviet threats. Here, the issue of religious affiliation between the two states became a key feature, where Johnson made repeated statements focussed on the affinity between Christianity and Judaism.

Traditionally, therefore, Democratic Presidents had been seen to be closer to Israel than Republican Presidents. It was Democrat President Truman who was one of

Figure 9.12   US Presidents and Israeli Prime Ministers (clockwise from top left): Harry Truman and David Ben Gurion, Dwight D. Eisenhower and Ben Gurion, John F. Kennedy and Ben Gurion, Lyndon B. Johnson and Yitzhak Rabin, Richard Nixon and Golda Meir, Gerald Ford and Yitzhak Rabin, Jimmy Carter and Menachim Begin, Ronald Reagan and Shimon Peres, George H.W. Bush and Yitzhak Shamir, Bill Clinton and Ehud Barak, George W. Bush and Ariel Sharon, and Barak Obama and Benjamin Netanyahu

Source (for all): Jewish Virtual Library

the earliest supporters for the establishment of the State of Israel, with Johnson also shifting to a more overt support of Israel during 1967. This was a position influenced by the role of oil companies and their senior executives in the Republican Party where these individuals, such as George H.W. Bush, had close business and, later, political links with key Arab regimes such as the Saudi monarchy.

However, the aforementioned shifts in the Israeli political scene to the right from the late 1970s saw a changing dynamic where Republican Presidents, particularly Ronald Reagan (1980–8) and George W. Bush (2000–8) would become the most vocal supporters of Israel. This revolved around both security concerns and questions of identity and cultural affiliation. In terms of security and strategy, the Reagan administration saw support for Israel as a key part of pursuing geostrategic aims in the Middle East in the face of the Soviet influence amongst Arab states. In addition, the links between the US and Israel based on democratic affinity were focussed on. However, this has been a controversial stance due to the continued US support for oil-producing authoritarian regimes including Saudi Arabia as well as support for, amongst others, Hosni Mubarak's rule in Egypt. As was discussed in Chapter 7, this became a theme of anti-American rhetoric in the Middle East and a key part of the rhetorical arsenal used by organisations such as al-Qaeda.

This affinity also included a focus on cultural elements. Here, for the Reagan and particularly the George W. Bush administrations, a sense of shared cultural heritage was used to underline the special relationship between the US and Israel. This was signified by subtle changes in language under Reagan, with references to the '*re*-birth' of the State of Israel to those of Bush who more explicitly stated that both Israel and the US 'are founded on certain beliefs, that there is an Almighty God' that have made the countries 'natural allies'. For Bush, these comments were made in the context of the so-called 'War on Terror' with a worldview based on existential connotations of 'good versus evil' (see Chapter 7).

Figure 9.13   From left: John Mearsheimer and Stephen Walt

Source: University of California, Berkeley

The Israel Lobby Controversy

Views of this special relationship have focussed primarily on the 'external' aspect, with views of US–Israeli relations, depending on one's view, as part of a broader strategic policy, a neocolonial exercise in the Middle East, or defence of democracy in the region. However, there is also a critical 'internal' element to this policy for the United States in terms of the influence of Israel, Israeli security and the Peace Process on US domestic politics.

In this regard, there is heated debate over the influence of this issue broadly, and a so-called 'Israel lobby' more specifically, on US politics. This came to the forefront of public debate with the publication of *The Israel Lobby* by University of Chicago Professor John Mearsheimer and Harvard Professor Stephen Walt. This book argued that there was a 'coalition of individuals and organisations who actively work to steer US foreign policy in a pro-Israel direction' (2007: 5).

The **Electoral College** system is the mechanism for electing the President of the United States. Each state is allocated a particular number of 'electoral votes' according to their population. A presidential candidate gains Electoral College votes if they win the ballot in a particular state. With 538 total votes, Presidents win office when they are able to secure 270 (50% + 1) Electoral College votes.

For the 2012, 2016 and 2020 presidential elections, the seven states with the largest Electoral College votes are first, California (55), second, Texas (38), equal third, Florida and New York (29 each), equal fourth, Illinois and Pennsylvania (20 each) and fifth, Ohio (18).

Whilst this, in and of itself, is not a controversial phenomenon, it is the implications that are controversial. For Mearsheimer and Walt, these influences have negative impacts on the US, working to isolate it in the Middle East, perpetuate the Israeli–Palestinian conflict, as well as distort US foreign policy decision-making in the Middle East and globally. Criticisms of this work variously argued that it was academically less than rigorous, that it was based on conspiracy and conjecture, or was an expression of an anti-Semitic and anti-Israeli trend in academia.

Overlaying this is the related issue of the influence of Israel and the Israeli–Palestinian conflict on US voting trends. The US has a Jewish population of an estimated 5 million people. Within this community there are a wide range of opinions of Israeli politics and the conflict with the Arab states and the Palestinians. However, there is a trend towards support for policies that are supportive of Israeli security. Here, this weaves into the fabric of US politics where candidates for elected office, particularly in those areas where there are large Jewish populations (see Table 9.6), will pay extra attention to this issue.

This gains importance in presidential elections, and the impacts of voting on the Electoral College system. Here, Jewish voters are concentrated in key 'swing states' such as Florida and New Jersey and their votes can directly affect the success of a presidential candidacy. However, it is worth remembering that the Jewish community is like many communities in the United States that will often vote on similar issues. As such, it is difficult to directly correlate this issue with the particular foreign policy positions of the US in the Middle East.

Table 9.6 US States with the Largest Numbers of Jewish Residents (2011 estimates)

	State	Percentage	Total
1	New York	9.1%	1,771,333
2	New Jersey	5.5%	485,164
3	Florida	4.6%	876,647
4	District of Columbia	4.5%	27,810
5	Massachusetts	4.4%	289,852
6	Maryland	4.2%	244,788
7	Connecticut	3.0%	107,421
8	California	2.9%	1,093,065
9	Pennsylvania	2.7%	344,058
10	Illinois	2.3%	295,993

CONCLUSION

Whilst it is infeasible to adequately cover all aspects of the Israeli–Palestinian conflict in a single chapter, a discussion of the key themes of the Peace Process help illuminate the intransigent nature of this conflict. The lack of agreement on key points of negotiation, from settlements to refugees to questions of territory, continues to define relations between the parties. However, these positions are further polarised through divergent norms and priorities, with the Israeli focus on self-defence and the Palestinian focus on self-determination. In this regard, it is difficult to identify points where the two parties are able to reach consensus for future negotiations. Here, the role of the US is vital. Much maligned as the lead negotiator due to the complicated relations it has with both parties, the US remains indispensable to the settlement of this dispute as it is the only party who commands the attention of both sides. However, it remains to be seen how this will eventuate, particularly in light of the ongoing regional security concerns outlined in Chapter 8 and the rapidly changing political environment, which will be discussed in Chapter 10.

Study Questions

- What factors led to the initiation of the Israeli–Palestinian Peace Process in 1991?
- What were the different approaches to negotiating peace?
- What are the main issues under negotiation and how do the parties approach these issues?

- What has been the role of external parties, particularly the United States, in these negotiations?
- How have the issues surrounding competing norms of self-defence and self-determination affected these negotiations?
- What are the bases for allegations and counter-allegations of the use of violence by both sides?
- What influence has identity politics had on the conflict?

FURTHER READING

Morris, Benny (2009) *One State, Two Societies: Resolving the Israel/Palestine Conflict.* New Haven, CT: Yale University Press.
One of the two revisionist histories outlined here, perhaps the seminal work from Morris in his review of the parameters of the Israeli–Palestinian conflict.

Pappé, Ilan (2006) *The Israel–Palestine Question.* London: Routledge.
The second revisionist account of the Israeli–Palestinian conflict, this volume reappraises Pappé's views of the conflict in the wake of the al-Aqsa *intifada*.

Rabinovich, Itmar (2004) *Waging Peace: Israel and the Arabs, 1948–2003.* Princeton, NJ: Princeton University Press.
This volume, from a former Israeli government negotiator, seeks to outline the major forces that have affected the trajectory of the Peace Process, both internal and external to the conflict itself.

Zertal, Idith and Eldar, Akiva (2007) *Lords of the Land: The War over Israel's Settlements in the Occupied Territories, 1967–2007.* New York: Nation Books.
A critical account of one of the key issues that have plagued the Peace Process, the issue of settlements, allowing for a broader discussion of the controversies of this conflict.

 Go to the companion website at www.sagepub.co.uk/macqueen for further material including free journal articles and links to other relevant documents.

REFERENCES

Baxter, Kylie and Akbarzadeh, Shahram (2008) *US Foreign Policy in the Middle East: The Roots of Anti-Americanism.* London: Routledge.

B´Tselem (2011a) 'Land Expropriation and Settlements Statistics', 1 January; www.btselem.org/topic/settlements

B´Tselem (2011b) 'The Separation Barrier', 1 January; www.btselem.org/separation_barrier

Fawcett, Louise (ed.) (2009) *The International Relations of the Middle East*. Oxford: Oxford University Press.

Israeli Ministry of Foreign Affairs (2007) 'The Anti-Terrorist Fence vs. Terrorism', 8 April; securityfence.mfa.gov.il/mfm/web/main/missionhome.asp? MissionID=45187&.

Knudsen, Are (2009) 'Widening the Protection Gap: The "Politics of Citizenship" for Palestinian Refugees in Lebanon, 1948–2008', *Journal of Refugee Studies*, 22 (1): 1–23.

Levitt, Matthew and Ross, Dennis (2006) *Hamas: Politics, Charity, and Terrorism in the Service of Jihad*. Washington, DC: The Washington Institute for Near East Policy.

Malley, Robert and Agha, Hussein (2001) 'Camp David: The Tragedy of Errors', *The New York Review of Books*, 9 August.

Mearsheimer, John J. and Walt, Stephen (2007) *The Israel Lobby and U.S. Foreign Policy*. New York: Farrar, Straus and Giroux.

Milton-Edwards, Beverly (2009) *The Israeli–Palestinian Conflict: A People's War*. London: Routledge.

Morris, Benny (1987) *The Birth of Israel: Myths and Realities*. New York: Pantheon.

Peleg, Ilan (2004) 'Jewish–Palestinian Relations in Israel: From Hegemony to Equality?', *International Journal of Politics, Culture, and Society*, 17 (3): 415–37.

Quandt, William (2005) *Peace Process: American Diplomacy and the Arab–Israeli Conflict Since 1967*. Washington, DC: Brookings Institution Press.

Rane, Halim (2009) *Reconstructing Jihad amid Competing International Norms*. New York: Palgrave Macmillan.

Ross, Dennis (2004) *The Missing Peace: The Inside Story of the Fight for Middle East Peace*. New York: Farrar, Straus and Giroux.

Ross, Dennis and Grinstein, Gidi (2001) 'Camp David: An Exchange', *The New York Review of Books*, 20 September.

Sayegh, Yezid (1998) *Armed Struggle and the Search for State: The Palestinian National Movement, 1949–1993*. Oxford: Oxford University Press.

Shlaim, Avi (2011) 'Reflections on the Israeli–Palestinian Conflict', *Asian Affairs*, 42 (1): 1–13.

State of Israel (1948) 'Declaration of israel's Independence 1948', 14 May <stateof Israel.com/declaration>.

10

Democratisation and the Arab Uprisings

Learning Objectives

This chapter will enable a greater understanding of:

- The debates around democratisation in the Middle East and Arab world.
- Various tensions related to the relationship between Islam and democracy.
- The multiplicity of factors behind the uprisings, including region-wide and country-specific trends.
- The role of information technology, including social media, during the Arab uprisings.
- The dynamics of the Arab uprisings since late 2010 through case studies of Tunisia, Egypt, Libya, Yemen, Bahrain and Syria.

TIMELINE

6 June 2010: Death of Khaled Said

7 December 2010: Self-immolation of Mohamed Bouazizi

27 December 2010: First mass protests in Tunis

4 January 2011: Death of Mohamed Bouazizi

14 January 2011: Tunisian President Ben Ali flees to Saudi Arabia

25 January 2011: First mass protests in Cairo's Tahrir Square

11 February 2011: Egyptian President Mubarak resigns

11 February 2011–30 June 2012: Egypt under the authority of the Supreme Council of the Armed Forces (SCAF)

14 February 2011: First mass protests in Bahrain

15 February 2011: First mass protests in Benghazi

17 February 2011: Manama's Pearl Roundabout Protests cleared by Bahraini security services

(Continued)

(Continued)

22 February 2011: Mass protests re-occupy the Pearl Roundabout in Manama

27 February 2011: Resignation of Mohamed Ghannouchi

27 February 2011: Formation of the Libyan National Transitional Council (NTC)

1 March 2011: Legalisation of *Ennahda* in Tunisia

7 March 2011: Dissolution of the Tunisia Secret Police

9 March 2011: Dissolution of the Constitutional Democratic Rally in Tunisia

14 March 2011: Bahrain requests GCC assistance to suppress protests

15 March 2011: Dissolution of the Egyptian State Security Investigations Service

17 March 2011: UN Security Council Resolution 1973

19 March 2011: Egyptian constitutional reforms approved at referendum

23 March–31 October 2011: 'Operation Unified Protector' in Libya

25 March 2011: First mass protests in Daraa', Syria

16 April 2011: Dissolution of the National Democratic Party in Egypt

29 July 2011: Free Syrian Army formed

23 August 2011: Syrian National Council formed in Istanbul

20 October 2011: Death of Muammar Gaddhafi

23 October 2011: Tunisian Constituent Assembly elected

19 November 2011: Capture of Saif al-Islam Gaddhafi

28 November 2011–11 January 2012: Parliamentary elections in Egypt

21 February 2012: Presidential elections in Yemen

26 February 2012: New Syrian constitution approved at referendum

23 May–17 June 2012: Presidential elections in Egypt

24 April 2012: New Libyan electoral law

14 June 2012: Egyptian Supreme Court annuls vote of parliamentary elections

7 July 2012: Elections in Libya

INTRODUCTION

In Chapter 5 we discussed the persistence of authoritarianism as a key feature of regional politics. For some, the Middle East and the Arab states were exceptional in global terms due to the resistance they displayed in the face of democratising trends globally. The wave of uprisings that swept the region since late 2010 have led many to argue that an 'Arab Spring' has dawned, leading to fundamental changes to the political landscape that equal an end to the dominance of authoritarian regimes and the rise of a new democratic Middle East.

However, it is unclear whether these uprisings are leading to this outcome, with the majority of authoritarian systems still in place and only marginal changes in many states that were witness to widespread unrest and the toppling of heads of state. This chapter will explore these uprisings, asking whether or not they signal a democratic transformation in the Middle East or something else. Here, discussion will first outline the main approaches to understanding democratisation in the region, picking up on the themes discussed in Chapter 5, before examining this in relation to the cases of uprisings in Tunisia, Libya, Egypt, Yemen, Bahrain and Syria. This will enable better engagement with the question of whether this is a democratic 'Arab Spring', as well as allowing us to engage with other questions around the vulnerability of particular regimes compared to others in terms of future potential unrest and challenges to authoritarian rule.

UNDERSTANDING DEMOCRATISATION IN THE ARAB MIDDLE EAST

Democracy is a global norm of immense influence. This can be best seen in the efforts of leaders of almost all political persuasions who claim to be 'democratic'. However, this general commitment to the idea of democracy and its normative power 'is a very recent phenomenon' (Held, 2006: 1). That is, the perception of the innate superiority of democracy is largely a post-World War II and particularly post-Cold War trend. Building on the discussion in Chapter 5, this section will briefly discuss some common understandings of democracy and the processes of democratisation. In particular, it will outline the factors that are most commonly focussed on as signifying 'democratic transition'. From here, this chapter will then move to a discussion of the uprisings in the Arab world since late 2010, with a particular view to the debate over whether this signifies a wave of democratisation in the region.

Democracy and Democratisation in the Middle East

The word democracy is an amalgam of the Greek words *demos* (people) and *kratos* (rule), the rule of and by the people. As such, the core of the democratic principle is the idea of equality of participation amongst the members, or citizens, of this community. However, this leaves open questions of what defines 'rule' by the people and who are the 'people' who hold this authority. In addition, questions remain as to how this rule is to be regulated, who ensures and enforces this equality of participation, as well as what happens when the 'rules of the game', the factors that ensure equal representation, are violated and how are grievances about a lack of equality are addressed.

These questions are addressed through various models of democracy. At a broad level, models of democracy can be classified as either direct or representative. Direct democracy is an idea that citizens have direct control over and input in the decision-making process. This is a form of democracy that becomes cumbersome with large populations, therefore is more common in terms of local governance. As such, democratic politics at the state level is most often managed through forms of representative democracy. Representative democracy centres on processes of appointing or electing people to represent the interests of the citizenry in institutions such as parliaments. Again, this leaves open questions of how representatives are selected, how these interests are managed and how responsive these representatives are to popular will.

Arendt, Hannah, *On Revolution* (New York: Penguin, 1963): 23:

Democracy is critical 'not because all men were born equal, but, on the contrary, because men by nature were not equal, and needed an artificial institution, the polis, which by virtue of its *nomos* would make them equal. Equality existed only in this specifically political realm, where men met one another as citizens and not as private persons. The difference between this ancient concept of equality and our notion that men are born and created equal and become unequal by virtue of social and political, that is man-made institutions, can hardly be over-emphasised.'

Whilst there are a wide range of debates over the structures and mechanisms of democracy, there is a more recent debate concerning how to foster democracy, or democratisation. In recent decades, this has become framed around the notion of *waves* of democratic *transition*. Huntington developed this notion of democratic waves, arguing that particular historical periods have seen clusters of 'transitions from nondemocratic to democratic regimes' occurring 'within a specified period of time ... that significantly outnumber transitions in the opposite direction' during the same period (Huntington, 1991: 15).

For Huntington, transitions to democratic governance had come in three waves: (1) the early 19th to the early 20th centuries; (2) decolonisation after World War II; and (3) the collapse of authoritarian regimes in southern Europe and Latin America from the mid-1970s, with each followed by a 'reverse wave' (particularly between World War I and World War II and through the 1960s and early 1970s). Central to this was the importance of institutions, particularly elections, by which participation is enshrined and power is transferred. These views impacted support for democratic transitions particularly in the US and organisations such as the World Bank.

These theories were approaches to 'democratisation', or the movement towards a democratic system. This *transitionalist* approach sought to isolate conditions relevant to the genesis of democracy as opposed to conditions relevant to the maintenance of democratic systems. This led to the proliferation of work on understanding how and why democratic transformations take place, and an effort to translate this into policies for governments and international organisations to sponsor, at least ostensibly, democracy (see O'Donnell et al., 1986; Linz and Stepan, 1996).

As was discussed in Chapter 5, there have been a variety of efforts to measure these transitions towards democracy or the relative status of democratic freedoms. Despite this, and despite the growing influence of democracy as a global norm, many authoritarian regimes in the Middle East were able to survive through taking on the trappings of democratisation such as parliaments and elections; however these have remained under regime control. This is what some have referred to as the emergence of so-called 'hybrid regimes', where democracies emerged alongside electoral authoritarian regimes, pseudo-democracies and politically closed regimes (Diamond, 2002: 22; Carothers, 2002: 8).

This resistance to pressures for greater democratisation have also been articulated in relation to the relationship between Islam and democracy. In particular, authoritarian regimes in the Middle East have often used the argument that they present the only barrier between a modicum of civil liberties and the rise of Islamist authority and the imposition of *shari`ah*, thus ending any democratic future. This was a debate that became pronounced after the Islamic Revolution in Iran, and has taken on renewed importance with the rise of Islamist parties in the wake of the Arab uprisings since late 2010.

Islam and Democracy

Despite the intense debate surrounding the role of Islam in the political sphere, the *Qur`an* itself does not prescribe a specific political system; however some have argued that it does put an emphasis on particular political and social preferences for a Muslim community. These include 'pursuing justice through social cooperation and mutual assistance ... establishing a nonautocratic, consultative method of governance ... and institutionalising mercy and compassion in social interactions' (El Fadl, 2004: 5). Controversially, others have argued that the relative lack of democratic systems in the Muslim world, the Middle East, or the Arab world lies within Islamic doctrine itself (Lewis, 2002). This has fed into debates concerning the role of Islamist parties in developing or established democratic systems. Here, concerns are expressed that apparent incompatibilities between Islamic political doctrine and that of democratic governance will lead to 'one man, one vote, one time' (Djerejian, 1992).

This debate can be further understood in relation to the question of sovereignty. In particular, can Islamist parties reconcile the claims to absolute sovereignty (*hakimi-yya*) on the part of the state with their position on the centrality of the *Qur'an* and the *shari'ah* as establishing the absolute sovereignty of God (*hakimiyyat Allah*) and God's word? This has been an issue central to discussions amongst Islamic intellectuals from the early 19th century, without any definitive position articulated. As was outlined in Chapter 5, the Islamic Republic of Iran has developed a system (*vilayet-e-faqih*) that seeks to balance spiritual with temporal authority. However, the Iranian political elites continue to face challenges to their authority based on the very structure of this system (Mayer, 2006). Elsewhere, the efforts to bring in Islamic law as the basis of political authority have been implemented in restricted political environments, such as in Saudi Arabia or Sudan, or have been implemented in a piecemeal fashion, such as in post-2003 Iraq.

This is not to discount the theoretical compatibility between Islam and democracy. Many scholars have identified how Islam recognises the notions of popular sovereignty, the rule of law, the accountability of political authority and equality amongst the political community (Chaudhry, 1997: 50–2). Indeed, many Muslim-majority states across the world are democracies, such as Indonesia (population 239,870,000), Bangladesh (142,319,000), Malaysia (28,300,000) and Senegal (11,658,000), or are partial democracies such as Pakistan (172,800,000), Nigeria (155,216,000), Kazakhstan (16,433,000) and Albania (3,170,000).

Here, elements of Islamic doctrine relating to consultation (*shura*) and consensus (*'ijma*), a history of constitutional governance (see Chapter 1) as well as components of the *shari'ah* are incorporated into the political system and exist alongside civil law codes. Despite this, there remains an uneasy relationship between religion and politics in Muslim states. This stems from, in part, the exploitation of Islam by authoritarian regimes to justify their rule as well as the dogmatic reinterpretations of Islamic doctrine presented by contemporary radical and militant movements that often seek to shut down dissent, thus closing the door on political pluralism.

The US and 'Democracy Promotion' in the Middle East

Whilst the major instances of American intervention in the post-Cold War Middle East were discussed earlier, US involvement has also, at times, been framed by the principle of democratisation or, more specifically, democracy promotion. This is a policy that is most often associated with the George W. Bush administration as part of the policy and rhetorical response to the terrorist attacks of 11 September 2001. Where the Bush administration, on the one hand, put the attacks down to a pathological hatred of the US way of life, this was articulated alongside an argument that the US support for authoritarian governments had bred resentment in the region, one that had expressed itself in these acts of terrorism.

As a result, the US developed a series of initiatives that sought to promote democratisation across the region. This was implemented through funding programmes located within the US Agency for International Development (USAID), the State Department, the National Endowment for Democracy (NED), as well as through new agencies such as the Middle East Partnership Initiative (MEPI) and the Millennium Challenge Corporation (MCC) amongst others. These programmes were designed to provide funding to support the formation of political parties and civil society organisations, as well as assisting in election monitoring and other activities.

> The **Middle East Partnership Initiative (MEPI)** was founded in 2002 as a complement to the impending invasion and occupation of Iraq. It worked alongside existing and other newly created funding agencies through small grant initiatives to support local civil society and political organisations in promoting political pluralism and democracy.

As such, these programmes, particularly MEPI and the MCC, were heavily influenced by the transitionalist approach to democratisation. This was particularly so in terms of the emphasis on formal political participation as the means to 'indigenous calls for enduring change' in the Middle East (MEPI, 2007). That is, the focus on elections as the key indicator of democratic development is criticised by many as ignoring both the resilience of authoritarian regimes and informal modes of political participation (Lust-Okar and Zerhouni, 2008; MacQueen, 2009).

In addition, both MEPI and the MCC incorporated development principles articulated by the World Bank and IMF that linked economic liberalisation to political liberalisation. However, these policy initiatives had limited effect on opening political space in the region. For some, where there was a benefit in assisting the vulnerable political parties, this was offset by the ability of authoritarian regimes to establish pseudo-democratic institutions such as flawed electoral systems of powerless parliaments.

UPRISINGS, WAR AND TRANSITION IN THE ARAB WORLD

Therefore, whilst the democratic landscape in the Middle East had changed since the 1990s, this did not necessarily mean a transition from authoritarianism to democracy. Instead, the nature of authoritarianism had changed during this period in response to a variety of global pressures, including that of democratisation as well as economic neoliberalism and globalisation. This resulted in a situation of false promises of political change, economic slowdown and growing expectations in the region through the 2000s, breeding greater resentment, frustration and desperation.

It was this frustration and desperation that fuelled the outbreak of unrest across the Arab world from late 2010. This section will explore the background to these uprisings, the most significant events in the region in several decades. Focus here will be on the myriad factors that fuelled the unrest in an effort to interrogate whether challenges to sitting governments across the Arab world were calls for democracy and in the cases where regimes have fallen, whether this has been the outcome.

The Background to the Arab Uprisings

There was no single factor behind the uprisings in the Arab world; instead it was an amalgam of various issues that impacted on different states in different ways. In broad terms, economic factors were central, particularly in terms of inflation and its impacts on basic food items such as bread and fuel, on unemployment, under-employment and job insecurity, and wealth disparities. In addition, political forces such as the lack of freedoms, the continuation of autocracy, corruption and the role of foreign interference also exacerbated unrest. Finally, social factors such as frustration and unmet expectations amongst the young population as well as tensions surrounding religion and social freedoms all contributed to the matrix of friction that fed into the outbreak of anti-government protests in late 2010.

Perhaps the most obvious of these tensions was the continuing lack of political freedoms across the region. This has been discussed at length throughout this volume. However, this does not reveal the whole picture. In particular, it does not explain why the uprisings happened at this point when authoritarianism has been a feature of regional politics for many decades. This is not to discount the impacts of dictatorship, but it does highlight the need to understand how a variety of factors have fed into the unrest.

One common theme highlighted has been the so-called 'youth bulge' where the fragile political and economic systems across the region have failed to accommodate the ambitions of the rapidly growing young population in the Arab world. However, according to the UN Statistics Department (Table 10.1), the youth population in the Arab world is not far in excess of the global average. Of the states that have experienced significant civil unrest between late 2010 and mid-2012 (Bahrain, Egypt, Libya, Syria, Tunisia and Yemen), Egypt, Libya and Syria have a youth population in excess of regional and global averages. However, other regional states, including Iraq, Saudi Arabia and Sudan also have large youth

Table 10.1 Demographics of the Arab States in the Middle East and North Africa (2011 UNSD estimates)

	% under 15 y/o	Annual Growth Rate	Urban Population
Algeria	27%	3.1%	67.1%
Bahrain	20%	2.1%	88.7%
Egypt	31%	1.7%	43.5%
Iraq	43%	3.1%	66.1%
Jordan	37%	1.9%	78.6%
Kuwait	27%	2.4%	98.4%
Lebanon	24%	0.7%	87.4%
Libya	31%	0.8%	78.1%
Morocco	28%	1.0%	58.8%
Oman	27%	1.9%	73.3%
Qatar	14%	2.9%	95.9%
Saudi Arabia	30%	2.1%	82.3%
Sudan	40%	2.4%	40.8%
Syria	36%	1.7%	56.2%
Tunisia	23%	1.0%	67.7%
UAE	17%	2.2%	84.4%
Yemen	44%	3.0%	32.4%
Regional average	*29%*	*2.0%*	*70.6%*
Global average	*26%*	*1.1%*	*50.5%*

populations in excess of the global average. Saying this, the region is growing at almost double the global average, putting continued upward pressure in terms of a growing youth bulge into the future.

Whilst the size of the young population may be in excess of the global average, it is not extraordinarily so. However, this factor does take on greater importance when combined with rates of unemployment, particularly youth unemployment. As was discussed in Chapter 6, unemployment across the region is a major issue, with youth unemployment being particularly high. According to the International Labour Organisation, the youth unemployment rate in the Middle East and North Africa (24.2%) is higher than any other region (central/southeast Europe – 20.8%, Latin America and the Caribbean – 15.7%). Whilst it is difficult to find exact unemployment statistics due to chronic under-reporting in official government data, it is safe to assume that this number is likely to be much higher.

The other notable statistic outlined in Table 10.1 is the high rate of urbanisation across the region. This may help explain one part of the unrest in terms of the lack of economic opportunities faced by those in the cities. This is a factor that is often worsened with rising levels of education, particularly tertiary education. Higher education levels can raise expectations amongst graduates, particularly in systems that have traditionally seen governments provide state employment programmes.

As was discussed in Chapter 6, neoliberal economic reforms including structural readjustment initiatives have seen a rolling back of state services, leaving many young people with a tertiary education little prospect of employment. Indeed, as Table 10.2 highlights, the states of the Middle East are almost all in the top 100 globally for literacy rates. In the words of the famed Syrian writer Saadallah Wannous, young people in the Arab world have been 'sentenced to hope' where the deprivation that they experience is 'relative' rather than absolute (cited in Rodenbeck, 2011). That is, higher levels of education lead to higher expectations, expectations that are difficult to meet in times of economic downturn or environments of political authoritarianism.

Again, this is not a consistent pattern across the region. As Table 10.3 outlines, education levels in Yemen have not markedly increased over the past two decades yet the country has witnessed widespread unrest, whilst tertiary education in Oman and the UAE has increased rapidly in the same period, with these states remaining relatively stable since late 2010. Here, factors specific to each country need to be factored into these understandings, such as the 'Omanisation' programme that has focussed on providing employment for Omani graduates over imported labour or the relative economic stability of the increasingly service-based UAE economy (Winckler, 2000).

Table 10.2 Literacy Rates of the Arab States in the Middle East and North Africa (UNESCO estimates)

	%	Rank		%	Rank		%	Rank
Libya	97.7%	13	UAE	90.0%	50	Algeria	75.4%	78
Qatar	94.7%	28	Tunisia	88.9%	54	Sudan	70.2%	90
Kuwait	94.5%	30	Syria	87.9%	59	Egypt	66.4%	97
Bahrain	91.4%	45	Saudi Arabia	86.1%	64	Yemen	62.4%	98
Jordan	91.1%	46	Oman	89.4%	69	Morocco	61.5%	100
Lebanon	90.0%	50	Iraq	78.1%	72			

Table 10.3 Education Rates of the Arab States in the Middle East and North Africa (UNESCO estimates)

	Secondary Enrolment			Tertiary Enrolment		
	1991	2010	Change	1991	2010	Change
Algeria	60%	75%	+25%	11%	31%	+182%
Bahrain	98%	95%	−3%	17%	21%	+24%
Egypt	69%	72%	+4%	12%	32%	+167%
Iraq	35%	38%	+9%	12%	13%	+8%
Jordan	78%	87%	+12%	22%	38%	+73%
Kuwait	99%	99%	0%	21%	24%	+14%
Lebanon	77%	81%	+5%	33%	54%	+64%
Libya	99%	99%	0%	52%	53%	+2%
Morocco	36%	42%	+17%	11%	10%	−9%
Oman	45%	81%	+80%	1%	24%	+2300%
Qatar	83%	94%	+13%	20%	10%	−50%
Saudi Arabia	99%	99%	0%	11%	37%	+236%
Sudan	21%	29%	+38%	6%	6%	0%
Syria	49%	72%	+47%	18%	20%	+11%
Tunisia	45%	79%	+76%	9%	23%	+156%
UAE	66%	82%	+24%	7%	23%	+229%
Yemen	40%	44%	+10%	10%	11%	+10%

This is a narrative that runs across other issues such as housing shortages, corruption, access to services, as well as the relationship between particular ethnic groups, religious groups, sectarian communities and family groups to the state (see Chapter 5). As such, the outbreak of unrest across the region may be understood in terms discontent against a variety of grievances as much as it was an effort to move towards a new democratic future. In other words, the 'negative' drivers of the unrest, protests *against* injustice, were as powerful if not more so, as the 'positive' drivers of protest *for* democracy. Whilst these grievances are largely country-specific, the sentiment and the desire for change became a regional theme. Here, the role of information technology, including satellite television and the internet, particularly social media, was critical.

The Arab Spring and Information Technology

These protests captured international attention, with rolling coverage of unrests as they unfolded in Tunisia, then across North Africa and the rest of the Arab world. This was not limited to those outside the region, with advances in access to information from the late 1990s allowing Arab citizens both to see first-hand how the international community sees the region and, increasingly so, to take control of these technologies and control how the world views the region. This section will outline the key advances in information technology, particularly satellite television and the internet, including the tools of social media, to understand how this fed into the growing unrest in the region.

Satellite Television and the Al Jazeera Phenomenon

The free flow of information is a key element in any democratic society. In recent years, this has been associated mostly with access to the internet and the innumerable news sites, opinion sites and tools of social media. However, the proliferation of satellite television preceded the growth of widespread internet access, with profound impacts. This was particularly so where affordable satellite TV access helped overcome control by state-run media services.

Whilst access to satellite stations from Europe and elsewhere helped citizens broaden their ability to get other sources of information, regimes were quick to establish dominance of satellite TV rights. From 1996, the Saudi-controlled Middle East Broadcasting Centre, the Egyptian Space Channel and Emirates Dubai Television as well as Lebanon's Future TV and the Lebanese Broadcasting Corporation acted as voices for regimes or key factions within these regimes. However, it was the Qatari-based Al Jazeera ('The Island') that revolutionised regional broadcasting, and provided a local voice for many Arabs on key local, regional and global issues.

Al Jazeera marketed itself as an independent Arab voice, promising to examine issues from foreign intervention through to domestic political issues that were previously considered taboo. This reputation was established early when the network aired a documentary on executions under *shari`ah* law in 1996 that saw the Saudi media company Orbit withdraw its financial support for Al Jazeera. Since this time, the network has grown into a global news network, providing coverage of key events from the 11 September 2001 attacks on the US, to the 2003 US-led invasion and occupation of Iraq, the ongoing Israeli–Palestinian dispute and more recently, the Arab uprisings. Its coverage of these issues has occurred alongside a series of programmes that explore key social and political issues within Arab and Muslim communities that continue to touch on topics that were previously off-limits to open debate.

In April 2003, **Al Jazeera** withdrew from Iraq after cameraman **Tarek Ayoob** was killed by US fire. In a controversial statement, senior Al Jazeera officials accused the US of intentionally targeting the network for its coverage of US actions in the country. This led to a falling out between the US government and the Doha-based network, with the availability of Al Jazeera in the US still highly restricted.

However, the network has not been without its critics. For instance, governments across the world have sought to limit the reach of the network. This has included efforts by the Algerian, Israeli, Palestinian, Egyptian, Libyan, US and Chinese governments to shut down access over critical coverage of sensitive political issues. In addition, the network has been accused of working under political influence despite its claims to independence and editorial objectivity. This relates specifically to the purported influence of the Qatari government over coverage. For instance, the network has been criticised for a lack of coverage over the unrest in Bahrain since 2011 whilst providing particularly critical coverage of the actions of the Syrian government at the same time. This criticism centres on the allegations of Qatari involvement in support of groups active in the Syrian uprising since 2011 (*Khaleej Times*, 2012).

Regardless of these accusations, the dynamic of access to information and the discussion of sensitive issues through satellite TV acted as a catalyst for the opening of political debate in many Arab states. Whilst it is difficult to quantify the exact impacts of this, the flow of information and diverse opinions in the region provided the tools for many to increasingly question the established political environment. This was a dynamic that was consolidated with the growth of internet access and the tools of social media.

The Internet, Social Media and Political Unrest

As with access to satellite news and entertainment, the growth of internet access in the Middle East has revolutionised access to information. Indeed, many within the region have embraced the technology not just to consume, but to become active producers of information through blogs, photo reporting and other activities. Again, however, the links between internet access and the outbreak of unrest remains opaque. For instance, there is not a direct correlation between the number of people with internet access and the outbreak of unrest. As Table 10.4 outlines, there are a variety of trends between the countries that have experienced significant unrest between late 2010 and mid-2012. For instance, Egypt has the largest internet market in the region; however the next four markets (Morocco, Saudi Arabia,

Table 10.4 Internet Statistics of the Arab States in the Middle East and North Africa (IWS estimates)

	Internet Usage			
	2000	*2009*	*Growth*	*% Penetration*
Algeria	50,000	4,100,000	+8100%	12.0%
Bahrain	40,000	402,900	+907%	55.3%
Egypt	450,000	12,568,900	+2693%	15.9%
Iraq	12,500	300,000	+2300%	1.0%
Jordan	127,300	1,500,500	+1079%	23.9%
Kuwait	150,000	1,000,000	+567%	37.1%
Lebanon	300,000	945,000	+215%	23.5%
Libya	10,000	323,000	+3130%	5.1%
Morocco	100,000	10,300,000	+10,200%	32.9%
Oman	90,000	465,000	+417%	13.6%
Qatar	30,000	436,000	+1353%	52.3%
Saudi Arabia	200,000	7,700,000	+3750%	26.8%
Sudan	30,000	4,200,000	+13,900%	10.2%
Syria	30,000	3,565,000	+11,783%	6.2%
Tunisia	100,000	2,800,000	+2700%	26.7%
UAE	735,000	2,922,000	+298%	60.9%
Yemen	15,000	370,000	+2367%	1.6%

Sudan and Algeria) have been relatively stable countries during this period. On the other side of this equation, small markets in Yemen, Bahrain and Libya are matched by markets in Qatar, Lebanon and Jordan.

This is the same for the degree of internet penetration in a particular state. Bahrain has the second highest percentage of internet penetration in the region, yet other countries with similar rates such as the UAE, Qatar and Kuwait have also been relatively stable. In addition, the rate of internet uptake does not necessarily correlate to unrest, with rapid uptake in Syria between 2000 and 2009, a state experiencing significant unrest, mirrored in Morocco, Sudan and Algeria. Indeed, this mixed picture continues with low uptake rates in Bahrain alongside Oman and a number of other countries.

Here, more detailed data are needed to identify whether internet penetration or the pace of internet uptake in particular communities within states has itself been a factor in fostering unrest. For instance, does internet access amongst university students, trade unionists or other groups result in more effective political action? Also, what particular content is more likely to have an impact on political activism than others?

Here, the tools of social media, particularly Facebook and Twitter, were conspicuous during the unrest that swept the Arab world from late 2010. However, the exact role and influence of these tools on the unrest is debated. On the one hand, there is a view that social media were central in both the articulation of dissent and a vital tool in helping organise protests and to avoid

Figure 10.1 The use of social media was a prominent theme of coverage of the Arab uprisings; however, its actual effects on motivating and helping coordinate unrest is debated

Source: Essam Sharaf

efforts to repress unrest. On the other hand, some have argued that the role of social media has been overstated where it was only an elite, particularly an English-speaking elite, that had regular access to the use of social media. As a result, this led many outside the region to suffer from a 'zoom effect' where this group was seen as representative of the broader sentiment across the country (Moisi, 2012).

This is a debate that will likely remain contested for many years. Suffice to say that the advance of information technology as a whole, from satellite media through to internet-based social media, has helped break down the control of information that was a key element in the maintenance of authoritarian rule. The exact role it played and its specific impacts are uncertain, but it is now both a key feature of regional life, and will impact on the way those in the region engage with political power and shape the expectations of people towards their government into the future.

THE ARAB UPRISINGS

This overview of structural factors behind the uprisings paints a rich, yet complicated picture of the factors underlying the challenge to the political status quo in the Arab world. This section will outline the specific instances of unrest in an effort to clarify some of this debate, as well as address the question of whether this movement is likely to lead to a more democratic future for states in the Middle East.

As events continue to develop, it is difficult to make concrete statements. However, some tentative conclusions are drawn, with an emphasis on the importance of factoring in conditions specific to each state where unrest has manifested.

Case Study: Tunisia

The uprisings in the Arab world began in Tunisia, a surprising development given the apparent stability of the country. This stability was built on the policies implemented by former President Zine el-Abidine Ben Ali since he took power in November 1987 that focussed on the privatisation of the Tunisian economy and the limitation of the role of religion in public life in the country. However, Ben Ali's rule was also characterised by harsh repression of opposition, from liberal advocates, human rights groups, through to the largest opposition movement in the country, the Islamist group *Ennahda* ('Renaissance'). The neoliberal economic policies and emphasis on secularism enabled Ben Ali's regime to deflect international attention and criticism until the outbreak of unrest in late 2010.

Despite this, unrest in Tunisia had been simmering for many years, particularly with the downturn of the Tunisian economy through the 1990s and 2000s, with its impacts felt particularly in the centre and south of the country. Whilst Tunisia remained relatively wealthy compared to the rest of the region, the growing wealth disparities in the country led to increased protests and the emergence of internet-based dissent. Alongside this, the deep-seated corruption within the Tunisian system began to stretch the loyalty of people from a variety of backgrounds.

Revelations via the **Wikileaks** website disclosed rampant corruption within the Ben Ali government. The scale of corruption, with an estimated 10% of the Tunisian economy siphoned off by the regime, was matched by the decadence of Ben Ali and his family. For instance, these report detailed massive expenditure on lavish dinners, consumerables and other indulgences. The President's wife, **Leila Ben Ali**, was a particular target of the leaks and she became a particular focus of the protestors during December 2010 and January 2011.

This became increasingly personified in the President and his family, with revelations via Wikileaks of the scale of fraud that occurred during this administration. For instance, the leaks that emerged in 2010 revealed the personal wealth of the President and his family at an estimated $5 billion, with accounts of decadent spending on consumer items at the same time that subsidies were removed on basic food items.

The Course of the Tunisian Uprising

The structural factors, particularly endemic corruption that framed the unrest, were given a focal point with the tragic death of Tarek al-Tayeb Mohamed Bouazizi after his self-immolation on 17 December 2010. Bouazizi was a street vendor in the poor southern town of Sidi Bouzid. In many ways, Bouazizi's story captures the frustration and desperation faced by many, particularly the young, across the Middle East. Forced to provide for ailing parents and five siblings, life for the 26-year-old Bouazizi was a constant struggle to eke out a living selling produce. Facing constant harassment by the state security services, Bouazizi sought to lodge official complaints, each of which was ignored. In response, and feeling no other option, Bouazizi went to the local municipality building, doused himself in petrol, and set himself on fire. Bouazizi died of his burns on 4 January 2011.

This led to the eruption of violence in Sidi Bouzid that spread throughout southern and central Tunisia through December. This also included a number of repeat self-immolations and suicides by Tunisian youth, with more than 100 Tunisian young people attempting suicide through self-immolation in the first half of 2011 with similar acts across the region, particularly in Algeria, Egypt, Yemen and Jordan. Protests had reached the capital by 27 December and by early January 2011, professional associations such as lawyers and trade unions went on strike in support of the protestors, bringing the country to a halt. This culminated when Ben Ali fled

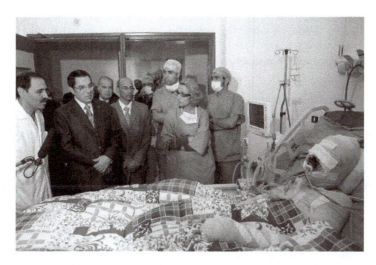

Figure 10.2   Ben Ali (second from left) visiting Mohamed Bouazizi in hospital on 28 December 2010. Bouazizi would die a week later, whilst Ben Ali would be deposed by 14 January 2011

Source: Public domain

Tunisia to Saudi Arabia on 14 January 2011, an act precipitated by the army turning on the internal security services, depriving Ben Ali of protection and a means of repressing the protests. Rule was assumed by former Speaker of the House Fouad Mebazza who appointed a transitional administration under Prime Minister Mohamed Ghannouchi and members of Ben Ali's Constitutional Democratic Rally (*Rassemblement Constitutional Démocratique*, RCD).

Anti-RCD protests continued through 2011, led increasingly by the trade union movement with senior government and military officials resigning *en masse* from the regime and the RCD, leading to the suspension of the party on 6 February. The continuation of protests forced the government to remove all former RCD members; however, Ghannouchi clung on to control of the transitional administration. Protests culminated by late February, with over 100,000 on the streets of Tunis, leading to the resignation of Ghannouchi on 27 February. The formally banned Islamist party *Ennahda* was legalised on 1 March followed by the dissolution of the Secret Police on 7 March and the RCD on 9 March.

Post-Uprising Tunisia

In addition to being the 'home' of the Arab uprisings, Tunisia has also seen perhaps the most stable and, in its early stages at least, successful transition from authoritarian to democratic rule. Central to this was the election of a new Tunisian Constituent Assembly on 23 October 2011. The re-emergence of *Ennahda* on the Tunisian political scene framed much of the debate in the run-up to the vote. In particular, this focussed on what the priorities of the movement would be vis-à-vis their religious programme.

This mirrored a broader debate where many highlighted the central place of Islamist parties as key opposition groups across the region and debates on their priorities within a democratic system. In particular, critics argued that there was a danger that Islamists would exploit the instability to entrench their rule and move towards establishing a theocracy. In contrast, others, including the Islamists themselves, have argued that there is no evidence of this intent.

Tunisia provided the first example of this when *Ennahda* won 89 of 217 seats in the Constituent Assembly election, ahead of centre-left parties *Congrés pour la République* (CPR, with 29 seats) and *Forum Démocratique pour le Travail et les Libertés/ Ettakol* (FDTL, 20 seats) and the populist

Figure 10.3 Rachid Ghannouci, leader of *Ennahda*

Source: Guillarme70

Pétition Populair pour la Liberté, la Justice et la Development/al-Aridha (26 seats). *Ennahda* eventually formed a unity coalition with CPR and *Ettakol* with political posts delegated to each party. In the wake of the election, the unity government as well as the new opposition parties have been debating the issues of secularism and religion in public life, including the lifting of the ban on the *hijab* in the public services and controls over the call to prayer. This has occurred alongside intense debates on economic issues such as privatisation and economic reconstruction as well as the drafting of a new constitution and the structure of the new political system, whether this is the *Ennahda*-favoured parliamentary model or the presidential model favoured by the CPR and *al-Aridha*.

Case Study: Egypt

As with most of the regional uprisings, the seeds of the unrest were laid in the structure of the regional state system and the lack of transparency and popular participation in political rule and the transfer of power. Egypt was no exception to this pattern, with many groups that would become active in the uprising crystallising during the protests against the results of the 2005 presidential elections that were won by Mubarak with 88.6% of the official vote over opposition leader Ayman Nour. These elections occurred in the context of charges of corruption, vote tampering and the exclusion of the major political organisations in the country including the Muslim Brotherhood and various liberal groups.

The issue of succession was important, where Mubarak's son, Gamal, was being groomed for the presidency. This was an issue that became increasingly central through the 2000s with the failing health of the Egyptian President and the rise of Gamal to the post of deputy secretary-general of the former ruling party, the NDP (National Democratic Party). This helped consolidate opposition against Mubarak where many across the political spectrum joined in opposition to the prospect of the Egyptian presidency becoming a dynastic office, similar to the trajectory of that in Syria with the ascension of Hafiz al-Assad's son, Bashir, to the presidency in 2000.

> Many authoritarian regimes have employed informal security services in various capacities. In Egypt, the *baltagiya* ('thugs') were a common feature of Mubarak-era repression of opposition protests. They were a key tactic employed by the regime in agitating for violence during the period of protests during 2011.

The continuation of the Emergency Law in Egypt that allowed the government to arbitrarily suspend the activities of political parties, detain activists and others without arrest, and generally suppress and divide the opposition also fed into growing unrest (see Chapter 5). This was reinforced by the increased levels of police, particularly internal security forces (*mukhabarat*) in the suppression of the opposition or suspected opposition figures, including the widespread use of torture and extra-judicial measures. Underlying all of this were the continuing issues of corruption and economic mismanagement that had wreaked havoc on the Egyptian economy.

Whilst political factors were critical, it was economic factors that further consolidated opposition to the Mubarak regime. The deterioration of the Egyptian economy through the 2000s, in particular the removal of subsidies and the shrinking public sector, hit Egypt's large working classes hardest. This was a consistent pattern in many Arab states, one that was worsened by the growing wealth imbalances in the country and ongoing endemic corruption. This corruption and questionable economic decision-making in the government was perhaps best encapsulated by the 2005 agreement signed with Israel to sell Egyptian natural gas.

The opening of government archives since 2011 has revealed that this deal, which supplies Israel with more than 40% of its natural gas requirements, saw Egypt selling this resource at almost half the global price (Bar-Eli and Trilnick, 2012). Those critical of this deal argued that it was the result of US pressure on the Mubarak

Figure 10.4 A cartoon of Khaled Said holding a caricature of Hosni Mubarak. Said's death at the hands of state security forces in June 2010 inspired a protest movement that fed directly into the unrest that broke out in Egypt in February 2011

Source: Carlos Latuff

government, part of the broader negotiations over US aid to Cairo (see Table 6.14). This fostered resentment of the ongoing quietism that had characterised Egyptian foreign policy since the peace treaty was signed with Israel in the late 1970s.

This simmering unrest included the killing of Khaled Said on 6 June 2010 by state security services. The disappearance and death of people in Egypt was not uncommon, but the tragic death of Said captured the attention of many Egyptians. Said was beaten to death by members of the internal security services for allegedly participating in online activism against the regime. Images of his body after his death were posted on the internet soon after, confronting many with a portrayal of the excesses of the government. This was consolidated through the use of Facebook and the page 'We are all Khaled Said' by Google executive Wael Ghonim, a site that became a forum where many Egyptians began to share stories of repression and anger at the government.

The Course of the Egyptian Uprising

Whilst protests against the regime were disorganised and relatively marginalised in Egypt from 2005 to 2010, the outbreak of unrest in Tunisia sparked a more organised confrontation with the regime. This confrontation would eventually draw in all of Egypt's key political players and remove Mubarak from the presidency. In this regard, the initial protests in Cairo's central Tahrir Square that began on 25 January 2011 differed from those across the region in their initial levels of planning for confronting the

Figure 10.5 Wael Ghonim, Google executive and founder of the site 'We are all Khaled Said' addresses the protestors in Tahrir Square on 9 February 2011

Source: Reuters/Dylan Martinez

Figure 10.6　Two million people gathered in Cairo's Tahrir Square demanding the resignation of President Hosni Mubarak on 11 February 2011

Source: Public domain

regime through non-violent activism. This level of coordination saw the major opposition groups in the country, from the Muslim Brotherhood to the liberal *Wafd* Party participate in the 'Day of Revolt'.

The key tools used by the protestors in Egypt and elsewhere were social media as well as mobile phones. In response to the initial protests, Mubarak sought to shut down both internet and mobile access across the country. However, the momentum for protest had begun, leading to successive days across the country, with Tahrir Square becoming the focus of activity where several hundred thousand Egyptians marched daily through to the end of January. This also saw a gradual escalation in tension, with growing reports of violence across the country.

This violence became an increasingly prevalent feature of the protests, one largely emanating from the regime towards the protestors as a means to break the back of the anti-government unrest. Various estimates put the death toll during protests from 800 to 1000 between 25 January and 11 February, with the bulk of casualties in Cairo and Alexandria (Human Rights Watch, 2011). This confrontation began to culminate through early February, when the regime deployed the *baltagiya* as well as the internal security forces to disperse the protestors in Tahrir Square, along with surreal scenes of Mubarak supporters charging at protestors on camel and horseback near Cairo's famed Museum of Egyptian Antiquities. In addition, Mubarak and his supporters within the administration sought to undermine popular support for the protests through dismissing police officers in major towns, claiming that the ensuing violence would be a sign of what political change would mean.

Whilst the protests had heightened tensions in the country, and put intense pressure on the regime, it was a move within the ruling establishment that eventually ended the 30-year rule of Mubarak. As was discussed in Chapters 1 and 2, the military held a particular role in Egyptian society, seen as the protector of the citizenry and champions of modernity. Whilst this reputation had become tarnished somewhat in recent years, it was their move that would determine the fate of the Mubarak regime and dictate events afterwards. On 11 February 2011, Field Marshal Mohamed Hussein Tantawi and newly appointed Vice President and head of the Intelligence Services Omar Suleiman informed Mubarak that he no longer had the confidence of the armed forces, forcing him to stand down.

Figure 10.7 Pro-Mubarak supporters on horse and camel-back charge protestors outside the Museum of Egyptian Antiquities on 3 February 2011

Source: European Press Agency

Post-Uprising Egypt

The removal of Mubarak from power came in the context of popular protests, but was precipitated by military intervention leading accusations that this was a military coup rather than a democratic revolution. The rule of the military between 11 February 2011 and 30 June 2012 under the Supreme Council of the Armed Forces (SCAF) became the focus of this debate, alongside the ongoing deliberations over the powers of the new parliament, the shape of the new constitution and the role of the army in the future of Egyptian politics.

Figure 10.8 From left: former Chairman of the Supreme Council of the Armed Forces (SCAF) Mohamed Hussein Tantawi and Vice President from 29 January to 11 February Omar Suleiman

Sources: Public domain, Public domain

The SCAF worked under the authority of Tantawi and senior military officials from the Egyptian army, navy and air force and operated as the government of Egypt. After the removal of Mubarak, the SCAF dissolved Egypt's parliament and suspended the constitution, with the stated central aim of managing political affairs until new elections could be conducted and a new constitution drafted. However, immediate tensions emerged between the SCAF, those active in the protest movement and the increasingly assertive Muslim Brotherhood.

Central to this tension was the initial formulation of a transitional constitution. On 19 March 2011, a series of reforms to Egypt's constitution were approved at referendum, with a majority of 77% to 23%, including presidential term limits, judicial oversight of elections and other issues relating to the balance of powers as well as provisions relating to the drafting of a new constitution after the parliamentary elections. However, this did little to mollify the increasing tensions and allegations that the SCAF were delaying future voting as a means to ensure they held on to a large measure of political authority in the country.

This led to delays in the holding of Egypt's first post-Mubarak parliamentary elections, in particular over the drafting of a new electoral law. This debate continued through to early November before elections were held in three stages from 28 November 2011 to 11 January 2012. Of those contesting the elections, the Muslim Brotherhood under their new political vehicle, the Freedom and Justice Party (FJP), were the clear frontrunners ahead of a range of established liberal parties and new parties on both the conservative side, such as the Salafist an-Nour Party, and across the political spectrum.

Figure 10.9 Egypt's parliament convenes for the first time since the fall of Mubarak on 11 February and the parliamentary elections of 28 November 2011–11 January 2012

Source: Asmaa Waguih

The victory of the FJP, with 235 of the 508 seats, was not a surprise. However, the success of an-Nour, in second place with 123 seats, shocked many observers, raising fears of an Islamist coalition that would fundamentally alter Egypt's political landscape. Indeed, the liberal parties such as the New Wafd Party (38 seats), the Egyptian Bloc (35 seats) and the Reform and Development Party (9 seats) were all largely marginalised by the vote, with their only hope of gaining access to power being through a coalition government with the FJP.

In the wake of the 25 January uprising in Egypt, former President Hosni Mubarak was charged with the murder of demonstrators during the protests, profiteering during his time in office and corruption over the controversial gas deal with Israel.

Mubarak's sons, Gamal and Alaa, were charged with profiteering and stock market manipulation, businessman Hussein Salem was charged with corruption over the Israeli gas deal, former Petroleum Minister Sameh Fahmy was charged over the Israeli gas deal, former Interior Minister and head of the Security Services Habib el-Adly was charged with murder and attempted murder of demonstrators, whilst six police officers were also charged with murder and attempted murder.

The verdict found Mubarak and el-Adly guilty of attempted murder, with both sentenced to life imprisonment. Salem and Fahmy were found guilty of corruption and sentenced to 15 years' imprisonment. Gamal and Alaa Mubarak, along with the six police officers charged, were all acquitted.

However, this outcome was thrown into question in the run-up to the presidential elections when Egypt's Supreme Court ruled on 14 June that the results of the election were to be annulled as unconstitutional. This ruling was based on a judgement that up to one-third of seats were elected in a way that did not conform to the draft electoral law passed in November 2011. This ruling was rejected by the FJP, with the current status of the new Egyptian parliament remaining uncertain.

Against this tumult, the Egyptian presidential elections were held over two rounds, from 23 to 24 May with a run-off poll on 16–17 June. There was intense controversy over which of the original 23 registered candidates would be eligible to run in the wake of the introduction of the new electoral laws in January 2012. The biggest controversy centred on the candidacy of Ahmad Shafiq who had served as interim Prime Minister in the last days of Mubarak's presidency as well as Minister for Civil Aviation from 2002 to 2011. However, on 12 April the new Egyptian parliament passed a law prohibiting former high-ranking Mubarak-era officials from being able to run for the office. This saw Shafiq disqualified, however this was overturned on 25 April.

Figure 10.10 The winner of the 2012
Presidential election
in Egypt, Muslim
Brotherhood candidate
Mohammed Morsi

Source: Drumzo

Alongside Shafiq, the other leading candidates were the head of the Muslim Brotherhood Mohammed Morsi, former Muslim Brotherhood member Abdel Moneim Aboul Fotouh, and liberal Hamdeen Sabahi. The debate around the election increasingly centred on debates over the potential dominance of the Muslim Brotherhood/FJP should Morsi win or a return to Mubarak-era politics under Shafiq. This debate sharpened when the first round of the vote did not lead to a majority for one candidate, instead seeing Morsi (24.78%) and Shafiq (23.66%) as receiving the two highest votes and eligible to contest the run-off ahead of Sabahi (20.72%) and Fotouh (17.47%).

The results of the second round were contested, with both candidates claiming victory in the days immediately after the vote. However, on 24 June Egypt's Presidential Elections Commission announced that Morsi had won the poll with 51.73% of the vote against Shafiq's 48.27%. This result, combined with the ongoing suspension of its parliament, leaves Egypt's post-Mubarak political scene and transition to democracy in a highly uncertain state. However, it has also highlighted how the new political landscape will be defined, between the powerful but highly diverse Islamist bloc, a smaller but vocal liberalist bloc and those who yearn for the relative stability of the Mubarak period.

Case Study: Libya

The Libyan political system under Muammar Gaddhafi was characterised by the lack of formal political institutions, arbitrary rule, harsh repression of opposition sentiment and personalised control by Gaddhafi, his family and a network of close associates. Whilst Gaddhafi had proclaimed that Libya was a model of direct democracy, this was a cover for the lack of any accountability of the actions of the central government where access to power depended on a person or group's relationship with the central authority.

This was a situation that shaped political life in Libya. For instance, Gaddhafi had kept a variety of small, well-trained militias under his personal control whilst leaving the Libyan army small in order to prevent the possibility of a military coup. This was replicated in terms of tribal and regional political dynamics where particular groups, such as those from Gaddhafi's home town of Sirte or regions in the south, had greater access to economic and politics resources whilst those in the east, particularly in Benghazi, were often excluded from the political process altogether.

Saying this, the economic situation in Libya was far different to that of Tunisia and Egypt, with its oil wealth and small population making it similar to the states of the Gulf. Indeed, as Table 10.3 indicates, Libyans had a high degree of both secondary and tertiary education, feeding a sense of relative deprivation in an environment that was, in economic terms at least, better than many other regional states. Indeed, this relative deprivation extended from the political realm through to the economic realm where, despite relatively high living standards, many Libyans struggled to gain access to government contracts unless they were part of a privileged elite.

Whilst the economic situation was one of relative perceptions, there was an absolute or objectively harsh human rights situation in Libya. As Chapter 5 outlined, Libya consistently ranked low on measurements of political freedoms, including freedoms of the press and human rights standards. As such, whilst there was a lack of internet penetration and slow uptake in Libya, the impacts of the broader information flow through satellite television and the internet would have likely hastened the undercurrent of discontent in Libya that led to the outbreak of civil war in the country in February 2011.

The Course of the Libyan Uprising

With instability continuing to roll through the region, unrest against the 41-year rule of Muammar Gaddhafi broke out in the eastern city of Benghazi on 15 February 2011. This came on the back of protests earlier in January in Libya's eastern cities against ongoing corruption and housing shortages. The regime's response oscillated between new welfare programmes and direct oppression; however, this failed to mollify unrest, with open rebellion breaking out by mid-February. This spread quickly throughout the east of the country, with calls for the removal of the Gaddhafi regime. This saw the situation escalate to the point where the Libyan regime and armed forces began to openly attack protestors.

The Libyan opposition formed the National Transitional Council (NTC) on 27 February, calling for the removal of the Gaddhafi regime and the reintroduction of the previous constitution including multi-party elections. The NTC was based in Benghazi, traditionally a centre of anti-government sentiment, and set about consolidating opposition to the regime. It was

Figure 10.11   Protests in the eastern city of Benghazi during April 2011

Source: Public domain

constituted primarily of civilians with initially a small number of defectors from the Libyan army. Despite its primarily civilian character, its confrontation with the regime rapidly became militarised, with allegations that the regime had employed helicopter gunships, snipers, artillery and other means against opposition fighters as well as allegations of using foreign mercenaries from Sub-Saharan Africa. This latter factor saw a series of reprisal attacks against the African community in the NTC-held parts of the country.

The regime was also accused of targeting NTC hospitals and civilian areas as well as using human shields during offensives and engaging in acts of torture, rape and other abuses. This led to increasing charges of crimes against humanity by the Libyan regime. Combined with the concern over reprisal attacks against insurgent forces and the population in the east as the government rolled back the territorial gains made by the NTC fighters, the international community began to discuss armed intervention, resulting in the establishment of a multilateral coalition force on 19 March 2011.

Figure 10.12   The no-fly zone and arrangement of NATO-led forces during 'Operation Unified Protector'

Source: Jolly Janner

This coalition was formed around UN Security Council Resolution 1973 of 17 March 2011 that authorised the use of force against the Libyan regime. Specifically, this resolution imposed a no-fly zone on Libya and called for an immediate cease-fire under what is known as the 'Responsibility to Protect' (R2P) Doctrine. R2P emerged out of debates in the UN in the wake of the genocides in Rwanda and Bosnia based on the premise that the UN is obliged to act under both Chapter VI and VII if a state is deemed to be active in 'genocide, war crimes, ethnic cleansing and crimes against humanity' (United Nations, 2005).

The activation of R2P raised intense debate over the nature of international intervention. In particular, some had argued that it opened the door for power-ful states to violate the sovereignty of less powerful states in pursuit of their own ends (Responsibility to Protect, 2009). On the flip-side of this debate, the principal advocate of the R2P doctrine, former Australian Foreign Minister Gareth Evans, argues that 'protecting the country's people from the kind of murderous harm that Gaddhafi inflicted on unarmed protestors' is central to the very logic of what the UN was established to do (Evans, 2011). This was not a programme of regime change, but one focussed solely on the protection of civilians from harm.

Resolution 1973 was implemented by NATO as 'Operation Unified Protector', led by the US, UK and Italy with supplemental involvement from Belgium, Canada, Denmark, France, Norway, the Netherlands, Spain and Sweden as well as regional states in Qatar and the UAE. Libyan forces were on the outer suburbs of Benghazi when the international intervention began on 19 March. The intervention effec-tively turned the course of the war, particularly in terms of mitigating the artillery and air advantages held by the regime. This saw their forces fall back through June and July, with intense fighting around Sirte, Misrata and Bani Waled. By the end of August, Muammar Gaddhafi's son and heir Saif al-Islam was arrested and Tripoli taken by the NTC fighters.

Post-Uprising Libya

Where events in Tunisia and Egypt have been tumultuous yet provide discernible steps towards opening the political system, the situation in Libya is far more uncer-tain. This is in large part due to the nature of the Gaddhafi regime. In particular, Gaddhafi's rule can be best characterised by an almost complete lack of formal politi-cal institutions, with authority wielded through personalised, informal links between local notables and the regime. As such, with the collapse of the Gaddhafi regime, there were no political institutions to be reconstructed and transformed. In other words, the post-Gaddhafi period under NTC rule is highly fluid and uncertain.

This uncertainty was amplified by the degree of violence that characterised the collapse of the Gaddhafi regime as well as the divisions between the various elements of the NTC. Indeed, the circumstances around the death of Gaddhafi on 20 October

Figure 10.13   Saif al-Islam
                   Gaddhafi
                   soon after his
                   capture on
                   21 November
                   2011

Source: Alexandra Valiente

2011 typified this instability. After the fall of Tripoli in August, Gaddhafi fled the capital with intense speculation over his whereabouts. As the NTC moved to take control of the last pro-Gaddhafi strongholds, he was discovered in his hometown of Sirte, east of the capital, where he was apprehended when attempting to flee. Backed by NATO air strikes, NTC fighters from the town of Misrata, which had witnessed heavy shelling by the Libyan army, apprehended Gaddhafi. The course of events after this is unclear, apart from Gaddhafi dying after the first moments of his capture.

After Gaddhafi's death, his son Saif al-Islam was captured on 19 November. The ICC had issued warrants for the arrest of both Gaddhafis during the conflict under Resolution 1973, with Saif held to face trial. However, this also led to controversy as those who had captured Saif, the Zintain militia, arguing that he should be tried in Libya and not in the Hague. This came to a head on 7 June when the ICC counsel for Saif, Australian Melinda Taylor and colleagues Alexander Khodakov from Russia, Esteban Pertalta

Figure 10.14   A still image from the video taken during the capture of Muammar
                   Gaddhafi on 20 October 2011. Gaddhafi was killed by his capturers
                   soon after

Source: Public domain

Losilla from Spain and Helen Assaf from Lebanon, were detained by the Zintain group for allegedly passing on classified information. Whilst they were released on 4 July, this act represented a broader tension where these groups were vying for influence over control of the new political system in the country.

From late 2011, the NTC announced its intentions to form an interim government that would plan for elections and the drafting of a new constitution. The head of militias from various towns, including Misrata, Derna, Zintan and Benghazi, were appointed to senior posts within the interim administration representing an effort to ensure that the disparate opposition groups remained part of the increasingly fragile NTC. A new electoral law was passed on 24 April 2012 that sought to balance the competing interests of these groups as well as the increasingly assertive religious establishment. This culminated in Libya's first elections in four decades on 7 July 2012, contested primarily by independent candidates with key tensions over how the new political institutions in the country would be structured, with the main point of debate being over whether Libya would be a centralised or federal political system.

Figure 10.15 Former Chair of the National Transitional Council in Libya and leader of the National Forces Alliance, Mahmoud Jibril

Source: Public domain

Case Study: Yemen

Whilst the grievances behind the uprisings in other parts of the region were a mixture of absolute and relative deprivation, Yemen perhaps represents the clearest case of absolute deprivation. As discussed in Chapter 6, the Yemeni economy has the lowest per capita GDP in the region, the highest official unemployment rate, the highest official inflation rate and according to the UNDP, is second only to the Palestinian Territories for those living below the poverty line and to Sudan on the Human Development Index. This was a dire economic situation with little sign of short-term improvement.

Alongside economic malaise, the political situation in Yemen was characterised by a lack of popular participation as well as a range of ongoing conflicts. Yemeni politics had been dominated by the rule of Ali Abdullah Saleh, who served as President of North Yemen from July 1978 and the unified Yemen since May 1990. However, whilst Saleh controlled official political authority, as well

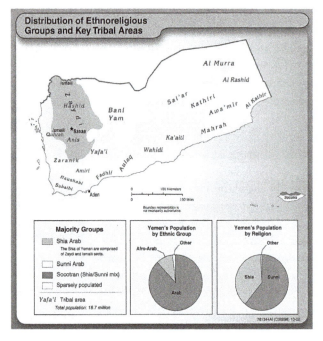

Figure 10.16 Distribution of ethno-religious groups and key tribal areas in Yemen
Source: Central Intelligence Agency

Figure 10.17 Anti-government protests at Sana'a University on 4 April 2011

Source: Public domain

as serving as commander of the Yemeni military, the state was riven by cross-cutting loyalties based on tribal allegiances, sectarianism and the growing influence of Islamist radicalism.

Sectarianism had been a simmering problem in Yemen, particularly amongst the Houthis, a large group within the Zaydi Shi`a community in Yemen. The Zaydi are the largest Shi`a group in Yemen, with Shi`a constituting an estimated 40%–50% of the population. This has been a source of tension where the Saudis, whose influence in Yemen is a persistent feature of the political landscape, accuse the Houthis of acting as a proxy for Iranian influence in the region. Here, Saleh sought to balance assuaging Saudi influence due to the Yemeni reliance on Saudi financial aid, whilst also attempting to avoid the emergence of tension within the Shi`a community. This was an untenable position, with sectarian tension emerging after 2004 (Phillips, 2010).

The Course of the Yemeni Uprising

As was discussed in Chapter 8, Yemen was in the throes of a number of conflicts by late 2010. This covered many fronts, including a Shi`a insurgency in the north, ongoing tribal conflict across the country, the re-emergence of a separatist movement in the south of the country and continued problems associated with the low levels of economic development in the country. By mid-January, protests on the latter issues, particularly in the capital Sana`a, drew on the themes that had emerged in Tunis and Cairo and turned towards a call for the removal of President Ali Abdullah Saleh.

From late January, protests of predominantly young unemployed people became a fixture of Sana`a and the southern city of Aden, with intermittent clashes with state security services. This tension culminated in an assassination attempt on Saleh on 3 June that saw him transferred to Saudi Arabia for medical treatment. After many delays and amidst ongoing protests, Saleh arrived back in Yemen in late September, agreeing to a Gulf Cooperation Council initiative for a transfer of power to Vice President Abd al-Rab Mansur al-Hadi on 23 November. This was followed by a formal election on 21 February 2012, electing al-Hadi, as the only candidate on the ballot, the new President of Yemen.

Post-Uprising Yemen

The assumption of power by al-Hadi was a watershed moment in Yemeni politics, and another example of a long-serving head of state falling in the wake of the uprisings in the Arab world. Whilst Saleh's intransigence saw the transfer of power become a long process, there is hope that the transition in Yemen, now underway, will gain pace. However, as has already been outlined, Yemen faces immense structural challenges to maintaining stability let alone democracy.

In particular, the poverty and lack of development across the country have been a major source of unrest. With little likelihood of rapid economic development in the near

Figure 10.18 Ballots being counted during the February 2012 presidential elections won by Abd al-Rab Mansur al-Hadi

Source: Yemen Fox

future, this is likely to be a major source of unrest for the new regime, one that may curtail efforts towards opening up the previously closed political system. In addition, the profound influence of tribal loyalties in Yemen limits the ability of the new regime to appoint new figures within key posts. This is particularly so for the military, where senior positions are often given to particular tribes in return for the loyalty of that particular group.

In addition, to this, the various conflicts faced by the government in Sana'a will dominate its attention for the foreseeable future. This will require efforts on the part of the new al-Hadi administration to maintain the unity and cohesiveness of the armed forces, as well as use political appointments as a tool for maintaining unity rather than turn towards full-scale democratisation that would likely lead to further instability. In addition to the ongoing controversies around US military action in Yemen, particularly the controversies over drone strikes (see Chapter 8), Yemen's post-uprising transition will be rocky.

Case Study: Bahrain

Where sectarianism is an emerging issue in Yemen, it has been the dominant political dynamic in Bahrain since its independence in December 1971. The majority of Bahrain's population is Shi'a (estimated 70%), whilst the al-Khalifa monarchy comes from the minority Sunni community (30%). Here, the Shi'a have accused the monarchy of marginalising them in terms of employment, housing, as well as broader social discrimination. This in part stems from the long-running Iranian claims on the small island kingdom.

Iran's claims are based the incorporation of Bahrain into the Persian Empire at various times in its history and the majority Shi'a population on the island (Iran refers to Bahrain as Mishmahig Island, or the 14th province of Iran). Whilst Iranian claims have only been voiced intermittently in recent years, the al-Khalifa monarchy and its allies in Riyadh, Doha and Abu Dhabi see this as a continuing pattern of efforts by Iran to influence events in the Gulf. It has also been used by the Bahraini and Saudi governments as rationale for the continued marginalisation of their Shi'a communities.

Shi'a economic and political marginalisation is exacerbated by the relatively modest economic growth in Bahrain. Where the economies of its Gulf neighbours have growth exponentially since the 1970s, Bahrain boasts only modest deposits of oil and gas, seeing it reliant on revenues from the service sector, assistance from its neighbours and the benefits of hosting the powerful US 5th Naval Fleet at the Naval Support Activity (NSA) Bahrain. NSA Bahrain has been the launching pad for all major US military operations in the region; including the post-2001 military operations in Afghanistan and Iraq (see Chapter 8).

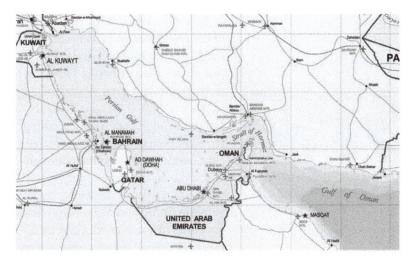

Figure 10.19   The states of the Persian (Arabian) Gulf
Source: Public domain

Political discontent had emerged previously in Bahrain, particularly in the 1990s with continued economic stagnation and political restrictions. These protests crossed sectarian divides, and called for the reinstitution of the Bahraini parliament and constitution that had been briefly implemented between 1973 and 1975. Whilst some reforms were introduced in 1999, the National Action Charter of 2001 was a more comprehensive move to quell discontent. However, the monarchy continued to mitigate the freedoms of the charter through the 2000s, highlighting what it labelled as foreign interference in Bahraini affairs (Nakhleh, 2011).

Bahrain's Failed Uprising?

The Arab uprisings provided a spark that re-lit this lingering tension in Bahrain. Protests were organised for 14 February 2011, the 10th anniversary of the referendum on the National Action Charter, demanding a revised constitution and a public investigation into allegations of government corruption and repression of dissent. Despite initially appearing conciliatory in the run-up to the protests, including the dispersal of 1000 Bahraini dinar payments to each household, King Hamad ibn Isa al-Khalifa responded with the use of security forces to disperse the protests as soon as they formed. This saw the rapid degeneration of the conflict to violent confrontation between the state security services and the protestors centred on Manama's Pearl Roundabout.

Figure 10.20 Protestors in Manama's Pearl Roundabout (or Pearl Square) in March 2011

Source: Bahraini Activist

This culminated with the forced clearing of the protestors on 17 February leaving four dead, over 600 injured and an estimated 70 people taken into custody. However, protests re-emerged with a mass rally on 22 February of over 200,000 people, roughly 25% of Bahrain's adult population, taking to the streets. Concessions were made, but protests continued in the capital through March, and took on an increasingly sectarian tone with counter-protests seeing confrontation between Sunni and Shi`a communities. The government intervened again on 13 March, breaking up the anti-government protests.

This situation deteriorated markedly on 14 March when Bahrain approached the Gulf Cooperation Council (GCC) for assistance. This saw Saudi Arabia deploy over 1000 troops on the island alongside 500 UAE police personnel, ostensibly to secure key government sites. This freed up the Bahraini security services to clear the protestors again and over the course of the following week five died in clashes. After this, many active in the protests were arrested, a number of whom died in custody through April, further heightening tensions.

From this, various dialogue efforts have been initiated, each meeting with limited or no success as protests continued through early 2012. This period has also seen

Figure 10.21 The home of the US 5th Fleet, the Naval Support Activity (NSA) Bahrain

Source: Public domain

increasing violence used by the protest movement, including petrol bombs, whilst the government continues to detain opposition figures and impose strict censorship controls on the flow of information out of the country. This latter factor has been of particular controversy with the Al Jazeera network, based in neighbouring Qatar, and the Al Arabiya network, based in neighbouring Saudi Arabia, accused of turning a blind eye to coverage of the Bahraini uprisings whilst providing extensive coverage of uprisings elsewhere. Combined with criticisms of Al Jazeera's coverage of the uprising in Syria, as is discussed above, this led to resignations at the network in 2011.

Therefore, the uprisings in Bahrain have had limited direct effect on the structure of the government, access to political participation by the majority of the citizenry, or the scope of powers held by the al-Khalifa royal family. They have sharpened the already volatile sectarian tensions in the country, something that has particularly significant regional ramifications given the history of tension between Iran and its Gulf neighbours. This is of added importance with the location of the powerful US 5th Fleet on the small island kingdom.

The events in Bahrain also spurred on discussions in the GCC of a possible political union between the six member states. Whilst there is little likelihood of

Figure 10.22 Saudi troops crossing the King Fahd causeway into Bahrain on 14 March 2011

Source: Samer Araabi

full political union between the states, discussions in May 2012 have indicated that there is likely to be a strengthening of ties between Saudi Arabia and Bahrain, one that would serve the security interests of both states against Iranian pressure as well as assist in offsetting domestic unrest and underwriting the Bahraini economy. However, this union is not likely to advance the cause of democracy in Bahrain, and therefore will potentially exacerbate the pre-existing tensions that led to the unrest that broke out on 14 February 2011.

Case Study: Syria

The key components of authoritarianism in Syria were discussed at length in Chapter 5. Here, the instability that characterised the Syrian political system through the 1960s and 1970s was replaced by a stable system of authoritarian governance under the rule of Hafiz al-Assad and the Ba`ath Party. Assad's rule was based on a mixture of state-led development, populist politics and repression of opposition forces underpinned by a reliance on control over the Syrian security services and the support of Syria's many smaller sectarian communities, including the President's own Alawi community, the Syrian Christian community, as well as important elements within the majority Sunni community.

Unrest had manifested in the early 1980s, with the short-lived rebellion by the Muslim Brotherhood that resulted in the 1982 Hama uprising and subsequent Syrian military assault on the city. Since this time, there were only small instances of unrest including some instability amongst the Kurdish community in the northeast. It was regional and international tension, rather than domestic unrest, that were the key challenges to the political dominance of the regime, a pattern that continued after the death of Hafiz on 10 June 2000 and the ascension of his son Bashir al-Assad on 17 July.

As such, with little domestic unrest during the rule of both Hafiz and Bashir al-Assad, it is difficult to pinpoint exact causes for the widespread violence that broke out in Syria in 2011. This is a pattern that is reflected in the highly diverse and diffuse nature of opposition movements that have emerged during this uprising. The economic situation in Syria had steadily deteriorated through the 1990s and 2000s, including a rolling back of state services and subsidies. However, this was offset by relatively strong economic growth in the north of the country, particularly around the city of Aleppo through the 2000s.

The human rights situation in Syria can perhaps be highlighted as a more salient factor underpinning this unrest. The regime in Damascus had employed coercive techniques consistently in confronting opposition forces, or targeting potential dissent before it emerged. This has also been evident in the efforts on the part of the Syrian regime to control the spread of information technologies

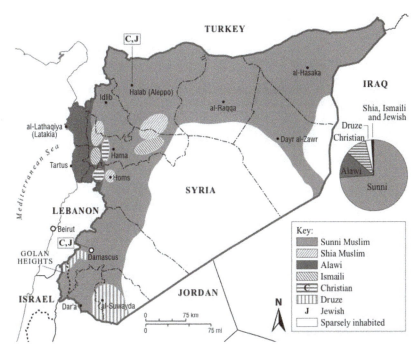

Figure 10.23 Religious and ethnic communities in Syria

Source: Kaplan, Seth D., *Fixing Fragile States: A New Paradigm for Development.* New York: Praeger, 2008, p. 100

in the country through the 2000s, including tight controls over social media and outside news sites.

Finally, the issue of sectarianism may also be a factor that led to the outbreak of violence. Here, resentment of the perceived privileged place of sectarian communities, particularly the Alawi, has been focussed on by many over the years as representative of the broader injustices of the Syrian mode of governance. Again, however, this is an opaque picture where many within the Alawi community have agitated against the rule of the Assad family whilst those within the majority Sunni community, most often perceived as bearing the brunt of government exclusion, are openly supportive of Ba`ath Party rule.

Syria's Civil War

Where unrest was expected to spark revolts across the region, Syria was often excluded from these projections due to the relative strength of the regime in Damascus, the diversity of the country and the apparent vulnerability of other states such as Jordan, Algeria and Sudan to unrest. However, despite repeated

Figure 10.24 Anti-government protests in the town of Naseeb near Daraa` in late 2011

Source: Abbad Diraneyyah

Figure 10.25 Members of the Free Syrian Army

Source: Grashoofd

stalled efforts to organise protests through February, a number of major demonstrations took place across Syria from mid-March. These were centred on the cities of Daraa`, south of Damascus and Homs, north of the capital.

These two cities were the focus for unrest for varying reasons. In Daraa`, resentment against the regime emerged in response to the influx of refugees in the town from the northeast of the country as a result of drought. This occurred at the same time as the regime stripped back services to regional centres such as Daraa`, creating an economic crisis in the town that bred increasing resentment. For Homs, anti-government sentiment had stretched back several decades as the town was the home of the Syrian Communist Party, a movement that was suppressed with the rise of the Ba`ath Party during the 1960s (see Chapter 4).

It was in Daraa` that the first large protests broke out on 25 March 2011 with 100,000 people marching. The immediate government response was the use of the security forces, resulting in an estimated 20 civilian casualties. This occurred alongside protests across the country, also in Damascus and the cities of Hama, Baniyas and Aleppo, in late March with a further 70 civilian casualties. By April, this unrest had turned highly confrontational, with rolling unrest across the country and casualties quickly moving into the hundreds.

From April, the US and later the EU imposed sanctions on the Syrian regime for their increasing use of artillery, tanks and snipers to disperse protestors. It was also at this time that an intense debate emerged over the nature of the opposition in Syria, with charges and counter-charges of human rights abuses, torture and coercion by both sides. This debate was complicated by the highly diffuse nature of the opposition in Syria. Unlike almost all other instances of uprisings across the region, the Syrian opposition had been divided from the beginning.

The colloquialism for pro-government 'gangs' or 'thugs' in Egypt is *baltagiya*; in Syria and many other parts of the Arab world it is *shabiha*. The **shabiha** are civilian groups allegedly paid for by the government (and, in some instances, by criminal networks), who act as enforcers, targeting protestors and other groups. They were allegedly involved in the 25 May 2012 massacre in the Houla region.

The most visible elements of the Syrian opposition to emerge were the Syrian National Council (SNC) and the Free Syrian Army (FSA). The SNC was a coalition group formed in Istanbul on 23 August 2011. Whilst it has acted to negotiate formally on behalf of the Syrian opposition, it has been widely criticised as acting as a proxy for Turkish interests in Syria and for being out of touch with the various groups active in the country.

The FSA announced its formation on 29 July 2011, and has been one of the most active participants in the fighting. It is constituted primarily of former Syrian military personnel, and remains not officially aligned with any one opposition movement. With an estimated size of some 70,000 members, its stated goal is the removal of the regime. However, it has also been criticised for alleged involvement in human rights abuses against supporters of the Assad regime as well as contributing to the overall degeneration of the conflict. In addition, critics claim that it has been the recipient of money and arms from Saudi Arabia, Qatar, Turkey and even the US and Israel in their moves to destabilise the Syrian regime.

This question of international involvement in the course of the conflict has become a key theme, where the Syrian regime has levelled charges at the Erdogan government in Istanbul, as well as the Saudi and Qatari regimes, that they are actively supporting the opposition in an attempt to remove the regime, hoping for the establishment of a friendly Sunni-backed government in Damascus as well as the removal of Iran's key ally in the Arab world.

On 25 May 2012 108 people were killed in the **Houla** region north of the city of Homs. Most of the deaths were civilian, with some 49 children and 34 women killed over the course of 24 hours. The Syrian army had shelled the cluster of villages that day, however UN investigations revealed that the majority were killed at close quarters. Whilst the government blamed opposition groups, survivors blamed pro-government *shabiha* militias for the violence and killings.

On the flip-side of this, the US and EU have decried the role of Russia and China in blocking a series of UN Security Council Resolutions aimed at explicitly condemning the Syrian regime's use of force against civilians, an act that may trigger a Chapter VII resolution akin to Resolution 1973 passed in relation to Libya. Russia has been a particular target for this criticism due to the close relationship it shares with Damascus, and the hosting of the Russian naval base in the western Syrian city of Tartous.

As these debates raged, the situation in Syria deteriorated markedly through 2011 and 2012, with ongoing violence raging across the country. Estimates vary widely, with the Syrian Observatory for Human Rights putting it in excess of 16,000 people by early July 2012. This included over 11,000 civilian casualties and over 4000 Syrian military personnel killed, with casualties among foreigners and others. As such, the uprising in Syria has descended into a full-scale civil war between the regime and a host of opposition groups including the FSA as well as militant Islamist groups, sectarian militants, criminal groups and others. It has also seen the violence spill over the border into northern Lebanon, flaring sectarian tensions in this fragile region.

The government did move to introduce a gesture towards political reforms, with the passing of a new constitution via referendum on 26 February 2012 that saw the removal of the single-party framework. However, many challenged these as superficial with the President retaining key portfolios such as defence and internal security as well as a veto over all parliamentary decision-making. As such, discussions about democracy and its relationship to the uprisings in the Syrian context have become overtaken by more immediate concerns over security and the rapidly growing death toll in the country.

CONCLUSION

With events unfolding at a rapid pace, the impacts of the uprisings across the Arab world are difficult to quantify. The immediate effect of the toppling of heads of state in Tunisia, Libya, Egypt and Yemen alongside ongoing conflict in Bahrain and Syria will change the dynamics of local and regional politics. However, the scale of this change varies from state to state. For instance, there is greater evidence of more profound structural transformation in Tunisia and Libya where entire systems of governance are being overhauled as opposed to Egypt and Yemen, where the removal of heads of state have left in place much of the structure that existed previously.

In this regard, the prospects for these uprisings resulting in a more democratic region are uncertain. The conditions that led to the uprisings varied from state to state, with a range of consistencies in terms of economic malaise and ongoing political repression. As such, it may be contended that the key feature of these protests was the 'negative' motivations, or protest against injustice. Calls for democracy were present, and often pronounced, but this was as much a call for accountability and transparency as it was a call for a specific form of representative democratic participation.

As such, the move towards a more democratic Arab world and Middle East may not be a direct result of these uprisings; but they will certainly mean a changed political dynamic in the region. Even in cases where the bulk of a political system remains in place, such as Egypt, the participation and dominance by previously marginalised groups will fundamentally alter relationships and political dynamics. There is no guarantee that these new players will be able to address the various causes behind the uprisings in the short or medium term. However, the legacy of these events may be one of highlighting how challenges to political authority are possible, potentially fostering the entrenchment of pluralist and participatory politics in the Arab world.

Study Questions

- What are the defining features of the debate on democracy and democratisation in the Middle East and the Arab world?
- What are the arguments that characterise the debate on Islam and democracy?
- How has the issue of democratisation and democracy promotion been approached in recent years by Western states and international organisations?
- What are the 'region-wide' factors behind the Arab uprisings?
- What are the 'country-specific' factors behind the Arab uprisings?
- How have uprisings differed in terms of grievance and outcome in Tunisia, Libya, Egypt, Yemen, Bahrain and Syria?
- Do the Arab uprisings signify a move towards a more democratic future in the region?

FURTHER READING

Campbell, Denis G. (2011) *Egypt Unshackled: Using Social Media to @#:) the System.* New York: Cambria Books.
A volume focussed on the role of social media and new media in the Egyptian uprising, providing an interesting account of these new social and political forces.

Cook, Steven A. (2011) *The Struggle for Egypt: From Nasser to Tahrir Square.* Oxford: Oxford University Press.
A reflection on the uprising in Egypt based on a lengthy examination of the political history of Egypt, critical in understanding the particularities of perhaps the most publicised of the 'Arab Spring' revolutions.

Hadded, Bassam, Bsheer, Rosie, Abu-Rish, Ziad and Owen, Roger (eds) (2012) *The Dawn of the Arab Uprisings*. London: Pluto Press.
An innovative edited volume that pools critical thought on the origins and possible future directions of the Arab uprisings, with a particular focus on the issues of new media, gender and human rights.

Lynch, Marc (2012) *The Arab Spring: The Unfinished Revolutions of the New Middle East*. Jackson, TN: Public Affairs.
A clear overview of the events surrounding the Arab uprisings from the perspective of US policy makers.

Go to the companion website at www.sagepub.co.uk/macqueen for further material including free journal articles and links to other relevant documents.

REFERENCES

Arendt, Hannah (1963) *On Revolution*. New York: Penguin.

Bar-Eli, Avi and Trilnick, Itai (2012) 'Israeli, Egyptian Officials in Secret Talks on Gas Deal Crisis', *Haaretz*, 29 April; www.haaretz.com/business/israeli-egyptian-officials-in-secret-talks-on-gas-deal-crisis-1.427049.

Carothers, Thomas (2002) 'The End of the Transitions Paradigm', *Journal of Democracy*, 13 (1): 5–21.

Chaudhry, Kirin Aziz (1997) *The Price of Wealth: Economies and Institutions in the Middle East*. Ithaca, NY: Cornell University Press.

Diamond, Larry (2002) 'Elections Without Democracy: Thinking About Hybrid Regimes', *Journal of Democracy*, 13 (2): 21–35.

Djerejian, Edward (1992) 'The US and the Middle East in a Changing World', Speech by Assistant Secretary of State for Near Eastern and South Asian Affairs, Meridian House International, 2 June; www.disam.dsca.mil/pubs/Vol%2014_4/Djerejian.pdf.

El Fadl, Khaled Abou (2004) *Islam and the Challenge of Democracy*. Princeton, NJ: Princeton University Press.

Evans, Gareth (2011) 'UN Targets Libya with Pinpoint Accuracy', *Sydney Morning Herald*, 24 March; www.smh.com.au/opinion/politics/un-targets-libya-with-pinpoint-accuracy-20110323-1c6pc.html.

Held, David (2006) *Models of Democracy*. Stanford, CA: Stanford University Press.

Human Rights Watch (2011) 'Egypt: Military Intensifies Clampdown on Free Expression', 17 August; www.hrw.org/news/2011/08/17/egypt-military-intensifies-clampdown-free-expression.

Huntington, S.P. (1991) *The Third Wave: Democratization in the Late Twentieth Century.* Norman: University of Oklahoma Press.

Khaleej Times (2012) 'Al-Jazeera: Controversial "Arab Spring" Platform', *Khaleej Times*, 27 March; www.khaleejtimes.com/Displayarticle09.asp?section=todays features&xfile=data/todaysfeatures/2012/March/todaysfeatures_March69.xml.

Lewis, Bernard (2002) *What Went Wrong? The Clash Between Islam and Modernity in the Middle East.* Oxford: Oxford University Press.

Linz, Juan J. and Stepan, Alfred (1996) *Problems of Democratic Consolidation: Southern Europe, South America, and Post-Communist Europe.* Baltimore, MD: Johns Hopkins University Press.

Lust-Okar, Ellen and Zerhouni, Saloua (eds) (2008) *Political Participation in the Middle East.* Boulder, CO: Lynne Rienner.

MacQueen, Benjamin (2009) 'Democracy Promotion and Arab Autocracies', *Global Change, Peace and Security*, 21 (2): 165–78.

Mayer, Ann Elizabeth (2006) *Islam and Human Rights.* Boulder, CO: Westview Press.

MEPI (2007) 'The Middle East Partnership Initiative Story', 20 January; 2002-2009-mepi.state.gov/outreach/index.htm.

Moisi, Dominique (2012) 'Don't Expect What Happened in Egypt to Happen in Russia', *Business Insider*, 3 January; articles.businessinsider.com/2012-01-03/europe/30583457_1_russian-protesters-dmitri-medvedev-young-protesters.

Nakhleh, Emile (2011) *Bahrain: Political Development in a Modernizing Society.* Lanham, MD: Lexington Books.

O'Donnell, Guillermo, Schmitter, Philippe C. and Whitehead, Laurence (eds) (1986) *Transitions from Authoritarian Rule: Prospects for Democracy.* Baltimore, MD: Johns Hopkins University Press.

Phillips, Sarah (2010) *Yemen: The Politics of Permanent Crisis.* London: Routledge.

Responsibility to Protect (2009) 'General Assembly Debate on the Responsibility to Protect and Informal Interactive Dialogue', 21 July; www.responsibilitytoprotect.org/index.php/component/content/article/35-r2pcs- topics/2493-general-assembly-debate-on-the-responsibility-to-protect-and-informal-interactive-dialogue-#debate.

Rodenbeck, Max (2011) 'Volcano of Rage', *New York Review of Books*, 24 February.

United Nations (2005) 'Follow-up to the Outcome of the Millennium Summit', United Nations General Assembly A/60/150, 15 September.

Winckler, Onn (2000) 'The Challenge of Foreign Workers in the Persian/Arabian Gulf: The Case of Oman', *Immigrants and Minorities*, 19 (2): 23–52.

Index

Page references to Figures, Photographs or Tables will be in *italics*